The Politics of Personal Law in South Asia

The viability of the Uniform Civil Code (UCC) has always been a bone of contention in socially and politically plural South Asia. It is entangled within the polemics of identity politics, minority rights, women's rights, national integration, uniform citizenry and, of late, global Islamic politics and universal human rights. While champions of each category view the issue from their own perspectives, making the debate extremely complex, this book takes up the challenge of providing a holistic political analysis.

As most of the South Asian states today subscribe to a decentralised view and share a common history, this study is an excellent comparative analysis of the applicability of the UCC. In this work, India figures prominently, being the most plural and vibrant democracy, as well as accounting for almost three-fourths of the region's population. This provides the backdrop for an analysis of the other states in the region.

This second edition will be indispensable for scholars, researchers and students of law, political science and South Asian Studies.

Partha S. Ghosh is Senior Fellow at the Institute of Social Sciences, New Delhi, India. Formerly, he was Professor of South Asian Studies at Jawaharlal Nehru University, New Delhi; Senior Fellow at the Nehru Memorial Museum and Library; ICCR Chair Professor at the Victoria University; Visiting Professor/Humboldt Fellow at Heidelberg University; and Ford Scholar at the University of Illinois. He had a long stint as Research Director at the Indian Council of Social Science Research. His most recent books are *BJP and the Evolution of Hindu Nationalism: Savarkar to Vajpayee to Modi* (2017) and *Migrants, Refugees and the Stateless in South Asia* (2016). He has contributed chapters to many edited volumes and published extensively in professional journals, magazines and newspapers.

'This book is important because it helps us understand the complex political choices that might be made in the area of personal law in South Asia.'

Muneer Mustafa, *Contemporary South Asia,*
18(3), September 2010

The Politics of Personal Law in South Asia
Identity, Nationalism and the Uniform Civil Code

Second Edition

Partha S. Ghosh

LONDON AND NEW YORK

Second edition published 2018
by Routledge
2 Park Square, Milton Park, Abingdon, Oxon, OX14 4RN

and by Routledge
711 Third Avenue, New York, NY 10017

Routledge is an imprint of the Taylor & Francis Group, an informa business

© 2018 Partha S. Ghosh

The right of Partha S. Ghosh to be identified as author of this work has been asserted by him in accordance with sections 77 and 78 of the Copyright, Designs and Patents Act 1988.

All rights reserved. No part of this book may be reprinted or reproduced or utilised in any form or by any electronic, mechanical, or other means, now known or hereafter invented, including photocopying and recording, or in any information storage or retrieval system, without permission in writing from the publishers.

Trademark notice: Product or corporate names may be trademarks or registered trademarks, and are used only for identification and explanation without intent to infringe.

First edition published in India by Routledge 2007

British Library Cataloguing-in-Publication Data
A catalogue record for this book is available from the British Library

Library of Congress Cataloging-in-Publication Data
A catalog record has been requested for this book

ISBN: 978-1-138-55165-7 (hbk)
ISBN: 978-0-429-50682-6 (ebk)

Typeset in Sabon by
Servis Filmsetting Ltd, Stockport, Cheshire

For Professors B. K. Shrivastava, Dietmar Rothermund, Kingsley de Silva and Stephen P. Cohen, all of whom helped me significantly at different stages of my academic life. As a token of my gratitude and affection I dedicate this book to them

Contents

List of Tables	viii
Preface to the Second Edition	*ix*
Preface to the First Edition	xi
Acknowledgements	xv

1	Introduction: Issues and Concepts	1
2	The Evolution of the Indian Discourse	43
3	It is Politics, Stupid!	76
4	On the Fringe: The Tribal Laws	117
5	The South Asian Mosaic	141
6	The Wider Context	200
7	Conclusion	222
8	Old Wine in the Old Bottle	236

Appendices	294
Glossary	332
Bibliography	337
Index	369

Tables

1.1	South Asian States and the CEDAW	37
2.1	British Legislations Intervening into Personal Laws	62
3.1	Communal Violence 1977–86	106
5.1	The Status of Muslim Personal Law in Pakistan	158
5.2	The Status of Muslim Personal Law in Bangladesh	168
5.3	The Status of Muslim Personal Law in Sri Lanka	189
6.1	Women's Representations in the Lower House of Parliament in South Asia, 1999 and 2004	220

Preface to the Second Edition

'It is politics, stupid.' That is exactly what it is. Nothing else can explain why in spite of so much hullaballoo about the introduction of a uniform civil code (UCC) it is only blare, no legislative action. As the interconnected issue of personal law/UCC has much to do with Indian politics, which almost always veers round the Hindu–Muslim question, it will be interesting to watch what will happen to the subject now that the Hindu nationalistic Bharatiya Janata Party (BJP) is in power, not merely as leading partner in the National Democratic Alliance (NDA) but as a party with an absolute majority in the Lok Sabha (lower house). Ruling in 18 of the 29 states, NDA will soon become the majority coalition in the Rajya Sabha (upper house). Although the political climate in India changes like mountain clouds, all indicators suggest that BJP will win the 2019 election. With such political confidence at command, the question is will the party enact a UCC, one of its avowed commitments from the beginning? The first edition of the book (2007) tried to answer the question. But at that time BJP was not as self-assured a party as it is now. It is, therefore, important to take the story forward through this second edition particularly because its powerful leader, Narendra Modi, is committed to a 'new India,' an important pillar of which is a uniform civil code for the entire country. But are there straws in the wind pointing to that direction?

Our argument in the volume is that in spite of its high-pitched rhetoric to have such a code, when it boils down to actual legislative action BJP will find discretion the better part of valour. The beauty of the situation is that it will still serve the party's drive to consolidate its Hindu base, for the more it corners the Muslims as a retrograde and socially backward people, the better it feeds into its Hindu constituency. In this hype, who cares to realise that a UCC must necessarily mean an end to all customary and social laws. Leave alone India's numerous tribes which have their constitutionally guaranteed

x   *The Politics of Personal Law in South Asia*

customary laws, many Hindu, Muslim and Christian caste groups also have their own laws. Even Parsis and Goan Hindus have their own laws. In Bangladesh and Pakistan, India's two comparable neighbours in this setting where Muslim majorities are pitted against Hindu minorities, it is the mirror image of India. There the Hindus, who cling to their personal law, are accused of being antireform, while Muslims are seen as reform friendly.

In bringing out this volume, many people have helped me in one way or the other. Though the list is long, some names must be remembered with profound gratitude. They are: Ajay Mehra, Faizan Mustafa, Hasnuzzaman (Bangladesh), Jehangir Patel, Indra Kaul, Indu Agnihotri, Mitra Sharafi, Mukesh Khatwani (Pakistan), Neera Chandhoke, Nutan Johry, Rasul Bakhsh Rais (Pakistan), Rohit De, Shiraz Patodia, Vikash Kumar and Zoya Hasan. My thanks also go to Shoma Choudhury and Shashank Shekhar Sinha of Routledge, who convinced me of the necessity of the study. I also thank the Routledge production team and their copyeditor for her/his thoughtful editorial dashes.

Partha S. Ghosh
New Delhi
November 2017

Preface to the First Edition

The issue of the uniform civil code (UCC) *vis-à-vis* personal laws is entangled within the polemics of identity politics, minority rights, women's rights, national integration and uniform citizenry and, of late, global Islamic politics and universal human rights. Champions of each category view it through their own prisms, making the debate extremely complex, more so in a plural and noisy democracy like India and, in a broader sense, in politically and socially plural South Asia. The purpose of this study is to disentangle the knots, or, in other words, to harmonise the threads of the debate to provide a holistic political analysis for, after all, politics is at the core of all public policy discourse.

At the centre of the debate is whether there should be a centralised view of the legal system in a given society or a decentralised view, both horizontally and vertically. At present most South Asian states, with the exception of the Maldives and Nepal, and also Bhutan in terms of a justice system for it does not have an effective civil code, subscribe to the decentralised view both in horizontal and vertical terms. The existing personal laws of different religious communities represent the horizontal approach while the family laws of the tribes as well as those of certain castes and *biradaris* of the Hindu and Muslim communities represent the vertical approach. Although all personal laws have their religious and/or traditional customary roots, and although South Asia is one civilisational space, much of which has a shared macro history, the sovereign existence of the seven states (now eight after the inclusion of Afghanistan in SAARC) has made them follow different trajectories in respect of the problematic.

India being the most plural and most vibrant democracy in the region, as well as accounting for almost three-fourths of its population and area, provides the most fertile intellectual soil to germinate all kinds of ideas concerning the viability of a uniform civil code.

xii *The Politics of Personal Law in South Asia*

Although Bangladesh has a checkered democratic career, it has an otherwise thriving intellectual and liberal tradition and as such does not lag much behind. Primarily spearheaded by its forward looking women's groups, the debate there significantly represents the broader issues of equality of the law across communities. Sri Lanka also has the wherewithal to provide fertile soil for the discourse for it too is plural and has an uninterrupted record of democracy (barring the referendum blot of Jayewardene's second presidency), but because of its decades-old Sinhala-Tamil ethnic conflict it has not been able to spend enough time and energy to address the matter. In Pakistan the debate is virtually non-existent but its politics provides clues for us to understand what can happen to the personal law of the majority community when it commands total domination. Devoid of any identity crisis in the conventional sense, to what extent can the community become reforms-prone? Curiously, however, both Bangladesh and Pakistan have, either scrupulously or out of sheer indifference, left the Hindu personal law untouched, allowing the community to lag behind its Muslim counterpart. Whether such neglect is desirable or not, and whether interference in Hindu personal law is politically feasible given the Hindu suspicion of majority domination there, is a moot point addressed in our study.

Nepal, Bhutan and the Maldives provide interesting experiences because the first was till recently a Hindu constitutional monarchy, the second a Mahayana Buddhist monarchy and the third a Wahabi Muslim totalitarian, euphemistically democratic, state. Maldives figures only marginally in our analysis for it does not have any other variety of Muslims leave alone non-Muslims. But both the Hindu-majority Nepal and Buddhist-majority Bhutan have sizable minorities and, therefore, it would be interesting to see how their respective polities address the personal law questions of the minority communities, if at all they do.

The study has been divided into seven chapters. The first chapter, Introduction: Issues and Concepts, posits the problematic in the context of the conceptual dichotomy between the centralised and the decentralised view of law together with the evolution of the concept of civil and common laws and then relates it to the overall South Asian scene from historical and sociological perspectives. In this context certain basic issues have been clarified: what is Hindu law, what is *shar'ia*, what are the different schools of Islamic jurisprudence, are South Asian Muslims different from their counterparts elsewhere, and what is the role of human rights in the discourse? The idea here is to provide a bowsprit to help readers get an idea about what they can

Preface to the First Edition xiii

expect from the book, which is exemplified in the research questions that it has listed.

The second chapter, The Evolution of the Indian Discourse, traces the evolution of law in India from ancient times to the debates in the Constituent Assembly of India that was convened in December 1946. Since the present legal system of the Indian subcontinent owes much to the developments during the colonial period, this period has been discussed in detail, though adequate space has also been devoted to the earlier phases of Indian history. Insofar as the Constituent Assembly debates are concerned, the chapter elaborately analyses the discourse on the eve of decolonisation, primarily in the context of constitution making. Two issues that particularly figured in the debate were how to reform Hindu personal law and how to prepare the ground for enacting a uniform civil code.

The third chapter, It is Politics, Stupid!, discusses the developments on the Indian political scene from the fifties through to the present. Starting with the passage of the Special Marriage Act (1954) and the Hindu Code (1955–56) the chapter looks into the politics of the discourse on the uniform civil code as it unfolded during the period. It explains the compulsions behind all the ruling coalitions going slow on the issue of introducing the uniform civil code, if not rejecting the idea outright. Simultaneously it explains why Muslims are so touchy about their personal law.

The fourth chapter, On the Fringe: The Tribal Laws, addresses the issue of tribal customary laws. Although there is some discussion on caste *panchayats* and caste customs in the discourse on UCC, seldom does one find any reference to tribal laws. This gap is filled by this chapter, which shows that even when there is a uniform civil code in India these tribes would be out of its purview. In this chapter more emphasis has been given to the North-East where many of the tribes of India are located; also, since the region is on the borders of India it also poses integrational challenges to the country.

The fifth chapter, The South Asian Mosaic, discusses the subject as it obtains in India's South Asian neighbours, namely, Pakistan, Bangladesh, Nepal, Sri Lanka, the Maldives and Bhutan, in that order. Since Pakistan and Bangladesh were part of India before 1947 and since both are predominantly Muslim countries, they provide interesting insights into how Muslims look at their own personal law and at that of others—reforms in Muslim personal law, yes; but, in respect of others, indifference. Nepal, Bhutan and the Maldives make interesting cases because they all have uniform legal codes or uniform justice systems, although they are all majoritarian codes or justice systems. In

xiv *The Politics of Personal Law in South Asia*

respect of Sri Lanka, besides Buddhist, Hindu and Muslim personal laws, the Kandyan law and the customary inheritance law of the Jaffna Tamils known as the Thesavelamai law figure adequately in the chapter.

The sixth chapter, The Wider Context, expands the parameters of the discourse by revisiting women's political empowerment, by referring to the experience of South Asians in western societies and by drawing from the perspective of international militant Islam.

The Conclusion presents a collection of some normative thoughts together with a pragmatic analysis of what is politically feasible and what is not.

At the end, a set of appendices, a glossary and a bibliography have been provided to facilitate better understanding of this complex subject as well as to encourage further research.

Partha S. Ghosh

Acknowledgements

In writing this book a number of organisations and individuals have helped me; to them all, I owe a deep sense of gratitude. The first and foremost is the ICSSR (Indian Council of Social Science Research), which funded this study that included my visits to the neighbouring countries to collect data. The Centre for Public Affairs, where the project was affiliated, meticulously administered the grant and never allowed me to face any difficulty in sorting out my accounts or dealing with related logistics. Almost immediately after the launching of the study in May 2003 I moved from Delhi to Guwahati to take up my assignment as a Visiting Professor at the Omeo Kumar Das Institute of Social Change and Development (OKDISCD). They extended all cooperation, never letting me feel that the project was not theirs. I extend my sincere thanks to all these organisations.

Among individuals who extended their academic and/or moral support at every stage of the research are Abu N. S. Ahmed, Ajay Mehra, Indranee Dutta, Anuradha Dutta, Bhupen Sarmah, Kalyan Das, Saswati Choudhury, Joydeep Barua, Pranab Borgohain, Praneeta Kalita, Harish Sharma, R. R. Prasad, P. M. Ramteke, P. R. Goswami and R. N. Saxena. T. N. Madan and Asghar Ali Engineer were kind enough to read portions of the manuscript and give valuable comments. Outside India I received cooperation from Humayun Kabir, Hasanuzzaman Chowdhury, Dipti Rani Sikdar and Meghna Guhathakurta (Bangladesh); Kingsley de Silva, Stanley Samarasinghe, Nalini Weragama, Dushyantha Mendis and Radhika Coomaraswamy (Sri Lanka); Gopal Krishna Siwakoti, Lok Raj Baral and Hamid Ansari (Nepal); Sudhir Vyas, Ketan Shukla and Pema Rinzin (Bhutan); Maryam Khaleel (Maldives); and Rasul Bakhsh Rais, I. A. Rehman and Farida Shaheed (Pakistan). In Paris my interactions with Christophe Jaffrelot, France Bhattacharya and Violette Graf were helpful on certain points.

xvi   *The Politics of Personal Law in South Asia*

It is not possible to name all the libraries that I, or my research assistants, visited and the personnel there who extended their assistance; still, a particular word of appreciation is due to the OKDISCD library and its ever-helpful Lohit Talukdar. In Delhi, the JNU library, the Nehru Memorial Museum and Library and the American Center library were ever cooperative. In Paris the library of MSH was particularly useful for writing the first chapter.

Three research assistants helped me at different stages of my research for different length of periods. Ritika Ganguly, who worked with me for the longest period to start with, did not spare any pains to build the base of my data, which helped her successors, Raju Mandal and Indrani Borpujari, to build further upon it. I deeply appreciate their cooperation.

In any acknowledgement note the family customarily figures. It is not an exception here either, but with a difference. I thank my wife, Indira, for being away from me during the course of writing this book. If I were on a *sanyas* in Guwahati, she was no less a *sanyasin* away in Delhi, paradoxically, however, most efficiently holding the family fort there. She was ever encouraging; so were my children, Arunabh and Suparna.

Last but not least, let me extend my thanks to all those hundreds of known and unknown individuals, like the proverbial unknown soldiers, who helped me in more ways than one. The criticisms and comments of the anonymous reviewer were extremely useful in sharpening some of my premises. My sincere thanks to her/ him. Roopa Dhawan deserves my profound appreciation for her meticulous editorial touches.

Partha S. Ghosh

1 Introduction: Issues and Concepts

> The Law of the Jungle—which is by far the oldest law in the world.
>
> —Rudyard Kipling, *The Second Jungle Book*

Why this Book?

Ever since the drafting stage of the Indian Constitution, and indirectly even prior to that, there has been a political debate in the country as to whether India, being a democratic and secular state, should have a uniform civil code (hereafter UCC), or, in other words, should it continue to allow its various religious and ethnic minorities to retain their personal and customary laws, which is traditionally the case. The debate picked up momentum in the eighties and nineties when the Hindu nationalists made, for the first time, a serious bid to capture political power. In their pro-*Hindutva* agenda, their demand for a UCC figured prominently. The way the idea was projected, it tended to suggest that the retention of the Muslim personal law was evidence of the pampering of the community by the Congress Party, an indulgence that was a veritable impediment to national integration. The debate fitted in well into the larger discourse over secularism versus communalism that virtually rent the entire political society asunder. Newspaper columns were replete with the highly opinionated and motivated views of columnists and letter writers to the editors, generating more heat than light. While Muslims in general felt concerned at the possible imposition of UCC, which they considered as brazen Hindu highhandedness, the average Hindu failed to understand why Muslims were so agitated when the move was apparently progressive and modern. That the issue was highly complex both sociologically and jurisprudentially they could seldom appreciate. What they also failed to realise was that all laws, in the ultimate analysis, were

2 The Politics of Personal Law in South Asia

political contraptions and a UCC or personal law was no exception. The present study purports to present a dispassionate analysis of the situation from a political perspective with the entire South Asian region as its focus. But India is the largest multi-religious and multi-ethnic democracy in the region, this kind of political discourse has its relevance for, and reverberations in, the politics of all its neighbours as they too are plural (barring Maldives) and by and large respect minority rights either by action or by default.

India is a predominantly Hindu country. Muslims constitute the largest minority (14 per cent), while Christians and Sikhs each account for about 2 per cent of the population. Buddhists, Jains and Parsis are small in number. For purposes of affirmative action (in Indian parlance, positive discrimination, reservation, or the quota system) and family law application, Buddhists, Jains and Sikhs are treated at par with the Hindus.[1] In 1955–56, all Indians other than Christians, Jews, Muslims and Parsis were given a common civil statute in respect of marriage, divorce, maintenance, minority guardianship, adoption and succession. Although many important provisions of the statute were not based on Hindu *shastric* tradition, it still came to be known as Hindu law, presumably because the predominant community to be governed by the statute was the Hindu community (Mahmood 1972: 463). There is a plethora of personal, regional and customary laws in India but the one that is most controversial is the Muslim personal law.

Muslim personal law in India is largely uncodified. There are no officially recognised *Shari'ah* courts either. The state courts generally administer the law on the basis of the Indo-Muslim (earlier 'Anglo-Mohammadan') judicial precedents. The most significant enactment governing the application of Islamic law to the Muslims is the Muslim Personal Law (Shari'at) Application Act of 1937. After India's independence in 1947 the scope of the law was extended to include three South Indian states, namely, Andhra Pradesh, Kerala and Tamil Nadu. There is also the Dissolution of Muslim Marriages Act of 1939. On the basis of this act the state courts can dissolve Muslim women's marriages, on their request, on grounds specified in the law, which are primarily drawn from the Maliki law. Following the passage of the Muslim Women (Protection of Rights on Divorce) Act in 1986, criminal courts are empowered to enforce some of the rights generally available to divorced Muslim women under the Islamic law (Mahmood 1995b: 87–88).

The purpose of this book is to analyse why, after so many decades of the constitutional directive to the effect that the Government of

Introduction: Issues and Concepts 3

India should make efforts to replace all personal and customary laws by one UCC, it has not yet been achieved and why, in other countries of the region, with the notable exception of Bangladesh, there is not even a debate on the subject. Why, whenever such an effort is made, for example in India or Bangladesh, it is opposed at various levels, making the exercise futile? These questions have been carefully examined here, keeping the focus primarily on India, which is most critical, while devoting a detailed chapter on the experiences of all the other six countries of the South Asian Association for Regional Cooperation (SAARC). (Afghanistan is not part of our discussion although it has become the eighth member of the SAARC.) Besides analysing the individual experiences of all the South Asian states, this book puts the discourse in a conceptual framework, referring to all relevant theoretical issues, without an understanding of which the essential elements of the debate cannot be adequately appreciated. Since law, as noted above, is essentially a political subject, the answers to our questions have to be found in the politics of the respective countries. It follows, therefore, that the sociopolitical climate of a country has to be conducive before it enacts a UCC for its people. Also, such an enactment hinges on the basic question of whether a country should have a uniform civil code in deference to the concept of equality of all citizens before law, or whether it should allow the respective communities that form the nation to enjoy their personal laws in deference to the concept that a democracy or any modern state system must respect minority rights and group identities of which personal law forms an important marker. Though these two concepts are apparently mutually irreconcilable, most nations across the globe have reconciled themselves to allowing both to coexist, with variance in degree only. Another point that has figured in the discourse, and which has also been discussed in the book, is whether codification of respective personal laws contributes to the eventual introduction of a uniform civil code or whether, on the contrary, it delays, if not completely destroys, the process by rigidifying a community's attachment to its personal law.

Research Questions

From the above standpoint, several broad questions have been raised and their answers attempted, which are as follows:

- Why is law a political question?
- Does the legal system, which includes personal and family laws, necessarily have its origin in religion?

4   *The Politics of Personal Law in South Asia*

- Can there be legal pluralism just like there is political pluralism?
- Is it true that a majority community is more willing to modernise its personal law because neither is its cultural identity in question nor is it under threat, perceived or otherwise?
- Are Hindus intrinsically in favour of a secular civil code while Muslims pathologically opposed to it, or are their positions much more nuanced than what appears?
- Would the introduction of a UCC mean the end of all religious and customary practices when even the Indian Penal Code (IPC) has not always been able to prevent the criminal justice system from being interfered with by such custom? For example, in spite of the fact that inter-caste marriages are legal, lower caste people who marry upper castes are sometimes victims of violence and even murder, usually sanctioned by village *panchayats*.
- What is the texture of the discourse in other South Asian countries?
- How do the South Asian communities respond to the family laws operative in the western democracies where they have settled in large numbers?
- Should personal law reforms wait indefinitely for community desires, or should the state be proactive to facilitate the process?

The above questions do not exhaust all the possible questions pertaining to the discourse. They are in way of sensitising readers to the types of issues that societies in South Asia confront while dealing with the subject. Broadly, all these issues can be viewed from four essentially interrelated perspectives, namely, the centrality versus the plurality of law, individual rights versus group rights, communal versus territorial identities of groups, and the relevance of giving primacy to women's rights. These and other related issues have been discussed here to make the discussion as comprehensive as possible, with the central point being that it is politics that guides all, more so in a democracy but even in non-democracies.

Politics and Law

Law has both written and unwritten sources. The written sources are the constitution, the law code and the court judgements. The unwritten sources are the so-called natural justice, cultural and family values and so on. Diversity of legal norms and practices is, therefore, inherent in the situation particularly in the realm of family laws, for each society has a different evolutionary experience. The very fact that each country has its own constitution and no two countries have exactly

Introduction: Issues and Concepts   5

identical laws underscores the point. Since laws are made by people who rule either at the political or at the societal level, the essence of law is politics.

One may argue that while giving a verdict in a court case the judge refers either to a legal provision or to a previous judgement and is, therefore, bound by a precedent. Where does politics come into the picture in such a situation? But is not the very choice of a precedent a subjective decision and, in making that choice, is not the judge influenced by several factors around him and the case? In the American context it has been empirically found that the notion *stare decisis,* meaning that judges defer the precedents and are bound by them thereby restricting their domain to law rather than politics, is rarely universally applicable. Not only do the same types of cases have the potential to draw different judgements depending upon their time and locale but even the choice of precedents is often motivated or is simply subjective. David Kairys, an American constitutional lawyer, writes in the introduction to his edited volume *The Politics of Law:*

> While seeming to limit discretion and to require objective and rational analysis, *stare decisis* in fact provides and serves to disguise enormous discretion. This discretion is somewhat broader in the higher courts, but it exists at all levels. Lower courts have an added institutional concern, since their decision can be reviewed, but they also have added discretion stemming from their relatively larger control over the facts and the credibility of witnesses. Functionally, *stare decisis* is not a process of decision making or a mechanism that ensures continuity, predictability, rationality, or objectivity. Precedents are largely reduced to rationalizations, not factors meaningfully contributing to the result; they support rather than determine the principles and outcomes adopted by judges. . . . Courts determine the meaning and applicability of the pertinent language; similar arguments and distinctions are available; and the ultimate basis is a social and political judgments. . . . Law is simply politics by other means.
>
> —(Kairys 1982: 15–17)

In the context of family laws in South Asia, as we will see in the succeeding chapters, the connection between politics and personal law, either in its continuity or in its reforms, is evident. In this regard religion plays an important role, particularly in those nations where Muslims form the majority. Even in other countries where Buddhism or Hinduism is the dominant religion, with or without secularism as

6   *The Politics of Personal Law in South Asia*

their state policy, the relevance of religion in determining family law patterns is no less. If India, which is a constitutionally secular country, has failed to introduce a UCC, it is on account of political hurdles.

Legal Traditions

Broadly, the whole legal structure can be divided into two segments— civil law and common law. The most important distinction between the two is that, whereas in civil law importance is given to legislation and theories of law, in common law precedents in judgements receive priority. Common law is thus a case based law. As such, there is an essential similarity, in most situations, between common law and customary law as both are case based and not legislated. This is true of the British experience and hence the American as well, for American law was largely borrowed from England. Since the South Asian legal systems are largely the legacy of British rule a better understanding of the history of common law would be useful because, as we will see in Chapter II, India inherited the Roman law twice.

Europe is the source of the present legal systems of almost all modern nations. Within Europe it was first Greece and then Rome, more effectively the latter, which contributed the most to the evolution of law and, through European colonial expansions, to the growth of legal systems in large parts of the developing world. Within Europe, however, two major parallel patterns emerged—one, civil law, and the other, common law, besides a few other smaller patterns. Civil law represents the sets of laws comprising Roman and Germanic traditions together with ecclesiastical, feudal and local experiences. Between the seventh and nineteenth centuries most of the continental European nations, which belonged to this system of law, undertook massive codification drives. Subsequently these laws spread to other parts of the world through colonialism and other forms of influence. The countries which subscribed to the model were Japan (1890–98), China (1929–31), Thailand (1925), Turkey (1926), and Ethiopia (1958–60). It was also introduced, together with local religious and customary laws, in the colonies, protectorates or trust territories of France (Algeria, Guinea, Mali, Morocco, Tunisia and other territories in Africa, the West Indies and Oceania), Belgium (the Congo, Rwanda-Burundi), the Netherlands (Indonesia, the Dutch West Indies), Portugal (Goa in India) and Italy (Somalia). The system also migrated to the Balkans and West Asia but there it was supplemented by Islamic law.

The system of common law is constituted by the law of England and that of those countries to which it migrated and, in the process,

Introduction: Issues and Concepts   7

included the local religious and customary features. The most notable English common law countries are the United States, Canada, Australia, New Zealand, the Republic of Ireland and the West Indies. The modified version of English common law prevails in India, Pakistan, Bangladesh, Sri Lanka, Myanmar, Malaysia and Singapore, besides Liberia and those parts of Africa and Oceania where the British ruled.

Besides the above two major patterns, the Nordic countries, namely, Sweden, Finland, Denmark, Norway, and Ireland, had their own system of law which was close to civil law but also had the characteristics of common law. Following the Bolshevik victory in Russia, the country introduced major innovations in its legal structure but its pre-revolution civil law structure was not completely replaced. In Poland it was more so.

The conceptual distinction between civil and common law notwithstanding, no watertight compartmentalisation between the two structures is possible. Even where legislation may seem to be the dominant influence, if one goes into the fine print, one would find that there is considerable scope for subjectivity of judges, which is bound to be based on societal influences. Lon Fuller in his book *Morality and Law* underlines this connection most tellingly.

> In the civil law countries the codes from which courts purport to derive their principles often provide little beyond a vocabulary for stating legal results. They are filled with clauses referring to 'good faith,' 'equity,' 'fair practice,' and the like—standards that any court could apply without the aid of a code. One of the best modern codes, the Swiss Code of Obligations, lays down very few rules and contents itself largely with charting the range of judicial discretion and with setting forth what might be called checklists for the judge to consult to make certain that he has overlooked no factor properly bearing on the exercise of his discretion.
> —(Quoted in Barnett 1998: 115)

The demand for codification, in India and other South Asian countries, of their personal and customary laws as well as the importance attached to their actual or potential interpretations by learned judges prove the coexistence of both civil and common law traditions in this region, together with the massive inputs from its history and traditions. To be more accurate, therefore, it may be said that India inherited the Roman law not twice but thrice, because while the second time was through the British adaptations, the third time was

8   *The Politics of Personal Law in South Asia*

through French (Chandan Nagar and Pondicherry) and Portuguese (Goa) adaptations.

For the purposes of the present study it would be also relevant to broadly understand the legal systems that prevail in the Muslim world. Including the Muslim countries mentioned above under various categories we may refer here to two groups in the Muslim world belonging to the Islamic legal system, one traditionally so and the other of recent vintage. Bahrain, Brunei, Comoros, Iran, Kuwait, the Maldives, Mauritania, Oman, Qatar, Saudi Arabia, United Arab Emirates and the Yemen Arab Republic formally and traditionally adhere to Islamic law as the source of their legal systems. The case of Iran is singular as it had an interlude of about a half a century of a Pehlvi-sponsored secularisation drive which was completely demolished by the Iranian revolution of 1979. Following the revolution Iran returned to its Islamic law with a kind of vengeance (Amin 1998: 134).

The Iranian revolution had a snowball effect in many other parts of the Muslim world. In some cases, however, the ruling cliques themselves appropriated the popular mood to further entrench their authority. The Senussi Order in Libya, the Mehdi uprising in Sudan and the Ma al-Aynaym in Mauritania all campaigned for the rejection of western values and the introduction of the Islamic order. All this was part of a general anti-West fever that gripped the Muslim world (Amin 1998: 134). In South Asia it hit both Bangladesh and Pakistan. Since Maldives was a hundred per cent totalitarian Islamic state it did not feel the change. Ziaur Rehman in Bangladesh and Zia-ul Haq in Pakistan forcefully championed this 'return to Islam' approach. But in the actual legal systems of both these countries, this so-called Islamic drive had little impact, as we have discussed in Chapter V.

Personal Law: Group Rights or Individual Rights?

There is a basic contradiction in the term 'personal law'. A person is an individual. As such, any right of an individual should mean that it is a personal right. But personal law connotes a set of legal rights pertaining to family affairs that an individual is entitled to not just by virtue of being an individual but by virtue of being a member of a religious or ethnic group or community. Though not talking about personal law, Bhikhu Parekh's distinction between 'the right of a community' and 'individually exercised community rights' would help us resolve this contradiction. A diasporic Jew is entitled to settle in Israel any time according to the country's Law of Return. It is a right given

Introduction: Issues and Concepts 9

to a religious/ethnic community spread across the world but this right is exercised by the individual members of the community. Similarly, a Sikh male's right to wear a turban or a Muslim's right to take time off from office work to pray is an individually exercised community right. There are, however, certain rights which are collective and cannot be exercised individually, as for example, the right of self-determination. On another plane, for instance, the Catholic Church's right to excommunicate any of its members, or its refusal to grant a divorce, is a 'collectively exercised collective right' at the cost of an individual right (Parekh 2000: 215–16). The Hindu caste *panchayat* decision or the Muslim *fatwa* would fall in the same category.

Personal law, therefore, is that set of matrimonial, inheritance and adoption rights that individuals claim on the basis of their being members of a particular community but which they want to exercise individually. Essentially it pertains to the discourse on individual rights versus group rights and the question of group identity, in most cases minority identity. From the politico-legal perspective the debate is nothing but an extension of the discourse on the centrality versus the plurality of law. The central logic of all democracies is that respect has to be shown to the majority view. But alongside, paradoxically, will not the majority view have to respect minority sentiments as well? If the majority fails to do so it loses its claim to have created an ideal democracy. Since almost every nation in the world hosts one or more minorities within its territory the question of minority rights is a universal one, more so in democracies because minorities there have a democratic avenue to ventilate their grievances, if any. Generally speaking, five idioms are used in discussing the subject, depending upon the nature of the state and the majority attitudes to the minorities, which may also vary from one minority to another. These idioms are: assimilation, suppression, silent toleration, indifference and respectful recognition. If one delves into the history of South Asia during the last two hundred years, one would come across all the above situations in some form or the other with regard to minorities, which could be of various types like religious minorities, linguistic minorities, tribal minorities, caste minorities, displaced groups sometimes forming stateless minorities, and so on.

The twentieth century is known to be the age of minority rights. Prior to that also different groups of people had lived in one single political territory and some of those groups naturally fell in the category of minorities, but it was only in the twentieth century that the relationship between the majority and minority was recognised as a distinct subject of discourse. The contribution made by modern

10 *The Politics of Personal Law in South Asia*

communication technology and the role of international agencies like the United Nations have been seminally significant in this regard. J. S. Furnivall, an economist and colonial administrator, was the first to draw attention to the situations in colonial societies where different peoples lived side by side though not necessarily interacting with one another. His reference of course was more to the colonial rulers and their ruled natives. Even after the end of colonialism different communities sometimes go different ways but quite often there is also an intrinsic drive for coexistence amongst them. The catch phrases now are multiculturalism and the salad-bowl experience.

Without going into the debate on individual versus group rights in more detail, let us quote here from Jay Sigler on the theory of minority rights. His explanation will further clarify the point we made above with reference to Bhikhu Parekh's ideas on the subject; both put together are sufficient for the purposes of this study. The points to be noted are (Sigler 1983: 195–96):

- Minority rights are group rights. They may be claimed by an individual, but they are asserted as a result of membership in a group that seeks a measure of differential treatment distinct from the majority of the population. *Equal treatment is not the basis of the rights* (emphasis added).
- Minority rights may include individual rights, as in the well recognised principle of nondiscrimination to be found in most of the world's constitutions and in the basic United Nations documents. This means that a member of a minority group should be able to claim that he or she, as an individual, has been denied rights available to others in the same nation. *Equal treatment under the law is an individual right, although it may be claimed by a minority group member* (emphasis added).
- Multicultural societies must, at least, consider whether they have significant groups that are effectively treated as minorities and should develop some principled bases for the recognition of the legitimacy of minority group status. This is a complex issue— group identity (language, colour, ethnicity, religion or race) may be different in different societies. Trivial or frivolous distinctions (left-handedness, red-headedness, fatness, tallness) are not to be considered. Physical disabilities, age, imprisonment, or other status conditions that may be entitled to some sort of special treatment do not confer minority group status because they are acquired conditions that do not meet the historical sense of minority status.

Introduction: Issues and Concepts 11

- Minority rights include the idea that individuals should be free to remain in the minority group or, if able, to leave it voluntarily. Individuals may abandon their religion, or marry members of another race, or surrender their linguistic rights.
- Minority rights should not be compulsory or a pretext for discrimination. Apartheid in South Africa and segregation elsewhere are clearly departures from the concept of minority right because they deny free choice to minority group members.
- A failure of multicultural societies to recognise the existence of a substantial minority is a denial of minority rights. A leading example is the treatment of the Kurds in Iraq and Turkey and of many other peoples who are often not even counted in official census figures.
- Under conditions of extreme deprivation, minority rights justify special treatment and advantages for groups victimised by persistent prejudice.
- Minority rights include rights to political representation and to social and economic justice.
- Minority rights do not include the right to revolution and secession except upon the same basis as do individual rights. Only the direct and substantial threat to life, limb and the integrity of family life would ordinarily justify group resistance to constituted authority.

In the context of personal law, the first point mentioned above is most relevant. Minority rights are group rights and the phrase 'equality before the law', ironically, may mean the negation of that right. For example, a UCC is supposed to treat all citizens as equal insofar as their personal laws are concerned but in the process it may hit at the personal law of some community that the latter considers as important as their religion or as co-terminus with their identity. The whole opposition to the proposed UCC in India by the Muslims of India is a case in point, a subject that has been discussed at length in subsequent chapters. What complicates the matter further is the existence of a large number of international covenants and instruments that uphold minority rights in the name of identity protection. Some such covenants are: the International Covenant on Civil and Political Rights (1967), the International Covenant on Economic, Social and Cultural Rights (1967), the Convention on the Elimination of All Forms of Racial Discrimination (1969), the Convention on the Elimination of All Forms of Discrimination Against Women (CEDAW, 1985), and the Declaration on the Rights of Persons Belonging to National or

12 The Politics of Personal Law in South Asia

Ethnic, Religious and Linguistic Minorities (1992). Champions of group rights in nation states find these covenants handy to safeguard their rights as communities and identities, although these covenants have no legal force and many nation states are reluctant to enact national laws in correspondence with these covenants. Still, these covenants at least 'point to democracy in a general sense as an emerging norm' and underline the fact that 'groups and organisations have gathered around the concept of human rights as a mobilising force against social injustice and inequity' (Coomaraswamy 2002: 510–11).

Hindu Law

Traditionally, Hindu law is a combination of *shashtr*ic injunctions and customary traditions. Since Hinduism is not based on one single scripture nor is there one single inspired text, to define Hindu law in precise terms is not simple. Prior to the codification of Hindu law that started during the colonial period (see Chapter II) Hindu law essentially revolved around the concept of *dharma*. Though in common parlance *dharma* means religion, in the cultural context it has a much wider meaning that encompasses righteousness. As such, *dharmashashtra*s were not religious treatises in the strict sense. *Dharma* meant the aggregate of duties and obligations—religious, moral, social and legal. Justice Sunderlal T. Desai in his authoritative introduction to Mulla's treatise on Hindu law says that 'much of the traditional law of ancient India would be termed as "morality" because that law was not "a direct or circuitous command of a monarch or sovereign to persons in a state or subjection to its author"' (Kishwar 1994: 2147).

Even *Manu Smriti*, which is generally considered to be the ultimate source of Hindu law, had underlined the concept of Hindu law in terms of castes, guilds *(shrenis)*, families and regions or districts. There was a multiplicity of *smritikars* and they all coexisted. Kishwar writes:

> Most of the leading smritikars make explicit statements to that effect. For example, *Medhatithi* and *Vijnaneshvara,* as also the *Mahabharata* and the *Arthashastra* of Kautilya, maintain the view that law as enjoined in the vedas and the smritis was of popular origin and the sanction behind that law was not the will of any temporal power. The smriti of Yagnavalkya gives a list of 20 sages as law givers. The mitakshara explains that the enumeration is only illustrative and dharmasutras of others are not excluded. There is no attempt to assign a hierarchical order to the authority of their authors. Brihaspati (one of the 20 important smritikars)

Introduction: Issues and Concepts 13

ruled that a decision must not be made solely by having recourse to the letter of written codes since if no decision was made according to the reason of the law or according to immemorial usage, there might be a failure of justice.

—(Kishwar 1994: 2148)

It was this concept of plurality that gave rise to the emergence of various schools of Hindu jurisprudence, the most well known being the Mitakshara and Dayabhaga. The central point, however, remained that any law was subject to constant review and reinterpretation depending upon changing times. During the nationalist phase the person who appreciated that point the most was Mahatma Gandhi who utilised it to the hilt to push forward his schemes of social reforms. He said:

> The interpretation of accepted texts has undergone evolution and is capable of indefinite evolution, even as the human intellect and heart are. . . . Nothing in the shashtras which is manifestly contrary to universal truths and morals can stand. Nothing in the shashtras which is capable of being reasoned can stand if it is in conflict with reason. . . . My belief in the Hindu scriptures does not require me to accept every word and every verse as divinely inspired. . . . I decline to be bound by any interpretation, however learned it may be if it is repugnant to reason or moral sense.
> —(Quoted in Kishwar 1994: 2148)

That Gandhi was killed by a Hindu fanatic proves the point that his modernism fundamentally challenged the Hindu social orthodoxy, a subject that has been brilliantly addressed by Ashis Nandy in his book *At the Edge of Psychology*. Actually both Gandhi and Nehru were committed to reforms in Hindu law but their approaches differed, to which we have briefly, and not so directly, referred in Chapter III.

After the introduction of the Hindu code it is no longer common to refer to Hindu law as Hindu personal law but in practice it is very much so. Werner Menski in his detailed study of Hindu law has demonstrated that 'as a conceptual system infusing the entirety of Indian law, as a practically applicable form of Hindu personal law regulation, and in its formal as well as informal manifestations, [it] has risen from the ashes of its supposed death [since the British]. Despite many pronouncements to the contrary, it has not declined at all in importance' (2003: 41).

14   *The Politics of Personal Law in South Asia*

Muslim Law

Muslims are broadly divided into Sunnis and Shias. South Asian Muslims are mostly Sunni. There are four major Sunni schools of Islamic legal thought (*fiqh*), namely, Hanafi, Maliki, Shafi and Hanbali. These were the names of the founders of the respective schools to which subsequent legal scholars or jurists owed their allegiance (see Glossary). Depending upon the cultural, political, and socio-economic milieus in which they developed and also upon the philosophy of reasoning, each school has differed from the other in some sense or the other. The Shia schools of law came into existence following a rift between the two groups of Prophet Mohammad's followers after his death. The subsequent political conflict between the two groups led to doctrinal differences. Imam Abu Jafar was the most eminent jurist of the main Shia school.

It took many decades after the revelation of the Qu'ran and the death of the Prophet for Muslim law to emerge. As such, the laws that the different schools outlined were not the direct revelations from God but were laws as developed through human judicial reasoning (*ijtihad,* in Arabic). The fact that these laws were manmade and not sacrosanct was often obscured by those attempting to gain moral and political authority by virtue of those laws. Equally obscured has been the diversity of Muslim laws, which reflects the different and changing concerns of the societies from which they emanated. Muslim laws, therefore, are changeable and need not be accepted unquestioningly by all Muslims. The four pioneering scholars after whom the four Sunni schools of law are named had no intention of making their views final and binding on all Muslims. Abu Hanifa said: 'It is not right on the part of anyone to adopt what we opine unless he knows from where we derived it.' Imam Hanbal urged: 'Do not imitate me, or Malik, or al-Shafi, or al-Thawri and derive directly from where they themselves derived.' Likewise, Imam Malik cautioned: 'I am but a human being. I may be wrong, and I may be right. So first examine what I say. If it complies with the Book [Qu'ran] and the Sunnah [the sayings and practices of the Prophet], then you may accept it. But if it does not comply with them, then you should reject it' (MWRAF 2000, quoted in WLUML 2003: 30).

It has been argued that for the last thousand years or more the gates of ijtihad have remained closed, resulting in the virtual end of the development of Islamic jurisprudence and the blind following of established models. However, it should be noted that this 'closing' was a politically inspired change in approach. Abu Zahra wrote that the

Introduction: Issues and Concepts 15

acceptance of *ijma* (a consensus about the schools of Muslim laws at that time) in the tenth century was only to maintain national unity and discourage individual deviations and that is why *ijma* was legalised as an 'authority after the sacred text'. Thus, further ijtihad does not amount to going against the Qu'ran or the Sunnah. The Shia schools anyway have never accepted the closing of the gates of ijtihad. At present both the codified and uncodified Muslim laws in most countries consist of an eclectic mixture of provisions from the various schools. The requirements of modern life have added further flavour to them, as is reflected in the need for state regulation of marriage and divorce. Local customary practices too have influenced the process, such as the refusal of courts in many cases to recognise women's property rights on divorce. Research studies show that often the judges state that they are applying a particular school of Islamic jurisprudence such as Maliki or Hanafi but elsewhere the same schools are interpreted differently (*ibid.*: 30).

Other Personal or Customary Laws

Besides the Hindu and Muslim personal laws, in South Asia there are also the Christian and Parsi personal laws, the Kandyan law in Sri Lanka, and many customary laws of different tribes or ethnic groups belonging to particular areas such as the Thesavelamai law of the Jaffna Tamils. Since all these laws have figured in our discussion at the relevant portions of the study, no separate explanation of them has been attempted here. A reference here is made only to Parsi personal law and the Goa Civil Code, which do not figure much in our discussion, yet help us understand the overall discourse both historically and conceptually.

Parsi Personal Law

Unlike Hindu and Muslim personal laws, which have religious bases, Parsi personal law has no religious foundation though all Parsis are Zoroastrians. Their personal law is largely based on Hindu customary laws and English common law. Before we discuss this law, which is relevant to one of smallest ethnic groups of the world, let us understand who the Parsis are and what their present status in Indian societies.

Parsis, one of the most successful communities of India in terms of professions, business and entrepreneurship, came to India from Iran (earlier Persia) in the seventh century to escape the religious

16 The Politics of Personal Law in South Asia

persecution of the Arab conquerors. The local Hindu king, in whose kingdom these early immigrants largely settled, allowed them to stay on four conditions, namely, that they would learn the local language, they would not carry arms unless asked by the king, their women would wear Hindu dress and that they would follow the Hindu system of marriage and only after sundown. Parsis have been following all these conditions till now and have added some more Hindu customs to their social lives. But one significant Hindu influence has not touched them—there is no joint family system amongst Parsis. According to the 2001 Census they are 69,601 in number, most of them living in the city of Mumbai.

The early British legal system differentiated between the personal law of Parsis living in the Presidency towns of Bombay, Calcutta and Madras and that of those living in other towns. As Hindu and Muslim personal laws became increasingly identifiable in the legal system, Parsis came to be governed by the English civil law. This was true so far as the Parsis of Presidency towns were concerned. In other places Parsis were to be governed by their customary laws; if there was no clear guidance in that regard, then by the rules of 'justice, equity and good conscience', which were supposed to mean 'the rules of English law if found applicable to Indian society and circumstances'. The application of English law, however, proved problematic. In 1835, a Parsi died intestate leaving a huge property behind. His eldest son claimed the entire property based on the English law of primogeniture. This claim unnerved the government, which realised the danger of applying English civil law in Indian conditions. Eventually, after several experimentations, the Parsi Law Association came into being in 1855 to systematically study the customs and usages of the community. In 1860 it submitted a Draft Code of inheritance, succession and matrimonial matters to the government and requested the latter to institute a Parsi Law Commission. The commission was set up, which submitted its report in 1862. Based on the recommendations of the commission, two enactments followed, both in 1865, namely, the Parsi Marriage and Divorce Act and the Parsi Intestate Succession Act. Notably, these acts did away with the distinction between Parsis of Presidency towns and those living elsewhere. Both these statutes were subsequently re-enacted with modifications. The first was replaced by the Parsi Marriage and Divorce Act of 1936 while the second by Chapter III of Part V of the Indian Succession Act of 1925 (Irani 1968: 278–81).

There are several court cases involving such questions as the advisability of clubbing all Parsis in one single community for legal purposes,

Introduction: Issues and Concepts   17

who exactly is a Parsi, and are Parsi and Zoroastrian interchangeable terms. Finally the situation that has emerged is that Parsi law is applicable to three categories of Zoroastrians. One, persons who are the descendants of the original Persian immigrants and are born of Zoroastrian parents; two, the children of Parsi fathers by alien mothers and who have been admitted to the Zoroastrian religion; and three, Zoroastrians from Iran who are either temporarily or permanently residing in India. In spite of these clarifications it is not unlikely that some questions may arise in a future court of law, challenging these definitions. Probably some kind of legislation in this regard, and not merely case laws, can remove the uncertainties (*ibid.*: 286).

The Goa Civil Code

Given the plurality of India some scholars have argued that the Goa experiment can be replicated on a national scale. But a peep into the evolution of family law in Goa will reveal that the process has been no less complicated, and continues to be so. Following the consolidation of Portuguese authority in Goa in 1511 under the leadership of Alfonso de Albuquerque, all Muslims were ordered to be slaughtered and it was hoped that out of fear the Hindus would convert themselves to Christianity. But it did not happen that way and the process of conversion remained rather slow. In the 1540s Hindu temples were destroyed and, to encourage conversions at least among sections of Hindu women, it was decided that Hindu women would be entitled to their fathers' properties if the latter had died without any male successors. But before inheriting such properties these women would have to embrace Christianity (Benton 2002: 114–18).

As Portuguese power expanded in the region, dealing with the legal matters of various categories of the population became increasingly difficult. The population consisted of a sizable number of Hindus, a large community of so-called Thomas Christians who were there even before the arrival of the Portuguese, groups of converted Indian Christians, and Portuguese residents divided into status groups depending upon their parentage and places of birth in Portugal. Which family law was to apply to whom therefore became a problem which got multiplied after the introduction of the Inquisition in Goa in 1560. Earler, in 1526, some efforts were made to codify the Hindu property and inheritance laws but due to opposition from the Hindus the exercise could not go very far. Increasingly the Portuguese had accepted the plurality of the law and respected Hindu legal norms. Following the Inquisition the Hindus were systematically harassed.

18 The Politics of Personal Law in South Asia

There was a problem in respect of Thomas Christians as well, who numbered between 100,000 and 200,000. It was alleged that their social practices were considerably tainted by Hinduism. But nothing could be done to meddle with these practices because the Thomas Christians were under the authority of the Syrian patriarch, who was recognised by the Vatican. In essence, therefore, 'the actions of Hindus and Christian converts in direct response to Portuguese legal policies underscores their familiarity with a multilayered legal order in which legal and cultural boundaries were linked but also fluid' (*ibid.*: 119–24).

The process of experimentation with civil laws of different communities of Goa continued till the Cordigo Civil Portuguese or the Portuguese Civil Code (PCC), which came into being in 1867, was introduced in Goa in 1870. With amendments added to it in 1910 and 1946, the code is still operative in the state. It is uniform for all communities with certain specific provisions for particular sections. For example, Hindu men there have the right to polygamy, but only under specific circumstances keeping in view the Codes of Usages and Customs of Gentile Hindus of Goa, of Daman and of Diu. This also is more in theory than in practice (Desai 1996). The Muslims of Goa have accepted the PCC. In 1981, when the Government of India appointed the Personal Law Committee and asked it to determine how the personal laws applicable in the rest of the country could be extended to Goa, it met with resistance from the progressive Muslims of the state. As against the views of the Goa Muslim Shariat Organisation, the Muslims of Goa under the leadership of the Muslim Youth Welfare Association and the Goa Muslim Women's Associations campaigned for the continuation of the PCC (Desai 1997).

The Goa Civil Code is, therefore, not strictly a uniform code. In any case everyone does not agree with the view for the following reasons. In the first place, there are three types of marriages—one, Catholic Church marriages; two, marriages of Catholics outside the fold of the Catholic Church; and three, marriages for non-Catholics. Marriages conducted by the Catholic Church are supposed to be sacramental. Catholics can have civil marriages without the involvement of the Church but this is generally not so simple because of societal pressure. The Catholic Church does not recognise such marriages. Catholics marrying in church need not register their marriages, for that job is supposed to be done by the Church itself. But in the process Catholics are treated separately compared to other communities as if they have their personal law which others do not have. Similarly, divorce is also governed separately depending upon under which law the marriage

Introduction: Issues and Concepts 19

has taken place. According to the agreement of 1946 between the Catholic Church and the Portuguese State, Catholics marrying under the Canon Law (church marriages) are excluded from the divorce provisions under the civil law. Canon Law 1141 stipulates that a marriage which is ratified and consummated is absolutely indissoluble. What the Church allows is judicial separation certifying as if the marriage has not taken place or has not been consummated. The Ecclesiastical Court of the Church, and not the civil court, can take such decisions. In 1974, in the *E. Nunes v. Fernandes* case, the Supreme Court struck down this practice as *ultra vires* of the Indian Constitution. Under the Codes of Usages and Customs of Gentile Hindus, divorce is permitted only on the grounds of adultery by the wife and, insofar as bigamy is concerned, it is possible if (i) there is failure by the first wife to deliver a male child till she is thirty, and if (ii) the first wife fails to deliver any child till she is twenty-five. The legal situation on these questions does not seem to be very clear as there is no court case. There are inequalities in respect of adoption and the rights of illegitimate children as well (D'Mello 1997: 513).

Centrist and Pluralist Concepts of Law

Let it be hypothesised for the sake of conceptual clarity that the UCC is a dream that should be cherished by all countries of the world. This dream subsumes certain ideals precious to all civil societies, namely, an unequivocal commitment to equal respect for all religions, freedom of conscience and freedom of expression. In short, it is the dream of democracy—a governing system that respects pluralism and the rule of law. It is a system that shuns fundamentalism of all hues and disapproves of intolerance towards others' ways of life. But therein lies the contradiction in the formulation. Are not all plural and democratic societies expected to grapple with the issue of minority rights? One of the most essential ingredients of minority rights is the right to maintain one's traditional rights. That ingredient is intricately woven into the issue of ethnic identity. Since all states are supposed to treat their respective citizens equally, how would they reconcile themselves to the maintenance of traditional rights of different communities and yet treat them equally? The question, therefore, is whether a UCC for all communities is a step in the right direction of nation building, or, is the retention of personal laws of different communities the right strategy to achieve the same goal. The issue is rather complex. National integration is not merely territorial integrity. It also means emotional integration of all segments of society leading to a common goal meant

20   *The Politics of Personal Law in South Asia*

to ensure the wellbeing of all. In this march, a uniform system of law is just one step, which arguably may be a major one. But no segment should be coerced to take this step for that can be counterproductive. If the minorities feel attached to their personal laws it must be because they do not feel confident of the intentions of the majority. Once that trust is developed it will be possible to work out a UCC by culling the good elements out of all the personal laws prevalent there or by simply taking recourse to broader human rights values. The question, therefore, is essentially political, not legal.

There are two basic approaches to study the interface between the state and the law—centrist and pluralist. The concept of legal pluralism and the sociology of law as a sub-discipline of sociology originated simultaneously, the latter actually contributing to the former. Like any field of social science, this binary approach to the study of law has been a part of the postmodernist discourse. Postmodernism as a concept is associated with the recognition of plurality in ways of existence as well as in ways of knowing. In contrast to the model of unified objects of knowledge, whether texts or artifacts, postmodernism refers to intellectual networks, open debates and the wide dissemination of knowledge and interpretations of knowledge. In opposition to the modernist ideal of the unified structure of science, postmodernism upholds 'the idea of irreducible difference and even incommensurability among the varieties of knowledge' (Smelser and Bates 2001: 1874; also Best and Kellner 1997).

Legal centralism suggests that democratic societies function under one uniform rule of law, based on sets of statutes, legal principles and professionally organised legal training (Tie 2002: 885). The Westminster and European legal systems primarily subscribe to this theory. As opposed to this, without going into the theoretical intricacies of the debate (for example, Tamanaha 1993), legal pluralism underlines the coexistence of two or more systems of law in one single political space. Legal pluralists thus suggest the existence of diverse legal practices through which the overall legal system works. In short, there are alternative forms of law across criminal, tort, family and constitutional laws for determining what constitutes valid evidence within a particular field. This undermines the idea that all law is conducted using the same rules. Moreover, legal pluralists refer to the manner in which people are regulated by a variety of 'laws, besides those of the state, such as the rules associated with religious practices, educational institutions, families, and professional organizations' (*ibid.*: 885).

The concept of legal pluralism is well known in jurisprudence and the sociology of law. Social anthropologists working among the

Introduction: Issues and Concepts 21

tribes of Africa in the 1960s argued convincingly that it was virtually impossible to understand other societies only through the premises of western legal concepts. Contrasting legal pluralism with legal centralism represented by a state-dominated legal system, three concepts of legal pluralism have been proposed. First, the multiplicity of legal systems in a single society and the existence of different legal levels therein. Second, 'a structural conception of pluralism based on corporate groups'. Third, 'a conception of semi-autonomous social fields based on processual characteristics'. The last is the key concept in the postmodern view of law. It has been widely adopted and is viewed as the most dynamic part of contemporary legal anthropology (Snyder 1993: 36–37).

In 1975 a major work by M. B. Hooker, *Legal Pluralism*, referred to the circumstances 'in the contemporary world which have resulted from the transfer of whole legal systems across cultural boundaries'. He explained in detail how the colonial encounters in Asia and Africa led to the growth of the concept of legal pluralism and in this context referred to the works of J. Duncan Derrett, Bernard C. Cohn and Marc Galanter on India, and those of J. N. D. Anderson on Islamic law. Hooker showed that in many colonies with the transplanted metropolitan legal systems and even after decolonisation, such pluralities continued, notwithstanding the emergence of the so-called nation states. Hooker wrote in his Preface that 'despite political and economic pressures, pluralism has shown an amazing vitality as a working system. It may well be that it—and not some imposed unity— should be the proper goal of a national legal system. Indeed, even within developed nations themselves, there are signs that a plurality of law is no longer regarded with quite the abhorrence common a decade ago' (quoted in Moore 1986: 19–21).

It has been argued that there probably can never be any really centrist legal structure, for all legal structures are in the ultimate analysis pluralist. Lon Fuller calls it the 'horizontal' conception of law. Throughout history this has been the case. As legal historian Harold Berman aptly writes:

> Legal pluralism originated in the differentiation of the ecclesiastical polity from the secular polities. . . . Laymen, though governed generally by secular law, were subject to ecclesiastical law, and family relations, inheritance, spiritual crimes, contract relations where faith was pledged, and a number of other matters as well. Conversely, the clergy, though governed by canon law, were subject to secular law, and to the jurisdiction of secular courts, with

22   The Politics of Personal Law in South Asia

respect to certain types of crimes, certain types of property disputes, and the like. Secular law itself was divided into various competing types, including royal law, feudal law, manorial law, urban law, and mercantile law. The same person might be subject to the ecclesiastical courts in one type of case, the king's courts in another, his lord's courts in a third, the manorial courts in a fourth, a town court in a fifth, a merchant's court in a sixth.

—(Quoted by Barnett 1998: 272)

This multiplicity of jurisdiction had an effect on the potential for enforcement abuse, about which Berman writes: 'The pluralism of Western law . . . has been, or once was, a source of freedom. A serf might run to the town court for protection against his master. A vassal might run to the king's court for protection against his lord. A cleric might run to the ecclesiastical court for protection against the king' (quoted by Barnett 1998: 272).

Even Islamic law, which is commonly understood as centrist for its emphasis on *Shari'ah,* is highly pluralistic as is reflected not only in its various schools of jurisprudence but also in the constant debates surrounding the nitty-gritty of family relationships in Muslim societies (see Chapter VI). In the context of an otherwise simple and uniform system of divorce in Islam, sociologist Imtiaz Ahmad highlights the widespread plurality in the situation.

There is a powerful line of reasoning among Muslims that does not fight shy of asserting with uncanny aggressiveness that Islam offers a complete blueprint for life for all times and cannot be changed. If the revealed text was quite explicit as average Muslims commonly believe is truly the case, there would indeed have been no basis for this kind of variation to prevail. Yet, the fact of the situation is that such variation currently exists, leading to a curious situation that one can talk in the same breath, as it were, of a Qur'anic law and a Muslim Personal Law. The two are not necessarily consonant, not at least on many points in respect of divorce practices. Formal Muslim scholarship has not been successful in dealing and coming to terms with this dichotomy, which continues to prevail even today, and is to a considerable extent unresolvable because the revealed injunctions are either self-contradictory (one revealed injunction cancels out another) or are not sufficiently precise so as to rule out conflicting interpretations. This has resulted in an unhappy and uncomfortable situation where, despite claiming to derive its authority from the Qur'an,

Introduction: Issues and Concepts 23

each school of Islamic law interprets it differently in a way that a diversity of forms and formal procedures is allowed to prevail in respect of divorce practices among different Muslim communities.
—(Ahmad 2003: 21)

Legal pluralism in the Islamic tradition is reflected at three levels: one, the coexistence and accommodation of different schools of Islamic jurisprudence; two, the cognisance of local and customary practices and the dispensation of justice; and three, the tolerance and accommodation of sectarian and denominational variations. During the caliphate of Umar ibn Abd al-Aziz there was a suggestion that he should bring about uniformity of Islamic legal practices but he resolutely rejected the idea. He said: 'I would not have been very happy if Muslim scholars had not had any differences in legal matters. The companions of the Prophet had certain differences in legal matters. Therefore, any one who follows the precepts of any of the companions is on the right path.' Abbasid caliph al-Mansur once told Imam Malik that he proposed to circulate the latter's books in every town and locality to standardise the law, to which Malik objected and advised the caliph to allow the local jurists have their say in legal matters. Similarly, Imam Malik dissuaded caliph Harun al-Rashid from displaying Malik's work *Al-Muwatta* in the Ka'bah with the purpose of making the Muslim masses follow a uniform system of Islamic law (Momin 2004: 16–18).

In India, Article 141 of the Constitution says that the law declared by the Supreme Court is binding on everyone. Now, it can be interpreted as 'rule of practice' in the civil law tradition or 'precedent' in the common law tradition. Whatever be it, the effect is the same. Justice J. S. Verma, who makes an intricate distinction between the civil law and common law systems by drawing from the Indian experience, comes to the conclusion that 'a responsive, honest, dedicated judiciary is the answer to all ills. I also venture to think that these distinctions assume importance in the area of private law. Today public law and Constitutional litigation and the powers of judicial review constitute a system of public law which invokes the best of both institutions' (Verma 2000: 46–53).

The most critical debate concerning legal pluralism is around the politics of law and the purpose of dispute resolution. While the politics of law cannot escape issues involving the interactions between and amongst the majority and minority communities in a given society, the question of dispute resolution cannot escape the various anthropological and philosophical issues involved in the phenomenon. The

24 The Politics of Personal Law in South Asia

anthropological approach to dispute settlement has picked up momentum since the mid-seventies. In this context a distinction was drawn between 'dispute processes' and 'dispute processing'. The first was concerned with social relationships in processes of conflict while the second with the somewhat standardised procedures for reaching a result. The first was thus more of an academic exercise, while the latter policy-oriented (Snyder 1993: 16–20). Insofar as philosophical issues are concerned there are essentially three approaches to conflict resolution, namely, conflict maximisation, conflict minimisation and conflict transformation. It has been argued that 'formal law routinely maximizes conflict between disputing parties in order to create a "resolution". It does so by defining the disputing parties in the black-and-white terms of guilt and innocence, a strategy that has the immediate effect of escalating differences between those parties' (Tie 2002: 886). In serious criminal cases this can be a good strategy for by heightening the conflicts intractable disputes can be addressed effectively.

In contrast, the conflict minimisation approach suggests that if the highly specific aspects of a dispute are addressed it makes the conflict more manageable. 'To this end, alternative dispute resolution might only focus on the most recent incidence of conflict within an ongoing dispute and avoid the underlying issues that fuel the strife' (Tie 2002: 886–87). Beyond the conflict maximisation and the conflict minimisation strategies is the conflict transformation approach. It 'attempts to transform the nature of conflict in ways that alter the social, economic, cultural, and personal antecedents of the disputes. It is highly applicable within situations of generalized discord in which the significance of the overall conflict outweighs the gravity of any particular points of dispute, as is routinely the case within civil wars between different ethnic, linguistic, or religious groups' (*ibid.*: 887).

From the above discussion it may be seen that both systems—legal centralism and legal pluralism—have their takers and both have their respective usefulness. It all depends on how the societies have evolved. Since European societies have by and large inherited Roman law, they are more or less uniform and the same system has migrated to the Americas together with the European settlers.

But when the Europeans colonised other parts of the world, though legal centralism was attempted it did not succeed fully. Confronted with alien systems of law and justice they quite often subscribed to legal pluralism. To take an extreme example, in New Zealand there is a provision for cultural authorities to submit reports to the sentencing judges in criminal suits involving indigenous communities. In India, after the annexation of Assam in 1826 the East India Company,

Introduction: Issues and Concepts 25

while dealing with the criminal justice system in the Kachari, Kuki, Manipuri and Naga areas, introduced a jury system and saw to it that it included persons from the same tribe to which the criminal or the victim belonged (Barpuzari 1996: 104). Even in the United States, which subscribes to legal centralism, many traditional laws are in operation in the American Indian reservations.

The debate between centrist and pluralist concepts of law, however, is much more complex than what we have discussed above. It is beyond the intellectual competence of the present author to dilate on the subject further, nor is it necessary for the purpose of this study. Let us conclude this subsection, therefore, with the following point. It should not be anybody's case that whatever has been happening should continue to happen. There was a time when civilised people used to think that to keep slaves was the norm for the gentry. The conquest of another country in search of slaves was perfectly all right because it was treated as a kind of favour done to those converted into slaves for otherwise they would have been killed. This brings in the question of social norms and their impact on lawmaking.

There is a common expression used: Law and Order. It is the duty of the state to enforce law and order, as if order can be ensured only by the use of law. The most dramatic criticism of this line of argumentation can be found in Robert Ellickson's *Order Without Law: How Neighbors Settle Disputes*. But law is not something that springs automatically and all of a sudden. Behind every law there is a set of social norms habitually respected. Thus there is an inevitable blend of legal centralism and social norms. Hence, as Epstein writes:

> The legal system either backs good social norms with force or overcomes bad ones with force. In both cases, legal centralism becomes the tool to secure some needed social conformity, as the separation of law and morals should be regarded as a regrettable lapse to be overcome by prompt legislative or judicial action. The set of purely social norms is thus regarded as falling in an awkward no-man's land between the world of purely subjective preferences (vanilla against chocolate ice cream) and the law of fully enforceable legal norms. The upshot is a diminished role for 'imperfect obligations'—those enforced by conscience and social pressures but not by law—which classical natural law theory believed to embody the *correct* societal response, for example, to the implementation of norms of benevolence. But we should be cautious before we jettison a principled reliance on this middle category, for there is no apriori reason to think that legal sanctions should

26 *The Politics of Personal Law in South Asia*

back all social norms. The separation of law from morals is sometimes a good thing, and sometimes a bad one.

—(Epstein 1998: 50)

The issue is how does one establish the correct relationship between
law and social norms?

The Issue of Muslim Extraterritoriality

Of all the personal laws discussed or referred to above, namely, Hindu
law, Muslim law, Christian law, Parsi law, the Goan civil code and the
customary laws in general, only the Christian (including the relevant
portions of the Goan civil code) and the Muslim law have extra-South
Asian origin. But the extraterritoriality of Christian law is cosmetic,
as it is the Indian Church, and not the Pope, which is the source of
guidance and interpretations, if any. Muslim law is neither guided by
any Church in India or anywhere else, yet its extraterritoriality springs
from the concept of the Islamic *umma* and the continued indispensa-
bility of the Qur'an and *sunnah* as the only and ultimate sources of
Muslim law. As such, Muslim law is not only political, as all laws are,
but its politics is extraterritorial. We have tried to explain below some
of the contours of the extraterritoriality of the South Asian Muslim
community.

Since, in our analysis, two important elements will almost always
figure in the background we will examine them in some detail here to
put the subject in perspective. These elements are: one, the importance
and use of religion in political society, and two, the nature and attitude of South Asian Muslims. The latter is relevant because South Asia
hosts the largest number of Muslims compared to any other region of
the world. They constitute the preponderant majority in three of the
seven South Asian states (four out of eight if Afghanistan is added). In
India, which is a Hindu majority country, Muslims are in huge numbers, almost equal to their numbers in Pakistan or Bangladesh. In the
regional historical context they, all put together, are pitted against an
even larger Hindu community. And, what is more important for our
analysis, they are sociologically torn between their extraterritoriality
and South Asian rootedness.

The world has witnessed the ascendancy of religion and its political
use almost everywhere during the last couple of decades. Let alone the
Islamic world, even large democracies like India and the United States
have experienced the rise of Hindu and Christian 'fundamentalism'
respectively. (Fundamentalism is indeed a misnomer for revivalism

Introduction: Issues and Concepts 27

and/or communalism.) The rise of the so-called Moral Majority in America with the ravings of right-wing tele-evangelists like Jerry Falwell and Oral Roberts, which supported Ronald Reagan in his presidential race, and that of Hindutva in India, which became the political ideology of the BJP (Bharatiya Janata Party), were its clear expressions. The umbilical connection between this religious phenomenon and the patriotic/nationalist discourse is clearly discernible. In a 1990–91 survey of about forty countries, mostly European and Latin American, but also including America, China, India, Japan and others, it was revealed that both the United States and India figured almost near the top in respect of the percentage of people 'giving high rating to importance of God in life' and percentage of people being 'very proud of nationality' (Inglehart and Carballo 1997: 38, cited in Huntington 2004: 366; also Williams 1998: 179). Since Muslim countries, by and large, did not figure in the survey it is not possible to make a comparative analysis but it is common knowledge that Islam and patriotism go hand in glove in most Muslim states, the overriding concept of *ummah* notwithstanding.

But religious ascendancy is not without its challengers within the communities themselves. This is the experience across nations. India's Hindu community provides one of the best examples in this regard, though even Muslims in many Muslim-majority nations display the same tendency. Often it is argued that it is not actually the clash of civilisations but it is the clash within civilisations.

Since, in our study, one of our central themes is the Muslim communities of South Asia and their general preference for the continuation of Muslim personal law as enshrined in the *Shari'ah* in opposition to a UCC, this section will grapple with this so-called Muslim ethnicity through a wide-angle lens.

South Asian Muslims number about 450,000,000. Except a small proportion of them who live in the Maldives, Nepal and Sri Lanka, almost the entire community is shared by Bangladesh, India and Pakistan, in that order. Bangladesh is the second largest Muslim country in the world after Indonesia. Ironically, however, global Muslim politics is dictated by events in West Asia, more particularly the Arab world, and not what obtains in South Asia. Why is it so? In an answer to this question lies the problematic of 'Muslims versus the others' syndrome, which several recent ethnic–religious conflicts around the globe have brought to our reckoning. At the core of this problematic are two interconnected phenomena—one, the extraterritoriality of the South Asian Muslim ethos, and two, the continuous and near-mesmeric influence of the Holy Qur'an.

28   The Politics of Personal Law in South Asia

The extraterritoriality of South Asian Islam probably draws it sustenance, at least what is visible to the eye, from the institution of the Haj pilgrimage, the importance of which is unparalleled in any other religion in a comparative situation. Even in India, where the Muslims are in a minority, considerable political importance is attached to the event. Not only is there a separate air terminal at New Delhi's International Airport (other airports like Guwahati too make special arrangements during the Haj season) to handle the Mecca-bound pilgrim traffic, even the air tickets of the Haj passengers are subsidised by the Indian state. Nobody, not even the pro-Hindutva BJP government, dared to discontinue the practice, although some noises were heard to that effect. The reason was that, according to the Seventh Schedule of the Indian Constitution 'pilgrimage to places outside India' falls in the Union List and, as per this provision, the Parliament had passed in 1959 the Haj Committee Act to organise the Haj and to institute the Haj Fund. Any change in the situation, therefore, required a parliamentary enactment, which the BJP was not sure would get passed in the Parliament given some of its NDA (National Democratic Alliance led by BJP) partners' opposition to the move. Moreover, the BJP itself wanted to enlarge its electoral base among the Muslims and it did, in fact, raise the quantum of Haj subsidy, though unwittingly. It had proposed to exclude 'the creamy layer' in justification of the raise but ultimately that did not work and as a result every Haj pilgrim enjoyed the enhanced Haj subsidy irrespective of economic status.[2]

On an average, more than 100,000 Haj pilgrims visit Mecca every year from India alone, while the total number of pilgrims that the city of Mecca hosts every year touches more than a million, flocking from all corners of the world. The Saudi Arabian government does not leave any stone unturned to make the stay of the pilgrims as problem-free as possible and ensures that the cities of Mecca and Medina remain out of the bounds for any non-Muslim. Closely connected to this sense of the common purpose of all Muslims is the idea of an Islamic *ummah*, which theoretically conceives of all Muslims living in a border-less territory—something like pan-Islamism, which, at least in theory, transcends all national barriers. The nucleus of this *ummah* is also nothing but Mecca. It may be argued that only better-off Muslims go for the Haj, which the poor members of the community cannot afford, but political demands too are always articulated by the richer sections and not the poorer ones.

The importance of the Haj and its Arab connection has an economic dimension as well. Ever since the discovery of oil in the Middle East and particularly after the oil money boom of the 1970s, Arabs have suddenly become rich, making Muslims around the world, with the exception of Indonesia and Malaysia, again oil-surplus countries, look to the Arab world for religious and political leadership. Since almost the entire cost of the Haj arrangements are borne by Saudi Arabia the latter creates a natural constituency for itself in the minds of all Muslims, particularly the pilgrims. It may be recalled that, till the oil money started making the difference, it was principally the Nizam of Hyderabad and some other princely states of India which used to fund the pilgrims' arrangements at Mecca and Medina during the Haj.

The importance of the Qur'an and its Arab connection is even more important. The fact that the Qur'an comprises the statements of Allah, the one and the only, and that it is written in Arabic makes it the bounden duty of all Muslims to say *namaz* in Arabic and read the Qur'an in Arabic as an act of piety, even though they may not know the language at all. Here also the phenomenon has no parallel in other religions. For example, the Bible, the sacred writings of Judaism and Christianity, is not a single book but a collection of books. These books were composed over a period of many centuries in three languages—Hebrew, Aramaic and Greek. The New Testament is the second part of the Bible and is about one half (about 260 pages) of the length of the Old Testament (about 550 pages). It comprises twenty-seven 'books' as compared to the Old Testament's thirty-nine. It has been translated into more than 1,000 languages without any special significance attached to the languages in which it was originally written.[3] So far as Buddhism is concerned, its original canons, the best known amongst which is the Tripitaka, in Pali, Prakrit or Sanskrit, are hardly remembered. In the course of its journey from India to other parts of Asia, Buddhism has lost much of its original linguistic and canonical characteristics and has assumed the local variations, which have sometimes been distorted beyond recognition. Take, for example, the Sanskrit word Amitabha (another epithet for the Buddha). It travelled to China to become Omita. By the time it reached Japan it became Amida. Similarly, Avalokitesvara transformed itself into Kannon; Bodhisattva to Bosatsu, and so on.

Hinduism has travelled beyond the Indian subcontinent only to Southeast Asia and along with the indentured labourers to the West Indies and some other places. Its classical texts are in Sanskrit and, since there are no hard and fast rules about its canons and prayers, one is not expected to learn them by heart, whether in Sanskrit or in any other language. Since the system of a priestly class (Brahmin) is still operative within the overall fabric of the caste system, most of the religious rituals, whether in temples or at homes, are performed

30 The Politics of Personal Law in South Asia

ceremonially by this class. A Hindu household generally needs a priest to perform all major life-cycle rituals. Moreover, since Hinduism, unlike Islam, which is a down-to-earth worldly religion, has a lot to do with spiritualism and transcendentalism, it is not obligatory for a Hindu to visit temples regularly, nor to ensure that the priest utters the hymns on his behalf. It is essentially a private and personal religion in which pluralism of thought and practice is inherent. Consequently, it is not congregational. Probably it is on account of this factor that it has survived the Muslim and Christian political domination spanning for almost about 1,000 years. Even after having ruled large parts of India for more than 600 years the Muslims remained a minority in India. The 1881 Census (technically the second but actually the first scientifically conducted such exercise) revealed that Muslims were less than 20 per cent of the total population of India. Behind the recent upsurge of political Hinduism and the movement built around the Babri mosque controversy, there is probably an effort to make Hinduism congregational because religion cannot be effectively used as a political tool unless it is congregational.

It may, however, be argued from certain empirical perspectives that there are probably similarities between Hinduism and South Asian Islam. Hindus apparently believe in many gods and is, therefore, essentially polytheistic, though at a higher philosophical level they all believe in *param brahma,* the one and only creator. But what is probably more relevant to understand about Hinduism at the popular level is the concept of henotheism, which means the belief in one God or deity without claiming that he is the only god—every deity is powerful. Now compare this with South Asian Islam. Like Muslims anywhere, South Asian Muslims too believe in one Allah and His last *paigambar,* Hazrat Mohammad, the earlier ones being Moses and Jesus. But while the concepts of Allah and his last *paigambar* are not to be tampered with at all, there has been a host of religious leaders and *pirs* in South Asia who command tremendous reverence in the day-to-day lives of Muslims and so-called non-Muslims like the Ahmediyas. Some such names are Mirza Ghulam Ahmad (1838–1908), the leader of the Ahmediyas or the Kadiyanis, Moinuddin-Chisti (d. 1235) of Ajmer, and Nizamuddin Aulia and Bakhtiar Kaki from Delhi. Besides, there are thousands of such shrines of saints scattered all over India where local Muslims (as well as Hindus) go for prayers and solace. [The case of the Sufi saint Sai Baba of Shirdi in Maharashtra is interesting. He has not only been completely appropriated by Hindus; his Brahmanisation and deification have also been achieved ritualistically (Sikand 2004c).]

Introduction: Issues and Concepts 31

The same is the experience of Bangladesh and Pakistan. According to the *Annual Report on International Religious Freedom: Pakistan* prepared in 2000 by the Bureau of Democracy, Human Rights, and Labor, US Department of State, many Pakistani Muslims consulted pirs (hereditary saints) or saints' shrines, where pre-Islamic practices were common. As many as 25 per cent of Pakistan's Muslims regularly consulted such *pir*s, and up to 50 per cent sought their help whenever in crisis (see *Pakistan: The Rot Deepens* 2003: 304). In Bangladesh the *pir* culture is even more popular. It may be noted that some shrines of Muslim saints do exist in the Arab world also but never do the devotees there pray for material or other gains as they do in South Asia. It may be hypothesised that this particular South Asian Islamic phenomenon is largely influenced by Hindu tradition.[4] Muslims of South Asia in general may not agree with this formulation as many of them may consider it blasphemous. But that is probably because, as my Bangladeshi friend and academic A. K. M. Abdus Sabur character-ises, 'Hinduism is doctrinally inclusive but socially exclusive, Islam is socially inclusive but doctrinally exclusive.'

The Arab-centricity of Islam has two competing dimensions—pan-Arabism and pan-Islamism. South Asian Islam is caught between the two, yet, under the tremendous impact of Hinduism, it has expe-rienced distortions as well in spite of those overriding influences. One may mention the caste orientation of South Asian Islam with its obvious pedigree in the Hindu caste system. The extreme case is that of Nepali Muslims who, under the dominant Hindu political dispensation, have been reduced to a Hindu caste within the rubric of the *varna* system (Chapter V). As a result not only is South Asian Muslim society stratified on caste lines, which has no sanction in Islam, it distinguishes the loyalty of a convert from the one born into the fold, again an un-Islamic notion and which has a lot to do with the Hindu social formation. An anthropological study of rural Kashmir highlights this point: '[T]he alleged teachings of the Qur'an notwithstanding [the Qur'an and *hadith* contend that genealogies count for nothing among Muslims], in actual practice the Muslims of rural Kashmir attach crucial importance to the fact of birth in the determination of a person's nature and his legitimate socio-cultural identity. Whether this is an Islamic notion or not, it certainly accords well with Hindu belief' (Ahmad 1978; Madan 2001: 239; Nazir 1993: 2879–900).[5] Even endogamy is practised amongst Muslims, as is the case with Hindus. It is the constant refrain of the teachers in *madrassa*s that this evil practice must be done away with in line with true Islamic values.

32 The Politics of Personal Law in South Asia

The above discussion would be incomplete without reference to the linguistic dimension of Muslim politics in South Asia. In this context the role of Urdu becomes relevant for our understanding. Urdu is the national language of Pakistan, though the mother tongue of only the minority Mohajirs, that too not all. Urdu is the official language of Jammu and Kashmir, though not the mother tongue of Kashmiri Muslims who form the majority in the state, let alone the Hindus of Jammu and the Buddhists of Ladakh. The language, however, is the mother tongue of almost all Muslims living in the Hindi-speaking states of India and in the eastern metropolis of Kolkata (earlier known as Calcutta). It is they who dictated the Muslim politics of India prior to the partition and even thereafter, and also Pakistan's politics for at least a decade, when Mohajirs mattered the most. It may be noted that it was mainly these Urdu-speakers, particularly those located in Kolkata who were behind the demand for Pakistan (McPherson 1974). Even at present the Urdu-speaking Muslims living in the Hindi-speaking states of northern India, such as Bihar, UP, Rajasthan and MP, dictate the trend of Muslim politics although a sizeable number of Muslims live in Andhra Pradesh, Assam, Kerala and West Bengal. Whether it is the Babri Masjid Action Committee or the All India Muslim Personal Law Board, their leaders either belong to northern states or at least speak Urdu. Over the years, on account of the Hindi-Urdu controversy during the last hundred years, Urdu has been identified with the North Indian Muslims alone. As a result, when one wants to grapple with the Muslim mood, one delves into the files of Urdu newspapers and magazines. It may be noted that such Indian dailies like *Rashtriya Sahara* and *Nai Duniya,* which are published in both Hindi and Urdu by the same management, reflect two different editorial policies catering to two different communities. In the aftermath of 9/11 it was found that the Urdu versions of the papers were relatively more anti-American while the Hindi versions were more circumspect. Their focus was against the Taliban and Islamic terrorism (Mehdi 2002: 29–30). In Bangladesh, of course, the linguistic variable has to be understood in the context of Urdu-oriented nationalism versus Bengali nationalism, which culminated in the creation of Bangladesh. This variable, however, is no longer relevant, although the older generation sports a sense of pride in knowing and speaking Urdu whenever necessary.

Most Muslims I have spoken to in the South Asian region feel that they are the most misunderstood community. They say it is on account of western propaganda. But to my mind it is due to an average Muslim's obsession with his religion, which others neither can

Introduction: Issues and Concepts 33

rationalise nor appreciate. All humans sport multiple identities, but for a Muslim, religious identity predominates. When Sri Lanka Tamils ask for an independent homeland no one brands them as Hindu separatists. When the Nagas in India's Northeast demand an independent status nobody sees them as Christian freedom fighters. But whether it is the question of the Chechens of Russia or the Moros of the Philippines people invariably see them as Muslim separatists. It is difficult to say if there is any Christian conspiracy behind this. But what is fairly certain is that the Muslims' invocation of Allah or their use of Arabic nomenclatures in their political struggles does contribute to this image building. It is to be noted that the word Allah, an Arabic word, has an essentially Islamic connotation while the word God or its other linguistic variations have no religion-specific or region-specific connotations. All non-Muslim communities have their own words for God but for all Muslims, wherever in the world they are, the word is Allah. It is this Arabic-rootedness of the religion, to which we have referred above, which dictates non-Muslims' perceptions and misperceptions about Muslims in general. Against this background, if Muslims think that they are a misunderstood lot, they have a point.

Like any other community in the region, Muslims too are not a monolithic community, notwithstanding the broad common heritage of South Asian Muslims. They also represent a multitude of views and perspectives. Depending upon their respective domestic political contexts they too form their independent judgements on issues. As such it would be a sweeping generalisation to say that Muslims of South Asia are all opposed to any change in their personal law. If they seem to be suggesting so, it is on account of the prevailing politics in Muslim societies in relation to either their own rulers, to other major communities with whom they interact or to global changes in the power equations. During the past two to three decades there is an emergence of 'International Islam' in which 'anti-Americanism' has served as the catalyst. The symptoms of this phenomenon are extremely varied and complex but in its South Asian context it may be argued that much of South Asian Muslims' anti-Americanism springs from their disaffection with their objective local conditions and their corresponding inability to ventilate their feelings against their rulers. This is true of Pakistani Muslims and probably true of their Indian counterparts as well. Their pent-up anger finds its outlet at the cost of the United States because it does not attract the wrath of their respective governments. It is necessary to understand this subtlety and react judiciously. South Asia is now at the crossroads. Forces of both civil society and primitivism are vying for political space everywhere in the region. And

34 The Politics of Personal Law in South Asia

'fundamentalism' of one variety thrives on the success of the other (see also Chapter VI).

In this context an understanding of the European scene would give an added clue to Hindu suspicion of Muslims in India. Muslims came to western Europe mainly as immigrants, hence the expression 'transplanted Islam'. Gradually this largely male population transformed itself from a transient group to a settler group with wives and children brought from their native lands. With this transformation the linguistic, racial, ethnic and nationalistic distinctions systematically started getting an organised and unified expression under the umbrella of Islam. By the early 1980s, such issues like *halal* meat, ritualistic slaughter and educational matters entered the public discourse in Europe. This was the time when multiculturalism was becoming fashionable in the West. After the collapse of the Soviet Union and the end of the Cold War, which more or less coincided with the Salman Rushdie affair and the headscarf controversy in France, the European public consciousness seemed to be convinced of the existence of a 'Muslim problem'. The community started getting stereotyped as intolerant, fanatical and fundamentalist although there was a huge liberal fringe everywhere. Historical prejudices against Muslims derived from the Crusades and the colonial European expansion coupled with negative images in the media constituted a major hurdle to the integration of Muslims into European society. The role played by Jamaat al-Tabligh was viewed with anxiety. The Jamaat al-Tabligh has its origin in India where it is called Tabligh-i-Jamaat. Mostly associated with the Deobandi school and the Chistiyah order, the Tabligh-i-Jamaat came into being during the colonial period to protect the religion from British 'modernist' policies. The movement concentrates on pietism and the re-Islamisation of daily life. Its approach transcends cultural and linguistic differences as well as internal divisions within the learned tradition of the community (Fierro 2000–2001: 579–87, also Dasgupta 2006).

The Centrality of Women's Rights

The controversy on the UCC or the discourse over reforms in personal law essentially boils down to women's rights. Women everywhere are treated in lesser terms compared to men. In his celebrated essay 'The Subjugation of Women', John Stuart Mill argued in 1869: 'It is said that women do not need direct power, having so much indirect power through their influence over their male relatives and connections . . . it is true that women have great power. It is part of my case that they

Introduction: Issues and Concepts 35

have great power, but they have it under the worst possible conditions, because it is indirect, and therefore irresponsible power ...' (quoted by Shaheed 2002: 171). The essay was immediately translated into more than a dozen European languages and soon became the bible for women's movements across the continent. One and a half centuries have passed since then but women's struggle for equality with men has not ended.

The subordination of woman to man is true in all faiths, maybe because, as Ashis Nandy argues, it is man's reaction to 'the natural selection imposed upon him by the female's original power to instinctively sense which mate was biologically fitter. This primal dominance arouses in man insecurity, jealousy and hostility towards woman. He has a phylogenetic awareness that his primordial role is "highly specialized as no more than a temporary and ephemeral appendage to life", as a "parasitic" fertiliser. Till now he has had no civilisational awareness that he has been trying to work through this basic hostility by limiting the full possibilities of woman through sheer oppression' (Nandy 1980: 33). Both Islam and Hinduism, whatever the fine prints in their respective religious texts may say, are no exceptions. All *mullahs* and *maulvis*, with the lone exception of one female *mullah* in North America, are male.[6] The same is true of Hindu priests. Leave alone non-Hindus and *dalit*s, even women belonging to upper castes are sometimes debarred from temple entry or ritualistic performances. The recent controversy in India over the entry, nineteen years ago, of the Kannada film actress Jaimala into the 'men only' Ayyappa temple in Kochi in Kerala, an otherwise progressive state with mostly the Marxists in political command and with a claim of a hundred per cent literacy, is a case in point. According to the Indian Young Lawyers' Association, the ban on women aged ten to fifty to enter the temple violates Articles 14, 15, 25 and 51A of the Indian Constitution, which talk of the right to equality, freedom of the practice and propagation of religion and the fundamental duty of promoting harmony. Even in Assam, which is another socially progressive Indian state, some of the *namghars* (prayer halls in the Shankaradeva tradition), for example the ones in the Barpeta district, prohibit the entry of women. Ironically, the avidly followed Shankaradeva tradition, considered to be enlightened and egalitarian, has verses that recommend the treatment of women as untouchables and animals. It is this general approach of gender injustice that has been at the root of the unequal legal rights of women across communities.

Most modern constitutions talk of non-discrimination and the equality of sexes but, notwithstanding this guarantee, discrimination

36 *The Politics of Personal Law in South Asia*

against women persists in almost all societies, more so in the developing ones. As such, women activists everywhere take recourse to international conventions to push forward their demand for equality of status in the legal sense. But the difference between these conventions and covenants on the one hand and national laws on the other persist, states themselves may or may not bind themselves to conventions and covenants, but in the case of individual citizens they are obliged to adhere to national laws whether they like it or not. It has been seen that in many cases states have signed particular conventions but when it comes to enacting national laws in correspondence with the commitments made in those conventions they either procrastinate, follow devious strategies, or refuse outright.

Beginning with the Universal Declaration of Human Rights in 1948, several humanistic conventions have been signed (see pp. 12–13). In 1963, twenty-two developing and East European countries, namely, Afghanistan, Algeria, Argentina, Austria, Cameroon, Chile, Columbia, Czechoslovakia, Gabon, Guinea, Indonesia, Iran, Mongolia, Morocco, Pakistan, Panama, the Philippines, Poland, Togo and Venezuela, put up a request to the Commission on the Status of Women (UN General Assembly, A/5606, 15 November) to draft a declaration on the elimination of all forms of discrimination against women. In the 1970s, largely on account of efforts made by non-government organisations (NGOs), the movement picked up momentum and through a series of UN-sponsored international conferences on women, the concept of women's rights as human rights emerged. In 1981 the Convention on the Elimination of all Forms of Discrimination Against Women (CEDAW), the so-called international bill of rights of women, was adopted and eventually, in 1985, it came into being. Thus the efforts took more than two decades to materialise.

CEDAW is an instrument to which women can take recourse to neutralise the patriarchy inherent in the laws that govern them, including the constitutions of their countries. A caveat may be entered here. It is often seen that while some nations do not mind signing such UN conventions and resolutions, when it boils down to coordinate national laws in correspondence with UN conventions they drag their feet. All but three Muslim majority countries have ratified the convention, although, like, for example, Bangladesh, Iraq and Morocco, often with reservations for Article 2, which commits the state, amongst other things, to undertake amendments of national laws aimed at bringing them in line with international norms. Table 1.1 shows the positions of South Asian states in respect of CEDAW. It is the constant refrain of the women's groups of Bangladesh, which are struggling for a

Introduction: Issues and Concepts 37

Table 1.1 South Asian States and the CEDAW

States	Signed	Ratified	Reservation/Declaration
Afghanistan	1980	2003	
Bangladesh		1984	Articles 2, 16–1(C)
Bhutan	1980	1981	None
India	1980	1993	Article 29(1) and Declaration on Articles 5(a), 16(1), 16(2)
Maldives		1993	Articles 7(a), 16
Nepal	1991	1991	None
Pakistan	1995	1996	Article 29(1)
Sri Lanka	1980	1981	None

Source: Mumtaz 2005: 30.

uniform and gender-just family code, that in spite of the government's ratification of the convention it shows precious little attention to their demands. However, ratification with reservations is not limited to Muslim majority countries alone. Both New Zealand, on behalf of the Cook Islands, and Britain have reservations with CEDAW. The United States is one of the few countries that have even refused to adopt the convention.

In respect of women living under Muslim personal law across the world, the International Solidarity Network of Women Living Under Muslim Personal Laws (WLUML) has been active since 1984 to make Muslim women aware of their rights. In 1986 WLUML drafted a Plan of Action highlighting the oppressive nature of Muslim law, which was a mixture of canons drawn from the Qur'an and local practices. The organisation made it clear that while similarities existed across Muslim societies differences amongst them were also striking. What worried the group the most was the resurgence of Islamic fundamentalism in many parts of the world, which was inherently anti-women notwithstanding its otherwise diverse political agendas from country to country. There was no dearth of money at the disposal of these fundamentalists, thanks to the Saudi and Iranian benefaction, to promote their respective versions of Islam. In Malaysia the pro-Islamist Al-Arkam, established in 1968 with the aim of refashioning Malaysian society in line with the Islamic ideal, has enough resouces to set up factories to provide employment to its supporters, to grant interest-free loans and to set up schools and other educational institutions. In Pakistan the Jamaat-e-Islami runs a hostel, a library, a publication unit and a well equipped hospital in Lahore. The writings of its founder Maulana Ala Maududi are made easily available to young people in various parts of Asia and Africa, aimed at indoctrinating the

38 *The Politics of Personal Law in South Asia*

youth to the cause of Islam, an essential component of which is male domination (WRAG 1997b: 4–5).

WLUML held its first Exchange Programme in 1988 in which the participants were to spend three months in a Muslim country other than their own to develop an international perspective on the status of Muslim women across the world. These experiences, in due course, resulted in a project called the Qur'anic Interpretation by Women meant to generate empirical information on the legal rights of Muslim women in different cultural contexts and to emphasise the importance of law as a proactive variable. In 1993, three participants of the Exchange Programme from India established the Women's Research and Action Group (WRAG) in Mumbai. The year was critical; it had witnessed large scale anti-Muslim riots in the country in the aftermath of the destruction of the Babri mosque and in Mumbai there was a series of bomb blasts engineered by Muslim terrorists with international links. Muslim women suffered on two counts. On the one hand, the general political climate was hostile against Muslims, with the ever increasing political strength of the Hindu right, while on the other, while dealing with Hindu fundamentalists their Muslim counterparts tended to emphasise the pristine form of Islam at the cost of Muslim women's rights. By the end of 1996 WRAG collected a fair amount of empirical data by surveying fifty districts spread across fifteen states, to bring home the point that the existence of Muslim personal law notwithstanding there was a considerable amount of regional variation. But what stood out as the major finding was that women in general, whether Hindu or Muslim, were an oppressed lot with unequal rights (WRAG 1997b: 10).

It may be seen that both the NGO sector as well as the mechanics of participation in UN conferences are essentially elite exercises, at least in South Asia. But politics in the region is increasingly becoming mass-based and the political class is emerging out of this base. As a result, while it is possible to work out a global networking on progressive social reforms, to translate them into national policies becomes a Herculean task. Still, from cross-national experiences it can be seen that when a country ratifies an international convention it is always under pressure from progressive forces to make amends in social legislations. Activists do often work on preparing arguments in their writs brought in courts based on these conventions. It sometimes happens that the judges too guide themselves on the basis of international norms and take cognisance of these conventions to give gender-sensitive judgements.

Of late, judicial activism in several democratic countries has influenced domestic legislation, a development that some legal activists

Introduction: Issues and Concepts 39

call the Bangalore Principles. In 1988, the Commonwealth Secretariat on the Domestic Application of International Human Rights Norms organised a colloquium chaired by the chief justice of India, P. N. Bhagwati. The other participants included Ruth Bader Ginsburg (now on the US Supreme Court), Anthony Lester (a leading human rights lawyer in England) and Michael Kirby (an Australian judge). The communiqué issued by the conference cited and approved the 'growing tendency for national courts to have regard to international norms for the purpose of deciding cases where the domestic law—whether constitutional, statute or common law—is uncertain or incomplete'. It defined the principles that should guide the judiciary to harmoniously blend local laws, traditions and circumstances with international humanistic norms (Bhagwati 2004: 251–52).

Before we end this section, one important point must be mentioned. There is an inherent contradiction between legal pluralism and feminism. Since most feminists are progressive as well they champion the cause of pluralism in all its dimensions, including the retention of personal law. This is reflected in India in their opposition to the demand for a UCC. Indeed, since the latter is being championed by the Hindu right there is an element of anti-Islam in the demand, yet the feminist opposition to it amounts to the perpetuation of gender-unjust personal laws across communities. Kumkum Sangari refers to the methodological challenges that feminist theory faces in this regard. She argues that 'personal law and most projections of the uniform civil code have been tied not only in a binary but also a symbiotic relation, and this has stifled, even deflated, a reappraisal of laws in their entirety'. Therefore, she further pleads, 'except in their secular and egalitarian aims and premises, new laws would have to be conceptually different from the uniform civil code in the way it has been projected so far' (Sangari 1999: 20–21).

The Human Rights Approach

Is it possible or is it not necessary to view the entire debate on the UCC or women's rights through the prism of human rights, and argue that whatever is repugnant to human rights norms are not acceptable as legal precepts? Some scholars argue that from a human rights perspective a UCC need not reject religion but must question all those dogmas and formulations of traditional religions which are not in harmony with 'justice, equity and good conscience'. The problem arises because some of these dogmas and formulations are inconsistent with the UN Declaration of Human Rights of 1948 and are not in a position to effectively solve many current social problems. They often become

40   *The Politics of Personal Law in South Asia*

subservient to the status quo model of religions and compromise with conventional worldly values, which are not in conformity with the spiritual patterns enshrined within those religions (Neelakanthan and Tyabji 1991).

The UN Declaration of Human Rights of 1948 has thirty sections; the important ones for the purposes of this book are:

1. Every individual without any discrimination on the basis of race, colour, sex, language, religion, political or other views, national and social status, properties, birth or any other aspect or distinction of any sort whatsoever shall be equally entitled to the rights and freedoms mentioned in this charter.
2. All persons shall be deemed to have equal status in the eye of law, and enjoy equal legal protection without any discrimination.
3. There shall be no intervention in any individual's privacy, domestic life, familial affairs, and correspondence, nor his dignity and honour shall be violated.
4. (1) Every adult man or woman shall have the right of marrying and having a home of his (or her) own without any distinction of race, citizenship (nationality) or creed.
   (2) Marriage shall be contracted with the free consent and approval of husband and the wife.
   (3) Family is the basic natural unit of the society, and is entitled to complete protection from the society and the state.
5. Every individual shall enjoy the freedom of thought, conscience and faith and this right includes the rights of change of faith, giving expression to his faith and to the preaching of faith and worship.
6. Every individual shall have the right of social protection for life with dignity and building up his personality and, through national effort and international cooperation and according to the resources of the state concerned, shall be entitled to economic, social and cultural rights.
7. (1) Every individual has the right to receive education.
   (2) The goal of education shall be the perfect building up of man's personality and inculcating deep respect for human rights and freedoms.
   (3) The parents shall have the option of selecting the type of education their children should have.
8. (1) Every individual has certain obligations too, imposed by the society, observing which makes possible the free and perfect freedoms of other people.

Introduction: Issues and Concepts 41

    (2) In connection with the rights and freedoms every person shall confine himself to those limits as ensure the rights and freedoms of other people.

    (3) These rights and freedoms cannot be used against the aims and objects and principles of the United Nations Organisation.

9. No part of this charter shall be interpreted as to acquire for any state, group or individual the right of engaging in an activity through which these definite rights and freedoms may be sabotaged.

The ideals enshrined in the declaration were too desirable to be universally implemented. Most of the third world countries which signed the declaration could not bring out corresponding social legislations in tune with those ideals because the realities of their political lives were quite at variance with them. The Muslim-majority countries categorically distanced themselves from it, claiming that the tone and tenor of the declaration was western or Judeo-Christian, which had little relevance for Muslim societies. Saudi Arabia did not sign the document. What particularly came in the way was the issue of gender equality, although some Muslim countries like Turkey, during the period of Kemal Ataturk in the 1920s and Tunisia under President Habib Bourguiba in the 1950s, had introduced far-reaching changes in the legal codes to ensure gender justice. The Charter of the Organisation of the Islamic Conference (OIC), which was founded in 1973, presented the most articulated Muslim point of view on the matter. Though the Preamble of the Charter had reaffirmed the commitment of the OIC members to the United Nations and to the fundamental human rights, the Cairo Declaration of the OIC, issued in 1980, underlined human rights in Islam, which were at divergence with international human rights. The emphasis in the Cairo Declaration was on people's obligations and responsibilities, and not on their rights. There were cosmetic references to gender equality without clearly mentioning equality of rights between the genders. Religious conversion was also to be discouraged, which was in contravention of the Universal Declaration of Human Rights. Freedom of speech and expression did not include the freedom to question the *Shari'ah*. It was clearly laid down that the *Shari'ah* 'is the only source of reference of the explanation or clarification of any of the articles of this Declaration'. Most notably, respect for democratic principles in general was conspicuous by its absence (Syed 2003b: 20–21).

It is thus seen that whether it is the Universal Declaration of Human Rights or the Convention on the Elimination of all Forms of

42 The Politics of Personal Law in South Asia

Discrimination Against Women, it is relatively easy to sign the documents but not easy to bring out corresponding legislations to uphold the ideals enshrined in the documents. While diplomacy is at play when a country signs an international protocol, it is domestic politics that comes in the way when that protocol is to be nationally implemented. In short all efforts aimed at gender justice must be geared to influence that politics, which in no society is easy, and if the society is not democratic it is even more difficult as a general rule though there are exceptions that we have discussed in Chapters V and VI.

Notes

1 Recently a controversy has arisen over the BJP government's passage of the anti-conversion bill in Gujarat, which clubs Buddhists, Jains and Sikhs together with the Hindus in preventing them from converting to other religions, primarily meaning Christianity and Islam. The Digambar Jain Mahasabha has protested against this clubbing.
2 In August 2006 in response to a petition filed in 1995 by B. N. Shukla of the Shiv Sena, the Lucknow branch of the Allahabad High Court ruled that all subsidies to pilgrims, including the Haj pilgrims, should be stopped. The response from the government was supposed to be submitted in October 2006.
3 According to Sanneh, Muslims prohibit the translation of Qur'an into other languages and in the process they conjoin the Islamic religion with Arabic culture. He says Islam 'is implanted in other societies primarily as a matter of cultural identity' (Sanneh 1989: 29). This view, however, can be contested because the Qur'an has been translated into Persian, Turkish and Urdu (by Shah Abdul Aziz) in full. Maulana Abul Kalam Azad wrote an exclusive commentary in Urdu of the Fatiha (the first seven verses of the Qur'an). Among the many English translations available is the one by N. J. Dawood, a Muslim from Iraq. In other South Asian languages too, such as Bengali and Tamil, its commentaries and virtual translations are available; they are not word by word translations. In the process the Qur'an has received a local cultural flavour. (On this point, see Eaton 2002: 7–10; See also Ahmad 2002: 2286.) There is also an English translation of the Qur'an, which has been certified as authentic by the Government of Saudi Arabia. This underlines the Arabic cultural dimension of Islam that Saleh mentions, and also probably the Saudi sense of preeminence in the Muslim world.
4 The author's discussions with Professor Ishtiaque Danish of the Jamia Hamdard University, New Delhi, in May 2003.
5 Madan, however, clarifies in his footnote that 'it is well known that Islam was never able to eradicate earlier social inequalities among the Arabs' (p. 263).
6 In China there are hundreds of certified female *Imams* but they are not allowed to lead men in prayers (Aiyar 2006).

2 The Evolution of the Indian Discourse

India owes a great debt to the British for the introduction of uniform and equal laws applicable to all citizens. Secularism and equality were writ large in the codified and other laws administered by the British. Let us not forget that the criminal and civil laws in operation before the advent of the British were in many respects unequal in their dealings with the citizen and discriminated in favour of those highly placed in the caste hierarchy.
—M. C. Setalvad, former Attorney General, 1965

The Amalgamation of Religious and Local Customs

In the evolution of law in India, which meant Pakistan and Bangladesh as well till 1947, both religion and local customs and practices have played the most dominant role, as is the case anywhere in the world. It is a complex story of the amalgamation of both textual religious tenets and customary practices. This explains the existence of different caste customs, which do not necessarily find support in the mainstream religious canons. A good example is that while the Hindu *dharmashastras* prohibit marriage within the *gotra* or *sapinda,* that is, between close relatives, in Punjab the local tradition encourages a widow to marry her husband's younger brother or male cousin (Dhagamwar 2003: 1484).[1] Still, based on the religious affiliations of the communities, these sets of laws came to be recognised as Hindu Law, Mohammedan Law, and so on. Buddhism, Jainism and Sikhism being homegrown religions, their adherents came to be considered within the fold of Hindu Law.

In pre-Muslim India, Hindu family law was dictated by Brahmins interpreting the *dharmashastras* or local and customary traditions as the case may be. Muslim rulers did not interfere with this system as they were reluctant to meddle with this problem. It may be noted

44   *The Politics of Personal Law in South Asia*

that from the beginning of Islamic expansion the need to coexist with non-Muslims was recognised. There were Jews, Christians and Zoroastrians, who were allowed to coexist with the Muslims, of course as second class citizens, by paying the tax known as *jiziya*. When Mohammad ibn Qasim conquered Sind he found that there could be another group, not necessarily one amongst the three groups yet big and organised enough to be treated like them. The result was the proclamation of the 'Charter of Liberty of Brahmanabad', which granted religious freedom to the Hindus. The proclamation said:

> You may feel free to build temples to your gods. You may carry on commerce and transactions with Muslims. Consider yourselves fully secure and work for your own welfare. Be charitable and kind to the Brahmans and the destitutes. Observe your festivals and follow your customs like your fathers and forefathers. Continue on your offerings to the Brahmans as before and according to the ancient custom; of every 100 dirhams of revenue, take out three dirhams to pay what may be due to the Brahmans and deposit the remainder in the public treasury to be accounted for by the staff and the deputy. Those of you who are officers and administrators will receive fixed salaries.
>
> —(Zaman and Akhtar 1993: 9)

The Sultanate rulers of Delhi who had introduced a somewhat organised system of justice continued with the practice. Although Islamic law had prescribed lower civil status for non-believers and as such unequal treatment of them, early Muslim rulers during the Sultanate period confessed that it was impossible to practise that in India. Thus while criminal law was uniformly applied to both Muslims and Hindus, by not strictly adhering to the canons of Shari'ah, family law was constituted of Muslim and Hindu personal laws as interpreted by *qazis, pundits* or village and caste leaders as the case might be (Hasan 1936: 304–45). Both Iltutmish (1211–36) and Balban (1266–86) had made it clear that it was impossible in India either to observe *dindari* (religious commandments) or *dinpanahi* (defending the Islamic faith). The best that they could do was to dispense justice (*adl*) with a sense of equal treatment, which meant not to disturb anybody's personal law (Nurul Hasan, in Chandra 2005: 67).

Mughals continued with the system with better organisation. They too applied Muslim law to Muslims, and Hindus were allowed to have their own tribunals. Till the reign of Shah Jahan there were thousands of cases of Hindu–Muslim marriages which did not require

The Hindu partner to convert to Islam. Shah Jahan, however, put an end to this by requiring Hindu men having married Muslims to convert into Islam but not the other way round (Shah Jahan Nama: 139, cited by Mukhia 1991: 65). In any case, however, most family law disputes were settled at community levels without interference by the government. According to Marc Galanter, 'The government's courts did not extend very deep into the countryside; there was no attempt to control the administration of law in the villages. Presumably, the Hindu tribunals proceeded as before Muslim rule, except that whatever ties had bound these tribunals to governmental authority were weakened; there was no appeal to the royal courts' (Galanter 1997: 17). If and when matters reached the Mughal courts, Hindu personal law was applied. The Maratha rule, which has the best preserved record of the Hindu justice system, bears testimony to the fact that legal pluralism was the order of the day and often law at the top was quite different from law at the local level (Lariviere 2005: 475–77).

Colonial Encounters with Customary Law

Custom had an important place in the Indian legal system prior to the imposition of Anglo-Saxon jurisprudence over the Indian legal system during British rule. In traditional Indian jurisprudence, dharma, royal order and custom were the three sources of law. Custom was known to have formed a 'special law' regulating various social groups, castes, corporations or guilds, and families belonging to the different regions of India. A delicate balance was maintained among the three sources, each of which reserved a distinct and specific authority (Vani 2002). Though the king enjoyed undisputed lawmaking and judicial authority, he was supposed to be discreet enough not to interfere with the common customs of localities and groups. Since it was his duty to uphold dharma and maintain public order he could not abrogate any custom if such abrogation was expected to lead to disorder or the breach of peace in society. The customs could be contrary to the *smriti* (traditions or knowledge of the rules of dharma which are remembered and transmitted by sages and which are the means of acquiring wisdom) or shastras (recorded literature or treatises inspired by the *smriti*) but the king would not intervene unless the usage was likely to create stress and discontent among the subjects by reason of its immorality or unjustness. Thus, customs of regions, castes, families and other groups were to be maintained intact. Otherwise the public would revolt, the subjects would turn against the king, and the army

46   The Politics of Personal Law in South Asia

and the treasury would be destroyed (Basham 1954: 100). This situation continued under the Muslim rulers, who also made no attempt to control the administration of law in the villages (Galanter 1989b: 16).

With the gradual development of positive colonial law, customary law started losing the position of eminence that it had earlier enjoyed. English law rested on a fundamentally different foundation—the primacy of written law or statutes. Even customs had to be sanctified by statutes to be legally valid. The judiciary was expected to assess the 'legality' of a custom, besides its justness, case by case. Notwithstanding this theoretical position, it was acknowledged during early British rule that Indians should be governed by their own laws in matters of family, religion and inheritance. Matters other than these continued to be governed by government courts on the common law principles of 'justice, equity and good conscience'. By the 1820s, courts began to be almost fully governed by the principle of *stare decisis* (decisions in earlier cases serving as precedents binding on later cases or lower courts).

Early Experiments in Codification

How did the laws evolve during the colonial period? Were the colonial rulers indifferent to customary and family laws and bothered only about criminal and mercantile laws, which were more relevant for the perpetuation of their domination? Why is it argued that Indians 'twice received' the European law while Europe received it only once when it absorbed Roman law? The early colonial history of India makes an interesting reading to answer these questions. The system of law that the British introduced in India was somewhat unique compared to their earlier experiences in the New World or the Caribbean. In those colonies the system of law was to become what had obtained in Great Britain. The indigenous people were either eliminated or totally supplanted. In any case, they were not the concern of the colonists insofar as the legal system was concerned. Only in Ireland, Scotland and Wales was some kind of innovation required. In Ireland the pattern was based on an unequal economic arrangement with the establishment of a Protestant plantation-owning elite and a depressed Catholic peasantry providing labour and rents to their masters. In contrast, India already had a functioning legal order, which could not be supplanted easily, nor was it necessary. The British adapted it to suit their colonial interests by keeping the English legal system in the back of their minds. In this venture the contribution made by Warren Hastings was seminal, though jurisdictional issues were constant

The Evolution of the Indian Discourse   47

sources of controversy between the company and the British parliament, which the Regulating Act of 1773 could hardly resolve. The establishment of the Supreme Court of Judicature at Fort William in Calcutta and the advice given to Governor General (Hastings) and Council to issue rules and regulations that were 'just and agreeable to the laws of England' complicated matters (Benton 2002: 135–49). Hastings was eventually impeached by the British Parliament for his alleged misrule.

Jurisdictional controversies notwithstanding, the evolution of law in the latter half of the eighteenth century showed that family law interested the British (company) as much as the criminal and mercantile laws and it was indeed true that India had to 'twice receive' the Roman law, as the latter was first adapted by the Europeans to suit their own conditions and that adapted version later had to be once again adapted to suit Indian circumstances, where at least two parallel streams of family law had functioned, namely, Hindu and Muslim personal laws. Both were allowed to continue, but in a more formalised way. The system that evolved was indeed not perfect because English judges with little understanding of the local situation had to apply Hindu and Muslim laws with the aid of salaried court officials (pundits for Hindu law and maulvis for Muslim law) who were seldom trusted by the judges (*ibid.*: 138–39). All this, however, led to the felt necessity to translate and codify the Hindu and Muslim legal texts. In the process, as Sumit Sarkar has argued, this 'colonial "personal" law centralised, textualised, and made operationally much sharper the boundaries between religious communities, and probably enhanced also to a significant extent the influence over the rest of society of high-caste and Muslim elites' (Sarkar 2002: 224–25), a point which Ayesha Jalal also makes. She argues that colonial rule contributed to 'privatizing religion' and to 'confuse notions of public and private' (Jalal 2001: 566–67). But these perspectives are not fully teneble because, even during the Delhi Sultanate and the Mughal rule, which together had a much longer sway in large parts of India than the British, the Hindus and Muslims were always treated as distinct social categories in respect of family laws. The British can be faulted only to the extent of giving too much importance to scriptural canons at the cost of the mind-boggling customary pluralities obtaining in all the communities of India, to which Madhu Kishwar has alluded in respect of the Hindu law (Kishwar 1994: 2145–149).

In the development of Hindu family law in the early phase of British rule in India, three persons figured most prominently: Warren Hastings (1732–1817), Sir William Jones (1746–1794) and

48   *The Politics of Personal Law in South Asia*

H. T. Colebrooke (1765–1837). Hastings, who was appointed as the first Governor General of Bengal, knew Persian and Arabic and had an earlier experience of governance in India serving the East India Company at Kassimbazar (Bengal). He is credited with the introduction of the office of Collector who was not only responsible for collection of revenue but also for the dispensing of justice. The justice system was divided into two segments—civil (the Dewani court) and criminal (the Faujdari court). In the Dewani court, the substantive law to be administered was Hindu law for the Hindus and Muslim law for the Muslims. In the Faujdari court it was 'Muslim' criminal law, meaning thereby the criminal justice system that had been in operation during the Mughal days, which was the substantive law. In essence Hastings rejected the prevalent European premise that the Indian state was despotic prior to the arrival of the British (Cohn 1996: 62).

But the problem that Hastings faced was how to determine what exactly Hindu law was, in the absence of one single text or the institution of a pope or similar religious patriarch. No Shankaracharya's writ ran all over the country. In their effort to grapple with the situation the British thought to train scholars in Sanskrit, for which they set up Sanskrit colleges in Calcutta and Benaras. This reflected the bias of the East India Company in favour of eastern India, which was rather natural because their journey to power had started from Bengal. In the process Benaras, Mithila and Bengali schools of law started receiving importance while the southern schools were completely neglected. Still, to streamline the process, Hastings, in 1772, appointed a group of eleven Sanskrit scholars to produce a Hindu law digest. In 1776, the digest was printed under the title *A Code of Gentoo Laws, or, Ordinances of the Pundits*. It was the first attempt at the codification of Hindu law though it had many deficiencies. To remove the deficiencies William Jones was called upon to produce something better (Kishwar 1994: 2145–146).

The contribution of William Jones is remembered for his painstaking endeavour to codify Hindu and Muslim laws, more so the former as it was to be based on different *shastras,* unlike only the Qur'an of the Muslims. The job that Jones had started was eventually completed after his death in 1794 by H. T. Colebrooke in 1797. In 1798, Colebrooke's *The Digest of Hindu Law on Contracts and Successions* was publishedCalcutta. Though Jones and Colebrooke had the same mission, their perspectives on Hindu law differed. Jones knew Roman law better but less of Sanskrit and Hinduism; Colebrooke knew Sanskrit and Hindu culture better but less of Roman law. Bernard

The Evolution of the Indian Discourse 49

Cohn explains this dichotomy between the two in the following words:

> While English jurisprudence of Jones's time sought certainty in the law, through either 'rationality' or an ultimate appeal to ideas of natural law, Hindu jurisprudence sought flexibility through fixed means to interpret what had been revealed to man in terms of principles of right action and proper duties. A British lawyer schooled in case law was skilled in finding precedent in the case record and by analogy relating this precedent to a particular case. The Hindu lawyer, a logician and dialectician, sought reconciliation of conflicting interpretations through analysis of meanings and intentions. It must be remembered that Colebrooke, unlike Jones, was not trained in English law and did not have knowledge of Roman law—aspects that marked Jones's intellectual approach to Hindu law. Colebrooke's solution to the problem of conflicting interpretations was to suggest that there were regional variations of differences that led to the 'construing of the same text variously'. Ultimately, Colebrooke attributed the variations to historical and cultural differences in India, 'for the whole Hindu people comprise diverse tongues; and the manners and opinions prevalent among them differ no less than their language'.
>
> —(Cohn 1996: 73)

Colebrooke's concept, though thoughtful, did not work in practice and the judges were at a loss to decipher the original text of a particular point of law. This was probably, as Menski has argued, because Colebrooke virtually bulldozed his interpretations of Hindu scriptures by disregarding the interpretations by Hindu pundits. Ignoring the plurality of Hindu jurisprudence he reduced them to two main Hindu codes, the Dayabhaga and the Mitakshara (Menski 2004: 14–15). As a result, in due course a strange kind of case law emerged, at the root of which there was a reference to a particular author supposed to represent a particular regional school but otherwise heavily influenced by interpretations of the same by British judges. All these came to be enshrined as Hindu law in such collections as Thomas Strange's *Elements of Hindu Law*. Cohn writes:

> After the reform of the judicial system in 1864, which abolished the Hindu and Muslim law officers of the various courts of India, and after the establishment of provincial high courts, publications of authoritative decisions in English had completely transformed

50 The Politics of Personal Law in South Asia

'Hindu law' into a form of English case law. Today when one picks up a book on Hindu law, one is confronted with a forest of citations referring to previous judges' decisions—as in all Anglo-Saxon-derived legal systems—and it is left to the skills of the judges and lawyers, based on their time-honored abilities to find precedent, to make the law. What had started with Warren Hastings and Sir William Jones as a search for the 'ancient Indian constitution' ended up with what they had so much wanted to avoid—with English law as the law of India

—(Cohn 1996: 75)

The British might have thought that they were able to unify all the tenets of Hindu jurisprudence; what actually happened was that the real Hindu law went underground, resulting in a thriving unofficial Hindu legal system (Menski 2004: 15).

Like the Anglo-Hindu law, the evolution of Anglo-Mohammedan law followed more or less the same pattern. Although, unlike the multiple sources of Hindu law, the Islamic *Shari'ah* was relatively simpler for it had primarily three sources, namely, the Qur'an, the Sunna and the Hadith, Islamic jurisprudence had a multiplicity of schools of thought. Besides, there were social rivalries amongst various sects and tribes, which often gave little credence to Islamic traditions and clung to their respective customary laws. At best they were maxtures of local customs and Islamic traditions. As a result many such laws got gradually codified because the British courts were quite often called upon to adjudicate in related disputes. It all started during the time of Hastings, as was the case with Hindu law. At his instance three Muslim clerics translated the influential Hanafi treatise *al-Hidaya* from Arabic into Persian, which was then translated from Persian to English by Charles Hamilton in 1791. But since *al-Hidaya* lacked any treatment of inheritance, William Jones had to translate, in the very next year, *al-Sirajiyya,* a treatise on inheritance. After this there was a relative lull in this translation exercise primarily due to financial reasons (Anderson 1993: 174–75).

Did these early colonial codification drives in any way contribute to a future uniform code? If one assumes that a UCC is desirable, keeping the factor of equality of all subjects before the law uppermost in one's mind, and one also concedes that the first step towards a UCC arguably has to be the standardisation of all community personal laws, then in that sense the British probably did contribute to the concept of a UCC. But the fact remains that the British motive was political, aimed at the perpetuation of their hold on India, which is reflected in the words of Charles Hamilton who translated *al-Hidaya*. He was clear in his mind that what the British needed was to keep the communities in good humour and, for that, even if retrograde social practices had to be perpetuated it would have to be faithfully done. He wrote:

> The permanency of any foreign domination requires that strict attention be paid to the advantage of the governed and to this great end, nothing can so effectively contribute except preserving their ancient established practices—civil and religious—and protecting them in the exercise of their own institutions for, however defective or absurd these may in many instances appear, still they must be more infinitely acceptable than any which we could offer; since they are supported by the accumulated prejudices of the ages, and in the opinion of their followers derive their origin from Divinity itself.
>
> —(Quoted in Ratnaparkhi 1997: 1–2; also see Vatuk 1999: 25–27)

The Politics of Hindu Law Reforms

The nineteenth century was the most critical period in respect of British interventions in Hindu personal law. We have noticed above that in the early colonial period the British did not meddle with the family laws of either Hindus or Muslims; they simply wanted to codify those laws to make them more functional. But when in the nineteenth century, because of the spread of English education, there was a sort of renaissance in the country, which found its first expression in Bengal, the seat of British power in India, it was once again for political reasons that the colonial rulers found it necessary to talk of reforms in family laws and societal customs. Of course, if such interventions boomeranged they were to be downplayed, or, at least, not to be replicated. The differentiated approach the British followed prior to the revolt of 1857 and thereafter reflected the essence of this strategy.

To drive home the point we would refer to three landmark events of the nineteenth century, namely, the enactment of the Suttee Regulation of 1829, the Hindu Widow's Remarriage Act of 1856 and the Special Marriage Act of 1872. The first two were prior to the revolt of 1857 while the third one was after that. All the three cases revealed the conflicting approaches to law held by three different forces—the conservative/orthodox social order, the progressive/reformist fringe of the same social order, and the imperial dispensation respectively.

52 The Politics of Personal Law in South Asia

The anti-*sati* legislation was largely due to the pressure built upon the British by the progressive forces in Bengal, at the forefront of which were the Brahmos, most notably Raja Ram Mohun Roy. The legislation certainly did not have the popular support and, for this reason, could not be fully effective. There were even efforts to nullify the Suttee Regulation. A group of orthodox Hindus formed a committee, obtained over 800 signatures and appealed to the Privy Council to restore the institution. It was only because of Ram Mohun Roy's efforts that the appeal was dismissed (Gulati 1994: 144).

The Hindu Widow's Remarriage Act too was the result of progressive pressure from Bengali intellectuals led by Ishwar Chandra Vidyasagar, though the Pune liberals were equally vocal. Many in the latter category had sworn to marry child widows in case they became widowers. Some of them even honoured their pledges. One such case was that of Dr Sakharam Arjun, who married a widow who had an eight year old daughter named Rakhma. Unlike in other states, widow remarriage was quite well accepted in the middle classes of Maharashtra, beginning with western Maharashtra. But this was because the law was initiated and followed by vigourous social campaigning. In general, however, including Bengal where the idea was mooted, the legalisation of widow remarriage remained largely on paper insofar as upper caste Hindus were concerned for whom the law was actually meant (Basu 2004). Behind its unpopularity there was the issue of succession to family property by the widows and the complexities associated with remarriage in that regard. What must not, however, be lost sight of is that, like all social legislations, the Hindu Widow's Remarriage Act was a facilitative legislation. It could not be enforced the way the Contract Act or the IPC could be. One could not force a person to marry a widow. But if someone was willing to defy society, custom or religion he could go ahead lawfully.

The revolt of 1857 put a brake on British efforts to reform Hindu personal law or, in general, to interfere with the social life of India. It was the belief of the British government that the interferences of the East India Company in the family laws of Indians were generally opposed by the society and the revolt was one of the expressions of that sentiment. As such, following the shifting of the administration from the Company to the Crown in 1857, it was proclaimed by Queen Victoria that all religious laws would be protected and that the administration would refrain from all interference in the social lives of various communities. The Queen declared: 'We do strictly charge and enjoin all those who may be in authority under us that they abstain from all interference with the religious belief or

The Evolution of the Indian Discourse 53

worship of any subjects on pain of our highest displeasure.' Probably the Indian concept of secularism had its origin in this development. British policy was to adopt, *vis-à-vis* organised religion, an attitude of live and let live. To see to it that the British government had full control over Indian affairs, the court administration was restructured to shift the ultimate judicial authority to the Privy Council (Agnes 2004a: 59–60).

The social history of nineteenth century India is very complex; it is not possible within the scope of this book to do justice to it. What must, however, be mentioned here is that, in spite of the British policy not to meddle with the family laws of the land after 1857, they sometimes did meddle and often in support of traditional values. Whether they did so out of conviction, out of plain ignorance or out of political considerations is of course a moot point. One important segment of this complexity comes to fore in the context of the Native Marriage Act of 1872. Had this act been enforced it would have rendered the Special Marriage Act of 1954 redundant. This 1872 Act was extremely progressive and much ahead of its time; it prohibited polygamy, legalised divorce, made inter-caste or inter-religious marriages valid and raised the age of marriage substantially. But it met with stiff resistance from conservative forces. The result was that, unlike the earlier experience with the Suttee Regulation Act of 1829 or the Hindu Widow's Remarriage Act of 1856 when the Company government had overpowered the conservative resistance, the British government succumbed and replaced it with the Special Marriage Act of 1872. According to the latter anybody could opt to marry under its provisions, but before that he or she would have to declare his or her being neither a Hindu, nor a Muslim, nor a Buddhist, nor a Jain, nor a Sikh. Virtually, then, it was meant only for the Brahmos.

In the subsequent decades one notices a nexus between conservative Hindu views on family laws and the adjudications by British judges tending to reinforce those views. Although Tanika Sarkar, being an avowed critic of the Hindutva philosophy, probably stretched her logic too far in questioning the legal status of an 'idol',[2] yet her central point is well taken:

> Towards the end of the [nineteenth] century, a strong body of Hindu lawyers and judges came to be formed whose conformity to Hindu practices (Hindutva) was often taken to be of decisive importance in judicial decision-making, even though their professional training was in western jurisprudence, and not in Hindu law. There was, moreover, an implicit grey zone of unwritten

54   The Politics of Personal Law in South Asia

law whose force was nevertheless quite substantial within law courts. Take a Serampore Court case of 1873, for instance, where a Hindu widow was suing her brothers-in-law for defrauding her of her share in her husband's property [sic.] by falsely charging her with 'unchastity'. Her lawyer referred frequently to notions of kinship obligations, ritual expectations from a Hindu widow and moral norms and practices of high caste women. Clearly, these arguments were thought to have value in convincing the judge and the jury, even though, overtly they had little legal significance. Far from laughing peculiarly Hindu susceptibilities out of court, English judges, even the Privy Council, seriously rationalized them. . . . Legal as well as ritual niceties about the proper disposition of idols were seriously and lengthily debated and sacred objects were brought into courts of law after due ritual purification of the space.

—(Sarkar 1993: 1871)

The Politics of Muslim Law Reforms

In the section 'Early Experiments in Codification' above we mentioned the translation of *al-Hidaya* and *al-Sirajiyya* as the first steps towards codification of Muslim law in India. Financial constraints, however, came in the way of taking the exercise further at that time. It took more than seven decades before the process was resumed in 1865 when Neil Baillie translated an abbreviated version of the *Fatwa Alamgiri* and a portion of the Shia text *Itna 'Ashariya*. The translation was called *A Digest of Mohummudan Law* (Anderson 1993: 174–75). The use of these various Muslim legal texts for the administration of justice, however, created resentment, for many Muslims thought that the judgements based on them did not properly reflect the essence of Islamic law. In 1882 the National Muhammadan Association pleaded, in their memorial to the British government, for the institution of *qazi* courts. They argued that ever since the abolition of the office of the *mufti* and *qazi-ul-quzzat* or Chief Justice there was no centralised system of justice pertaining to Muslim personal law with full appreciation of Islamic tradition. Whatever be the truth, the fact was that ever since the days of Hastings the Anglo-Mohmmedan law evolved in fits and starts and, in this evolution, which included the compilation of Muslim personal law, the persons who contributed the most were C. Hamilton, Neil B. E. A. Baillie, William MacNaughtan and Syed Ameer Ali (Anderson 1993: 174–76, Jalal 2001: 143–50).

The Evolution of the Indian Discourse 55

Unlike Hindu law reforms, Muslim law reforms, however, did not take place in the nineteenth century. This was largely due to the fact that while there was a vocal reformist fringe within the Hindu community which encouraged the British to intervene in Hindu social matters, there was no comparable reformist voice within the Muslim community. Even Sir Syed Ahmed Khan's (1817–98) reformist zeal remained primarily confined to teaching the English language to Muslims so that they could compete at par with Hindus in the job market. As a result, whatever interventions were there in Muslim personal law on the part of the colonial dispensation they were in the form of codification only, largely culled out of the case laws. It was only in the second quarter of the twentieth century, by the time when the Hindu-Muslim controversy had already driven a wedge into the composite struggle for freedom from the British yoke, that the latter took interest in Muslim law reforms. But unlike the Hindu law reforms of the nineteenth century, inspired by Hindu progressive forces, these Muslim law reforms were engineered by Muslim League politicians whose primary motivation was to poach into the potential Muslim constituency of the Indian National Congress. It was against this background that in the 1930s three important events took place, which reflected two different realities. The first reality was reflected in a set of two events, namely, the passage of the Muslim Personal Law (Shariat) Application Act in September 1937 and the Dissolution of Muslim Marriages Act in 1939, while the second reality was reflected in the Lahore High Court's judgement on the Shahidganj mosque that was issued in January 1938.

The Shariat Bill had been originally tabled in the Central Assembly on 9 September 1935 by the Muslim League. The political agenda of the League was to forge unity amongst all Muslims by introducing a uniform *Shari'ah* for all Muslims of India, who did not necessarily follow a single family-law pattern at that time. Many Muslim communities of India followed local Hindu customs of joint family property based on male leadership, where women had no right to inherit. This suited the Muslim landlords of Punjab more than the proposed Shariat Act, which not only covered marriage and divorce but also inheritance that included agricultural land. According to the *Shari'ah* women inherit half of the familial property given to their male siblings. No wonder the Shariat Bill could not be passed easily because of the pressure mounted against it by Muslim landlords. Ultimately Jinnah rescued the bill from oblivion by introducing an amendment in the bill that excluded agricultural property from its purview, thereby enlisting the support of Muslim landlords, particularly of Punjab and UP.

56   The Politics of Personal Law in South Asia

Jinnah's critics rightly thought that this move was a ploy to register his support of wealthy Muslim landlords who wanted to maintain their authority to dispose of their property, unrestricted by Islamic law. This support of the landlords eventually contributed to Jinnah's demand for Pakistan. The argument that was, however, put forward was that the act would enhance the status of Muslim women and would give them the right to property (Agnes 1996b: 63; Jalal 2001: 384; Risso 1992: 56–57).

The implementation of *Shari'ah* across the board had its liabilities too as the League realised. According to the *Shari'ah,* if either party in a conjugal situation abandoned his or her religion the marriage naturally stood dissolved. It used to so happen that some Muslim women, to get rid of their oppressive husbands, would give up Islam, thereby getting out of the wedlock. But this also meant losing Muslim women to other communities. To prevent this from happening the Dissolution of Muslim Marriages Act of 1939 provided Muslim women with the opportunity to divorce their husbands without their having to give up their religion. Political motivations notwithstanding, it must, however, be conceded that the Muslim League did indeed introduce

> . . . a landmark reform in the history of Islamic (predominantly Hanafi) law in India. The concept, borrowed from the Maliki school, was based on the recommendations of the renowned Islamic scholar and an advocate of women's rights, Maulana Ashraf Ali Thanvi and was supported by jurists like Asif A. A. Fyzee. The enactments granted Muslim women two crucial rights—property inheritance and divorce, almost two decades before the Hindu women acquired similar rights.
>
> —(Agnes 1996b: 63)

But the primacy of the *Shari'ah* as a tool to promote the sectarian interest of the Muslim League, achieved through the passage of the Muslim Personal Law (Shariat) Application Act of 1937 and through the Dissolution of the Muslim Marriages Act of 1939, was tempered by the Lahore High Court judgement in the Shahidganj mosque dispute that was passed between the above two acts, in January 1938. The judgement upheld the supremacy of the British Indian law over the *Shari'ah* by drawing its authority from the Punjab Law Act, which in 1872 had overruled Muslim personal law. The Muslims of Lahore were upset by the judgement, which did not agree with the *Shari'ah* proposition that once a mosque always a mosque. They tried to register the support of Jinnah in their favour but the latter ultimately gave

The political factor that weighed against his efforts was Sikander Hayat Khan's disinterest in the affair, for he had alliance with the Hindu and Sikh landlords who had a stake in the judgment (Jalal 2001: 385). In any case, the above three developments of 1937, 1938 and 1939 proved two things, one, that law is always a political game, and two, that in the process the disadvantaged too sometimes gain as a byproduct, as happened in both the cases of the Shariat Act of 1937 and the Dissolution of Muslim Marriages Act of 1939—Muslim women had some gains.

Regional Variables

Alongside the compilation and recording of different canonical and customary laws, the British rulers also took note of the fact that it was necessary to consider the legal tenets differently, keeping in view regional specificities. Thus, in the Bombay province, Mount-stuart Elphinstone, the Governor of the province from 1818 to 1827, recognised the discrepancy between the ancient Hindu texts applied in the Bengal courts and the modern practice that was in vogue in the Maratha states. He also acknowledged that 'in many cases, what did work in practice were known customs, founded indeed on the *Dharma Shastra,* but modified by the convenience of different castes and communities, and no longer deriving authority from any written text' (Vani 2002). Elphinstone proposed a system for the province that would incorporate both the written and unwritten laws. This was to be done by producing a digest through an exhaustive investigation. Hindu lawyers, *shastris,* heads of castes and others were to be interviewed on law, custom and public opinion. In addition, court records would be studied to elicit information on these subjects obtained in the course of judicial investigation. While a digest was produced in 1827 covering some Deccan districts, the ultimate aim of Elphinstone to put to use a Bombay Code however did not materialise. The Code provided that in the absence of an act of Parliament or a regulation, the law to be observed would be the usage of the country in which the suit arose; if none were discernable, the law of the defendant was to be applied; in the absence of specific law, 'justice, equity and good conscience' should prevail. This was intended as a mechanism to protect the dynamic interplay between the Brahmanical tradition, as represented by the dharmasastras and custom, along with traditions of dispute management.

In Madras, J. H. Nelson, member of the Indian Civil Service and district judge, objected to the imposition of 'foreign law' on South

58   *The Politics of Personal Law in South Asia*

India. The Hindu 'great tradition' was foreign to the inhabitants of South India, who were not Aryans and who were generally ruled by their own customs. He suggested a short enabling act for the guidance of Madras judges which was to recognise and proclaim the general rights of Indians to consult their own inclination in all matters of adoption, alienation, testation and the like. Government was to refrain from all interference with substantive law. However, the loss of provincial autonomy under the Charter Act of 1833, which created a Central Legislature in Calcutta, frustrated these efforts.

Punjab, being a newly acquired territory, was deemed to require a strong executive with wide discretionary powers, as it was considered 'primitive'. The operation of Bengal Acts and Regulations was withheld till the end of the nineteenth century. In Punjab, custom was the primary rule of decision in questions regarding succession, special property of females, betrothal, marriage, divorce, dower, adoption, etc., with Muslim and Hindu law coming second. Official sanctity was accorded to custom by the practice, since the 1850s, of recording customs during land settlements by revenue officials. Village customs were recorded in the *'riwaj-i-am'* by collectively interrogating villagers of the same tribe or district and recording their joint answers. Based on these records, a series of volumes on customary law in the Punjab were published. A compilation of decisions of courts on points of customary law was also attempted and achieved in the 1870s, with the objective of producing a precise codification of custom as judicially recognised in the province. However, this very recording of custom fundamentally transformed its nature.

Several regulations and acts promulgated between 1753 and 1935 to serve different regional communities reserved a legal space for custom. All these laws provided that custom will be the rule of decision 'unless it is opposed to justice, equity and good conscience or unless it has been abolished or altered by a legislative enactment' (Vani 2002). Customs at variance with the general Hindu and Mohammedan law, which was administered by the courts, were heavily dependent upon the nature of evidence, the burden of proof essentially being on the person taking recourse to those customs. Indeed, the statutory reservation of the validity of custom through several enactments was not very helpful in the face of increasing and extensive codification of laws and the centralisation of the functions of lawmaking, law enforcement and dispute-management authorities. By 1882, there was an almost complete codification of commercial, criminal and procedural laws, with the exception of the personal laws of Muslims and Hindus. According to Marc Galanter, the impact of the western colonial legal

The Evolution of the Indian Discourse   59

system on customary law was that custom became a fixed body of law (through codification), indistinguishable from statute and case law; opinions and evidence given by villagers on custom, in courts or in the process of land settlement, were isolated from their contexts and utilised to describe single transactions or offences. This gave rise to a sense of individual right not dependent on community opinion or usage, actively enforced even in opposition to community opinion. Specifically, dispute management was abstracted from the totality of customary law (Galanter 1989b: 19–36). It has also been pointed out that rules of evidence imported from the colonial legal system and imposed by statute and convention on the Indian court procedures were the main reasons for the disappearance of customs. Strict criteria were imposed to prove the legal validity of custom.

Continued Involvement

In spite of the general reluctance on the part of the British to meddle in the societal affairs of the Indian communities after the revolt of 1857, there were many enactments concerning the personal laws of different communities, as we can see from Table 2.1. Some such acts were certainly progressive in terms of giving some benefit to women. For example, the Hindu Married Women's Property Rights Act of 1937 conferred benefits on Hindu women though it had several pitfalls. Flavia Agnes is of the view that the act 'conferred upon Hindu widows a limited right of life interest. Through a legal fiction, the widow was granted the right to step into the husband's shoes, and succession to her husband's property was suspended until her death. Although an important milestone, the act caused legal anomalies and confusions' (Agnes 1996b: 63). To remove those anomalies the Government of India, by a resolution dated 25 January 1941, appointed the Hindu law Committee under the chairmanship of B. N. Rau. The other members of the committee were Dwarkanath Mitter, J. R. Gharpure, Rajaratna Vasudeo and Vinayak Joshi. Their task was to examine the various bills aimed at amending the Hindu Married Women's Property Rights Act of 1937, and to suggest measures so as to remove possible injustices to daughters. The committee was also to look into the amendment that had been suggested by K. Santhanam in the Hindu Law of Inheritance and the bill introduced by G. V. Deshmukh concerning Hindu women's right to a separate residence and maintenance. The committee was of the view that the existence of various schools of Hindu law created anomalies in the situation and there should be one uniform Hindu code. All this led to the formation of

60 *The Politics of Personal Law in South Asia*

the second Hindu Law Committee in 1944, assigned the specific task of bringing about a comprehensive Hindu code. A note explaining the exact aim of the committee was issued on 5 August 1944, which read as follows:

> One of the objects of the Committee is to evolve a uniform civil code of Hindu law which will apply to all Hindus by blending the most progressive elements in the various schools of law which prevail in the different parts of the country. The achievement of uniformity necessarily involves the adoption of one view in preference to others on particular matters. The committee desire that code should be regarded as an integral whole, and that no part should be judged as if it stood by itself.
>
> —(Kannabiran 1996: 16)

The members of the committee made an extensive tour of the country, meeting all kinds of people, discussing with them the various possibilities and taking copious notes. By February 1947 they had prepared a complete draft code. When the draft was introduced in the Central Assembly in 1947, before Independence, it was not approved on account of vociferous opposition. The matter was again debated in the Constituent Assembly but it again met with stiff resistance, as is discussed below.

A Stocktaking

On the whole the British did a good job in the evolution of law in India, which was, as much as possible, based on justice and equity. Though, compared to the criminal justice system, their contribution in unifying and modernising the family laws of different communities was less, still, given the rigid social norms based on watertight caste stratifications, they did intervene positively to the extent it was politically correct. For reasons explained in the above subsections these interventions were mostly in respect of Hindu law but other personal laws too were not outside the ambit of their policy.

It is evident from the record that a uniform civil code was not on the British agenda unlike the uniform criminal code. Criminal law had already become uniform since the days of the Mughals, which the British further streamlined and standardised. The earliest of such effort was the Indian Penal Code (IPC), promulgated in 1861, which is effective till this day with certain amendments. It supplanted the so-called Muslim 'criminal' law. The fact that the Muslim community did

The Evolution of the Indian Discourse   61

not protest showed that there was no particular conservative outlook to be associated with the community. Of particular importance is that the supplanting of Muslim criminal law by the IPC showed that there was nothing sacrosanct about Islamic law either that could not be modified. In any case, as we have noted earlier, the Muslim rulers did not use the Shari'ah in respect of the criminal justice system. The IPC was translated into Urdu by Maulvi Nazir Ahmed, for which he was crowned by the British with the title 'Shamsul Ulema', which means 'the sun of theologians'. According to Asghar Ali Engineer, Muslim criminal law is as much part of the Islamic *Shari'ah* as is Muslim personal law, and therefore, 'the argument that the *shari'ah* is divine and immutable . . . is not very convincing. Such an argument could then have applied to the abolition of the Muslim criminal law too' (Engineer 1993). It was not only criminal law that was unified and codified; a major portion of civil law dealing with sales, contracts, negotiable instruments, trusts, company law, transfer of property, and procedures for settlement of cases and disputes was brought under uniform civil codes.

But so far as the personal laws of various communities were concerned, there was no effort on the part of the British to either unify or synchronise them. They were sometimes interfered with, and also codified, but to these codifications all communities apparently acquiesced (see Table 2.1). The point to be noted, therefore, is that progressive though most of these legislations were, the British could take such steps because they were somehow convinced that their actions would not lead to any mass opposition. Or, at least they were convinced that the community opinion makers were in support of these reforms; they often spearheaded them.

Evidence, however, suggests that besides political considerations which always weigh heavily in lawmaking there were two contradictory undercurrents that dominated British legal thinking; one was the genuine concern of a good number of officers to do something positive to attack the many obnoxious social customs such as sati, and the other their nagging ambivalence about how much interference with the indigenous law was really the optimum. Here is the story of a British officer, Charles Harding, of the Bengal Civil Service, as narrated by Sir W. H. Sleeman in his memoirs, *Rambles and Recollections of an Indian Official*. The story goes like this. In 1806, Harding prevented the widow of a Brahmin from committing sati. But a year later, her family somehow or the other persuaded her to sit on a funeral pyre at Ramnagar, three kilometers upstream from Varanasi. But as soon as the pyre was lit, she jumped into the river to save herself. Though

62 The Politics of Personal Law in South Asia

Table 2.1 British Legislations Intervening into Personal Laws

Hindu Law	Hindu Inheritance (Removal of Disabilities) Act, 1928
	Suttee Regulation Act, 1829
	Caste Disabilities Removal Act, 1850
	Hindu Widow's Remarriage Act, 1856
	Age of Consent Acts of 1860 and 1891
	Hindu Wills Act, 1870
	Prohibition of Female Infanticide Act, 1872
	Hindu Disposition of Property Act, 1916
	Hindu Inheritance (Removal of Disabilities) Act, 1928
	Child Marriage Restraint Act, 1929
	Hindu Gains of Learning Act, 1930
	Arya Marriage Validation Act, 1937
	Hindu Married Women's Property Rights Act, 1937
	Hindu Women's Right to Property (Sind Extension to Agricultural Land) Act, 1943
	Hindu Marriage Disabilities Removal Act, 1946
Muslim Law	Muslim Personal Law (Shariat) Application Act, 1937
	Dissolution of Muslim Marriages Act, 1939
Parsi Law	Parsi Marriage and Divorce Act, 1865 (re-enacted in 1936)
	Parsi Intestate Succession Act, 1865 (re-enacted in Part V, Chapter III, Indian Succession Act, 1925)
Christian Law	Native Converts Marriage Dissolution Act, 1866
	Indian Divorce Act, 1869
	Indian Christian Marriage Act, 1872
Secular Civil Law	Code of Criminal Procedure, 1961 (prior to this, under Hindu Law a Brahmin could not be punished on the evidence of a Sudra, nor under Muslim law a Muslim on the evidence of a non-Muslim [Chatterjee 1996: 54])
	Indian Succession Act, 1865 (re-enacted in 1925)
	Special Marriage Act, 1872 (re-enacted in 1954)
	Contract Act, 1872
	Specific Relief Act, 1877
	Negotiable Instruments Act, 1881
	Transfer of Property Act, 1882
	Guardians and Wards Act, 1890

she did not know how to swim she managed to remain afloat till a police boat rescued her in Varanasi. The town was in uproar at the news, and the community leaders suggested that Harding, the concerned officer, return the widow to the pyre if he wanted to preserve the peace. Having exhausted all the rational arguments at his command to no effect at all, Harding took recourse to an ingenious argument. He convinced the crowd that it was not he who had saved the widow but actually Mother Ganga. How else could she have survived

The Evolution of the Indian Discourse 63

without knowing how to swim? Her sacrifice on the pyre was obviously unacceptable to Mother Ganga. The point was well taken and the widow survived. In 1826, Lord Amherst had asked for the views of seven European district magistrates of central India on whether a ban on sati would be acceptable to the people. All seven said it would not. But when Lord William Bentinck did ban sati in 1829, there was no protest (Akbar 2003).

About the second undercurrent, here is some supportive evidence. A mid-nineteenth century British legal perspective on the matter reads as follows:

> . . . in lieu of this simple and rational mode of dispensing justice, we have given the natives an obscure, complicated, pedantic system of English law, full of 'artificial technicalities', which . . . force them to have recourse to a swarm of attorneys . . . that is . . . *professional rogues* . . . by means of which we have taught an indigenous people to refine upon the quibbles and fictions of English lawyers. . . . The course of justice, civil as well as criminal, is utterly confounded in a maze of artifice and fraud, and the natives, both high and low, are becoming more and more demoralized.
>
> —(Galanter 1989b: 39)

Even as late as 1945, similar sentiments were expressed by a scholarly British district officer: 'We proceeded, with the best of intentions, to clamp down upon India a vast system of law and administration which was for the most part quite unsuited to the people. . . . In Indian conditions the whole elaborate machinery of English law, which Englishmen tended to think so perfect, simply didn't work and has been completely perverted' (*ibid*.: 38).

On the whole, however, the British efforts, though slow and of limited consequence, were steps in the right direction insofar as personal laws were concerned. Given the societal conservatism of India, nothing more probably could have been expected. After Independence the Indian intelligentsia did not fail to recognise the British contribution to the Indian legal system. Barring a few Gandhians, no one felt romantic about going back to the indigenous system of law and justice. M. C. Setalvad, India's former attorney general, while delivering the Patel Memorial Lecture in Delhi, 1965, had no hesitation in saying that India 'owes a great debt to the British for the introduction of uniform and equal laws applicable to all citizens. Secularism and equality were writ large in the codified and other laws administered by the British'. He reminded his audience: 'Let us not forget that the

64 The Politics of Personal Law in South Asia

criminal and civil laws in operation before the advent of the British were in many respects unequal in their dealings with the citizen and discriminated in favour of those highly placed in the caste hierarchy' (Setalvad 1967: 49–50).

The UCC in Nationalist Discourse

Within the framework of the nationalist movement no political group, not even Congress, was particularly concerned with the issue of a uniform civil code. Notably, in the report of the Committee appointed by the All Parties Conference popularly known as the [Motilal] Nehru Committee Report of 1928, which was supposed to counter the Simon Commission and determine the principles of the Constitution of India, there was neither any reference to the subject nor to the question of personal laws of various communities (text of the Report in Hasan 2002: 429–72). But if one looks into the antecedents of the establishment of the Nehru Committee and the emphasis it put on the collective approach to take care of the minority question, particularly the one pertaining to the untouchables, it may be seen that Congress was opposed to the idea of individual citizens insofar as social reforms were concerned, the fundamental premise of B. R. Ambedkar's politics (Jaffrelot 2005: 56). It was against this background that, at the Karachi session of the Congress held in 1931, the party assured the minorities that they would be allowed to follow their personal laws.

In the unity conference held in 1932 at Allahabad no Hindu leader, including Madan Mohan Malaviya who was a known Hindu campaigner, however, objected to the Muslim proposal for setting up *Shari'ah* or *qazi* courts. The proposal was referred to a subcommittee convened by K. N. Katju, who later became the defence minister of India and chief minister of Madhya Pradesh. The conference eventually accepted the Muslim proposal. The demand for reform in the Hindu personal law was, however, increasingly audible from the women members of the Congress. Captain Laxmi, speaking at the All India Women's Conference (AIWC) meeting of 1933, stated: 'The members of the Legislative Assembly who are all men will not help us in bringing any drastic changes which will benefit women'. The organisation continued with its efforts and, at the urging of one of its leading members, Renuka Ray, 24 November 1934 was declared the 'Disabilities Day'. AIWC also undertook to make a comparative analysis of the personal laws of different communities to see if a uniform civil code could be developed. All these efforts bore some fruit; Congress did decide to strive for a uniform civil code. But, following

The Evolution of the Indian Discourse 65

the Government of India Act of 1935, when it got an opportunity to share power, it did not show enough interest in the matter (Agnes 1996b: 63). It should, however, be appreciated that, first, it could hardly remain in power for long in the provinces that it ruled, and second, the outbreak of World War II overtook the nationalist movement and altered the discourse substantially. In any case, in the conflict between the conservative Muslims and the reformist Muslims, Congress had decided to side with the former because it were they who were for a one-nation theory while the latter, represented by the Muslim League, were for a two-nation theory that eventually culminated in their demand for the partition of India. Thus while the Congress had political compulsions to go slow on the uniform civil code, the Muslim League had political compulsions to stress the value of Muslim personal law in the life of the community. That way the League wanted to unite the Muslims, thereby negating the concept of a uniform civil code. Ironically, neither the Congress nor the League wanted a uniform civil code but their intentions were diametrically opposite.

The Constituent Assembly Debates

The Constituent Assembly of India, which held its sessions from 9 December 1946 to 24 January 1950, considered whether it was possible to introduce a family code uniformly applicable across the communities. One of the greatest champions for the cause was B. R. Ambedkar, the chairman of the Drafting Committee. Even a Hindu traditionalist like K. M. Munshi, unlike others belonging to the same ideology within the Congress, which we will discuss in Chapter III, was in favour of a uniform code and emphasised the need 'to consolidate and unify our personal law in such a way that the way of life of the whole country may in course of time be unified and secular' (Quoted in Jaffrelot 2004: 144). But the contemporary politics of one-upmanship between the Congress and the Muslim League, which was to culminate in the partition of India, weighed heavily in the minds of the members and came in the way of the acceptance of such a code.

Prior to the partition it was the constant propaganda of the Muslim League that Muslim personal law would not be respected in 'Hindu India' after Independence. The Jamaat-e-Ulema-e-Hind (the organisation of Muslim theologians) and the Deobandis in general, which were opposed to the Muslim League and subscribed to the Congress theory that India was one nation, took this up as a challenge and tried to convince the Muslims of India that just as the British did not touch

66   The Politics of Personal Law in South Asia

the essentials of Muslim personal law the Indian government would also not tamper with them. Indeed the Deobandis were conservative on social questions pertaining to Muslims but their commitment to a unified India was beyond doubt (Sikand 2005: 25–31). In the 1940s, therefore, when the Pakistan movement was picking up momentum, their support to the Congress was of critical importance to the latter. As such, making a commitment to respect Muslim personal law after Independence made political sense. Hence the *ulema* sought an assurance to this effect from Gandhi and Nehru, and received one. Against this background, Nehru persuaded the Constituent Assembly not to press for a uniform civil code. Placing the subject in the list of Directive Principles of State Policy was a compromise that seemed to satisfy all. The Article, numbered 35 in the draft constitution, which in the adopted constitution became 44, read as follows: 'The State shall endeavour to secure for the citizens a uniform civil code throughout the territory of India'.

It was, however, not easy to arrive at this consensus. There were three occasions when the matter figured in the debates. Primarily, the contexts were: one, individual versus community rights within the discourse on fundamental rights; two, religion and secularism; and three, and directly, the question of incorporating the above said article in the constitution. Indeed, all three discourses were closely interrelated and often overlapping. The justiciable fundamental rights that both K. M. Munshi and B. R Ambedkar had put in the draft articles in March 1947 indirectly referred to a uniform civil code. Munshi's proposal stated: 'No civil or criminal court shall, in adjudicating any matter or executing any order, recognize any custom or usage imposing any civil disability on any person on the ground of his caste, status, religion, race or language'. Ambedkar's draft said that all subjects of the Indian state shall have the right 'to claim full and equal benefit of all laws and proceedings for the security of persons and property as is enjoyed by other subjects regardless of any usage or custom based on religion and be subject to like punishment, pains and penalties and to none other'. These suggestions, however, were overtaken by the fact that on 30 March 1947 the Fundamental Rights Sub-Committee decided to put the uniform civil code issue in the Directive Principles part. This did not satisfy all and some felt strongly in favour of an affirmative position. Considering it to be 'very vital to social progress', Rajkumari Amrit Kaur emphasised the importance of the uniform civil code. In a joint letter of 14 April 1947 she, along with Hansa Mehta and M. R. Masani (all three were the members of the Sub-Committee) strongly pleaded in favour of transferring the provision from the Directive

The Evolution of the Indian Discourse 67

Principles to Fundamental Rights. It may be noted that Kaur was a Christian, Masani a Parsi, and Mehta a Hindu. They wrote:

> We are not satisfied with the acceptance of a Uniform Civil Code as an ultimate social objective set out in Clause 39 [Article 35 in the Draft Constitution and Article 44 in the adopted Constitution] as determined by the majority of the Sub-Committee. One of the factors that has kept India back from advancing to nationhood has been the existence of Personal Laws based on religion which keep the nation divided into watertight compartments in many aspects of life. We are of the view that a Uniform Civil Code should be guaranteed to the Indian people within a period of five to ten years in the same manner as the right to free and compulsory primary education has been guaranteed by Clause 23 within ten years.
>
> —(Dhagamwar 1989a: 2; Jha 2002: 3178)

The controversy, however, subsided and the clause continued to remain in the Directive Principles.

In spite of the fact that nothing substantive was done towards codifying a uniform civil code for India, the Muslim fear persisted. It came to the fore when the draft article in the Directive Principles dealing with the issue came up for debate on 23 November 1948. By that time India had become independent, it had been partitioned, the worst Hindu-Muslim riots had rocked the public consciousness, and millions of Hindus and Muslims had migrated to Pakistan and India respectively. Also, India and Pakistan had fought their first war over Kashmir. And, most importantly, a Hindu fanatic had killed Mahatma Gandhi, on 30 January 1948. Against this background, Indian Muslims were in a predicament. They were worried about their future in India and as such were diffident in pushing their case aggressively. The Hindu leadership of the Congress had a mixed bag to carry. In the first place, they had to think of the social development of India on modern lines; second, they had their commitment to Muslims not to fiddle with their identity markers and third, they had the added compulsion to show Pakistan their democratic commitments in which their respect for minority rights had to figure prominently. All these concerns played their roles in the debate on the uniform civil code.

In the Constituent Assembly there were no female members from the Muslim community. As a result, the Muslim women's perspective was conspicuous by its absence. Amongst the Muslim members who held progressive views was Tajamul Husain from Bihar, as was particularly reflected in his views expressed during the debate on

68 The Politics of Personal Law in South Asia

secularism and religion. But he was not present in the debate on the Draft Article 35. The four members who moved amendments to the Article, were: Mohamad Ismail Sahib (Muslim member from Madras), Naziruddin Ahmad (Muslim member from West Bengal), Mahboob Ali Baig Sahib Bahadur (Muslim member from Madras) and B. Pocker Sahib Bahadur (Muslim member from Madras). Besides, there was Hussain Imam (Muslim member from Bihar), who did not propose any amendment but strongly argued in favour of preserving Muslim personal law. Article 35 of the Draft Constitution read: 'The State shall endeavour to secure for citizens a uniform civil code throughout the territory of India'. To this Mohamad Ismail Sahib moved the following proviso to be added: 'Provided that any group, section or community of people shall not be obliged to give up its own personal law in case it has such a law'. He argued that personal law was part of Islam and as such Muslims would not compromise on the matter. He referred to the experience of Yugoslavia where the personal laws of Serbs, Croats and Slovenes were equally respected. Questioning the wisdom behind a uniform civil code he argued that it was 'evidently to secure harmony through uniformity. But I maintain that for that purpose it is not necessary to regiment the civil law of the people including the personal law. Such regimentation will bring discontent and harmony will be affected. But if people are allowed to follow their own personal law there will be no discontent or disaffection. Every section of the people, being free to follow its own personal law will not really come in conflict with others' (*Constituent Assembly Debates,* Vol. VII, 4 November 1948–8 January 1949: 540–41).

Naziruddin Ahmad proposed the following amendment to the article: 'Provided that the personal law of any community which has been guaranteed by the statute shall not be changed except with the previous approval of the community ascertained in such manner as the Union Legislature may determine by law'. He argued that while the 175 year old British regime had enacted several laws that interfered with the civil laws of various communities, but on fundamental matters like marriage, inheritance, etc., there was conscious effort on its part not to meddle with them. 'I have no doubt that a stage would come when the civil law would be uniform. But then that time has not yet come. We believe that the power that has been given to the State to make the Civil Code uniform is in advance of the time. As it is, any State would be justified under article 35 to interfere with the settled laws of the different communities at once' (*Constituent Assembly Debates,* Vol. VII, 4 November 1948–8 January 1949: 541–43).

The Evolution of the Indian Discourse 69

Mahboob Ali Baig Sahib Bahadur moved that the following proviso be added to the article: 'Provided that nothing in this article shall affect the personal law of the citizen'. Referring to the fact that civil law was a larger concept that included laws of property, transfer of property, law of contract, laws of evidence, etc., he surmised whether the framers of the article had only the personal laws in mind. If so, then 'they are overlooking the very important fact of the personal law being so much dear and near to certain religious communities. As far as the Mussalmans are concerned, their laws of succession, inheritance, marriage and divorce are completely dependent upon their religion' (*Constituent Assembly Debates*, VII, 4 November 1948–8 January 1949: 543). On the same lines B. Pocker Sahib Bahadur moved the following proviso: 'Provided that any group, section or community of people shall not be obliged to give up its own personal law in case it has such a law'. He argued that the demand for the retention of personal law was not typically a Muslim demand. Many Hindu organisations had also expressed their anxiety. He raised the fundamental question of the representativeness of the Constituent Assembly and whether the members were returned specifically to deal with the issue.

> If such a body as this interferes with the religious rights and practices, it will be tyrannous. . . . What is it that you are making the basis? Is it open to us to do anything of this sort? By this one clause you are revolutionizing the whole country and the whole setup. There is no need for it. . . . Even assuming that the majority community is of this view, I say, it has to be condemned and it ought not to be allowed, because, in a democracy, as I take it, it is the duty of the majority to secure the sacred rights of every minority. It is a misnomer to call it a democracy if the majority rides roughshod over the rights of the minorities. It is not democracy at all; it is tyranny.
>
> (*Constituent Assembly Debates*, Vol. VII,
> 4 November 1948–8 January 1949: 544–45)

The responses to all the proposed amendments came from K. M. Munshi, Alladi Krishnaswamy Ayyar and B. R. Ambedkar, who all found them superfluous. Munshi argued that the Article was just an enabling clause and the whole idea was that 'as and when the Parliament thinks proper or rather when the majority in the Parliament thinks proper an attempt may be made to unify the personal law of the country'. He took strong exception to the branding of the uniform civil code as 'tyrannical to minorities'.

70 *The Politics of Personal Law in South Asia*

Nowhere in advanced Muslim countries the personal law of each minority has been recognized as so sacrosanct as to prevent the enactment of a Civil Code. Take for instance Turkey or Egypt. No minority in these countries is permitted to have such rights. But I go further. When the Shariat Act was passed or when certain laws were passed in the Central Legislature in the old regime, the Khojas and Cutchi Memons were highly dissatisfied. They then followed certain Hindu customs; for generations since they became converts they had done so. They did not want to conform to the Shariaht; and yet by a legislation of the Central Legislature certain Muslim members who felt that Shariaht law should be enforced upon the whole community carried their point. The Khojas and Cutchi Memons most unwillingly had to submit to it. Where were the rights of minority then?

—(*Constituent Assembly Debates,* Vol. VII,
4 November 1948–8 January 1949: 547–48)

Munshi strongly advocated the uniformity of civil law to serve as a vehicle of societal growth in which, in the larger interest, some sacrifices were inevitable. Even the on going process of reforming Hindu law was in tune with the same ethos, he said. 'Look at the Hindu Law; you get any amount of discrimination against women; and if that is part of Hindu religion or Hindu religious practice, you cannot pass a single law which would elevate the position of Hindu women to that of men. Therefore, there is no reason why there should not be a civil code throughout the territory of India'. Pleading with the Muslim members to shed their 'isolationist outlook on life', Munshi said:

This attitude of mind perpetuated under the British rule, that personal law is part of religion, has been fostered by the British and by British courts. We must, therefore, outgrow it. If I may just remind the honourable Member who spoke last [Husain Imam] of a particular incident from Fereshta which comes to my mind, Allauddin Khilji made several changes which offended against the Shariaht, though he was the first ruler to establish Muslim Sultanate here. The Kazi of Delhi objected to some of his reforms, and his reply was—'I am an ignorant man and I am ruling this country in its best interests. I am sure, looking at my ignorance and my good intentions, the Almightly will forgive me, when he finds that I have not acted according to the Shariaht'. If Allauddin could not, much less can a modern government accept the proposition that religious rights cover personal law or several other

The Evolution of the Indian Discourse   71

matters which we have been unfortunately trained to consider as part of our religion.
—(*Constituent Assembly Debates*, Vol. VII,
4 November 1948–8 January 1949: 547–48)

Supporting the position held by Munshi, Alladi Krishnaswamy Ayyar said that Muslim law included a whole set of laws, including criminal law. But when the British introduced a uniform criminal code the Muslims did not object. The same was true with the law of contract.

The future Legislatures may attempt a uniform Civil Code or they may not. The uniform Civil Code will run into every aspect of Civil Law. In regard to contracts, procedure and property uniformity is sought to be secured by their finding a place in the Concurrent List. In respect of these matters the greatest contribution of British jurisprudence has been to bring about a uniformity in these matters. We only go a step further than the British who ruled in this country. Why should you distrust much more a national indigenous Government than a foreign Government which has been [*sic.*] ruling? Why should our Muslim friends have greater confidence, greater faith in the British rule than in a democratic rule which will certainly have regard to the religious tenets and beliefs of all people?
—(*Constituent Assembly Debates*, Vol. VII,
4 November 1948–8 January 1949: 549–50)

B. R. Ambedkar did not accept the proposed amendments and promised to make a more detailed response when the amendments to certain fundamental rights would be moved as will be discussed later. But he took the opportunity to refer to several developments in respect of Muslim law during the 1930s to drive home his point. He mentioned that up to 1935 the North-West Frontier Province (NWFP) was not subject to the Shariat law. Many important aspects of the civil law of the province were governed by Hindu law. So much so that in 1939 the Central Legislature had to abrogate the application of Hindu law to the Muslims of the NWFP and to apply the Shariat law to them. Not only in the NWFP, but also in parts of Bombay, the Central Provinces and the United Provinces the same situation prevailed till 1937 in respect of succession amongst Muslims. In order to make it uniform for all Muslims, an enactment was passed in 1937 applying the Shariat law to the rest of India. Ambedkar also referred to the

72 The Politics of Personal Law in South Asia

contemporary practice of the matriarchal system of the Marumakka-thayyam law that was being applied to both Hindus and Muslims of North Malabar. However, Ambedkar tried to assuage Muslim sentiments by talking about his position on the optionality of the uniform civil code. His argument was:

> It [the Draft Article 35] does not say that after the Code is framed the State shall enforce it upon all citizens merely because they are citizens. It is perfectly possible that the future Parliament may make a provision by way of making a beginning that the Code shall apply only to those who make a declaration that they are prepared to be bound by it, so that in the initial stage the application of the Code may be purely voluntary. Parliament may feel the ground by some such method. This is not a novel method. It was adopted in the Shariaht Act of 1937 when it was applied to territories other than the North-West Frontier Province. The law said that here is a Shariaht law which should be applied to Mussalmans provided a Mussalman who wanted that he should be bound by the Shariaht Act should go to an officer of the state, make a declaration that he is willing to be bound by it, and after he has made that declaration the law will bind him and his successors. It would be perfectly possible for Parliament to introduce a provision of that sort; so that the fear which my friends have expressed here will be altogether nullified. I therefore submit that there is no substance in these amendments and I oppose them.
>
> —(*Constituent Assembly Debates,* Vol. VII,
> 4 November 1948–8 January 1949: 550–52)

The amendments were not accepted and Draft Article 35 was added to the constitution (later to become Article 44).

The issue of the uniform civil code figured once again in the Constituent Assembly debates on 1 and 2 December 1948 when the Draft Article 13 (Article 19 of the Constitution of India) came up for debate. Once again Mohamed Ismail Sahib tried to add a protective clause in respect of freedom of religion to the effect that this freedom meant also 'to follow the personal law of the group or community to which he belongs or professes to belong'. He took the opportunity to refute all the arguments that K. M. Munshi had put forward in defence of Article 35 dealing with the uniform civil code, as has been discussed. Strongly holding the position that religion and personal laws were closely linked and one could not be divorced from the other, he said that Munshi 'as an illustrious and eminent lawyer ought

The Evolution of the Indian Discourse   73

to know that this question of personal law is entirely based upon religion. It is nothing if it is not religious'. He also refuted Munshi with regard to his arguments about the state of affairs in Egypt and Turkey. In both the countries, Ismail Sahib argued, the personal laws of minorities were respected (*Constituent Assembly Debates*, Vol. VII, 4 November 1948 to 8 January 1949: 722–23). These arguments were supported by Maulana Hasrat Mohani (Muslim member from the United Provinces), who stated:

> I would like to say that any party, political or communal, has no right to interfere in the personal law of any group. More particularly I say this regarding Muslims. There are three fundamentals in their personal law, namely, religion, language, and culture which have not been ordained by human agency. Their personal law regarding divorce, marriage and inheritance has been derived from the Qoran and its interpretation is recorded therein. If there is any one, who thinks that he can interfere in the personal law of the Muslims, then I would say to him that the result will be harmful.
>
> —(*Constituent Assembly Debates*, Vol. VII,
> 4 November 1948–8 January 1949: 759)

Responding to the Muslim apprehensions M. Ananthasayanam Ayyangar said that there was no question that the state would ride roughshod over Muslim personal law. 'The law of the land as it exists today gives sufficient guarantee so far as that is concerned. But our friends who moved the amendments wanted a double guarantee that their personal law ought not to be interfered with. My submission is that it is impracticable, for, in an advanced society, even the members who belong to a particular community may desire their personal law to be changed' (*Constituent Assembly Debates*, Vol. VII, 4 November 1948–8 January 1949: 777–78). Wrapping up the debate on the question of fundamental rights, B. R. Ambedkar made the following final statement in respect of uniform civil code:

> Coming to the question of saving personal law, I think this matter was very completely and very sufficiently discussed and debated at the time when we discussed one of the Directive Principles of this Constitution which enjoins the State to seek or to strive to bring about a uniform civil code and I do not think it is necessary to make any further reference to it, but I should like to say this, that if such a saving clause was introduced into the Constitution,

74 The Politics of Personal Law in South Asia

it would disable the legislatures in India from enacting any social measure whatsoever. The religious conceptions in this country are so vast that they cover every aspect of life, from birth to death. There is nothing which is not religion and if personal law is to be saved, I am sure about it that in social matters we will come to a stand-still. . . . After all, what are we having this liberty for? We are having this liberty in order to reform our social system which is so full of inequities, so full in inequalities, discriminations and other things, which conflict with our fundamental rights. It is, therefore, quite impossible for anybody to conceive that the personal law shall be excluded from the jurisdiction of the State. Having said that, I should also like to point out that all that the State is claiming in this matter is a power to legislate. There is no obligation upon the State to do away with personal laws. It is only giving a power. Therefore, no one need be apprehensive of the fact that if the State has the power, the State will immediately proceed to execute to enforce that power in a manner that may be found to be objectionable by the Muslims or by the Christians or by any other community in India. . . . No Government can exercise its power in such a manner as to provoke the Muslim community to rise in rebellion. I think it would be a mad Government if it did so. But that is a matter which relates to the exercise of the power and not to the power itself.

—(*Constituent Assembly Debates,* Vol. VII,
4 November 1948–8 January 1949: 779–780)

Notes

1   Elsewhere, Dhagamwar mentions an interesting case. Resolution 10 [of the Anandpur Sahib Resolution] demanded a change in the Hindu Succession Act to take away a woman's right to inherit her father's property, and to confine her rights of succession to only her father-in-law's property. Needless to say, this would open the flood-gates to enforced marriages between the widow and her deceased husband's brother. Levirate marriages are not unknown to North India. It is the compulsion that would be anti-women, as indeed Resolution 10 is. After the November 1984 [anti-Sikh] riots, many young widows had to take divorce from their fathers-in-law before they could remarry. This divorce was on the poignant ground that there was no surviving son in the family to marry the widow. The law does *not* recognise a grotesque and bizarre phenomenon such as divorce from the father-in-law or indeed anyone other than the legally wedded and living spouse. A widow is, therefore, totally legally free to marry. She needs no such document or "divorce",

yet social forces are such that she cannot marry within the community without it' (Dhagamwar 1989a: 65).

2 She mentions the absurdity of an English judgment that referred to the existence of 'a Hindu idol as a legal person: "Nothing impossible or absurd in it . . . after all an idol is as much of a person as a corporation,"' (Sarkar 1993: 1871). Legally speaking, the judge probably had a valid point in the concerned case, which, in the absence of a detailed discussion by Sarkar on the subject, cannot be elaborated on any further here. A person is a legal entity bound by law. It may not be one of flesh and blood. The Church is a person, so are corporations, *waqfs,* universities and also deities, and therefore they can hold property within the legal framework. They pay taxes, sue and can be sued.

3 It is Politics, Stupid!

> Article 44 of the Indian Constitution, which directs the state to enact a uniform civil code for all citizens, has been both a perennial as well as a source of permanent embarrassment ever since the Constitution was adopted. Some are annoyed because the article is still in cold storage. Others are embarrassed because the article continues to exist. The individuals in the first category give supreme consideration to fundamental rights guaranteed to all citizens, particularly the right to equality before law and the right to life. The second group feels equally strongly that family law is or should be outside the purview of the Constitution.
>
> —Vasudha Dhagamwar, in *Economic and Political Weekly,* 2003

It is Economics, Stupid!

The huge poster that adorned the campaign office of the Arkansas governor Bill Clinton at Little Rock who was running for the American presidency in 1992 read: 'It is Economics, Stupid'. That short phrase said all—Clinton was to give primacy to America's economic recovery. American voters listened to him and allowed him to lead them for two consecutive terms. Our understanding of the Indian discourse on the uniform civil code or reforms in personal laws in post-independent India is that it is nothing but politics that dictates it and hence this paraphrasing of that Clintonian wisdom.

The Embarrassing Directive

More than half a century has passed since the Constitution of India has granted the power to the state to implement a uniform civil code but the politics of the country has not allowed any government to exercise that power. On the contrary, in spite of several exhortations by the courts, the political class has reinforced its commitment not to meddle with the personal laws of the minorities, most notably that of the Muslims. The predicament of the situation is reflected in the following words of Vasudha Dhagamwar:

> Article 44 of the Indian Constitution, which directs the state to enact a uniform civil code for all citizens, has been both a perennial as well as a source of permanent embarrassment ever since the Constitution was adopted. Some are annoyed because the article is still in cold storage. Others are embarrassed because the article continues to exist. The individuals in the first category give supreme consideration to fundamental rights guaranteed to all citizens, particularly the right to equality before law and the right to life. The second group feels equally strongly that family law is or should be outside the purview of the Constitution.
>
> —(Dhagamwar 2003: 1483)

Several years later, in 1973, the Ministry of Law and Justice brought out a commemorative volume of the Constitution of India in which it was suggested that it was the judiciary that had, in the early 1950s, diluted the importance of the Directive Principles by making the latter subservient to Fundamental Rights, highlighting that while the Fundamental Rights were justiciable the Directive Principles were not.

> Thus, in spite of the precautions taken by the framers in stating expressly that the Directive Principles were fundamental and obligatory, the courts failed to understand their significance. By giving undue emphasis to their non-justiciable character, they whittled down their vital importance. At a later stage, this view of the Supreme Court, was developed in such a manner as to threaten the Directive Principles with virtual atrophy and extinction. Recently, therefore, Parliament had to come forward with the Twenty-fifth Amendment and provide that no law seeking to enforce the Directive Principles in clauses (b) and (c) of article 39 shall be held invalid on the ground that it violates the fundamental right in article 14, article 19, or article 31.
>
> —(Government of India 1973a: vii)

Indeed the Twenty-fifth Amendment did not do something innovative. The note that B. N. Rau, Constitutional Adviser to the Constituent Assembly, had submitted to the Drafting Committee had

78 *The Politics of Personal Law in South Asia*

said that it was 'a matter requiring careful consideration whether the Constitution might not expressly provide that no law made and no action taken by the State in the discharge of its duties' under the Directive Principles 'shall be invalid merely for reason of its contravening' the Fundamental Rights. He was apprehensive that in the absence of such an express provision 'the private right may override the public weal' (Government of India 1973a: viii). The fact, however, remains that the Directive Principles have virtually remained a bunch of pious thoughts and successive governments have honoured most of them by ignoring them, notably the directive to introduce a uniform civil code.

Somewhat tangentially, an interesting observation can be made here. The Constituent Assembly, on the one hand, just stopped short of introducing a uniform civil code while, on the other, just stopped short of declaring India a secular state. Besides the fact that K. T. Shah's suggestion to declare India as secular and define the word unequivocally was twice rejected, probably on the ground that it tended to send an anti-religious message, which Indian politics was not tuned to, it has also been argued that Congress politics was willy-nilly a pro-Hindu politics, which could not afford to delink religion from politics (Mallampalli 1995: 80–91). Ashis Nandy agrees with this line of argumentation, though from a different perspective, when he writes: 'My criticism of secularism is an aggressive reaffirmation of these proto-Gandhian traditions and a search for post-secular forms of politics more in touch with the needs of a democratic polity in South Asia. . . . In this effort I have been guided by Gandhi's maxim that those who think that religion has nothing to do with politics understand neither religion nor politics. I leave it to the next generation of South Asians living in South Asia to judge if it has been all a waste of time' (Nandy 2004: 14; for more on this point, see Ghosh 1999: 159–67).

What suited Hindus, Muslims and other religious groups during the days of the Constituent Assembly was religious tolerance, which could be incorporated in the Constitution even without characterising it as 'secular'. There was no hurry either, therefore, to implement UCC because the continuation of personal laws of different communities underlined the state's commitment to religious tolerance without compromising its authority to strive for the same at some point in future if the situation became sufficiently conducive. That during the Emergency (1975–77) Indira Gandhi amended the Constitution in 1976 to declare India a 'socialist' and 'secular' state is another story, which is not relevant for our analysis here. Politics being at the core of the problem in introducing a uniform civil code, it would be instructive

It is Politics, Stupid! 79

to trace the development of this politics. In the previous chapter we have discussed the evolution of the discourse till the promulgation of the constitution. In this chapter we will carry the story forward, beginning with the passage of the Hindu Code bills and the politics surrounding them.

The Codification of Hindu Law

The decade of the 1950s was a decade of a forward march towards replacement of the traditional Hindu personal law by a modern and standardised code, which would have little to do with the Hindu dharmashastras. In this march, three elements were noticeable. First, the approach was modernist and highly influenced by professional lawyers and other members of the intelligentsia who had scant regard for the traditional institutions which the Gandhians were advocating. Second, while reforming and standardising Hindu law, *shastric* tradition was not considered sacrosanct. Within the Hindu fold it was a secular move. Third, for those who did not want to use any personal law of any community in contracting a marriage, a secular option was to be made available to them.

Returning to the indigenous system of justice was ruled out, though on very small matters the relevance of the *nyayapanchayats* at the village level was recognised. The system was no substitute for the organised legal system of India that the Gandhians had wanted it to be. The Law Commission of 1958 categorically said that although even a brief analysis of the traditional Indian system would show that it was just not practicable to expect it to cope with the complexities of the law in a modern welfare state, yet village panchayats, with simplified procedures and jurisdictions over petty matters, could be established. The experiment, however, did not work well, primarily because village societies were faction ridden and the election of the *panchas* (*panchayat* judges) got entangled with state and national level electoral politics.[1]

Following India's independence Nehru entrusted his first Law Minister B. R. Ambedkar, who belonged to the Scheduled Caste Federation, with the task of codifying the Hindu personal law as the first step towards a uniform civil code. Ambedkar formed a committee with himself as its chairman. The other members were K. Y. Bhandarkar, G. R. Rajagopal of the Ministry of Law and S. V. Gupte of the Bombay Bar. The committee made only minor revisions to the draft that was presented to the Constituent Assembly in 1947 before Independence. But even before the bill could be put up to the

80 The Politics of Personal Law in South Asia

Constituent Assembly (Legislative) some vocal sections of Hindu public opinion raised the bogey 'Hinduism in danger'. Ambedkar and his team, however, was undaunted and continued with their efforts with all seriousness and presented the draft bill to Nehru's cabinet, which unanimously approved it. Emboldened by this exercise, on 5 February 1951 he introduced the bill to the Parliament. But to his utter surprise, many Hindu members, including some who had approved it in the cabinet earlier, now resisted it. Sardar Patel as the home minister and the Deputy Prime Minister, Syama Prasad Mookerjee as the industry minister who belonged to the Hindu Mahasabha, and Pandit Madan Mohan Malaviya, a traditionalist Congressman, strongly opposed the bill. Pattabhi Sitaramayya, the Congress president, also opposed it, particularly keeping in view its negative impacts on Hindu votes in the election of 1951–52 (Jaffrelot 2005: 116). Mookerjee said that it would 'shatter the magnificent structure of Hindu culture and stultify a dynamic and catholic way of life that had wonderfully adapted itself to the changes for centuries' (Zakaria 2003b). Even women belonging to the Hindu Mahasabha came to the forefront to oppose the bill. Already a year ago, in a long letter to President Rajendra Prasad, Janakibai Joshi, the President of the All India Hindu Women's Conference that belonged to the Hindu Mahasabha, had written on 4 February 1950 that any move to replace the concept of Hindu marriage as sacrament by making it contractual would destroy the entire family system of the Hindus. 'The Hindu family should be taken as a unit and fragmentation of the property should not be allowed so as to go away to other family through daughter [sic.]' (Akhil Bharat Hindu Mahasabha Papers, File No. C. 184, Nehru Memorial Museum and Library, New Delhi, as cited by Chakravartty 2005: 26).

Malaviya declared that nothing should be done to 'damage the Hindu system, which was enshrined in our scriptures'. Congressman Mukul Beharilal Bhargava opposed the bill on the grounds that it incorporated provisions of Christian and Muslim laws. Furthermore, Rajendra Prasad, the first president of the nation, threw his weight against the bill leading to its withdrawal in September 1951. In a letter to Patel, Rajendra Prasad wrote that 'new concepts and new ideas are not only foreign to Hindu law but are susceptible of dividing every family'. He did not make such comments in public but privately campaigned against the bill by arguing that the provisional parliament had no authority to decide on such critical matters. In utter disgust Ambedkar resigned from the cabinet on 27 September 1951 because he felt that even Nehru, with all the political strength at his command, did not stand behind him. In a subsequent statement Ambedkar

It is Politics, Stupid! 81

said: 'I have never seen a case of chief whip so disloyal to the Prime Minister and the Prime Minister so loyal to a disloyal whip' (Jaffrelot 2005: 116–17). He lamented that Hindus were incapable of bringing in reforms in their archaic system. He accused them of creating such an atmosphere that even other communities would not be encouraged to reform themselves (Zakaria 2003b). Vasudha Dhagamwar writes: 'The first round for the Uniform Civil Code had already been lost in the Constituent Assembly where, though no amendments to Art. 35 [Article 44 of the Indian Constitution] were allowed, verbal assurances of the kind demanded by dissenting members had been given by Dr Ambedkar. With his resignation the second round was lost, for the man who had a clear vision in matters legal and constitutional, had departed from the scene' (Dhagamwar 1989a: 5).

Nehru's fortnightly letters to the chief ministers are replete with evidences of his commitment to the cause of having a uniform code of Hindu personal law. Although the major opposition to the idea had come from Hindu traditionalists, in the forefront of which was the RSS and the Anti-Hindu Code Committee, it was not confined to them alone, as we have noted above. Some sections of the Sikh community too opposed it as Hindu law included that community as well. On 3 December 1950, addressing a meeting in Amritsar, Master Tara Singh accused the Congress of driving a wedge between the Hindus and the Sikhs, and a few days later, on 13 December, he addressed a Sikh congregation in Delhi, denouncing the introduction of the Hindu Code Bill, saying that the 'Sikh religion today is in great danger and in order to protect it, great sacrifices are needed'. His main aim, of course, was to get a separate state for the Sikhs, the so-called 'Punjabi *suba*' (Parthasarathi 1985: II, 290).

In spite of these oppositions the Hindu Code Bill was ultimately passed by the Parliament in 1955–56, owing largely to Nehru's persuasive skill and because of the fact that the first Parliament that was elected in 1952 had forty-two women members. Moreover, the new law minister, H. V. Pataskar, also played an important role; he made impassioned speeches in Parliament, quoting from Hindu scriptures to underscore the point that women did enjoy equality of rights in the Hindu tradition. It was the same kind of strategy that Vidyasagar had used to poach into the conservative Hindu opposition against his efforts to get the Hindu Widow's Remarriage Act promulgated in 1856. Still, considering the fact that one comprehensive bill was more unlikely to sail through in the Parliament, it was put up in parts, which worked. The bill was enacted in three parts, namely, the Hindu Marriage Act, 1955; the Hindu Adoptions and Maintenance Act,

82   *The Politics of Personal Law in South Asia*

1956; and the Hindu Succession Act, 1956. Nehru argued in favour of the bills not from the point of view of Hindu religion but from his sense of Hindu history. Nehru was very happy that ultimately some progress could be achieved in the legal status of women falling within the purview of Hindu law. Writing to the chief ministers on 10 May and 15 June 1956, he characterised the passage of the bills as 'an epoch' amounting to 'a social revolution'. 'They have broken the barrier of ages and cleared the way somewhat for our womenfolk to progress. I have long been convinced that a nation's progress is intimately connected with the status of its women' (Parthasarathi 1985: IV, 369, 384).

The Hindu Code was not a secular code but the importance of it lay in the fact that it upheld the authority of the Parliament to legislate in matters of personal law and that in so doing it did not take recourse to any religious sanction associated with that law. The Code turned away from the Hindu shastric tradition by abandoning the varna considerations, one of the most essential elements of Hindu social organisation. By favouring greater individualism, emphasis on the nuclear family, the possibility of divorce and the equality of varnas, the Code attacked certain core traditions of the Hindu social system like the caste system, the indissolubility of marriage, the preference for the extended joint family and the custom of inheritance by males only. Thus the Hindu Code became the first step in the direction of the uniform civil code for it was validated on the grounds of India being a secular state. Whatever elements of Hindu flexibility could be used were used to make them take the first pill, for ultimately the movement towards a uniform civil code had to be based on the nature of citizenship in the secular state (Baird 1978: 83). Highlighting the far-reaching impact of the Code on the evolution of civil law in India, Galanter writes:

> For the first time, the bulk of the world's Hindus live under a single central authority that has both the desire and the power to enforce changes in their social arrangements. It has been pointed out that, throughout the history of Hinduism, no general and sweeping reforms were possible, just because of the absence of centralized government or ecclesiastical institutions. Reformers might persuade others and they might gain acceptance as a sect; but there was no way for them to win the power to enforce changes on others. They could supplement existing practice but they could not supplant it, because there were no levers which could be grasped to accomplish across-the-board changes. The

It is Politics, Stupid! 83

modern legal system has made possible enforcement of changes among all Hindus by a powerful central authority. The Code subjects Hindus to a degree of uniformity unprecedented in Hindu legal history. Regional differences; the schools of commentators; differences according to *varna*; customs of locality, caste, and family; many special statutes and estates, and (largely) distinctions of sex have all fallen by the wayside. Some narrow scope is allowed for custom, but for the first time a single set of rules is applicable to Hindus of every caste, sect and region.

—(Galanter 1997: 30)

The Pitfalls of the Hindu Code

The process, however, remained incomplete. Caste practices continued to influence the family laws of Hindus despite the Code. Derrett has listed matters that remained open to customary variation: the prohibited degrees for marriage, the maximum age of adoption, the right to dissolution of marriage by a caste tribunal, the right to be a *sanyasi* (hermit), the right to maintenance out of indivisible estates, and other joint family rights (Derrett 1963: Section 13). In the crucial area of Hindu undivided family property, women remained excluded. 'This resulted in the piquant situation in which a woman could be prime minister of India but not the *karta* (head) of a Hindu joint family' (Dhavan 2003). The Hindu undivided family system indeed was a relevant social concept in the pre-industrial era when the entire family worked together; at present, too, it is convenient for farming communities and villages but it has become a tax haven for urbanites and businessmen.

Feminist scholars also found fault with the Hindu Code, on the grounds that, in the process of standardising Hindu law, the Code obliterated many positive elements that obtained with the lower caste Hindus or those communities which followed the matrilineal system of inheritance. For example, the Nairs in Kerala, the Meiteis in Manipur, the Meenas in Rajasthan, and the Jains had more gender-just system, which the Hindu Code neutralised (Menon 2002: 80). Flavia Agnes argues that to countenance the impediments to the passage of the act some crucial women's rights had to be compromised to appease detractors. For example, since Rajendra Prasad had threatened to veto the abolition of coparcenaries, it had to be retained. Similarly, daughters' right of inheritance was nullified by introducing the concept of testamentary succession. By enacting the Code the state abdicated its responsibility to secularise and homogenise family laws for good. For

84 The Politics of Personal Law in South Asia

instance, Hindus were taken out of the application of statutes applicable across communities such as the Guardians and Wards Act of 1890. The Hindu Adoption and Maintenance Act of 1956 restricted the scope of this Act. Concessions were made to Hindu coparcenaries within taxation laws. By emphasising the term 'Hindu' the provisions of the Caste Disabilities Removal Act of 1850 that prohibited loss of rights upon conversion were set aside and thus converts from Hinduism were denied benefits under the act (Agnes 1996b: 64). As to Muslims, the judiciary seems to have ignored the act from the very beginning or else no Muslim marriage could have been dissolved on account of conversion (Bhattacharjee 1994: 93). Agnes writes:

> The reforms did not introduce any principle which had not already existed somewhere in India. Despite this, the reforms were projected as a vehicle for ushering in western modernity. There were, however, several liberal customary practices which were discarded by the Hindu code for the sake of uniformity. In their stated determination to put an end to the growth of custom, the reformers were in fact putting an end to the essence of Hindu law, and ironically, persisted in calling the codification 'Hindu'.
>
> —(Agnes 2004a: 80–81)

The Special Marriage Act, 1954

Insofar as a common civil code is concerned, a reference to India's Special Marriage Act, 1954 would be instructive. It is a secular act and any two male and female adult citizens can take advantage of it irrespective of their religious affiliations. It also provides opportunity to those who are already married according to their personal law to apply for registration of their marriages under this Act and make its provisions applicable to them. The Act provides for liberal grounds of divorce, a severance from the joint family of the Hindu marrying under it, and the application of the Indian Succession Act in relation to succession to property, to the exclusion of the Hindu Succession Act or any other personal law. Setalvad says:

> The Act may perhaps be described as 'a uniform civil code of marriage' and a step towards the uniform civil code for all citizens contemplated by the Constitution. Those who take advantage of its provisions will be Indians governed by a uniform law of marriage though belonging to different religions. The Hindu or the Muslim marrying under it, though he ceases to be governed by his

It is Politics, Stupid! 85

personal law in important matters, will not cease to be a Hindu or a Muslim.

—(Setalvad 1967: 52)

It may, however, be noted that, in 1976, the Act was regressively amended to provide that Hindus marrying under it would continue to be governed by the Hindu Succession Act (Verghese 2003). [Parenthetically it may be noted that the aborted Native Marriages Act of 1872 was the forerunner of the Special Marriage Act of 1954 in that it was also meant to be secular. The Special Marriage Act of 1872, however, diluted that position and virtually turned it to one for the Brahmos only who claimed neither to be Hindus nor Muslims (see p. 58)].

Muslim Resistance

While the Hindus, however reluctantly, were progressing towards a standardised Hindu family code the Muslim community was increasingly getting concerned about the probability of their being targeted next. With this apprehension in mind the Working Committee of the Indian Union Muslim League observed in 1955 that 'the personal law of the Muslims is a vital part of their religion and the substitution of it by any other law is a direct negation of religious freedom guaranteed in the constitution' (Shakir 1972: 85). Since the 1950s was, by and large, a peaceful decade insofar as Hindu-Muslim relations were concerned in spite of so much bloodshed in the wake of the partition, Muslim anxiety about their identity was less pronounced. But the Jabalpur riots of 1961, when Jawaharlal Nehru was still in command, broke the lull and heightened Muslim anxiety. Although a shaken Nehru responded by setting up the National Integration Council to promote emotional integration in the country, a section of the Muslim leadership seemed to doubt Nehru's capacity to stem the deterioration in the Hindu-Muslim relationship. For example, Dr Abdul Jaleel Faridi, the founder of the Urdu newspaper *Qaed* and a social activist, and Sayed Mahmood (a man very close to Nehru and minister of state for external affairs) were disillusioned with the Nehruvian policy and formed the All India Muslim Majlis-e-Mushawarat in 1964. Headed by Faridi, the organisation was supposed to serve as an umbrella body representing various Muslim groups, thereby presenting the Muslim grievances in a coherent manner. As an advisory council, the Majlis-e-Mushawarat was not a political party but was instrumental in articulating the Muslim point of view on the question of their overall status

86   *The Politics of Personal Law in South Asia*

in Indian society and more particularly on the question of Muslim personal law.

While Muslims in general welcomed the move, the right wing of the Hindu community watched the development with suspicion. Since the Jabalpur riots were followed by a chain of riots in Ranchi, Jamshedpur, Aligarh and other towns, which took place in the wake of anti-Hindu riots in East Pakistan, and as all these riots were soon to be followed by the outbreak of the India-Pakistan war of 1965, Muslim anxiety about their future in India heightened. The death of Nehru in the meantime (1964) was an additional cause of anxiety, though he had hardly been able to prevent these riots, despite the fact that they occurred in the states that were ruled by his own Congress Party (Engineer 1999b: 264–65).

It was against this background, or, when these developments were taking place, that the demand for the retention of Muslim personal law became more strident, particularly in the aftermath of the International Congress of Orientalists, held in New Delhi in January 1964 and attended by some 600 delegates, mostly from India and West Asia. The conference offered a special symposium on 'Changes in Muslim Personal Law'. Mohammadali Currim Chagla, the then education minister of India and the former chief justice of the Bombay High Court (1948–58) chaired the session. He set the tone of the deliberations by strongly advocating a uniform civil code for India. This view was strongly supported by delegates from Egypt, Iran and Turkey, who expressed the need of legislation to reform Muslim personal law in their own countries and spoke about the possibility in India as well. J. N. D. Anderson, the only non-Muslim participant in the conference, discussed the specific methods by which this could be achieved: *takhsis-i-qada* (the right of the just ruler 'both to confine and define jurisdiction of his courts'), and twentieth-century *talfiq* (coordinating different opinions of jurists in different schools of law to give relief to women in cases of marriage and divorce) and *ijtihad* (independent reasoning to arrive at a legal principle).

There was, however, one dissenting voice in the conference. It was that of the Iranian Shia scholar, Syed Hossein Nasr. Arguing that *Shari'ah* and Islam were one and the same thing he said that tampering with *Shari'ah* would amount to tampering with Islam. He went to the extent of arguing that the institution of polygamy should be retained as it was in the *Shari'ah*. The Indian press largely ignored the proceedings, which could have contributed to a lively debate. The *Indian Express* did not appreciate Chagla's raising the spectre of a uniform civil code and editorialised: 'Perhaps the time has not come

It is Politics, Stupid! 87

for a resolute official stand'. The question was obviously sensitive and Indian Muslims probably opposed any change. The potential for communal conflict and anti-Congress sentiments among Muslims at the polls had a cautionary effect on the government (Risso 1992: 61).

The Majlis-e-Mushawarat, which represented mostly conservative Muslim opinion, stood firmly against any move that interfered with Muslim personal law. Two factors possibly contributed to its conviction. In the first place, the level of communal rioting was higher in 1964 than in previous years, and second, the death of Nehru in May 1964 might have made Muslims feel even more insecure about their future status in India. In 1963–64 there were 1,125 riots causing 1,733 deaths, compared to the 1960–63 period when the corresponding figures were 343 and 181 only (Ali 1991: 27).

The discourse on Muslim personal law and the position held by the Majlis-e-Musahwarat on the question polarised the Muslim community into traditionalists and modernists. The traditionalists defended the application of personal law as inherently just, while the modernists called it utterly unjust in the prevailing socio-economic milieu. In the early 1970s, under the leadership of Hamid Dalwai, a creative writer in Marathi, and his Muslim Satyashodhak Samaj, a group of forward-looking Muslims articulated the grievances and demands of the weaker sections of the Muslim community. They were the first in the history of the Muslim world to organise a Muslim Women's Conference, which was held in Pune in December 1971, which demanded the introduction of a uniform civil code as prescribed in the Directive Principles of the Indian Constitution (Shah 1981: 114; Shakir 1972: 122–25). There was a moderate group as well, called 'the reformists'. They argued in favour of the continuation of the personal law with suitable modifications. These categories were not exclusive; they overlapped into gray areas. Still, by and large, dividing lines were drawn between the traditionalists and the progressives (Risso 1992: 66).

Emboldened by the views of the progressives, particularly Chagla, the Government of India, in the late 1960s and early 1970s, contemplated changes in Muslim personal law in respect of maintenance for divorced Muslim women together with similar changes for Hindus and other communities. Ever since the bill on polygamy had been shelved, the attention of the government had shifted to the problem of divorced Muslim women who were entitled to maintenance only for the three-month *iddat* period. This evoked protest from the Muslim traditionalists who argued that the three-month logic did not tell the whole story. According to Muslim personal law, after the

88   *The Politics of Personal Law in South Asia*

expiration of the *iddat* period, the financial burden of the women is borne by her father or other male relatives, failing which by the whole Muslim community through the wakf board. Theoretically the point was strong but the system probably worked better in predominantly Muslim societies where the social pressure was effective. In predominantly Hindu India, where divorce itself was considered a social curse, the Muslim practice could not be taken for granted. Members of a divorced Muslim woman's family might well consider that the woman had brought dishonour on them all and as such might not be willing to receive her, leave alone support her (*ibid.*: 66–67).

Amendments in the Criminal Procedure Code and Muslim Protest

Despite opposition from Muslim traditionalists, the government, under the leadership of Indira Gandhi, went ahead and amended certain provisions of the Criminal Procedure Code (Cr. PC) in August 1973, in respect of maintenance for dependents including wives, which included divorced wives as well. Divorced women, including divorced Muslim women, were, therefore, to be entitled to maintenance, a provision which was not there in Muslim personal law. According to the latter, as mentioned earlier, a Muslim man was required to support his divorced wife only for a period of three months (the *iddat* period), during which there could be reconciliation between the estranged couple leading to the restoration of conjugal life. If reconciliation did not take place, then the divorce was complete and the divorced wife was not entitled to any maintenance.

The amendment debates in Parliament sparked off reactions from the Muslims. In 1972, at a meeting in the seminary of Deo-band, the late Qazi Mohammed Tayyab suggested the formation of a lobby group. Following this, a meeting was convened in Mumbai, on 27 and 28 December 1972, of various Muslim groups to plan for an All India Muslim Personal Law Board (AIMPLB) with Tayyab as its first president. The motto of the AIMPLB was

> to thwart any effort to interfere, by either the government or the courts, with its interpretation of the Islamic law (or *shari'ah*). In effect it meant that this body of clergy and likeminded politicians and activists would oppose any change, even if that change was beneficial to the community. It gave to itself veto rights on Islamic law; its continual slogan was: 'Islam is in danger!'; and its mission was to herd an insecure community into a vote bank that it would

It is Politics, Stupid! 89

deliver to those who were ready to recognize its sole spokesman role for the Indian Muslim community.

—(Akbar 2003).

That the Muslims were unhappy with the ruling Congress Party was reflected in the Mumbai municipal elections held in the spring of 1973. Most Muslims did not vote for the Congress candidates, who suffered setbacks. The amendments, however, were carried through in Parliament in August 1973.

It was almost during the same time that the Muslims also opposed the government move to introduce a uniform code of adoption. The personal laws of Muslims, Christians, Parsis and Jews do not recognise the practice of adoption; hence, persons belonging to these communities who wish to adopt a child can take a child only in 'guardianship' under the Guardians and Wards Act of 1890. This does not provide the child the same status as a child born biologically to the family. The Act confers only a guardian-ward relationship. The right to adopt a child is, however, available to the Hindus under the Hindu Adoption and Maintenance Act of 1956. To remove this discrimination, the government introduced the Adoption Bill in Parliament in 1972 which was to be applicable to all communities. But it had to be withdrawn due to Muslim opposition. (A similar effort in 1980 also failed because of the same reason.)

Opposition to the new Cr. PC provisions continued. Several Muslim members of Parliament, for example, Shamim Ahmed Shamim (Jammu and Kashmir), C. H. Mohammed Koya (IUML [Indian Union Muslim League], Kerala) and Ebrahim Suleiman Sait (IUML, Kerala) argued that the amendment directly infringed on the *Shari'ah.* Several other politicians and community leaders met Indira Gandhi to ventilate their anxiety and it seemed, by December 1973, that the government was in a mood to compromise. An amendment to another provision of the Cr. PC (Section 127) stated that if a divorced woman's interests were looked after by her customary and personal law then she was not entitled to maintenance under the aforesaid provisions. In the case of divorced Muslim women they were not to receive their maintenance if they had received their *iddat* support. Muslim leaders were not completely happy but they appreciated the government's commitment not to interfere with their personal law (Williams 2006: 128–29).

Though there were inherent legal complications in the amended Cr. PC provisions, several cases involving divorced Muslim women were adjudicated between 1979 and 1982 (*Bai Tahira v. Ali Hussain Fissali*

90   *The Politics of Personal Law in South Asia*

Chota, 1979; *Fuzlunbi v. Khader Vali,* 1988; *Zohara Khatoon v. Mohammad Ibrahim,* 1981; and *Smt. Khatoon v. Mohammad Yamin,* 1982). In all these cases the Muslim personal law was not upheld. Muslims in general felt threatened by these developments and decided to initiate a proper debate with the Indian state. Some Muslim intellectuals launched two periodicals to present well articulated Muslim perspectives on the subject, namely, the *Islamic and Contemporary Law Quarterly* and *Muslim India,* both from Delhi.

The *Islamic and Contemporary Law Quarterly* was launched in 1981 by the Department of Islamic Studies of the Indian Institute of Islamic Studies, New Delhi. The president of the Institute, Hakim Abdul Hamid, wrote: 'Non-Muslims seem to have funny ideas about the laws of Islam. Innumerable Muslims, too, do not properly understand them, and therefore, misuse them' (Risso 1992: 70). With Tahir Mahmood as its editor, the journal became a forum of opinion both for and against Muslim personal law. As for *Muslim India,* its first issue appeared in 1983 under the editorship of Syed Shahabuddin who had served as president of the Majlis-e-Mushawarat and also as a member of the All India Muslim Personal Law Board. He was also a Janata Party MP. *Muslim India* provided an important forum for discourse on Muslim personal law when the Shah Bano case came to the Supreme Court for judgement in 1985.

The Shah Bano Case

The case of *Mohammad Ahmad Khan v. Shah Bano* concerned the same provisions of the Cr. PC as earlier similar cases. In this case also, Muslim personal law was not upheld. Shah Bano, a divorcee who had filed for maintenance in the court of a judicial magistrate, was awarded maintenance to the effect of Rs 25 a month (subsequently raised to Rs 179.20 by the High Court). The husband, however, refused to make the payment and appealed to the Supreme Court, arguing that under the Muslim personal law he was not expected to pay maintenance to his divorced wife. The Supreme Court upheld the essence of the verdicts of the lower courts, saying that the statements in the textbooks on Mohammedan law written by such noted authorities like Mulla, Tyabji, Paras Diwan and Ameer Ali were inadequate to address all the contingencies arising out of divorces or multiple marriages. The judgement said: 'Section 125 was enacted in order to provide a quick and summary remedy to class of persons who are unable to maintain themselves. What difference would it then make as to what is the religion professed by the neglected wife, child or parent? Neglect by

It is Politics, Stupid! 91

a person of sufficient means to maintain these and the inability of these persons to maintain themselves are the objective criteria which determine the applicability of Section 125. Such provisions, which are essentially of a prophylactic nature, cut across the barriers of religion'. The judgement further stated:

> We are not concerned here with the broad and general question whether a husband is liable to maintain his wife, which includes a divorced wife, in all circumstances and at all events. That is not the subject matter of Section 125. That section deals with cases in which a person who is possessed of sufficient means neglects or refuses to maintain, amongst others, his wife who is unable to maintain herself. Since the Muslim Personal Law, which limits the husband's liability to provide for maintenance of the divorced wife to the period of *iddat,* does not contemplate or countenance the situation envisaged in Section 125, it would be wrong to hold that the Muslim husband, according to his personal law, is not under an obligation to provide maintenance. The argument of the appellant that, according to the Muslim Personal Law, his liability to provide for the maintenance of his divorced wife is limited to the period of *iddat,* despite the fact that she is unable to maintain herself, has therefore to be rejected. The true position is that if the divorced wife is able to maintain herself the husband's liability to provide maintenance for her ceases with the expiration of the period of *iddat.* If she is unable to maintain herself, she is entitled to take recourse to Section 125 of the Code. The outcome of this discussion is that there is no conflict between the provisions of Section 125 and those of the Muslim Personal Law on the question of the Muslim husband's obligation to provide maintenance for a divorced wife who is unable to maintain herself.

The reference to Muslim personal law in the judgement took the Muslim community by storm. Muslims interpreted it as an interference with Qur'anic law and convinced Shah Bano accordingly, thereby making her retract from her earlier position. Through an open letter addressed to Muslims, published in the newspaper *Inquilab,* 13 November 1985, she said:

> Maulana Mohammad Habib Yar Khan, Haji Abdul Gaffar Sahib and other respectable gentlemen of Indore came to me and explained the commands concerning *nikah,* divorce, dower and

92 *The Politics of Personal Law in South Asia*

maintenance in the light of the Qur'an and the Hadith. . . . Now, the Supreme Court of India has given the judgment on 23 April 1985 concerning maintenance of the divorced woman, which apparently is in my favour. But since the judgment is contrary to the Qur'an and the Hadith and is an open interference in Muslim Personal Law, I, Shah Bano, being a Muslim, reject it and dissociate myself from every judgment that is contrary to the *Shariat*.

—(Quoted in Tabassum 2003: 35–36)

The community expressed its anger electorally as well. The results of the by-elections of 1985 showed a loss of Muslim votes to the Congress. The opposition Muslim candidate Syed Shahabuddin was returned from Bihar's Kishenganj constituency. The experience of the 1973 Mumbai civic elections seemed to be repeating itself. Soon an independent Muslim MP introduced a bill to 'save Muslim personal law'. On 21 December 1985, leading a 17–member delegation, the chairman of the AIMPLB, Syed Abdul Nadri, met Prime Minister Rajiv Gandhi to lodge his protest. The delegation included Ibrahim Suleiman Sait, MP and President of the Indian Union Muslim League, who demanded that Section 125 of the Cr. PC be amended to exclude Muslims. Earlier, on 27 July 1985, G. M. Banatwalla had moved a private member's bill in the parliament to amend Section 125 and 127 of the Cr. PC to ensure that no court should interfere in Muslim personal law (Deshta 2002: 50).

In the face of Muslim opposition, the Congress government, led by Rajiv Gandhi, was in a serious political dilemma, particularly because several progressive Muslims had strongly supported the Supreme Court judgement. On 26 February 1986, many such people had complained, in their memorandum submitted to Rajiv Gandhi, that the 'secular fabric' of India was in danger. The memorandum had said:

We believe that Muslim women have the right to maintenance—a right that they enjoy in several Muslim countries, through the rational and progressive interpretation of Islamic principles, as in Morocco, Iraq, Egypt, Turkey, Libya, Tunisia, Syria and Algeria. . . . We emphasize the necessity of safeguarding the interests of all sections of the minorities. That's why the demand to exclude Muslim women from the purview of section 125 Cr. PC would adversely affect rights and interests of Muslim women.

—(Engineer, 1997: 217–21)

It is Politics, Stupid! 93

There was also an appeal signed by 104 important Muslims drawn from all fields, which virtually looked like an eminent Muslims' Who's Who that demanded no change to be allowed in Section 125 of the Cr. PC (*Muslim India,* March 1986: 135). Such voices were also raised in the Parliament. CPM MP Hannan Mollah from West Bengal claimed that hundreds of Muslim women had approached him to register their protest against the government's proposed act. He said that 'the gates are now being opened wide for the obscurantist elements in other communities to make a grand entry as if we have not enough trouble with such elements (*Parliamentary Debates,* 17 April 1986, Column 235).

For the Congress, however, the consideration of Muslim votes seemed to be the most important factor. As a result, setting aside all progressive advice, the Congress government, which had an overwhelming majority in the Parliament, decided to table a Bill called the Muslim Women (Protection of Rights on Divorce) Bill. The Bill aimed at doing away with the relevant Cr. PC articles and providing for remedies for divorced Muslim women according to Muslim personal law. Any controversy pertaining to its implementation could be taken to court but not the question of maintenance *per se*. There was a lively debate in Parliament on the bill, a debate which needs to be analysed in some detail to make sense of the rationale for the bill as well as to understand the political considerations that were at play.

The Politics of the Muslim Women's Bill

In the eighth Parliament (1984–89) Congress had an overwhelming majority with 415 seats out of 542, that is, 77 per cent. The BJP, which had just been formed before the election, had only two seats. The Janata Party, which ruled India from mid-1977 to mid-1979, had ten members and the CPM twenty-two. Given this party line-up in parliament, there was no danger of the bill being defeated by any stretch of the imagination. Still, it must be conceded that the Congress did the necessary homework to prepare the draft and argue for it. Essentially, the party pushed through three arguments during the debate; one, that by taking out the Muslims from the purview of Section 125 of the Cr. PC, the bill only set right a mistake or a mistaken interpretation thereto; two, that the bill reflected the majority sentiment of the Muslim community, which its vocal and progressive fringe did not represent; and three, that Muslim personal law provided a better deal to divorced Muslim women than the relevant section of the Cr. PC.

94 *The Politics of Personal Law in South Asia*

Presenting the bill in parliament on 5 May 1986, Minister of Law and Justice, A. K. Sen, made the following statement in respect of the first point mentioned above:

> Originally in 1898 Sir Fitzjames introduced a Bill, which was enacted into the Criminal Procedure Code of 1898. It contained a provision, Section 488, which was described by Sir Fitzjames as a provision against vagrants and the whole purpose was, if a wife was unable to maintain herself or if a man's children are not looked after, then a summary procedure was obtainable in the criminal court by which the husband was made to pay what was considered to be a maintenance not exceeding Rs 500 for his wife and children. At that time, the obligation was confined only to wives and not to ex-wives. . . . In 1973 when the Criminal Procedure Code was passed, it was passed in two sections— Sections 125 and 127 including sub-section (3) of Section 127. Section 125 for the first time introduced an explanation which said, a wife will include an ex-wife, a wife who has been divorced, so that for the first time the obligation to maintain a divorced wife was cast by the Criminal Procedure Code on the husband divorcing the wife. The law about alimony is contained in the respective law—for the Christians, the Indian Divorce Act, for the Hindus, the Hindu Marriage Act, and for the Muslims, their own personal law. . . . When the matter was debated in Parliament, the Minister of State for Home Affairs said, on objection being raised on behalf of the Muslims, that under the Muslim personal law, the obligation to maintain an ex-wife lasts only up to the *iddat* period and that beyond that the obligation reverts to the original family. And if the husband discharges his obligations under the personal law, namely pays the mehar contracted to be paid at the time of marriage, makes over all the property belonging to the wife and also pays the maintenance during the *iddat,* he should not be saddled with any obligation to maintain beyond the *iddat.* . . . The stand of the government was that no Muslim person should be offended because under Section 127 (3) the moment a person discharges his obligation under the personal law, the order under Section 125 will cease to be operative. That is so. Therefore, there is an inbuilt provision in this very Criminal Procedure Code whereby the personal law of the husband concerned was made the determinant factor for the continuance of the order under Section 125, so that if a Hindu paid whatever was ordered as alimony at the time of his divorce under the Hindu Marriage Act, he would not be

It is Politics, Stupid! 95

saddled with any further order under Section 125. Similarly with a Christian and similarly with a Muslim.

—(*Parliamentary Debates*, 5 May 1986, Columns 302–306)

The problem arose, explained Sen, because in the Shah Bano case the Supreme Court, after deciding that the Section 125 of Cr. PC did not conflict with the Qur'an or the *Shari'ah*,

> went further and said that they noted with regret that the Government has failed in his [*sic.*] duty to bring about a uniform code for all the community [*sic.*] reasoning thereby as if the uniform code which has to be framed under Article 44 was to be enforced against all communities forgetting the history of Article 44 of the Constitution and you will remember how the matter was raised here, debated here and we gave our expression about the Article 44 and if I may repeat once more about the history of Article 44 and what was said at that time, it may be of some relevance.
>
> —(*Parliamentary Debates*, 5 May 1986, Column 311)

Sen then elaborated at length on the commitment that was given by Ambedkar in the Constituent Assembly that no uniform civil code would be imposed unless the communities themselves were prepared for it (see Chapter II for details). He also clarified how much importance the Muslims attached to *Shari'ah* as the marker of their identity. When some members sniggered at his comment that the Muslims considered *Shari'ah* as 'a law ordained by God' Sen rebuked the members by saying: 'There is no question of laughing about it. To the Muslims it is article of faith' (*Parliamentary Debates*, 5 May 1986, Column 314).

With regard to the second point mentioned above, Sen and many members from the treasury bench who spoke in favour of the bill repeatedly tried to convince parliament that they had met the community leaders several times and ensured that the bill had the support of the majority in the Muslim community. In his enthusiasm to drive home his point Sen even exaggerated the number of Muslims in India, which according to him was 140 million (*Parliamentary Debates*, 5 May 1986, Column 310) while it was evidently much less.[2] Concluding his long statement, Minister of Steel and Mines, K. C. Pant, said: 'I stress the perception of minorities. . . . I think, this bill will engender a feeling of trust and confidence in the minorities and I think that at this particular juncture of our history, the creation

96   The Politics of Personal Law in South Asia

of this sense of trust and confidence is far more important than the imaginary political battles and shadow-boxing which we are doing in this House' (*Parliamentary Debates*, 5 May 1986, Columns 392–93). Almost all Muslim members of parliament favoured the bill, with the notable exception of Arif Mohammad Khan of the Congress. There were CPM Muslim members too in his category but they were voicing their party's position on the bill. The Janata Party was vertically divided on the bill. While Pramila Dandavate opposed the bill tooth and nail, Syed Shahabuddin was completely in favour of it. Madhu Dandavate was worried that the party would not be split on the issue, though he too was opposed to the bill. Shahabuddin's statement is worth quoting here:

> I do not consider the Bill is perfect. Like any man made law, it has its defects and its inconsistencies. Yet, I support it even at the risk of being termed as a fundamentalist, dubbed as an obscurantist, as a reactionary, regarded as a socially backward and even called a mentally retarded. . . . We don't consider this Bill is the end of the matter. It is the beginning of the debate, of the process of reform in Muslim society, of the opening of a new chapter in our national life. This debate will continue, from house to house, from Bill to Bill, and from stage to stage. There, our contribution will be that we will always allow freedom of expression to all our members. . . . There is some confusion between Islam and *Shariat* and Personal Law. There has been a codification of Muslim Personal Law in many Muslim countries but in no country has codification traveled outside the orbit of the *Shariat* with the only exception of Turkey. You cannot pick and choose in good conscience from the *Shariat*. *Shariat* is an integrated whole, is universal, valid for all times and for all societies. If therefore you come to the question as to what are the essentials of religion, even the Supreme Court has decided that essentials of any religion must be decided with reference to internal evidence of that religion and not by the passing fancy of the time or by the transient fashion of the time or by the intellectual climate of the age in which we live.
> —(*Parliamentary Debates*, 5 May 1986, Columns 500–502)

The third kind of reasoning that the government put forward in favour of the bill was that instead of doing harm to divorced Muslim women the proposed bill would ensure a better deal for them. Countering the arguments of all those who thought that the Cr. PC route was better to take care of divorced Muslim women, Sen said that 'what happened was that the old law, Sec. 125 which is still existing—what did it give to the Muslim divorced woman? Only if the husband was able to maintain her, he was liable to pay maintenance but not exceeding Rs 500' (*Parliamentary Debates*, 5 May 1986, Column 515). The bill was passed by the Lok Sabha, as expected, by a overwhelming majority of 372 with 54 opposing (*Parliamentary Debates*, 5 May 1986, Column 624). Two days later the Rajya Sabha also passed the bill. Ultimately, in May, it received presidential assent. Subsequently, the government made a categorical statement in parliament that it was the consistent and declared policy of the government not to make any change in the personal law of any community unless the community itself asked for it (*Parliamentary Debates*, 19 November 1986, Column 3).

The passage of the bill totally polarised political and intellectual opinion within the country. By and large all Hindus, modernist Muslims, lawyers' associations, women's organisations, and the English language press condemned the legislation as retrograde. Progressive Muslim women argued that the government only listened to conservative Muslim opinion and ignored the progressive voice (Hasan 1994: 59–73). There were similar reverberations in Pakistan (Naqvi 1986). Justice V. R. Krishna Iyer, who had decided the Bai Tahira case in 1979, quickly wrote a book against the Act (Iyer 1987). Danial Latifi and Sona Khan (Shah Bano's lawyers), both Delhi-based advocates, in a public interest writ petition to the Supreme Court, marshalled both religious and secular arguments to say that a kind of apartheid had been introduced in the country by which the weakest of the weak, that is, women of a minority community, had been further victimised (Tabassum 2003: 36–37). In a memorandum submitted to the prime minister, the Pune-based Muslim Satyashodhak Mandal said that the government only listened to 'religious and obscurantist leaders'. It should 'consider what is best for the Muslim women, for the society and for this country and decree, without waiting to verify whether such decrees have religious sanctions or sanction of a majority of Muslims' (*Muslim India*, April 1986: 156).

Battle lines were drawn between the champions of Muslim personal law and those who stood either for reforms in Muslim personal law or the cause of a uniform civil code. In the forefront of the latter were the Hindutva chauvinists who had been clamouring against the so-called appeasement of Muslims by the Congress Party as well as, by a strange coincidence, progressive Muslims and women's organisations. However, these views probably did not really reflect the majority Muslim sentiment. Rajiv Gandhi was probably being politically

98 The Politics of Personal Law in South Asia

correct, believing that, by introducing the Muslim women's bill, he was reflecting the voice of the Muslim masses, who, because of their poverty and illiteracy, were more prone to stick to their traditional mores than accept progressive ideas. Mushirul Hasan's book gives detailed evidence of Muslim backwardness and underdevelopment, though the rationale of the book is to counter the Hindu right's argument that the community is pampered (Hasan 1997, also Zakaria 2003a).

If one wants to hold a brief for Rajiv Gandhi's action, one can argue that, from the perspective of the development of the Muslim community his logic for introducing the act held water. Following the passage of the bill there was a spate of cases in courts. Most of the judgments irked Muslim husbands because the amounts they were made to pay to their divorced wives were often more than what they would have been required to pay under the Cr. PC. Obviously, therefore, the act was not anti-Muslim women as it was made out to be; it provided scope for the judiciary to opt for a liberal interpretation of the act to the benefit of divorced Muslim women. On 28 September 2001 a five-judge bench of the Supreme Court put its seal of approval on these positive interpretations (Agnes 2004b: 390). From yet another perspective it can be argued that village-based social–anthropological studies show that, law or no law, three things come in the way of gender equality, namely, the male domination of social norms, female illiteracy and the lack of economic independence of women. Patricia Jeffrey's research in rural Bijnor in UP shows that Section 125 of the Cr. PC had a very limited role to play in preventing women from becoming destitute after their failed marriages. As such, the Muslim Women's Act of 1986, which removed their right to appeal under the same Cr. PC section, had little negative impact on the economic situation of divorced Muslim women. Given these ground realities, the efficacy of the UCC in ensuring gender justice is highly suspect. Probably, there already exists, in rural India, a 'uniform customary code' with regard to gender politics at the domestic level (Jeffrey 2001: 23–24).

Still, to understand the politics behind the passage of the bill, it has to be seen both from the angle of the Congress as well as from the general tenor of the then Muslim psyche. Ever since the late 1970s India was in turmoil. In Kashmir, Islamic militancy was on the rise, in Punjab, the Khalistan movement was becoming increasingly violent with the potential of driving a permanent wedge in the hitherto harmonious relationship between the Hindus and the Sikhs, and in Assam, the anti-foreigners agitation, which had an anti-Muslim communal angle, had all the trappings of a secessionist struggle. The

It is Politics, Stupid! 99

assassination of Indira Gandhi at the hands of her Sikh bodyguards (1984), and the anti-Sikh riots that followed, dramatically demonstrated the danger to societal harmony. Although her son and successor Rajiv Gandhi did manage to arrest the drift to some extent and soon signed two landmark accords, the Rajiv Longowal Accord and the Assam Accord, both in 1985, there was no scope for complacency. Hindutva forces were raising their heads as never before and Muslims were naturally anxious.

Congress had a traditional base amongst the Muslims, which had been drifting away since the late sixties, as we have seen above. After the return of Indira Gandhi to power in 1980, she realised that she would not only have to make a dent into the Hindutva constituency, which was reflected in her 1982 Jammu poll strategy, she would also have to re-enlist the support of the Muslims, who were disillusioned with her party ever since the days of the Emergency (1975–77), as certain policies followed at the time had directly hit the community. To regain Muslim trust, the traditional wisdom of the Congress considered Muslim conservatives more relevant compared to urban-based intellectuals and feminists. Soon after her return to power, Indira Gandhi visited Deoband to participate in the seminary's centenary, where, in her speech, she not only heaped praises on the Deobandi *ulema* for their knowledge of Islam and their contribution to india's plurality but also referred to the efforts of their forebears in the country's freedom struggle. In the same year her government issued a special 30-paise stamp in honour of the Deoband seminary. The Deobandis, too, basked in the glory of their patriotic past and their newly regained relevance in national politics (Sikand 2004d: 13).

In tune with this political strategy it was quite expected that, under Rajiv Gandhi's leadership, the party would also go by the voice of the Muslim traditionalists. The latter were prepared for a *quid pro quo* with the Congress during the Shah Bano controversy. The Muslim women's bill amply provided that opportunity. If one reads the statements of the Congress members in parliament during the course of the debate on the bill, one can smell this political compulsion. It is noteworthy that Rajiv Gandhi chose not his own party's Muslim leaders for consultation on the bill but those more established Muslim leaders who had the known credentials to represent conservative Muslim sentiments. They were Syed Abdul Hasan Ali Nadwi, chairman of the All Indian Muslim Personal Law Board; Minnatwala Rehmani, secretary of the Board; G. M. Banatwala and Suleiman Sait of the Indian Union Muslim League; and Syed Shahabuddin of the Janata Party (Jayal 2001: 122).

100 *The Politics of Personal Law in South Asia*

Here, a brief analysis of the Muslim leadership may be in order. It is broadly divided into two groups. To the first belong the conservative forces that include the *ulema* in general and the *mullahs* in particular. Not necessarily subscribing to everything held by these groups, yet still in the category of conservatives, particularly insofar as Muslim personal law in concerned, falls the All India Muslim Personal Law Board. All these categories put together have wide appeal amongst the Muslim masses in rural areas, where 70 per cent of India's Muslims live. The second group consists of those Muslim intellectuals who are generally located in urban areas and who mostly belong to professional categories as academics, journalists, lawyers, doctors, engineers and so on. Social activists, including feminists, figure prominently in this category. They write mostly in English and draw their support from progressive forces both within the country as well as abroad. Within the community, they largely talk amongst themselves and pat each other's backs for mutual survival. Although the two groups are critical of each other, there is an essential similarity between them. Neither asks for a uniform civil code, barring a few in the second category. Even those who vociferously champion the cause of reform in Muslim personal law argue that the *Shari'ah* contains all the elements of modernist changes in the law, so that there is no need to go beyond its purview. In support of their position they draw the attention of their target audience to the reforms ushered in by Muslim majority countries within the parameters of Islamic law. Thus what they essentially argue is for reforms as available *within* the *Shari'ah* and not *of* the *Shari'ah*.

Since, in a mass democracy like India, the number of heads matters more than the intrinsic worth of an argument, it is important to understand which of the two groups command the popular support amongst the vast majority of poor and illiterate Muslims. Since a large majority of Muslims are rural-based, the local mullahs and madrassa teachers have better communication with them than the urban progressive intellectuals. Since the Deobandis and the AIMPLB talk by and large in the same orthodox language, there is a structural relationship between the two systems of opinion building, and both have a much wider reach than the progressive and modernist urbanised Muslim intellectuals. Moreover, since the latter too do not question the *Shari'ah per se,* and only talk of implementing the better guidelines therein, the average Muslim fails to understand this intricate hairsplitting, preferring to trust those people who speak his language, sport traditional beards and wear the traditional Muslim dress. Obviously these people have a wider mass appeal, which the politicians can ignore only at their own cost. Congress had established such a communication from the days of the Khilafat movement down to the days of partition, when the Deobandis stood behind the party in favour of India as one nation. Rajiv Gandhi, therefore, was only following a well-tested party line when he decided to support Muslim conservatives in enacting the Muslim Women's (Protection of Rights on Divorce) Act, 1986.

Because of this nexus between Muslim conservatism and Indian national politics in general (the role of Congress in this connection is incidental, for any political party would have behaved the way the Congress did if it could be ensured of mass Muslim support), the debate on the UCC, insofar as reforms within Muslim personal law is concerned, gets very narrowly focused. Non-Muslims are virtually debarred from questioning the *Shari'ah* as if only Muslims have the right to do so. Leave alone the judges of the supreme courts and high courts (who, whenever they have directly questioned the propriety of certain aspects of Muslim personal law, have invited the wrath of the Muslims), even an average non-Muslim is not expected to do so. At times, even Muslims like Salman Rushdie or Taslima Nasreen are looked down upon for their comments on Islam. Syed Shahabuddin argues that Rushdie, by his comments, has lost his credentials to remain a Muslim and should say so openly. He argues that only Muslims have the right to talk of Islamic tenets, meaning thereby that questioning those tenets is tantamount to blasphemy. Becoming an expert in Islam is fine but criticising it as a doctrine is not permissible, according to those who share Shahabuddin's logic (Shahabuddin 2004).

The Hindutva Backdrop

The Shah Bano controversy must be seen in the context of Hindu-Muslim relations during the previous few years. As we have noted above, by the 1980s, Muslim opinion was getting crystallised to counter any move by the Indian state that tended to interfere with the personal law of the community because it was considered to be an affront to its identity. This process had started earlier but picked up momentum after the demise of Pandit Nehru. During this period, Hindu nationalism was also spreading its wings. In 1964, the RSS had created the Vishwa Hindu Parishad (VHP), literally the World Hindu Council, in response to the activities of Christian missionaries, particularly in India's north-east. This was against the backdrop of statehood being granted to Nagaland (1964), where the population consisted

102   *The Politics of Personal Law in South Asia*

of Christianised tribes. Hindu nationalists saw this development in the light of the 'denationalisation' process that threatened national integration. S. S. Apte, an RSS functionary, who was appointed by the RSS *sarsanghchalak* (supremo), M. S. Gowalkar, as the general secretary of the VHP, justified its creation in the following words:

> The declared object of Christianity is to turn the whole world into Christendom—as that of Islam is to make it 'Pak'. Besides these two dogmatic and proselytizing religions there has arisen a third religion, communism. . . . The world has been divided into Christian, Islamic and Communist, and all these three consider the Hindu society as a very fine rich food on which to feast and fatten themselves. It is, therefore, necessary in this age of competition and conflict to think of, and organize, the Hindu world to save itself from the evil eyes of all the three.
>
> —(Jaffrelot 1993: 522)

The process continued unabated during the 1970s, which witnessed several momentous developments that directly or indirectly encouraged it. Starting with the Bangladesh crisis through the first oil shock (1972), the emergence of Sanjay Gandhi as the extra-constitutional power centre in the central government and his alleged connection with the RSS, the J. P. movement, the Emergency, and ultimately the rise of the Janata Party and its fall over the ticklish issue of whether some of its members could owe dual loyalty to the party as well as the RSS, contributed measurably to bolster the Hindu face of Indian politics. The Emergency in particular contributed to the phenomenon. Imprisoned by the Indira Gandhi government, RSS leaders first felt like fish out of water. Balasaheb Deoras, the RSS chief, even pleaded with Indira Gandhi that, in return for his and his colleagues' release from the Yeravada jail and for lifting the ban on his organisation, the RSS would be available to the government for national uplift. When his appeal fell on deaf ears, the organisation concentrated on networking within the jails with other political prisoners, thereby legitimising its role in Indian politics, which had not been possible ever since the taint it had acquired following Mahatma Gandhi's assassination in 1948. The seeds of Hindutva politics of the following decade were sown during the Emergency (Rajagopal 2003).

By the end of 1970s, foresighted politicians were able to feel the pro-Hindu pulse of the nation. Congress, the more seasoned political party, realised it better, which the BJP took time to understand. The respective politics of these parties during the first half of the 1980s revealed

It is Politics, Stupid! 103

this (Ghosh 1999: 86–87). On the social level a new form of Hindu militancy was gaining momentum. In November 1983, the Vishwa Hindu Parishad (VHP) organised an *Ekatmata yagna*. Literally meaning 'sacrifice for integration', it was a march in which 400 litres of water from the source of the Ganga at Gangotri was carried 50,000 miles across the length and breadth of the country to advertise the concept of Hindu solidarity. The march, consisting of three main processions and forty-seven smaller processions, aimed at reaching out to sixty million people. The first main procession was from Hardwar in UP to Kanyakumari in Tamil Nadu, the second from Kathmandu, the capital of ' Hindu' Nepal, to Rameswaram in Tamil Nadu, and the third, from Gangasagar in West Bengal to Somnath in Gujarat. These three processions crossed each other at the centre of the country at Nagpur, to signify Sangam, the confluence of three rivers, which has great religious importance. 'India cannot be kept united without uniting the Hindus', the VHP leaders claimed. During the march, religious leaders delivered fiery speeches, the central theme of which was: 'Hinduism in danger'. They ranted against politicians who pampered the Muslims because they were their vote-banks. This growing nexus between religion and politics was noticed by all concerned. Significantly, the organisers of the Ekatmata yagna tried to highlight the reach of Hinduism beyond the borders of India as well. One of the chariots used was from Nepal, there was a delegation from Myanmar carrying water from the river Irrawady, a delegation from Bhutan, vessels of water from Bangladesh and Pakistan as well as from the religious site of Ramsar in Mauritius (Benei 1998: 135; Ghosh 1999: 88).

Following the assassination of Indira Gandhi in October 1984, the Congress functionaries and politicians of Delhi played a notorious role in the anti-Sikh riots that rocked the city and other parts of India. In the parliamentary elections that soon followed, all the seven seats of Delhi went to the Congress. At the national level it was a landslide victory for the party. While the opposition parties attributed this victory to the 'sympathy wave' generated by Indira Gandhi's assassination, Hindu chauvinistic forces realised that behind the sympathy was the dormant Hindu fear that the nation was in danger from the political demands presented by the minorities from time to time. 'It brought home to them', noted an analyst,

> that the elusive 'Hindu vote' which they had been chasing since Independence and given up as lost, was actually in the making, but instead of it being acquired by a Hindu party, it was once again being usurped by the Congress. The 'Hindu vote' did not, of

104   *The Politics of Personal Law in South Asia*

course, encompass the entire Hindu community but it was large enough for a party to make a living out of it. The only difficulty was that the Congress (I) had generated that vote not on a pro-Hindu or an anti-Muslim card but on a carefully orchestrated anti-Sikh platform. For the BJP, and more particularly the RSS, Sikhs had always been part of the Hindu brotherhood and they could not make themselves whip up anti-Sikh hysteria, which they were so adept at doing vis-à-vis the Muslims.

—(Chatterjee 1992: 19–20)

This political judgement was translated into electoral strategy by L. K. Advani who took over as president of the BJP in 1986. By harping on the 'pseudo-secularism' and 'minorityism' of the ruling Congress, he charted a clear and unambiguous path in favour of Hindu resurgence. In his first presidential address at the party's plenary session in New Delhi in May 1986, he said: 'If anyone were to ask me which is the most distinctive trait of BJP's personality, I would say that BJP is the voice of unalloyed nationalism. Ours is a "Nation-First" party. It aspires to be the heartbeat of India'. He denounced cow slaughter that was allowed in many parts of India and the destruction of as many as forty-five Hindu temples in the state of Jammu and Kashmir, although the figure was actually much less. Advani declared that 'for many politicians, and political parties, secularism has become only a euphemism for political appeasement of minority sections which tend to vote *en bloc*. These politicians unabashedly propound the thesis that there is no such thing as minority communalism' (Malik and Singh 1994: 76).

Already, a ferment was in the making under the leadership of the VHP as we have seen. Religious leaders like the Sankaracharyas (chief priests) of different monasteries contributed to the process significantly. The 144th Jagatguru Shankaracharya of Puri, one of the most venerated personages of Hinduism, unleashed an attack on the government for taking away 550 acres of his monastic land, but 'can you imagine', he said in anger, 'the Government touching even an inch of mosque or church property'. He argued that the government had 'negated secularism. There must be a common law for all inhabitants of this country'. In the cause of Hindu unity, he led a procession of more than 1,000 Hindus to the Kumbh Mela (a great Hindu pilgrimage held at Hardwar, Nasik and Allahabad every year and a major one every twelve years) in April 1986 and united them on a three-point pledge: Stop the slaughter of Hindus in Punjab; Ban cow slaughter; and Pass uniform laws for all religions. Evidently, the

It is Politics, Stupid! 105

Shankaracharya and Advani were speaking from the same platform (Ghosh 1999: 90).

Against this background, the controversy over the ownership of the Babri mosque, situated in Ayodhya in UP, surfaced in 1985 following a court judgment. In that year, a group of Hindu activists revived the demand to allow Hindus to worship inside the shrine as it contained the idol of Lord Ram. A district judge ordered the opening of the gates, which initiated one of the worst phases of Hindu-Muslim relation. An innocuous local issue assumed proportions of national importance in which Hindu chauvinistic groups like the BJP, the VHP, the RSS, the Bajrang Dal and other regional groups like the Shiv Sena of Maharashtra emerged at the centre stage. These groups, put together, are known in Indian political parlance as the *Sangh Parivar,* which subscribes to the theory that India belongs to the Hindus, or, alternatively, Hindu nationalism and Indian nationalism are synonymous. This group drew up a plan to demolish the mosque and build a Ram temple there. A group of Muslims who constituted the Babri Masjid Action Committee (BMAC) insisted on the sanctity of the mosque but conceded that a temple could be built adjacent to it. This was, however, not acceptable to the Hindu chauvinists. The maximum that the BJP was willing to concede was that the mosque be shifted to another place brick by brick, for which, it argued, the requisite technology was available. To sensitise Hindus throughout the country, the campaigners for the Ram temple, most notably the VHP, organised the manufacture of the so-called *Ramshilas* (bricks anointed in the name of Lord Ram) over the length and breadth of India as well as in the United States, the United Kingdom and Canada to be taken to Ayodhya for the construction of the temple. The supplanting of the Supreme Court judgment in the Shah Bano case by the Muslim Women (Protection of Rights on Divorce) Act of 1986 charged these sentiments further. Riots that were reported from the UP town of Barabanki and Kolkata, both of which resulted from Muslim protest against the Shah Bano judgment, clearly reflected deteriorating Hindu-Muslim relations (Williams 2006: 167–68). The BJP took full advantage of the situation and completely identified itself with all the pan-Hindu forces (Ghosh 1999: 91–92). Advani later admitted that the act 'was a watershed events. . . . The mood of the Hindus began building up after [this]' (*Sunday Times of India,* 14 October 1990). Against this background, it would be evident that the logic that the Muslims opposed the Supreme Court judgement in the Shah Bano case just because it contained references to the *Shari'ah* was only half valid and amounted to missing the central point. By

106 *The Politics of Personal Law in South Asia*

Table 3.1 Communal Violence 1977–86

Year	Number of Incidents	Persons Killed
1977	188	36
1978	230	110
1979	304	261
1980	427	375
1981	319	196
1982	474	238
1983	404	202
1984	456	444
1985	50	252
1986	764	418

Source: *Muslim India* (New Delhi), February 1994: 83.

the mid-1980s, the Hindu-Muslim communal scene had become so vitiated that it was quite expected that Muslims would react to the judgement exactly in the way they did. Between 1977 and 1986 there were 3,616 communal incidents in which 2,532 people lost their lives (see Table 3.1).

The Muslim criticism of the judgment was, therefore, the product of both a historical process as much as it was a doctrinally inspired move. A peep into the past would bail this point out. While it was true that from the beginning of Independence Muslim leadership was safeguarding their personal law, it may be recalled that several judgments of the courts prior to the Shah Bano case had rebuked personal laws, including that of the Muslims, and had talked about the advisability of a uniform civil code. In the 1970 case of *Shahulameedu v. Subaida,* Justice V. R. Krishna Iyer had even characterised some aspects of the Muslim personal law as 'obscurantist.' His judgment, *inter alia*, read:

> The Indian Constitution directs that the State should endeavour to have a uniform civil code applicable to the entire Indian humanity and, indeed, when motivated by a high public policy, S. 488 of the Criminal Procedure Code has made such a law, it would be improper for an Indian court to exclude any section of the community born and bred up [*sic.*] on Indian earth from the benefits of that law, importing religious privilege of a somewhat obscurantist order. I have no doubt that it behoves the Courts in India to enforce Section 488(3) of the Code of Criminal Procedure in favour of Indian women, Hindu, Muslim or other. I will be failing in my duty if I accede to the argument of the petitioner that

Muslim women should be denied the advantages of para. 2 of the proviso to Section 488(3).

—(Menski 2001: 391)

Iyer concluded that 'there is hardly any doubt that neither the reliance on Art. 25 of the Constitution nor the refuge under the sanctions of the Koran can save a Muslim husband from meeting his statutory obligations. . . .' (Menski 2001: 392). Muslims had not raised any hue and cry then that the court had tried to interfere with *Shari'ah*.

The *Talaq* Controversy

More or less at the same time as when the Shah Bano controversy was hitting the headlines, another controversy with regard to Muslim personal law was in the making, though it took a few more years before it actually surfaced. It pertained to the practice of triple *talaq* as enshrined in the *Shari'ah,* and its frequent misuse by irresponsible husbands. In 1984, Shahnaz Sheikh, a victim of the triple *talaq,* filed a writ petition in the Supreme Court demanding the abrogation of the Muslim personal law as it violated Articles 14, 15, 16 and 25 of the Constitution that guaranteed justice and equality to all citizens irrespective of their faith. The petition was supported by organisations like the Forum Against Oppression of Women (FAOW) and the Lawyers' Collective. AIMPLB was disturbed by this development as it thought the government might positively respond to the petition, thereby shaking Article 13 as well as Article 25 of the constitution. In a memorandum written to Prime Minister Indira Gandhi on 25 August 1984, the board pleaded that it was the board's 'duty, to Nation and to the Community, to convey . . . that the Muslim Personal Law based on the Shariat is immutable and an inseparable part of the Islamic faith, that any change in the Shariat, direct or indirect, through legislation or judicial interpretation, would amount to *MUDAKHALAT-fid-DEEN,* i.e., interference in religion. . . .' In its panic the AIMPLB even questioned the autonomous research funding body, the Indian Council of Social Science Research (ICSSR), for promoting research on the subject. It asked the government to 'reconsider the advisability of extending support and even subsidy by some semi-Government funding agencies like the ICSSR to the motivated campaign against the Muslim Personal Law, in the name of academic activity' (*Muslim India,* September 1984: 417–18).

Still, the controversy remained at the subcutaneous level until the 1990s when it picked up momentum. It started on 4 April 1993 with

108 *The Politics of Personal Law in South Asia*

a UP High Court judgment in the case of *Rahamtullah v. State of UP* and *Khatoonisha v. State of UP,* in which Justice Tilhari struck down *talaq-e-biddat,* popularly known as triple *talaq.* The verdict, which was issued by the Lucknow Bench of the Allahabad High Court, not only said that *talaq* at one sitting was unconstitutional, it also talked about the superiority of the Hindu Marriage Act over Muslim personal law. The judgment said:

> Divorce brings a plight of vagaries . . . and upheaval in the life of a woman. . . . The Hindu Marriage Act introduced divorce and a divorced woman has been declared to be 'entitled to claim maintenance from her husband'. Under Muslim law, the plight of a woman divorced by her husband is more pathetic. It is the husband who has the free hand to divorce his wife . . . even orally, by declaring *talaq* thrice . . . the poor Muslim woman has been held to be entitled to maintenance for a limited period of three months and then left to the vagaries of fate.
>
> —(quoted in Gangoli 2003: 381–82)

Some commentators thought that the judgment smacked of the Hindu right for it referred to the superiority of the Hindu Marriage Act. They also noted that soon thereafter the same judge gave a verdict in favour of allowing *darshan* (the right to worship) to Hindu devotees at the spot where the Babri mosque once stood and where a makeshift Ram temple had been constructed. Gautam Navlakha, a left-oriented commentator, cautioned the progressive and womens' groups not to be carried away by the pseudo-concern shown in the judgment for the plight of Muslim women. 'Is the judgment and the support thereof based on women's rights, or on communal arguments of Muslim obduracy and backwardness', he asked (Navlakha 1994: 1264).

The judgment divided the Muslim community the way the judgment in the Shah Bano case had done so earlier. The All India Muslim Personal Law Board and the All India Babri Masjid Action Committee were once again in the forefront objecting to this interference with Muslim personal law and threatening to move the Supreme Court against the judgment. The AIMPLB Executive Committee passed a resolution saying that the judge should 'have refrained from pronouncing any opinion on the legality/constitutionality of divorce. . . . The judiciary should respect the principles of non-interference in the matters of scriptural laws' (*Muslim India,* June 1994: 262). Eventually, on 4 August, the Supreme Court stayed the operation of the verdict till the apex court disposed of the case.

It is Politics, Stupid! 109

The institution of divorce in India must be seen in its sociological context. Although divorce is a simple procedure according to Muslim personal law it is not as simple as it is commonly believed, in spite of the fact that empirical data show that the incidence of divorce among Muslims is higher compared to other communities, most notably the Hindus. A survey conducted by the census authorities in 1961, covering 507 selected villages, with a sample of 133,775 over a period of fifty years found that the incidence of divorce among Muslims was 6.06 per cent while among Hindus it was 3.21 per cent among Buddhists 3.07 per cent, Jains 1.68 per cent, Sikhs 0.91 per cent and Christians 0.47 per cent (*Muslim India*, February 1996: 73). A comparatively recent survey (1995) based on Delhi and Aligarh samples showed that the incidence of Muslim divorce was as low as 0.15 per cent (*Muslim India*, March 1995: 120) but the sample was probably too small to be taken seriously. In any case, one must not lose sight of the fact that the Muslim community is the worst off compared to other communities in terms of all social indicators, which partly explains the phenomenon.

Imtiaz Ahmad argues, in his edited volume on the same subject, that the debate over Muslim divorce practice in India must be seen from two perspectives. First, it is a fallacy that there is only one single pattern that has been prescribed in the *Shari'ah*, and second, the assumption that the Indian Muslim community is an altogether distinct group uninfluenced by majority community norms is not accurate. In respect of the first, Ahmad argues that, contrary to popular perceptions and common belief that Muslim law is derived from the Qur'an and as such must be uniform for all Muslims, there is considerable evidence of legal pluralism among Muslims on the matter. The fact that different schools of law and theology hold highly divergent views on the validity of the divorce procedure is itself proof of that. Those who follow the Hanafi and Shafi systems as well as some sub-sects among the Shias uphold triple *talaq* to be divinely sanctioned and therefore part and parcel of the *Shari'ah*. They would, therefore, oppose any change in it. On the other hand, most Shias, the followers of the *Ahl-e-Hadis* and those who follow some other theological and legal persuasions reject this procedure altogether and deny the validity accorded to it by other theological and legal schools (Ahmad 2003: 40).

Second, the case studies on divorce presented in his edited volume show that it is hardly true that the practice of triple *talaq* is always an individual act and that too a sudden or momentary decision on the part of the husband. More often than not there is social sanction behind the move. Social science research studies have conclusively

110   *The Politics of Personal Law in South Asia*

established that Muslims in India are under the continuing influence of the Indian cultural ethos. Even though Muslims claim adherence to the Qur'an and *Shari'ah*, the fact is that in many aspects of their attitudes and behaviour they deviate from textual religious values and norms, primarily because of the continuing hold of cultural orientations and practices that enjoy legitimacy in the Indian environment (Ahmad 2003).

In any case, the *talaq* controversy bore at least some fruit. The *ulema* entered into discussions to draft a standard *nikahnama* (marriage agreement) for the country's Sunni Muslims. The *nikahnama* that was proposed stipulated that triple *talaq* should not be resorted to by the man. If he did, he was liable to pay double *mehr*. The stipulated form of *talaq* would be *talaq-e-ahsan*, the Qur'anic form most preferred by the Prophet. It meant pronouncing *talaq* once in the presence of four respected members of society, two from each side, preferably those who witnessed the marriage. This form of divorce allowed for a three-month period when reconciliation could be attempted, failing which the divorce became effective. On the question of second marriage, the *nikahnama* proposed that the husband would not remarry without the first wife's consent. If he did, he would have to pay her double the *mehr*. The first wife would have the first right to the matrimonial home and would not be compelled to share it with the second wife. It also recommended that mehr should not be in cash but in shares, land or gold or silver, all of which would appreciate in value. An accompanying note to the *nikahnama* would lay down guidelines on calculating the mehr according to the man's income and status (*Times of India* 1995).

The discussions on the matter, however, went unabated, and all kinds of *talaq* cases continued to pour into the courts for judgment. The procrastination on the part of the AIMPLB to come out with a standard *nikahnama* was subjected to severe criticism from activists like Asghar Ali Engineer, who argued that the personal law board should launch an awareness campaign to educate Muslim men not to follow this sinful form of divorce and instead resort to the form that is clearly spelled out in the Qur'an. He lamented that there was no such awareness movement, as a result of which Muslim men continued to be Islamically illiterate, not knowing that triple divorce was a sinful form of divorce, which the Prophet had strongly denounced. Maulana Ashraf Thanvi and others had taken a bold step in 1939 in drafting the Dissolution of Muslim Marriage Act, which gave great relief to suffering women. 'Can the members of Muslim personal law board not show such wisdom and draft a comprehensive law codifying the

Muslim personal law on the lines of the 1939 Act'?, Engineer asked (Engineer 2004). Maulana Sayed Rabey Al-Hasani Naqvi, President of the AlMPLB, had said: 'Our laws are based on divine inspiration and triple *talaq* comes from the same inspiration, that is, Shariat. We have no powers to amend or abolish it. So the triple *talaq* is irrevocable.' Therefore, Naqvi argued that though triple *talaq* was a social evil it should not be removed by legislative reform. Commenting on such contradictory logic, M. C. Bhandare, a former Congress MP and a human rights lawyer, said: 'It is difficult to understand how what is divine can at the same time be evil' (Bhandare 2004).

Ultimately, on 1 May 2005, at the end of a three-day conference at the historic Tajul mosque in Bhopal, the AlMPLB formally adopted the much-talked-about model *nikahnama*. The community response to it was mixed. While many thought that it was a forward step towards codification of Muslim personal law others considered it a superfluous exercise. Mushirul Hasan, Vice Chancellor of the Delhi-based Jamia Millia Islamia University and a noted progressive voice in the country, was happy that at long last the *ulema* had accepted the necessity of reform. Rehana Sultana, Director of the Centre for Women's Studies at the University of Hyderabad, said that the recommendations made in the *nikahnama* would reduce the incidence of *talaq* as it would no longer be as simple for men to use the triple *talaq* utterance. Imam Bukhari of Delhi's Jama Masjid was, however, not impressed at all: 'Islam does not have a model *nikahnama*. There is only a *nikahnama* that everyone follows. There is nothing new that the AlMPLB has come out with. The Qur'an already talks whom a Muslim can marry [*sic*.], while the Hadith spells out how a woman should be treated.' Muslim women activists were not happy with the nikahnama. The All India Muslim Women's Law Board, which was floated in early 2005, rejected triple *talq* as a means of divorce. Other such bodies like the Muslim Women's Rights Network, Majlis, the India Centre for Human Rights and Law, and the Forum Against Oppression of Women picked holes in the *nikahnama*. They said that it still remained highly male-centric and there was no effort to ensure gender equality (*The Telegraph* 2005).

Beyond 'the Muslim Problem'

Since, in Indian politics, communalism connotes Hindu-Muslim communalism the personal law controversy is viewed from that perspective alone. Indeed it is true that Muslims get more worked up when their personal law is touched compared to, say, Christians or Hindus.

112 The Politics of Personal Law in South Asia

The type of Muslim response one experienced in the Shah Bano case was probably unlikely had Hindus or Christians been involved. But everything is not all that fine in respect of Christian and Hindu family laws either, as we will see below.

Almost during the time when the Shah Bano controversy was the top newspaper story, the Supreme Court in its verdict in the divorce case of *Jorden Diengdeh v. S. S. Chopra* (1985) had said:

> It is thus seen that the law relating to judicial separation, divorce and nullity of marriage is far, far from uniform. Surely the time has now come for a complete reform of the law of marriage and [to] make a uniform law applicable to all people irrespective of religion or caste. It appears to be necessary to introduce irretrievable breakdown of marriage and mutual consent as grounds of divorce in all cases. The case before us is an illustration of a case where the parties are bound together [*sic.*] by a marital tie which is better untied. There is no point or purpose to be served by the continuance of a marriage which has so completely and signally broken down. We suggest that the time has come for the intervention of the legislature in these matters to provide for a uniform code of marriage and divorce and to provide by law for a way out of the unhappy situations in which couples like the present have found themselves. We direct that a copy of this order may be forwarded to the Ministry of Law and Justice for such action as they may deem fit to take.
>
> —(Menski 2001: 393)

The demand for reforms in the Indian Christian Marriage Act of 1872 was already gaining momentum. In 1983, the Joint Women's Programme (JWP) entered into a dialogue with bishops, the clergy, lawyers and the laity of various churches to find means of improving the status of Christian women. These efforts culminated in the drafting of three bills, namely, the Christian Marriage Bill 1994, the Indian Succession Amendment Bill 1994, and the Christian Adoption and Maintenance Bill 1994, all of which were sent to the government in February 1994. A year later, on 24 February 1995, the Kerala High Court passed a significant judgement. In the case of Mary Sonia Zachariah the court quashed one of the anti-women provisions in the Indian Divorce Act (IDA) of 1869, applicable to Christians, on the grounds of discrimination against women. Section 10 of the IDA made it mandatory for a wife to prove 'incestuous adultery', 'adultery coupled with cruelty' and 'adultery coupled with

It is Politics, Stupid! 113

desertion' for seeking divorce. While quashing the multiple preconditions for divorce for Christian women, the three-member judicial bench observed that Christian women seeking divorce need to prove only one of the grounds—adultery, cruelty or desertion. The court pointed out that 'the provision which compelled the deserted and cruelly treated wife to live perpetually in a marriage which ceased to exist was harsh and oppressive. Section 10 of the Indian Divorce Act of 1869 was suitably redrafted to achieve the desired result of putting Christian women on par with other Indian claimants for divorce in the same situation. Such may be an appropriate strategy to harmonise various personal laws, more suitable for the country's legal development than trying to introduce a uniform civil code (Chatterjee 1996: 35; Menski 2001: 396).

In the hype of the controversy over the Shah Bano case, the question of Hindu women's rights got overshadowed, as if everything was fine at that end. The question that should have been legitimately raised was whether, given the fact that the Hindutva forces were up in arms against the Muslim Women's Act (indeed, progressive forces were also opposed to the act), they were in favour of Hindu women's rights in the same fashion. But such questions did not bother the political class. The Hindu right had realised the necessity of creating their women's wings but did not have any women's rights agenda. Thus the BJP Mahila Morcha, the VHP Maitri Mandal and Durga Vahini, together with their different regional versions, concerned themselves primarily with the Ram Janmabhoomi movement. In any case, towards the end of the 1990s, these bodies witnessed their decline (Sarkar 1999).

As regards the judiciary, in one after another of its judgements it asked the state to introduce the uniform civil code in deference to the Directive Principles but its assumption in most of the cases was as if everything was fine with Hindu women's rights. In the famous bigamy case of *Sarla Mudgal v. Union of India and Others* (1995) the Supreme Court said: 'Since Hindus had accepted reforms and sacrificed for the national unity, the minorities should now give up their commitment to the two nation theory and agree to a uniform civil code which would strengthen national integration'—as if there was no necessity of any further reforms in the Hindu law. Just prior to the above Supreme Court judgement, a Congress member, Veena Verma, had introduced a Private Member's Bill in Parliament called the Married Women's (Protection of Rights) Bill, 1994. In its Statements of Objects and Reasons, the bill underlined the exploitation faced by women: 'The woman has no right in the house of her husband or to his property. The laws confer the right of property on a woman only after the death

114   *The Politics of Personal Law in South Asia*

of her husband and not during marriage. If a woman's right in the property of her husband is recognized, she will overcome her sense of helplessness and economic insecurity' (Agnes 1996b: 65).

Following the debate in Parliament, which was by and large supportive of the bill, H. R. Bhardwaj, the Law Minister, picked up only those elements of the debate that had opposed the bill, stating:

> We cannot insist that a husband must give 50% of his property to his wife. The women's movement in India is different from the West. We cannot really think that women will be better only by making legal provisions. . . . We will also have to see how the question or property can be settled under diverse personal laws. . . . There was a suggestion to examine whether a flat allocated to a man under government schemes should be in joint names of husband and wife. But Income Tax regulations and other problems crop up.
>
> —(*ibid.*: 65)

Commenting on the ministerial explanation, feminist lawyer and activist Flavia Agnes wrote:

> The question of diverse personal laws was raised by the Minister and not by any Muslim Member of Parliament. It is also interesting to note that the hesitation was not entirely based on diverse laws of succession but also on taxation laws. When the reforms are a setback to the economics of patriarchy, perhaps it is easier to stall them by communalizing the issue. Due to an overwhelming support, the Minister was compelled to assure the house before the bill was withdrawn on 31 March 1995 that it will be re-introduced as a government bill. The important point to note is that the debate was not communalized within majority-minority binaries.
>
> —(Agnes 1996b: 65)

Since the Congress Party, then in power, itself scuttled the bill, the Hindu right did not have to activate itself. But it is common political sense that, given the opposition to the Hindu Code bill in the 1950s and given the ascendancy of the Hindutva forces in the 1980s and 1990s, any progressive move in Hindu law would have been opposed in the name of upholding Hindu heritage and tradition. In the states that the BJP then ruled no legislation was initiated that would strive to improve the legal status of Hindu women. In Haryana and Rajasthan the party even supported the caste *panchayats* that passed resolutions denying certain rights to women. In Rajasthan, the BJP MLA, K. L. Meena, and the BJP Mahila Morcha organised a massive rally against Bhanwari, a Sathin (village-level government social worker), who had been raped by members of the powerful Gujjar community. The rally was also directed against the women's groups that had come forward to support Bhanwari's case (Singh 1996: 57).

Vasudha Dhagamwar convincingly argues that the existence of personal laws, which include Hindu personal law, has not only created an unjust social situation but has even intruded into the arena of the criminal justice system, making a mockery of criminal law in the rural areas. As a result, not only does bigamy take place by circumventing the law or, even within the ambit of law, by taking recourse to incomplete marriage rituals; even crimes within the definition of the IPC are perpetrated in the name of personal and customary laws. When a young *harijan* and his wife in UP were beheaded by their caste, Mahendra Singh Tikait, leader of the powerful agricultural lobby of North India, justified the killing on the grounds that anyone violating caste norms deserved to be punished. The state did not contradict him. The line demarcating personal law from criminal law, or for that matter even constitutional law, often gets blurred, making it difficult to determine where one ends and the other starts. Dhagamwar argues:

> If A and B marry that comes under personal law. Their personal law or custom will determine if they can marry. If they marry against the panchayat's will—though as per statutory law—and the panchayat fines or ostracises them, that is within the power of the panchayat. But if the panchayat executes them for it, then, clearly, we say, *that* is murder. It comes under criminal law; it is not within the powers of the panchayat. . . . But the lines are not always clear. The panchayat may not kill. It may take away their possessions; blacken their faces, put a garland of shoes on their neck, force them to ride a donkey and drive them out of the village with a life-time ostracism. Is this personal law? Is it a caste or tribal decision? Or is it a violation of Fundamental Rights? Is it also an offence under the Indian Penal Code (IPC)? How are most people to know where criminal law begins?
>
> —(Dhagamwar 1996b: 14)

Dhagamwar's anxiety is well taken. But the question that arises is: Is personal law the cause of the malady or it is the consequence of that malady? She herself shows how penal laws, which are universally

116 *The Politics of Personal Law in South Asia*

applicable, are sacrificed at the altar of personal laws. The problem, therefore, lies in the backwardness of Indian society, or, for that matter, of the entire South Asian society, and no amount of uniformity of family law would clear the mess. Still, one may agree with her that a uniform civil code is a proactive move in the desired direction. And one may add, to achieve that goal, the appropriate political climate has to be created.

Notes

1   The debate on the utility of the *nyayapanchayat* has not died down during all these decades and the Congress Party has expressed its willingness to introduce the system from time to time. The main rationale has been to decentralise the administration of justice and reduce the burden of pending cases on the courts. There are about thirty million such pending cases as of 2005 (Bandopadhyay 2005).
2   According to the 1981 Census the Muslim population was 11.4 per cent which in 1991 became 11.67 per cent. In 1981 there was no Census in Assam and in 1991 there was no Census in Jammu and Kashmir (J&K). Since both the states contained sizable Muslim populations this should be factored in. In 1991 the population of the country was about 839 million. In 1986, therefore, the Muslim population in India was certainly much less than the 140 million that Sen claimed it was.

4 On the Fringe: The Tribal Laws

Indian tribesmen do not cheat and exploit the poor and the weak. They are mostly ignorant of caste and race prejudice. They do not prostitute their women or degrade them by foolish laws and customs. They do not form themselves into armies and destroy one another by foul chemical means. They do not tell pompous lies over the radio. Many of their darkest sins are simply the result of ignorance. A few of them are cruel and savage, but the majority are kind and loving, admirable in their home, steadfast in their tribal loyalties, manly, independent, honourable.

—Verrier Elwin, 1943

Why Discuss Them?

Tribal laws are not personal laws. If so, why discuss them within the ambit of this book which is primarily devoted to the q uestion of personal laws and, wherever relevant, to that of customary laws? The reason for doing so is because the underlying theme of this study is to understand whether the plural legal systems of South Asia, more particularly that of India, can ever attain uniformity of law through a uniform civil code or family code. In India and Bangladesh such a discourse is politically visible in their respective formulations—the uniform civil code in India and the uniform family code in Bangladesh. In Sri Lanka, Pakistan and Nepal, too, there are symptoms of this discourse in the activities of women's right groups and those of human rights organisations (See Chapter V). But seldom in this discourse does the issue of tribal laws figure. Even if, at some point, these countries, starting with India in all likelihood, are able to develop uniform civil codes for their peoples by streamlining the essential elements within the personal laws of religious communities, no one seems to be concerned about how these countries would deal with their tribes, who follow their own family laws.

118   *The Politics of Personal Law in South Asia*

In the Indian Constituent Assembly, there was only one occasion when a direct reference was made to tribal laws in the context of a uniform civil code. It was when the article dealing with the uniform civil code in the Directive Principles of State Policy was being debated. One Muslim member from Bihar, Hussain Imam, while pleading for an amendment in the Draft Article 35 (later to become Article 44 in the Constitution of India) by inserting a protective clause in favour of Muslim personal law, said:

> In the Scheduled areas—I know of Jharkhand and Santhal Parganas [now the state of Jharkhand in the Indian Union]—we have given special protection to the aboriginal population. There are certain circumstances, which demand diversity in the civil laws. . . . Look at the Assam [then comprising the present tribal majority states of Meghalaya, Mizoram and Nagaland] tribes; what is their condition? Can you have the same kind of law for them as you have for the advanced people of Bombay? You must have a great deal of difference.
>
> —(*Constituent Assembly Debates,* Volume VII, 4 November 1948–8 January 1949: 546)

Throughout the history of the Indian subcontinent there has been an acute tension between non-tribal and tribal peoples, as their respective perceptions of law differ fundamentally. Although Vasudha Dhagamwar's recent study (2006) does not particularly talk about tribal laws, it analyses the way the tribal people were forced to subscribe to the laws of the state particularly after the British arrived on the scene, and why and how they resented these developments. This hiatus continued even after the British left. The so-called rule of law has little meaning for the tribals who, writes Dhagamwar, 'have long since concluded that the law was not for them. It was difficult to understand, it was expensive, and time consuming. Law was meant to exploit and oppress them. At all costs, one should avoid the law. It worked only for the rich and the powerful' (Dhagamwar 2006: 352).

The tribal family laws are not only distinct, they are also numerous, since there are many tribes and sub-tribes in South Asia. Since Islamic law does not recognise tribal laws the subject is not so important in Pakistan or Bangladesh though Pakistan has many tribes in Baluchistan, the North-West Frontier Province (NWFP), the Northern Areas and the Federally Administered Tribal Areas (FATA), and Bangladesh has them in the Chittagong Hill Tracts (CHT) region. In

On the Fringe: The Tribal Laws   119

both these countries tribal laws broadly fall within the category of customary laws and they are not justiciable. But in India, their laws are recognised by the Constitution, which employs the terms 'custom' and 'customary practices' when it says that 'all laws in force before the commencement of this Constitution shall continue in force therein until altered or repealed or amended' (Article 372). The effect of this provision is to continue the entire body of civil laws as prevailing in India before the Constitution came into force, which includes not only laws like the Law of Torts, Hindu laws and Mohammedan laws but also customs having the force of law (*Gapaian v. State of Madras* 1958, AIR Madras: 539). Article 13 of the Constitution says that the term 'law' includes 'customs' and 'usages' having the force of law, though such a law cannot infringe any of the fundamental rights conferred by Part III of the Constitution.

In certain regions of India the tribal people are in a majority, if not in a predominant majority, making the question even more relevant. Out of a total of twenty-eight states in the indian Union there are such states, namely, Arunachal Pradesh, Chhattisgarh, Jharkhand, Meghalaya, Mizoram and Nagaland. Barring Chhattis-garh and Jharkhand, which are so-called tribal states without a tribal majority, the remaining four are almost entirely tribal. These four states are located in india's north-east, bordering Bangladesh, Bhutan, China and Myanmar. Since it is not possible to discuss the entire gamut of tribal law in South Asia within the scope of this volume, nor is it necessary for our purpose, we will take the case of the tribal laws of india's north-east only, which have all the trappings of the discourse relevant for our analysis, namely, the plurality of legal systems, the coexistence of state and non-state legal structures, ethnic identity, and law and national integration, and look at them as encouragement to and discouragement of diversity. In short, the politics behind the continuation of tribal laws.

What is Tribal Law?

To understand what tribal law is one must first understand what a tribe is. From the indian experience during the past 200 years it can be seen that it has been rather simpler to identify a tribe than to define a tribe. Indeed, those politicians and administrators of the B ritish period who drew up lists of tribes must have had their own conceptions of tribes, but those conceptions were never clearly explained. Indian anthropologists were equipped with their disciplinary tools to define a tribe but when they were obliged to identify the tribes they

120   *The Politics of Personal Law in South Asia*

cleverly took recourse to the phrase 'tribes in transition', as if the tribes were not in transition throughout recorded history (Beteille 1991: 59). In way of finding a solution to the problem both from historical and civilisational perspectives, Beteille writes:

> Where tribe and civilization co-exist, as in India and the Islamic world, being a tribe has been more a matter of remaining outside of State and civilization, whether by choice or necessity, than of attaining a definite stage in the evolutionary advance from the simple to the complex. We cannot therefore dismiss as anomalous the Indian practice of regarding as tribes a large assortment of communities, differing widely in size, mode of likelihood and social organization. They are all tribes because they all stood more or less outside of Hindu civilization and not because they were all at exactly the same stage of evolution. . . . The permeability of the boundary in India, in the Islamic world and perhaps also in China obliges us to adopt a flexible rather than a rigid attitude towards the definition of tribe. It makes the presence of borderline cases an inescapable feature of the system, but does not permit us to argue as if all cases were borderline cases.
>
> —(Beteille 1991: 76)

The British had a vague notion about the concept of tribe. The census commissioners faced considerable difficulties in deciding where the category of tribe ended and caste began (Jha 1998: 145). But in 1881, when the first proper all-India census was conducted, some amount of clarity emerged when the word 'forest tribe' was introduced. Till almost the 1940s, anthropological writings used to suggest that tribes, with their constant interaction with non-tribes, eventually became castes. But later it became clear that it was not necessarily so and indeed the tribes no longer transformed themselves into castes. They continued to retain their distinctive identities. The difference between a caste and a tribe is clear. In terms of social organisation, tribe and caste are different. While a caste is regulated by the hereditary division of labour, hierarchy, the principles of purity and pollution, as well as civic and religious disabilities, a tribe is characterised by the absence of any of the above. Thus the basic principles that govern them are different. A tribal society is governed by kinship bonds and hence all individuals there are equal. In tribes, lineage and clan tend to be the chief unit of ownership as well as of production and consumption. In caste structures inequality, dependency and subordination are integral to the system (Xaxa 1999: 1519).

With or without a proper conception of tribes available to the British administrators, it was in the 1930s that a list was drawn to identify the tribes of India, which has formed the basis of the current listing. The Census of 1931 started, for the first time, the process of designating or 'scheduling' tribes in India. The process was not without controversy. On the one hand were the British officials belonging to the Indian Civil Service (ICS), the so-called 'official anthropologists', while on the other were the nationalist anthropologists. The former argued that the aboriginal tribes had a distinct identity while the latter considered them as part of the larger Hindu identity (Beteille 1991:77). Still, on the whole, the debate on tribes was on the periphery of the nationalist movement. Otherwise the list of backward tribes that was drawn in 1936, which was a follow-up of the special provisions for their uplift mentioned in the 1935 Government of India Act, would not have formed the basis of drawing the Scheduled Tribes list in the Constitution of India promulgated in 1950.

Tribal Law as Customary Law

Having discussed how the tribes have been understood as distinct from the so-called civilisational mainstream of India, it would be instructive to see how their legal systems too bore the mark of distinctiveness. Before analysing the Indian situation, if we talk in broad general terms while keeping the South Asian mosaic in focus, we would realise that tribal laws are essentially customary laws. But since customary laws are also found among various caste and linguistic groups, we would have to treat tribal laws as an independent legal category, to highlight their distinctiveness for the purposes of our discussion. Just to recapitulate, we have thus three categories—personal law, customary law and tribal law. Personal law is not territory-specific and its application is generally determined by the community to which persons belong by birth or the religion to which they adhere. Thus personal law is a broad category. In contrast, customary law is generally territory-specific. Different tribal laws that govern the numerous tribes of Bangladesh, India, Pakistan, Sri Lanka or any other country, or for that matter, the Thesavelamai law that governs the land rights of the Sri Lanka Tamil community of Jaffna (the Sri Lanka Tamils cannot be categorised either as a caste group or a tribal group, it is a linguistic and racial ethnicity), the Kandyan law of Sri Lanka, etc., all fall within the category of customary law (discussed in Chapter V). But there are exceptions to territory-specificity even in the customary law. For example, in South Asia, which has a caste system, many caste

122 *The Politics of Personal Law in South Asia*

laws have popular acceptance though they may not have legal recognition. And the caste system as such is not territory-specific; castes are spread across territories, more in the forms of horizontal social formations. To avoid this confusion, we will use the term 'tribal customary laws', since they operate in India as a distinct category and have legal recognition as such.

In India tribal customary laws can be comprehended as sets of traditional rules and norms considered intrinsic for tribal identity formation. These rules and norms often markedly differ from the general legal system, both in the domains of civil and criminal laws. By way of defining tribal customary law, it may be seen as 'a pattern of regulating behaviour of individuals and groups within a limited area and sphere because of popular sanction behind it and due to historical antecedents. As a result customs are sharpened into regulations and they can be branded as fundamentals of customary law' (Mitra 2000: 6). To make any effort at understanding tribal customary law, we must begin with looking at what custom is.

Custom is not a term that can be constrained by one definition. However, in common parlance it can be understood as the uniformity of conduct of people under like circumstances. As per the *Macmillan Dictionary of Anthropology,* the term custom refers to cultural traditions or habitual forms of behaviour within a given social group. The concept of custom implies not only the statistical occurrence of a given behaviour but also a prescriptive dimension: customary behaviour is that which is required or expected of the members of society under any given circumstance. To behave contrary to custom may attract sanctions ranging from social disapproval to ostracism or other forms of punishment. Custom is also defined as a usage by virtue of which a class of persons belonging to a defined section in a locality is entitled to exercise specific rights against certain other persons or property in the same locality (*State of Bihar v. Subodh Gopal Bose,* AIR 1968, SC 281). According to *Block's Law Dictionary* (8th edition, 2004), when custom, by its common adoption and long varying habit, has come to have a force of law, it may be termed as customary law or legal custom. The *Dictionary* further defines a legal custom as a custom which operates as a binding rule of law, independently of any agreement on the part of those subject to it.

In any case, customary laws predate the state or the nation and perform the functions of social control attributed to law in state systems. They can be defined as 'the unwritten or un-codified codes of conduct hallowed by age-old observance in a particular sociocultural unit. These acquire public sanction in due course because of their

On the Fringe: The Tribal Laws 123

uninterrupted continuity. The same are sanctified by unquestioned authority emanating from the ancestors of any given ethno-cultural group' (Goswami 1981: 18). Customary rules and practices are to be understood in contrast to constitutional law and written or codified rules of personal or public conduct created by acts of legislature which are referred to as statutory law. The main points of difference between statutory law and customary law relate to their creation, forms, applicability, enforcibility, popular acceptability, amendability, and the superiority of one over the other when they are in conflict, as explained below.

Statutory laws are a set of laws created through legislation at specific times but customary laws evolve through ages of interactions and transactions amongst the members of the community. In form, a statute thus is a written enactment and hence codified, unlike a customary law, which is seldom found in codified form. The latter is the expression of the positive will of the people handed down from one generation to its successor through social mechanisms of cultural transmission. Lately, however, there has been a tendency, in the wake of the resurgence of identity politics, to make attempts to revive customary rules and regulations, or innovate on such rules and regulations, and to write them down.

In terms of their extent and application, statutory laws are uniform in nature and extend to all those parts of the country that are mentioned in the extent clauses of those statutes. The customary laws, in contrast, are restricted to smaller areas, are region-specific and, in most cases, applicable to kinship-based societies. Obviously, therefore, they are not uniform in nature and differ from community to community, tribe to tribe. As a result, in many cases where two or more tribal laws are in question they have to be adjudicated through the formal judicial system by applying statutory laws and not customary laws. To bring about an amendment in the statutory law is a long process but in customary law it is simple and flexible, not requiring any formal procedure. Any community congregation can put a stamp of legitimacy on these changes.

One of the major conceptual differences between the two sets of laws is that, while customary laws gain strength from the habitual obedience of community members, statutory laws exist even without people recognising them. In semi-autonomous societies people are often unaware of their violations, whereas in respect of customary laws, it can never so happen. But customary laws remain effective only till collective interests remain intact. As soon as individualist interests start overtaking community interests, customary laws lose

124 *The Politics of Personal Law in South Asia*

their efficacy, which we will refer to in the context of Bhutan in the next chapter and which we have also discussed in the last section of this chapter. In this context it may be mentioned that, in case there is a conflict between statutory law and customary law, the former prevails. Though Article 13 of the Constitution of India recognises customary laws having the force of law, judicial precedents certify that customary laws have subservient status compared to statutory laws (Pant 2002: 6–13).

However, all customs do not have the force of law. For a custom to be valid, it must not be contrary to justice, equity and good conscience. In considering whether a custom is reasonable or unreasonable one should not be influenced or guided by modern ideas, for that which appears to be unreasonable to many of us might have been considered as eminently reasonable and necessary for the wellbeing of a community in bygone days. What is important is that it is the assent of the community that gives a custom its validity as well as its flexibility (Goswami 1981: 21–22). As is evident from various decisions of the Supreme Court, customs and customary laws constitute only a source of law and not law as such; also, they become such a source only when they are recorded in statutes or recognised by courts as such and mentioned in judgments (Upadhyay 2003: 46–44). In a 2001 case, the Supreme Court said that 'a party relying on a custom is obliged to establish it by clear and unambiguous evidence . . . For a custom to have a colour of rule of law, it is necessary for the party claiming it to plead and thereafter prove that such custom is ancient, certain and reasonable' (2001, AIR, SC 938). Whether a custom is ancient, certain and reasonable, to be part of customary law itself gives virtually 'uncontrolled discretion' to judges to recognise or reject a custom.

It may be noted that one of the most remarkable features of customary law is that it does not make any clearcut division between criminal and civil offences as is done in modern jurisprudence. Any discussion on customary law would remain incomplete without reference to the tribal's faith in the oath or ordeals. When there is no concrete evidence to prove the offence, the suspected or alleged offender is given an alternative, either to admit his/her guilt, or to undergo the traditionally prescribed ordeal, or to swear by the prescribed oath. Popular belief in the automatic punishment of the offender often makes the latter confess guilt, whereupon prescribed punishments follow without malice on anybody's part. An outstanding feature of the primitive judicial system is that each party involved in a quarrel or crime openly and freely defends their respective position without bearing any bad feeling against the other. Justice is inevitably quick; such

On the Fringe: The Tribal Laws   125

quick dispensation of justice makes tribals abhor the modern legal system, which is notorious for its inordinate delays (Ansari 1988; Goswami 1981: 24–25). There are also many other strengths of the traditional system, which advocates of tribal customary law point out. Some of these strengths are:

(i) Since rural, including tribal, communities have little exposure to the different statutory forums available for redress of their problems, they prefer to avoid formal courts and sling to their traditional justice systems.

(ii) Justice in tribal society is based on the concept of restitution that brings relief, whereas in the formal courts litigation is normally adversarial in nature and relief is not guaranteed to the aggrieved party. The case normally depends on the strength of the party and the lawyer. It is not necessary that justice shall be meted out and the truly aggrieved party will win.

(iii) Under the traditional system of justice, an accused remains an honourable member of society once he or she has been punished and there is no stigma attached; whereas in the modern system, even after being punished the accused is not able to be reformed or rehabilitated due to the stigma that society attaches to his or her crime or violation.

(iv) In the formal system, court expenses can be very expensive for the litigant—lawyer's fees, travelling expenses, etc., whereas village institutions are situated at a more accessible distance and do not involve any court or advocacy fee. Sometimes the disputing parties have to bring some ceremonial gifts to the mediators and often a party offers a feast to the community if it is a major dispute.

(v) People prefer to go to traditional institutions for resolution of conflicts; one reason being that the penalty, many a time, is set according to the paying capacity of the violator; or else at times it need not be paid immediately or can be deferred to a later date (Pant 2002: 93–94).

It may, however, be underlined that tribal customary laws in India are not un-influenced by the state legal system. For example, the introduction of cash fines in the tribal justice system does not only reflect the monetisation of the tribal economy but also the impact of state legal system 'stock-in-trade' restitutive sanction. Similarly, not only has state law prevented the Naga custom of head-hunting, the institution has actually been brought into disuse by the community itself. A penal offence like murder is also now completely within the state legal

126 *The Politics of Personal Law in South Asia*

system (Baxi 1986: 88). But insofar as civil disputes or small crimes are concerned the state legal system, by and large, does not interfere with tribal customary laws except in such disputes where a tribal and a non-tribal are involved, as in the case of mixed marriages, as for example the one we have seen in the case of a Khasi woman married to a Sikh under the Christian Marriage Act of 1872 (see pp. 120–121). Since for the purposes of this book it is neither possible nor necessary to address the entire gamut of the controversy over tribal laws in juxtaposition to the issue of the uniformity of laws and nation building, we will take up the q uestion only in respect of the tribes of India's north-east as a case study to make a few broad points.

India's Tribal North-East

Our argument here is organised in the following manner. First, we will discuss the intellectual discourse on tribes in general in the pre-Independence period; second, we will analyse why the tribes in the north-east were treated differently from other Indian tribes; and third, we will discuss the justice system that operates in the region, together with the efforts that are underway to codify the tribal laws there.

The Texture of the Discourse

There is little on the tribal question in the pre-Independence nationalist discourse. There is virtually nothing on the issue of tribal customary law and their justice system (Guha 1996). Therefore, whatever little was possibly there on the subject must be culled out of the intellectual debate surrounding tribal culture and the future model of development that was being talked about. In this context the names that figured most prominently were those of Amritlal V. Thakkar (popularly known as Thakkar Bapa), G. S. Ghuriye, Nirmal Kumar Bose and Verrier Elwin. Besides, there were the Catholic missionaries with their proselytising motto.

But before their respective approaches are analysed the backdrop of the historical context of the period must be examined. While in the 1920s and 1930s the backward classes and dalit movements had considerably influenced the nationalist discourse, in the 1940s the Hindu-Muslim communal question had virtually overshadowed everything else. Against the background of these divisive tendencies and the nationalist efforts to contain them, it was natural that the tribal question would also be seen through that prism. Those who saw the question from the point of view of national integration were

On the Fringe: The Tribal Laws 127

asking for the assimilation of the tribes into the national 'mainstream', while those who viewed it from the angle of group rights or minority rights were asking for the retention of their autonomous existence. To understand the relevance of this debate for our purposes here, it must, therefore, be related to the central point of the discourse on the uniform civil code, that is, national integration with individual citizens as its constituents versus national unity in diversity by upholding group rights and group identities, a subject that consumed a lot of the energy of the members of the Constituent Assembly. This aspect is critical for our understanding of why tribal customary laws have not only been retained, there is a massive effort underway to codify them, thereby making them more permanent, which we will discuss later in this chapter.

At the time of India's independence there were two major schools of thought on how to deal politically with the tribes of India. The first school, the assimilationist school, was represented by A. V. Thakkar, G. S. Ghuriye and Nirmal Kumar Bose. The essence of their argument was that there was evidence of some tribes getting totally assimilated into 'mainstream' Indian culture. As such, without showing any disrespect for the cultural distinctiveness of tribes, all institutional incentives should be provided to encourage 'marginal' peoples to assimilate into the Indian 'mainstream'. Such a process would contribute to building national identity and the mutual give and take between the 'marginal' and the 'mainstream' communities would enrich the overall Indian culture (Stuligross 1999: 499–500).

The second school, the integrationist school, was primarily represented by Verrier Elwin. Elwin had come to India from England in 1927 as a missionary but soon developed serious differences with both the Church of England and the British Indian Government. He quit his mission in 1932 and his church in 1935. Later he became a citizen of India and, before his death in 1964, established himself as a great champion of tribal development. Between 1954 and 1964 he was the adviser on tribal affairs to the Northeast Frontier Agency (NEFA, now the state of Arunachal Pradesh). He argued that tribal culture was superior to the so-called 'mainstream' culture in several respects, as for example women's position in the society, and the assimilationist approach would destroy these tribal qualities. Referring to other such finer aspects of tribal culture, Elwin wrote in 1943 that Indian tribesmen

> do not cheat and exploit the poor and the weak. They are mostly ignorant of caste and race prejudice. They do not prostitute their

128   *The Politics of Personal Law in South Asia*

women or degrade them by foolish laws and customs. They do not form themselves into armies and destroy one another by foul chemical means. They do not tell pompous lies over the radio. Many of their darkest sins are simply the result of ignorance. A few of them are cruel and savage, but the majority are kind and loving, admirable in their home, steadfast in their tribal loyalties, manly, independent, honourable.

—(Quoted in Guha 1996: 2377)

Indeed, Elwin's position on tribal matters underwent significant changes depending upon the changes in national politics during the tumultuous decades preceding India's independence and after (Guha 1996: 2375–389). As an adviser to Pandit Nehru on tribal affairs, he eventually warned against 'museumification' of the tribes, which would stifle their development; he sought their integration as communities into the Indian national state. He did not favour the idea that the tribal people should be left to themselves. While serving as an adviser to NEFA he raised the q uestion: How could a democratic government be indifferent to any of its regions and allow it to stay isolated from the rest of the developmental processes sweeping the country? He gave three reasons why this so-called isolationist tactic was flawed.

In the first place it [the policy of isolation] has rarely been implemented in practice. There are some twenty million tribal people in India, and before Independence little was done to them. At the same time, they were not in actual fact left alone. They were exploited by landlords and zamindars, robbed by money-lenders, cheated by merchants, and their culture was largely destroyed by foreign missionaries. Secondly, the belief in the happy care-free Noble Savage is a myth, except perhaps in the South Seas long ago. In NEFA at least the people had not enough food; they suffered from abominable diseases; they died young; they were heavily burdened with anxiety; their life was distracted by war, kidnapping, slavery and cruel punishments. They were not even free: weaker tribes had to pay tribute to the strong; rich and powerful Chiefs grew richer on the labour of hundreds of serfs; freedom of movement was severely restricted by inter-village conflict. And thirdly, while isolation was possible in the last century, it is impossible today. Modern industry is transforming the whole world; the humanitarian ideals of a welfare state no longer permit the neglect of any section of the population; political necessities forbid the existence of any administrative vacuum on the

On the Fringe: The Tribal Laws 129

international frontier; tribal leaders themselves demand greater opportunities. And no one (least of all the scientist) wants to keep the tribal people as museum specimens for the benefit of science.
—(Elwin 1999: 47)

The recommendations of the two schools of tribal policy got reflected in two schedules of the Indian Constitution. While the Fifth Schedule was aimed at assimilating all tribals into the Indian 'mainstream', as was recommended by the first school, the Sixth Schedule was designed for particular north-eastern tribal communities, as was recommended by the second school. It was on the lines of the latter that Assamese leader Gopinath Bardoloi, as the head of the Northeast Frontier (Assam) Tribal and Excluded Areas Sub-Committee of the Advisory Committee of the Constituent Assembly, recommended an administrative setup for the administration of hill areas based on the concept of regional autonomy in all matters affecting their customs, laws of inheritance, administration of justice, land, forests, etc. These recommendations formed the basis of the Sixth Schedule that led to the establishment of the Autonomous District Councils (ADC) in the tribal areas of India's north-east.[1] The subcommittee recommended in clear terms:

As regards civil cases (among the tribes there is little distinction between criminal and civil cases) we recommend that except suits arising out of special laws, all ordinary suits should be disposed of by the tribal councils or courts and we see no objection to the local councils being invested with full powers to deal with them, including appeal and revision. In respect of civil and criminal cases where non-tribals are involved, they should be tried under the regular law and the Provincial Government should make suitable arrangements for the expeditious disposal of such cases by employing Circuit Magistrates or Judges.
—(*Constituent Assembly Debates*, Volume VII,
4 November 1948–8 January 1949: 112)

The ADCs were meant to serve as institutional mechanisms by which tribal communities could be integrated into the modern and bureaucratic political system of India with minimum sacrifice to community values and traditions (Jyrwa 1996: 22–23; Stuligross 1999: 506). The political purpose of introducing the ADC system was three fold: one, to take institutionalised democracy to the grassroots levels in the tribal areas, thereby contributing to national integration; two, to

130   *The Politics of Personal Law in South Asia*

gradually replace the tribal chieftain system by democratically elected leaders; and three, to devolve powers, both financial and administrative, to newly emerging tribal leaders to take care of local development, thereby protecting tribal autonomy over resources.

The Specificity of the Tribal North-East

The tribal population of the north-east is comparatively very small compared to the central belt of India. It accounts for only 11 per cent of the overall tribal population of India, while the central belt covering the nine states of Andhra Pradesh, Chhattisgarh, Gujarat, Jharkhand, Madhya Pradesh, Maharashtra, Orissa, Rajasthan and West Bengal accounts for 86 per cent. Yet, the north-east commands enormous political importance, partly because of its geographical location and partly because of its numerous past and present secessionist and autonomist movements (Doley 1998: 14–49). To put the matter in the overall perspective of the tribal politics of India, it may be noted that according to the census of 2001 the tribal population is about 89 million, constituting 8.6 per cent of India's population. In 1951, it was 5.3 per cent. The names of the distinctive tribes are mentioned in the Constitution of India and as such they are called Scheduled Tribes (STs), which, according to the People of India Project of the Anthropological Survey of India, are 461 in number (Xaxa 2003: 70–71). The rise in the ST population is primarily explainable by the fact that, since the STs have certain special privileges in terms of jobs and taxes within India's version of affirmative action called protective or positive discrimination guaranteed by the Constitution, those tribes which do not figure in the Constitution often hanker for their inclusion in the constitution's schedule, and sometimes they succeed too. As such, ST is a political category like the Scheduled Castes (SCs) and their legal rights too therefore fall within a certain political discourse, which is essentially Identlty-centric. This Identlty-centric political discourse naturally wraps the tribal law discourse within its fold. The champions of the uniform civil code in India had better take this dimension into account, lest their success, if any, were to remain incomplete.

The Evolution of the Justice System in the North-East

Administration of justice in tribal INE is significantly different from the rest of India. It has been so all along. In the past, village councils admlnlstered both criminal and civil justice in all cases, based on

On the Fringe: The Tribal Laws 131

age-old customary practices. It was only among the Mizos and Kukis that the chiefs had absolute judicial authority but even they used to seek the advice of the community elders. In Arunachal Pradesh, village councils were the lawmaking and dispensing authority among most tribes except where chieftainship prevailed, such as among the Noctes, the Wanchoos and the Tangsas. The village councils were well organised institutions among the Adis and the Monpas. The members of the Adi *kebangs* (village councils) were acknowledged leaders of the society with reputations for honesty, integrity and oratorical powers. They were chosen for life. All disputes in the village were settled by the *kebang* after detailed enquiries. Inter-village disputes were settled by an inter-village council established for a group of villages called *bongo*. Over the bongos, there was a superior body called bog. *Bokang* settled inter-bongo disputes of the same tribe. Thus, among the Adis, the traditional judiciary was three-tiered. Among the Nishis, there was the *mel* and the Mishimis had the *abbal*, which, however, had less powers. They could function only when both parties to the dispute agreed to abide by their decisions. The members of these bodies were really a class of professional mediators who were supposed to know the true significance of the customary laws and were approached by the parties because of their wisdom and knowledge.

Among the Kukis of Manipur, the Kuki chief was the final arbiter of all disputes among his subjects. On the other hand, the Manipuri Nagas had a flair for having a many-tiered judicial organisation, where the council of elders was the original trial court and the upper tiers were appellate bodies. For instance, among the Mao Nagas of Manipur, the lowest tier was the clan council; it decided only petty disputes. The next higher tier was the council of village elders, which was the real original court. It tried all cases of the villagers. Appeals from this court went to the third tier, the group council of elders of villages. Appeals from the six-village group council's decisions were made to the eighteen-village group council of elders, which was the apex body and formed the fourth tier.

In Tripura, the Maharaja had originally established a separate hill court, which had exclusive jurisdiction to try cases between parties where one belonged to a hill-tribe. This court was, however, abolished in 1879 and the ordinary courts of the Maharaja were authorised to try such cases. But the Maharaja explicitly laid down a rule that in trying disputes among tribesmen, the customary laws should invariably be followed (LRI, 1990: 660–81). Despite the official jurisdiction of the Maharaja, the village councils of the various tribes, in actual practice, disposed of the overwhelming majority of these cases without

132   The Politics of Personal Law in South Asia

any interference from the Maharaja's official machinery of justice. For instance, the Jamatia had a two-tiered judiciary. At the lowest level, there was the *chaudhury* elected by the villagers. He had a village council to assist him, with the priest and messenger of the village being two important members of the council. At the higher level, there was the *acra* (*sardar*) selected by the villagers. He was assisted by some office bearers. While the *acra* disposed of major criminal and civil disputes, the village council tried to amicably resolve minor disputes.

At the grass-roots level among the Karbis in Assam, there was the *sarthe* or the *gaonbura*, who was assisted by the council of elders called *mei*. The *sarthe* and the *mei* disposed of minor disputes. The *habai* was the next higher tier and was in charge of a number of villages. The next tier was that of the *lyndokpo* or the Karbi king. He was at the apex of the judiciary and was assisted by ministers and officers. Again, in the North Cachar Hills, the Dimasa Kachari king was the fountainhead of justice. The traditional village council, with eight officials headed by the gaonbura (*khunang*) tried petty cases. Where women were involved as parties, elderly village women were invited to participate in the trials by the *khunang*.

The British rulers recognised traditional village authorities, but cut down their powers drastically. For example, in Mizoram, they retained the chieftainship system but his power to try criminal cases was limited only to non-heinous or petty offences. In the Mikir Hills (the old name of Karbi Anglong), the *lyndokpo* and the *habai* were not recognised by the British and in place of the *habai,* the institution of *mouzadar* was introduced. At the village level, the *sarthe* was allowed to continue, though some *gaonburas* were appointed by the British government as *sarkari gaonburas*. In Arunachal Pradesh, the traditional village authorities were not recognised and the deputy commissioner was authorised to appoint his own village authorities.

In Manipur and Tripura, the British government did not meddle with the judicial system of the two Maharajas and introduced no rules for administration of justice as was done in the Mikir Hills, the Lushai Hills (now Mizoram) or NEFA (now Arunachal Pradesh). The Maharajas, on their parts, did not interfere with the traditional systems of justice prevailing among the hill-tribes. In 1935, the Manipur Maharaja passed the Rules for the Management of the State of Manipur, which included, among other things, Rules for Administration of Justice in the Hill Areas. Towards the end of the Manipur Maharaja's rule, the Manipur Hill Peoples' Regulation (1947) was enacted. It provided for a four-tiered judicial administration for the hill areas—the village authority, the circle authority, the Hill Bench and the Chief Court,

On the Fringe: The Tribal Laws   133

with nominal powers given to the village authority. However, with the end of the Maharaja's rule following Independence in 1947, this system also came to an end.

In Tripura, the Maharaja tried to introduce the *gramya mandalis* in 1938 which would have restricted judicial powers. However, this could not be translated into action as the Maharaja's rule came to an end following World War II. Thus, during the British period, while the powers and structure of the village authorities in the hill districts of Assam (including the present territories of Mizoram, Arunachal Pradesh, Karbi Anglong and the North Cachar Hills) were modified or curtailed by written rules, the village authorities of Manipur and Tripura continued to function as usual without much interference. But in practice, even in the hill areas of Assam, the village authorities continued to exercise their old powers, the only exception being the homicide cases (LRI 1987: 1–2).

On the whole, during the colonial period, after having established their authority over the north-east, the British brought some changes in the administration of justice, though not as profound as in other parts of the country (*ibid.*: 1–2). In pursuance of their policy of least interference with the tribal way of life, the Assam Frontier Tract Regulation (Regulation 2) of 1880 provided for the tribes to rule themselves according to their own customs and traditions. Some changes were introduced in 1919, 1921 and 1935 but they were minor. It was as late as 1945 that, through the promulgation of the Assam Frontier (Administration of Justice) Regulation of 1945, it was reiterated that most of the disputes and cases in those areas were to be adjudicated by tribal customary laws and practices. Of course, since 1916 the Indian Penal Code was in force there to facilitate the holding of trials by regular courts, trials involving serious criminal offences (Chowdhury 1997: 16–17).

Notably, the conversion of most of the tribes of the north-east into Christianity in the nineteenth century had little impact on tribal customary laws. Following the British entry into Assam in 1826 when Sadlya became an important centre of tea trade, the first Baptist Mission was establlshed there. During the remaining part of the century Christian missions belonging to various denominations spread to many other parts of the region. By and large, the relationship between the missionaries and the colonial government was one of mutual respect, for their interests complemented one another. But when the missionaries began to interfere with the traditional customs of the tribes, which they resented and which had the potential of creating a breach of peace, the British government sided with the

134   *The Politics of Personal Law in South Asia*

tribes. Political and strategic interests were uppermost in their minds. For example, following one such controversy between the Naga Ao tribe and the local missionary, the British government passed a decree in 1910, specifying the festivals and rituals in which the Christians should participate (Dena 1988: 117–19; Imchen 2003: 60; Roy and Rizvl 1990: 22–29).

In the Constituent Assembly the issue of the autonomy of tribes in the north-east figured prominently in the context of the debate over the Sixth Schedule. We have noted above the Bardoloi Committee report and the setting up of the ADCs. The debate held on 6 and 7 September 1949, however, concentrated more on matters of details. Insofar as the continuation of tribal customary laws was concerned, there was no major disagreement and, with minor amendments, the Sixth Schedule of the Draft Constitution was adopted (*Constituent Assembly Debates,* Volume IX, 30 July-18 September 1949: 1003–084).

But the case of Nagaland was somewhat different. As independence was nearlng, nationalists stepped up efforts to convince the Nagas to join the Indian Union. In the process both the Nagas and the Indian interim government agreed to uphold the Naga customary laws. An accord was signed between the Assam Governor, Sir Akbar Hydarl, and the representatives of the Naga tribes, following their discussions on 26–28 June 1947, the first clause of which referred to the continuation of 'Naga customary or such law as may be lntroduced with the consent of duly recognized Naga representative organisation' (Text of the Naga-Hydarl Accord in Misra 2000: 201–03). Incldentally, the Bardoloi Committee, which had subsequently drafted the Sixth Schedule, was not able to visit the Naga Hill district because of insurgency there, as we have noted above. Since the ADC scheme, therefore, was not to apply to the Nagas, their traditional local government structure was maintained, consisting of the Village Council, the Range Council and the Tribal Council (subsequently reorganised in 1971–72 as Nagaland village, area council and regional council respectively). These bodies administered the Naga tribal customary laws (Bhagabati 1997: 20).

After Independence, when the tribal areas of the north-east were brought under the purview of the Sixth Schedule of the Constitution, it was provided that certain categories of criminal offences and civil disputes would be adjudicated by the mechanism of the Autonomous District Councils. According to Clause 5(3) of the Sixth Schedule 'the Code of Civil Procedure [CPC], 1908, and the Code of Criminal Procedure [Cr. PC], 1898, shall not apply to the trial of any suits, cases or offences in an autonomous district or in any autonomous region'. Although Arunachal Pradesh and Nagaland are outside the purview of the Sixth Schedule it does not mean that the laws operative in the rest of India operate there. In Arunachal Pradesh the Rules for Administration of Justice promulgated during British rule are in force, while in Nagaland the traditional village councils administer justice. The hill tribes of Manipur are governed by the Manipur Hill Areas Village Authorities Act of 1956 and, ever since 1979, the Tripura Tribal Areas Autonomous District Council has been administering justice in the areas under its iurisdiction (LRl 1987: 2–3).

The Plural Justice System

As is evident from the above discussion, there is a plurality of legal systems in the Sixth Schedule areas of the north-east. On the one hand, there are the formal modern central laws, while on the other there are traditional customary laws emanating from within the community, which are being recognised by modern institutions as well. In addition, the Sixth Schedule states have been empowered to enact laws for the areas within their jurisdiction through their Autonomous District Councils. The laws made by the Autonomous Councils are closer to customary laws and social practices of local communities, and are applicable in cases where both the parties in a dispute are tribal. Para 3 of the Sixth Schedule of the Constitution is especially important, as it empowers the District Council to make laws with respect to the following:

(a) the management of any forest not being a reserved forest;
(b) the use of any canal or water-course for the purpose of agriculture;
(c) the regulation of the practice of *jhum* or other forms of shifting cultivation;
(d) the establishment of village or town committees or councils and their powers;
(e) the appointment of a succession of chiefs or headmen;
(f) the inheritance of property;
(g) marriage and divorce; and
(h) social customs.

A major diference between Sixth Schedule states and non-Sixth schedule states concerns the application of Acts of Parliament and the State Legislatures in these states. The Sixth Schedule bars the application of the Acts of Parliament and the State Legislatures to the Autonomous District Council Areas in the subject matter where the latter are authorised to make laws.

136   *The Politics of Personal Law in South Asia*

According to Clause 5(3) of the Sixth Schedule, the Code of Civil Procedure, 1908, and the Code of Criminal Procedure, 1898, shall not apply to the trial of any suits, cases or offences in any autonomous district or autonomous region. The Sixth Schedule envisages the establishment of a three-tiered system for the administration of justice. At the top are the magistrates, followed by SDOs and DCs who can try offences punishable with death, transportation or imprisonment for five years or more. The Autonomous District Councils put in place by the Sixth Schedule can set up courts with higher powers than those exercised by the village councils under the British Rules for Administration of Justice. Next are the village courts, empowered to try only petty cases; the imposition of fines or compensations is considered enough in respect of such petty cases.

The above system was put in place only in Mizoram, Karbi Anglong and the North Cachar Hills. In Arunachal Pradesh, where the Sixth Schedule was not adopted, the DCs, SDOs and magistrates try heinous crimes and the village authorities the non-heinous ones. Where well organised village councils existed from before, the DC usually appoints their members to the village authorities, but where (as in the Mishimi and Nishi areas) no such permanent organisations existed, the DCs generally appoint the *sarkari gaonburas,* the *anchal samity* members or the *gaon panchayat* members to constitute village authorities for a limited period, sometimes to try only one case.

In Manipur, the Manipur Village Authorities in Hill Areas Act was passed in 1956. The members of the village authority are to be elected by the villages, but the village authority is not the village court. The members of the village court are to be appointed by the state government from among the members of the village authority, and their tenure is to be coterminous with that of the village authority. The Act of 1956 has conferred powers on the village court to try certain offences under the Cattle Trespass Act and certain petty offences under the Indian Penal Code.

Tripura introduced a system of *nyayapanchayat* in 1959 all over the state, including the hill areas; 138 *nyayapanchayats* were established in 1967. However, this experiment met with little success and they were finally abolished in 1983. By the enactment of the Tripura Tribal Areas Autonomous District Council Act, 1979, the Autonomous District Council system was introduced in Tripura. It also required an amendment of the Constitution to include the hill areas of Tripura in the Sixth Schedule. The District Councils of Tripura are yet to frame the rules for administration of justice and consequently, there is no *nyayapanchayat* or village council court in Tripura; all cases, criminal

On the Fringe: The Tribal Laws   137

and civil, are supposed to come before the regular magistrates and *munshiffs*. In reality, however, the traditional village councils that existed prior to the British continue as before to settle disputes in the villages.

As regards rules of procedure, the Autonomous District Councils are to frame their own rules for the administration of justice and lay down procedures for the trial of cases at different levels. At the level of the village court, customary law and practice determine the procedure. At the level of the Subordinate District Council court and the District Council court, the spirit of the Civil and Criminal Procedure Codes is to be followed.

The Codification Project

As the recognition of the sources of law is not easy and courts can be unpredictable, advocates of customary laws have realised that to be recognised as such, these laws need to be recorded as legal rights. Law 'in' society (including customary laws) has to be seen as part of law 'for' society (formal laws laid down by statutes and courts), otherwise the policymakers and lawmakers would not take it seriously (Upadhyay 2003: 4644–645). Thus, to give formal sanction to customs under the modern legal regime, efforts are on for their codification.

Many efforts have been made in the past, and are still being made, to understand and codify tribal customary laws to the extent possible. Besides individual scholars, the most notable contribution in this regard at the institutional level has been made by three organisations, namely, the Law Research Institute of the Guwahati High Court, the Indian Law Institute at New Delhi and the Anthropological Survey of India, headquartered in Kolkata. In the process of the compilation of data, it is kept in mind that the researchers should not necessarily use modern terminologies alone, as it is quite possible that the way an offence is understood and designated by a person familiar with Anglo-Indian law might not be the same as understood and interpreted by tribals. This has been highlighted by Upendra Baxi in his response to the project design prepared by K. S. Singh, Director-General, Anthropological Survey of India, who, in the mid-1970s, undertook a massive project to study the customary laws of seventy tribes. Baxi writes:

I think that your note on the project is fairly comprehensive. I remain, however, a little anxious concerning the use of certain

138 *The Politics of Personal Law in South Asia*

categories of Anglo-Indian law in the project note. For example, the note refers to 'theft', 'homicide', 'murder', 'ownership', 'usufructuary right', 'property' right, etc. The use of these categories, howsoever handled, is likely to create a systematic bias in the understanding of the tribal law. For one thing, we seem to presume that identical or even similar conceptions such as these exist in the tribal law; and for another that these categories could really be useful in either understanding, describing, or evaluating the structure of tribal society and its legal systems. It is, therefore, very essential, in my opinion, not to use these categories of the Anglo-Indian law but instead to classify the conduct in question as accurately as possible in terms of the nature of claims involved between parties and protected or sacrificed by the state of tribal law.

—(Singh 1993: 423)

Singh appreciated Baxi's concern and urged his research team that 'the terms which we have mentioned in our schedule guidelines and the context of the conceptions that exist among the tribes should be examined. The investigators should find out the cultural and ethnographic context of the terms in the tribal legal system while analysing concrete cases' (Singh 1993: 428). In the codification of the tribal customary laws of INE the contribution of the Law Research Institute has been seminal.

The Issue of Women's Rights

Regarding women's legal rights, tribal women activists from the north-east argue that it is inappropriate to view their problems merely from the binary perspective of the uniform civil code versus community family laws. Jarjum Ete, a noted activist from Arunachal Pradesh, writes that 'there are vast gray areas which constitute the essence of life and of struggle for the women of the North East— with the innate need to uphold the heritage and rich cultural values of their tribes while simultaneously struggling against new forms of oppression within their communities in the name of tradition' (Ete 1996: 43). Like anywhere else, women's rights activists in the tribal areas of the north-east are primarily concerned with issues such as marriage, separation and property rights. There are also related questions pertaining to child marriage, multiple or forced marriages, the abduction of women and the common problem of abandoned women and children. Why should it be, Ete argues, that women alone should bear the onus

On the Fringe: The Tribal Laws   139

of tribal tradition while men can get away with non-tribal behaviour in the name of modernity? In February 1989, the Arunachal Pradesh Women's Welfare Society (APWWS, established in 1979) presented a charter, which contained the following demands:

1. Marriages of all Arunachal Pradesh communities should have a uniform system of solemnisation and should all be registered.
2. The communities should treat their women better, keeping in view the changes taking place in society.
3. The state government should do more to eradicate such practices as forced marriages, child marriages and multiple marriages.
4. Inter-tribal marriages should be encouraged and there should be mass conscientisation in this regard.

Subsequently, the organisation demanded the implementation of the 73rd Amendment of the Constitution, which provided for one-third representation for women in the *panchayats*. It also pleaded for reforms in the customary laws. But the maledominated politics did not heed these demands. On the contrary, on 4 November 1994 the State Assembly passed without any debate the AP Bill for Protection of Customary Laws and Special Practices 1994. The blanket provisions in the Bill tended to protect even regressive customs, including those that undermined the status of women (Ete 1996: 43–45). The President of India, however, was persuaded by the women activists not to give his assent to the bill.

Tribal Laws and Globalisation

It is generally accepted from a modernist perspective that economic growth hinges on two basic elements—property and contract (Kitch 1986: 122). India's north-east, with its largely common-property norms, is thus not suitable for economic development which would match the rapid economic growth envisaged for India in the present globalised world. But how long can the region resist the pressures of the process of liberalisation and globalisation? If one goes by the experience of the English Commons—a system in which a village cooperatively controlled public land—the structure collapsed under the pressures of the industrialisation of England over the centuries; the structure was found inefficient and bogged down by inefficient customs (*ibid.*: 122–23). In essence, therefore, the market economy and the customary socio-legal system cannot coexist for long. One has to succumb to the pressures of the other. What is conceivable, therefore,

140 *The Politics of Personal Law in South Asia*

as has happened in other places in similar circumstances (for example, with the English Commons) is that social relationships, such as marriages, may continue to be governed by customary laws but economic relationships will be increasingly governed by private property considerations and contractual obligations. How to peacefully manage this transition is the greatest challenge for the tribal elites of the north-east as well as for the Indian state.

Note

1 The five-member Gopinath Bardoloi Committee visited all the tribal areas in the north-east except the Naga Hills District. It could not go there on account of insurgency. Notably, the Committee completely ignored the plains' tribes, for example, the Bodos (Stuligross 1999: 502).

5   The South Asian Mosaic

A culture which leaves unsatisfied and drives to rebelliousness so large a number of its members neither has a prospect of continued existence nor deserves it.

—Sigmund Freud, *The Future of Illusion*

The Region

Our discourse on personal law reforms, the uniform civil code and their connection with the discourse of nationalism would be incomplete if we confine it to India alone. The region of South Asia, being one civilisational space and having more or less one common historical experience, would provide us with a better perspective of the problematique. In recent international literature, South Asia as a region connotes seven states, Bangladesh, Bhutan, India, the Maldives, Nepal, Pakistan and Sri Lanka. They all form the regional institutional grouping called SAARC (South Asian Association for Regional Cooperation). Though, at the 13th SAARC Summit held in Dhaka in November 2005, Afghanistan has been added to the organisation, and though Myanmar too is considered part of the region by many international relations analysts, for our purposes here we will confine our discussion to the original seven states of SAARC, for Afghanistan is still in the process of normalisation and social research in that country is yet to be practicable. We will take up the question countrywise in the following sequence: Pakistan, Bangladesh, Nepal, Sri Lanka, the Maldives and Bhutan.

142   *The Politics of Personal Law in South Asia*

Pakistan

The Islamic Ideology

To understand the status of personal laws in Pakistan, it would be instructive to understand the nature of Pakistani state and the texture of its Islam-oriented politics. Ever since the adoption of the Lahore Resolution of the Muslim League in 1940, which for the first time clearly resolved in favour of creating Pakistan in the name of Islam,[1] the political class of Pakistan has become hostage to Islamic politics, not necessarily ideologically subscribing to it all the time. There has been a constant undercurrent of strain between the modernists and the traditionalists in Pakistan politics, giving the army an opportunity to take full advantage of the situation, though, within the army itself, there are traditionalists and modernists. If one analyses the changing contours of Pakistan politics over the years, around the changing role of the 1949 Objectives Resolution, which is the central element of Pakistan's constitutionalism, one would understand this intrinsic political tension (Conrad 1997).

Immediately after the creation of Pakistan, the conflict between the modernists, represented by the Muslim League in general and Jinnah in particular, and the traditionalists, represented by the Jamaat-e-Islami in general and the *ulema* and *mullahs* in particular, surfaced. Jinnah's inaugural speech in the Pakistan Constituent Assembly on 11 August 1947 was a clarion call for the establishment of Pakistan as a secular state. From the principal forum of the new state he said categorically:

> You may belong to any religion or caste or creed—that has nothing to do with the business of the state. . . . We are starting with this fundamental principle, that *we are all citizens of one state.* . . . I think we should keep that in front of us as our idea and you will find that *in the course of time Hindus will cease to be Hindus and Muslims will cease to be Muslims, not in the religious sense because that is the personal faith of each individual but in the political sense, as citizens of the state.*
> —(Choudhury 1967: 21–22, emphasis added)

In February 1948, in a broadcast directed at the people of the United States, Jinnah reiterated his position: 'In any case Pakistan is not going to be a theocratic State—to be ruled by priests with a divine mission. We have many non-Muslims—Hindus, Christians, and Parsis—but they are all Pakistanis. *They will enjoy the same*

The South Asian Mosaic 143

rights and privileges as any other citizens, and will play their rightful part in the affairs of Pakistan' (Government of Pakistan 1948: 93, emphasis added). Despite the background under which Pakistan was created and the conflict between the modernists and the traditionalists as reflected in the discussions of the Aims and Objectives Committee of the Constituent Assembly of Pakistan, Jinnah took a political risk. While the League did not dispute the traditionalists' view about the importance of Islam in Pakistan, the two groups disagreed on the question of who would have the final say in interpreting the Qur'an and the *Sunnah*. On this point, the League 'temporized; it was willing to grant concessions to the traditionalists, but not to surrender to them' (Abbott 1968: 216).

In 1949 the Constituent Assembly, in tune with the Act of 1935, which was still the living constitution of Pakistan, passed the Objectives Resolution. Following the footprints of Jinnah, Liaquat Ali Khan, the Prime Minister of Pakistan, while moving the 'Objectives Resolution' in the Constituent Assembly, declared that 'the people are the real recipients of power. This naturally eliminates any danger of the establishment of a theocracy' (Choudhury 1967: 25). The resolution said that 'adequate provision shall be made for the minorities to freely profess and practise their religions and develop their cultures' and that 'adequate provision shall be made to safeguard the legitimate interests of minorities and backward and depressed classes' (Birnbaum 1956: 6).

But after having created Pakistan on the basis of a two-nation theory, such a quick *volte face* was not politically possible. The orthodox elements were unhappy with the Interim Report of the Basic Principles Committee, 1950, the so-called first draft constitution, as its provisions had diluted the Islamic character of the state. The *ulema* and the Board of Islamic Teachings were up in arms against the draft and threatened to bring in a vote of no-confidence against the government. Prime Minister Liaquat Ali Khan saved the day by welcoming suggestions from the traditionalists for the making of the Constitution. In response, all the major Islamic groups met in Karachi in 1951 and presented a twenty-two-point charter of demands that should form the basis of the Pakistani state (Pleshov 2004: 79–81). These points were:

1. Ultimate sovereignty over all Nature and all Law belongs to Allah, Rabb-ul-Amin.
2. The Law of the land shall be based on Qur'an and *Sunnah*, and no law shall be passed nor any administrative order issued which would be in conflict with Qur'an and *Sunnah*.

144 *The Politics of Personal Law in South Asia*

3. The State shall be based not on geographical, linguistic or any other materialistic concepts but on the principles and objectives of the Islamic scheme of life.

4. It shall be incumbent upon the state to uphold the Right and suppress the Wrong as postulated in Qur'an and *Sunnah*, to take all necessary measures for the revival and exaltation of the tenets of Islam, and to make provision for Islamic education in accordance with the requirements of the various recognised schools of thought.

5. It shall be incumbent upon the State to strengthen the bonds of unity and brotherhood among all the Muslims of the world and to inhibit among the Muslim citizens of the State the growth of all tendencies born of un-Islamic prejudices towards distinctions on the basis of race, language, territory or other materialistic considerations so as to preserve and strengthen the unity of the Millat-i-Islami.

6. It shall be the responsibility of the government to guarantee the provision of basic human necessities, i.e., food, clothing, housing, medical relief and education to all citizens, irrespective of religion or race, who are temporarily or permanently incapable of earning their livelihood due to unemployment, sickness or other reasons.

7. The citizens shall be entitled to all the rights conferred on them by the Islamic law, i.e., they shall be assured, within the limits of the law, of full security of life, property and honour, freedom of religion and belief, freedom of worship, freedom of person, freedom of expression, freedom of movement, freedom of association, freedom of occupation, equality of opportunity and the right to benefit from public services.

8. No citizen shall at any time be deprived of these rights except under the law, and none shall be awarded any punishment on any charge without being given full opportunity of defence and without a decision of a court of law.

9. The recognized Muslim schools of thought shall have, within the limits of the law, complete religious freedom, the right to impart religious instructions to their followers, and shall have the freedom to propagate their views. *Matters relating to their personal status shall be administered in accordance with their respective codes of jurisprudence. It will be desirable to make provision for the administration of such matters by their respective Qazis* [judges in a Muslim court of law; emphasis added].

10. The non-Muslim citizens of the state shall within the limits of the law have complete freedom of religion and worship, mode of life,

culture and religious education. *They shall be entitled to have matters relating to their personal status administered in accordance with their own religious laws, usages and customs* [emphasis added].

11. All obligations assumed by the state within the limits of the Shariah towards the non-Muslim citizens shall be fully honoured. They shall be entitled equally with the Muslim citizens to the rights of citizenship as enunciated in paragraph 7.

12. *The Head of the State must be a male Muslim* in whose piety, ability and soundness of judgment the people or their elected representatives have confidence [emphasis added].

13. The responsibility for the administration of the state shall primarily vest in the Head of the State, although he may delegate any part of his powers to any individual or body.

14. Governance by the Head of the State shall not be autocratic but consultative, i.e., he will discharge his duties in consultation with persons holding responsible positions in the government and with the elected representatives of the people.

15. The Head of the State shall have no right to suspend the Constitution wholly or partly or to run the administration in any other way but on a consultative basis.

16. The body empowered to elect the Head of the State shall also be empowered to remove him by a majority of votes.

17. In respect of civil rights the Head of the State is not above the law.

18. All citizens, whether members of the government, officials or private persons shall be subject to the same laws which shall be applied to all by the same courts of law.

19. The judiciary shall be separate from and independent of the executive in the discharge of its duties.

20. The propagation and publicity of such views and ideologies as are calculated to undermine the basic principles and fundamentals of the Islamic state shall be prohibited.

21. The various zones or regions of the country shall be considered the administrative units of a single state. They shall not be racial, linguistic or tribal units but only administrative areas which may be given such powers under the supremacy of the Centre as may be necessary for administrative convenience. They shall not have the right to secede.

22. No interpretation of the Constitution which is in conflict with the provisions of the Qur'an and *Sunnah* shall be valid.

Since almost all the Islamic sects spoke in favour of the twenty-two points, the government too had to approve it. The State Commission

146 *The Politics of Personal Law in South Asia*

that it had set up to study the charter had recommended its adoption. The Report of the Basic Principles Committee, 1952, the Second Draft Constitution, incorporated provisions that underlined the Islamic character by providing for the establishment of a board of ulema that was to monitor if any law was repugnant to the Qur'and the *Sunnah* (Choudhury 1967: 31). But the constant reference to an 'Islamic constitution' by the *ulema* led to many clashes in urban areas, particularly in respect of whether or not to treat the Ahmediyas as Muslims. In January 1953 a group of thirty-three Islamic theologians deliberated for eight days to come out with a draft constitution, which closely reflected Jamaat chief Maulana Abu'l A'la Maudoodi's concept of 'theodemocracy'. In short, the idea was that Pakistan should be declared an Islamic republic, the *Shari'ah* should be the basis of all laws, the justice system should be structured around *Shari'ah* courts, the Supreme Court should include five members of the *ulema,* all questions relating to religion are to be interpreted by the *ulema,* Ahmediyas should be declared non-Muslims, and so on (Pleshov 2004: 84–85). These propositions were in direct opposition to those of the modernists.

The confrontation between the modernists and the traditionalists, which was inevitable, came to a head in the same year, when the city of Lahore was rocked by disturbances over the issue of whether the Ahmediyas (or Qadiyanis) were full-fledged Pakistani citizens. The Pakistan government put down the riots with the help of the army and instituted a commission of enquiry. The report of the enquiry commission, commonly referred to as the Munir Report, named after its head M. Munir, who was a Supreme Court judge, attacked the interpretations of Islam made by the *ulema*. The Report said: 'Pakistan is being taken by the common man, though it is not, as an Islamic state. This belief has been encouraged by the ceaseless clamour for Islam and Islamic State that is being heard from all quarters since the establishment of Pakistan.' Charging the *ulema* for holding a narrow outlook in interpreting Islam and thereby creating cleavages in Pakistani society, the Report further said: 'The *"ulema"* are a very learned class and entitled . . . to great respect. But like all learned persons whose energy has been devoted to specialization, they have developed a single-track mind and a single-track mind has dangerous possibilities. . . .' And then, more tellingly: 'Our politicians should understand that if Divine Commands cannot make or keep a man Musalman, their statutes will not' (Ahmad and Grunebaum 1970: 190–94; Noorani 2002: 62).

Still, although the Muslim League was determined not to be overpowered by the orthodox elements, it could not preach a theory of delinking the state from religion. It was apprehensive that the

The South Asian Mosaic 147

Jamaat-i-Islami would make political capital out of the issue and dislodge the League from power. Its strategy included a set of compromises. The party would, on the one hand, agree to a rather liberal interpretation of the Qur'an, but on the other, it would be reluctant to treat non-Muslim citizens at par with Muslim citizens. It did not subscribe to the extremist view that the Ahmediyas or the Qadiyanis were non-Muslims and therefore not entitled to official positions, but, at the same time, it could not guarantee equal political rights to the minorities, for example, the Hindus. The Basic Principles Committee Report of 1954 guaranteed that the 'legitimate interests' of non-Muslims would be protected, but its provisions debarred a non-Muslim from becoming a head of state, a remote possibility in any case given the demographic composition of the country (Birnbaum 1956: 6). The first constitution of Pakistan that was promulgated in 1956 declared Pakistan as an 'Islamic Republic'.

During the Ayub Khan regime (1958–69) some half-hearted efforts were made to secularise the state; however, they were not expected to succeed because they were not really meant to. Ayub's Basic Democracies ploy was not only aimed at destroying competitive politics based on the party system, its purpose was also to establish his Islamic credentials (Ziring 1999: 260–61). His 1962 constitution clearly incorporated several Islamic clauses though it cosmetically declared Pakistan a 'Republic' and not an 'Islamic Republic'. As such, within a year, when he was forced by Islamic forces to agree to rename Pakistan an ' Islamic Republic' with greater thrust on the use of Islamic ideology for the purposes of governance, he did not show much resistance.

Like Ayub Khan, Zulfiqar Ali Bhutto (1972–77) too started with the cosmetic promise of secularising Pakistan polity, but relented before long. In the 1977 election manifesto of his Pakistan People's Party (PPP) the word 'secularism' was dropped and in its place was inserted the phrase '*Musawat-i-Mohammadi*'—literally translated as 'the equality of Muhammad', that is, Islamic egalitarianism. Besides, the PPP manifesto promised to replace Sunday with Friday as the weekly holiday and make the learning of the Holy Qur'an an integral part of the school curriculum. It also promised to establish a federal Ulema Academy and other institutions. Following the elections, in which the PPP got a thumping majority, largely on account of the rigging of the polls, the government not only kept its election promises with regard to Islam but went even further. It announced a set of *Shari'ah* laws banning gambling, horse racing, and the drinking of alcohol. On 1 July 1977, four days before he was ousted from

148 *The Politics of Personal Law in South Asia*

power by the military, Sunday was replaced with Friday as the weekly holiday (Ghosh 1989: 24).

In General Zia-ul-Haq, who ruled the country from 1977 to 1988, the Islamic ideology of Pakistan found its staunchest champion. Immediately after he captured power on 5 July 1977 through a military coup, he declared: 'Pakistan, which was created in the name of Islam, will continue to survive only if it sticks to Islam. That is why I consider the introduction of Islamic system as an essential prerequisite for the country.' Within a few days, martial law was declared and several Qur'anic punishments were introduced through the Hudood Ordinances (1979). In 1984 the Qanun-e-Shahadat (law of evidence) became the law, which replaced the Evidence Act of 1872 to bring it in 'conformity with Islam'. It diminished the value of women's evidence in law courts under particular circumstances, with far-reaching implications for women's rights.

To indoctrinate the Pakistan army in Islamic ideals, a process which was underway since the creation of Pakistan, Zia introduced far-reaching changes in the training of officers and troops. Urdu replaced English as the language of parade commands and the pre-Partition mottos of several units were replaced by verses from the Qur'an or lines from iqbal, Pakistan's national poet. Other steps included complete prohibition in the services, the upgrading of unit mullahs to the rank of religious teachers, etc. In the annual performance reports of the officers, which determine their promotional prospects, a column on the observance of religious rituals was Introduced (Ghosh 1989: 26). But, notwithstanding all that Zia did, he could not go to the extent of making Pakistan theocratic. His proposed Shari'ah Bill (1985) too did not get enough legislative support. Zla's Islamic ideology was indeed hollow for, on the question of interest-free banking, the most difficult thing to implement in modern times, he had no desire to see it implemented as per the *Shari'ah*. Through a complex mechanism of buying and selling of mortgaged or hypothecated goods of customers, the banks called the proceeds 'profits', which were actually 'interests', thereby cosmetically circumventing the Islamic ban on interests (Alavi 1988: 109). Similarly, his Hudood ordinance also remained largely on paper.

But whether Zia-ul-Haq's Islamisation drive worked effectively or not, the Islamic tone set by him lingered on even after his death in 1988, largely because his Islamism had the full support of Jamaat-i-Islami and Tabligh-i-Jamaat, the influence of which went on increasing in Pakistani society because of international aid. The restoration of democracy and the electoral process that followed his death did

The South Asian Mosaic 149

not thus obliterate the Zia legacy. Even the regime of Benazir Bhutto (1988–90), which made women more visible on the media, lifted the ban on their participation in spectator sports and improved their job status, did precious little to do away with the laws of the Zia regime. So was the case with Muhammad Nawaz Sharif, who became the prime minister in October 1990 following the interim government of Ghulam Mustafa Jatoi (August–October 1990). Sharif went a step further by passing the Enforcement of *Shari'ah* Bill in the National Assembly in May 1991, which Zia had not been able to effectively do. Sharif actually had no choice. His Pakistan Muslim League had come to power with the support of Jamaat-i-Islami and other religious groups, and during the electoral campaign he had made such a commitment to the ulema that he would ensure the passing of the Bill. The Shariat Act was intended to ensure the continuing process of bringing civil law into conformity with Islamic injunctions. Although it did not happen in reality, it was, at least in theory, meant to undercut the authority of the civil courts (Newberg 1995: 220–21). In 1999 Nawaz Sharif was deposed and Pakistan was once again brought under a military dictatorship led by General Pervez Musharraf, which virtually coincided with an extreme form of Islamic militancy in many parts of the world, an important theatre of which was Pakistan.

It is apparent from the above discussion that the tenor of Pakistan politics has always been such that any modernist approach to politics which even remotely advocates separation of religion and state becomes an anathema for the political class. In its extreme form, this class considers only that person to be a true Pakistani who is a Sunni and also, preferably, a Punjabi, or at least a Sunni Pathan. Ahmediyas have not been considered Muslims ever since 1974, and the Shias, who form a minority, are often on the receiving end of frequent anti-Shia violence. In this sort of climate it is no wonder that, of late, the Pakistani state is countenancing a serious challenge from the so-called *jehad* 'industry'. Although under strong US pressure in the aftermath of 9/11, the present regime of Pervez Musharraf is trying its best to cope with the problem, a Herculean task. Musharraf has banned several extremist groups and has tried to exhort his people about the true concept of jehad, originally conceived as a war against poverty and social evils, but it is probably too late for him to extricate Pakistan from the clutches of the Frankenstein of religious politics. There are between 40,000 to 50,000 *madrassas* in Pakistan, which, according to Moinuddin Haider, the former interior minister of Pakistan, preach a brand of Islam which is not good for the country. In the garb of religious teaching they fan sectarian violence. His efforts to

150　*The Politics of Personal Law in South Asia*

get them registered yielded little result. Only about 4,350 responded positively. As there is an intricate nexus between these *madrassas,* religious extremism and international Islamic funding, something like a 'Jehad International, Inc.' has emerged. One may trace the origin of international Islamic funding to the ideological conflict for the leadership of the Islamic world, between the Shiite 'revolutionary' Iran and the Sunni Wahabi Saudi Arabia in the 1980s. Saudis succeeded because of their financial strength. They supported the *madrassa* education in many Muslim countries and also did not fail to project Iran's Shiaism as an anathema to Sunnism. (Fuller 2002: 55). It must, however, be underlined that it is too simplistic to conclude that all *madrassas* breed fanaticism and militancy. Some of them are used by the military regime to counter the democratic forces (Sikand 2004b: 10–12). Moreover, it can be empirically shown that most Muslim suicide terrorists have a modern education and belong to urban middle class families, though the rank and file jehadis are mostly from rural areas (Rashid 2006: 372).

Muslim Personal Law

It is against this political backdrop that one may analyse the status of Muslim personal law in Pakistan and the process of reforms therein. Sunni Muslims are generally followers of the Hanafi school and Shias mostly belong to the Ithna Ashari school. There are also some Shafi and Ismaili followers. All personal laws that were operative in undivided India continued to be valid after the creation of Pakistan. Between 1948 and 1952, however, new laws were enacted to extend the NWFP Shari'at Application Act of 1935 to the provinces of Punjab and Sind and the princely states of Bahawalpur and Khairpur. These laws enlarged the scope of the Muslim Personal Law (Shari'at) Application Act of 1937. In 1955, shortly before the first constitution of Pakistan was promulgated in 1956, a commission called the Commission on Marriage and Family Laws was set up to survey the prevailing marriage and family laws, with a view to suggesting measures that would ensure women 'their proper place in the society in accordance with the fundamentals of Islam'. The seven-member commission headed by the former Chief Justice of Pakistan, Mian Abdul Rashid (who had replaced Dr Khalifa Shuja-ud-Din upon his death), popularly known as the Rashid Commission, submitted a report that evoked a considerable amount of controversy, mainly because the reforms it suggested included limiting the rights of Muslim men to polygamy, the abolition of triple *talaq,* compulsory registration of all marriages and

The South Asian Mosaic 151

divorces, and changing the scheme of succession regarding orphaned grandchildren. Many leading theologians opposed the report, most notable amongst whom were Maulana Abu'l A'la Maududi, Maulana Ihtisham-ul-Haq and the Mufti Muhammad Shaafi' Deobandi.

It may be noted that, at the time the commission was set up, the Islamic forces were ascendant in the nation's politics, and the constitution that was soon to be introduced had underlined the importance of Islam in the governance of the country. No wonder the orthodox elements were up in arms against the reforms suggested by the commission. Maulana Ihtisham-ul-Haq forcefully expressed his dissent, saying: 'Certain depraved elements have again raised their heads and are conspiring to rob the weaker sex of their cherished treasure of chastity by holding out false prospects of their rights in an attempt to push them again into the abyss of disgrace in which they had been rotting in the dark ages.' These oppositions got reflected in the constitution, which declared that no law repugnant to Islamic injunctions would be passed and all existing laws would be reviewed and revised to ensure their conformity with those injunctions (Coulson 1963: 240–48; Mahmood 1995b: 74; Menski 2000: 318). The constitution of 1956, however, was abrogated in 1958 following a coup.

Taking advantage of martial law, General Ayub Khan subjected Muslim personal law to modification. The most notable step that he took in this direction was the Muslim Family Law Ordinance (MFLO) of 1961. It did not derive its legitimacy from the 1955 Rashid Commission on Marriage and Family Laws, although certain recommendations made by the Commission, such as restrictions on polygamy and triple *talaq*, did find their place in the ordinance in some form. What probably gave some strength to Ayub Khan's courage to introduce the MFLO was that, in the meantime, certain Muslim countries had introduced reforms in Muslim law in their respective countries, namely, Tunisia (1957), Morocco (1958) and Iraq (1959). The Tunisian code had prohibited polygamy and made divorce dependent on court verdicts (Coulson 1963: 240–48).

MFLO was a brief document consisting of thirteen short sections. Its main features included:

1. All Muslim marriages must be registered. A marriage that is not solemnised by the *Nikah* Registrar has to be reported to him by the person who has solemnised it.
2. Polygamy is discouraged. Only if found 'necessary and just' by an arbitration council headed by a civil official, and after the first wife's consent has been obtained can bigamy be allowed.

152   *The Politics of Personal Law in South Asia*

3. Divorce through 'triple *talaq*' is abolished and one would have to follow a certain process through the Arbitration Council before it is granted. (But there were certain clauses that diluted this provision.)
4. In respect of succession, an orphaned grandchild would receive the share equivalent to that which its father or mother would have received if alive. This provision was the most controversial one and the *ulema* strongly criticised it as it was in contravention of the Qur'an and the *Sunnah*.

The Arbitration Council was to consist of the chairman of the Union Council constituted under the Basic Democracies Order, 1959, who must be a Muslim, and a representative of each of the parties to any one of the three principal subjects figuring in the ordinance, namely, polygamy, divorce and the wife's claim for maintenance. Regarding restriction on polygamy, the MFLO followed the recommendations of the Rashid Commission *in toto,* but in respect of divorce the Commission's recommendations were substantively watered down. While the Commission had recommended that divorce should depend only on the court verdict, Section 7 of the Ordinance merely said that after pronouncing the talaq the husband should, in writing, inform the chairman of the Arbitration Council and the wife, otherwise he would be liable to one year's imprisonment or a fine up to Rs 5,000, or both. Even in respect of the divorced wife's maintenance, the ordinance did not live up to the expectations of the Commission. But notwithstanding all the pitfalls of the ordinance, and even after conceding the fact that for political compulsions it could not abide by the more progressive recommendations made by the Rashid Commission in terms of codification of Islamic law, it followed the tradition of Anglo-Mohammedan law (Coulson 1963: 248–57). In the following year the West Pakistan Muslim Personal Law (Shariat) Application Act, 1962 repealed the 1937 Muslim Personal Law (Shariat) Application Act as well as the provincial legislation on the application of Muslim personal laws, notwithstanding any custom or usage, to all questions of personal status or succession where the parties were Muslims. It stated, *inter alia,* that 'the limited estates in respect of immovable property held by Muslim females under the customary law are hereby terminated'. This stance was the opposite of that taken by the 1937 Act but was to apply prospectively (An-Na'im 2002: 232).

There could be several political explanations for Ayub Khan's decision to introduce these reforms, besides the fact that several Muslim countries had already introduced reforms pertaining to women's legal

The South Asian Mosaic 153

rights, as mentioned above. Such explanations could be as follows. One, since Ayub Khan had already established his pro-Islamic credentials in Pakistan he did not have to worry too much about orthodox opposition to his reforms. We have noted above that his Basic Democracies was a device to cleverly project something in tune with the Islamic theory of governance. Two, after he had come to power in 1958 he had used the Islamic ideology for the indoctrination of the armed forces. Armed Forces Day was celebrated with much fanfare and the soldiers were given to believe that they were not only defending their motherland against a belligerent and vicious neighbour, that is, India, but also fighting for the cause of Islam against that ' idolator infidel' (Qureshi 1972: 568). A third explanation is that it was a clever move to consolidate his dictatorship. Ayub Khan had successfully penetrated into the civil society institutions like TV, writers' forums, arts and theatres, etc., and had established state control over them. Through MFLO requirements like registration of marriages or prevention of polygamy, he also ensured the presence of the state in matters of family law. In 1969 when the movement for the restoration of democracy picked up momentum, the primary demand of which was the re-introduction of the parliamentary system in place of the presidential system, orthodox forces added their own item to the democratic agenda, that is, the abrogation of MFLO. Their problem, however, was with the progressive elements in the MFLO and not with the allegedly subtle political design of Ayub. Three, a somewhat farfetched explanation could be that Ayub was trying to advertise his progressive image internationally, particularly in the United States, the support of which country was crucial to his political survival. It may be noted that just two years after the promulgation of the MFLO, Pakistan, together with twenty-one other developing countries, requested the Commission on the Status of Women of the UN General Assembly to draft a declaration on the elimination of all forms of discrimination against women.

Although both the constitutions of 1962 and 1973 underlined the fact that all existing laws must be brought in conformity with the injunctions of Islam as laid down in the Holy Qur'an and Sunnah and that no law should be enacted which was repugnant to such injunctions, MFLO was not generally questioned because its provisions were not in opposition to the *shari'ah*. It all depended on how one interpreted it. But notwithstanding the fact that the Muslim Family Law Ordinance was quite progressive in the context of Pakistan, it could not be as effective as it was expected to be, because of the strong undercurrents of Islamic politics and the traditional nature of the

154 *The Politics of Personal Law in South Asia*

society. Moreover, there were always demands from the traditionalists to do away with the MFLO (Metcalf 2004: 243).

After the military coup of General Zia-ul Haq in July 1977 when the introduction of the Islamic system became the essential prerequisite for the country, the supremacy of the *Shari'ah* was established in all branches of law (Mahmood 1995b: 77). Through various Hudood ordinances, the Qur'anic penal laws on theft, fornication, the false accusation of unchastity, the prohibition of alcohol, etc., were introduced. Jurisdictional conflicts between the Supreme Court and the Federal *Shari'ah* Courts, however, continued. The latter lacked jurisdiction over the constitution, over Muslim personal law and personal laws of other communities, and over laws relating to court procedures and fiscal rules. The Hudood ordinances relating to criminal justice remained mostly on paper. No wonder that later, in 2003, when the *Shari'ah* laws were imposed in the Northwest Frontier Province, there was no discernible difference in the situation. Although this development was hyped up as the beginning of theocracy in Pakistan, a closer look at the laws showed they were merely the literal translation into Urdu of the Enforcement of the *Shari'ah* Act adopted by the federal parliament and gazetted on 18 June 1991 (Nayak and Nayak 2001: 43–75; Rehman 2003).

Whatever be the impact of the Zina Ordinance of 1979 on the criminal justice system, a subject that is not within the purview of this book, it contributed to the circumvention of the provisions of the MFLO. Polygamy was prohibited, but there was precious little that the government could do to prevent it. Similarly, triple *talaq* or plain abandonment of the wife also continued because, in many cases, aggrieved wives accepted the situation under social pressure. Sometimes vindictive husbands and their relatives tried to use the Zina Ordinance to harass divorced wives. In many such cases, however, the Federal *Shari'ah* Court dismissed such petitions as malafide (Menski 2000: 322–23). In the case of *Allah Rakha v. Union of Pakistan* (2000) the supremacy of *Shari'ah* over the MFLO was reiterated. In this case the Federal Shari'ah Court ruled that while *Shari'ah* was a God-given law and MFLO was a man-given law the former would naturally receive precedence over the latter in case of a conflict between the two. The case proved that the 1961 reform was just a reformist fig-leaf meant for the educated and modernist middle class, while for an average Pakistani it meant little (Menski 2004: 10).

There were thus several means of circumventing the MFLO and in this the Zina Ordinance too came handy. For example, fathers who did not approve of their daughters' marriage choices filed cases of

The South Asian Mosaic 155

kidnapping against their 'husbands' under the provisions of the Zina Ordinance, making husbands criminally liable for having a sexual relationship outside marriage, because their wives were forced to stand witness against their husbands. Since the 1970s, access to the Special Marriage Act (SMA) has all but ceased because of strict penal provisions concerning blasphemy that make it impossible for someone to renounce Islam. Since Ahmediyas/Qadiyanis were declared non-Muslims in Pakistan in 1974, it has not been clear if the MFLO applies to marriages involving Ahmediyas or if a Muslim woman's marriage to an Ahmediya man is valid. The courts have preferred to avoid dealing directly with this controversial issue and have instead ruled on the immediate issue at hand (the demand for maintenance and the validity of *talaq*). In the three known cases, it appeared that the husband was attempting to evade his legal responsibilities by claiming that the marriage was not valid, and in each the court ruled in the woman's favour without directly dealing with the issue of validity *(Nasir Ahmed Shaikh v. Mrs Nahid Ahmed Shaikh* NLR 1986 Civil 659; LN 1986 Lahore 597; *Muhammad Rashid v. Mst. Nusrat Jahan Begum* 1986 MLD 1010 Lahore). In Syed families, especially in Shia Syed families, women are not permitted to marry non-Syeds. If there is no suitable match for a daughter, some feudal Syed families of the Sindh province will ask her to forgo her right to marriage. She then makes a formal renunciation on the Qur'an. This tradition is known as 'marriage with the Qur'an', or *haq bakhshwana* (literally, foregoing the right). The woman is thereby condemned to a life without a husband or children and may live as a recluse. Families inflict such a fate on their daughters to avoid their marrying persons of lower social status, as well as to ensure that property remains within the family (WLUML 2003: 75, 102–3, 106). In June 2005, the Council of Islamic Ideology, an advisory body of the Islamalisation of laws, drafted a bill to punish with imprisonment anyone who became a party to a woman's marriage to the Qur'an. The draft bill proposed to amend Section 285–B of the Pakistan Penal Code (which prescribes life term for anyone who desecrates the Qur'an) by rewording the section as follows:

> 295–B. Defiling of and marriage with the Holy Quran: Whosoever wilfully defiles, damages or desecrates a copy of the Holy Quran or an extract therefrom or directly or indirectly allows the Holy Quran to be used for purpose of its marriage with a female or fraudulently or dishonestly induces any person to swear on the Holy Quran never to marry anyone in her lifetime or knowingly

156 *The Politics of Personal Law in South Asia*

uses it in any derogatory manner or for any unlawful purpose, shall be punishable with imprisonment for life.

The draft bill said that the so-called marriages with the Qur'an had no legal standing and amounted to punishable offence under the Shari'ah law (HRCP 2006: 20–21). The bill, however, has not yet been moved in parliament.

It is evident from the above discussion that, given the social and political situation currently prevailing in Pakistan, reform in Muslim personal law is most unlikely. The Shari'ah commands considerable respect in Pakistan. The influence of Jamaat-e-Islami and Tabligh-i-Jamaat is noticeable in the society and, through their women's wings, they systematically spread the concept of the 'ideal' woman in Muslim society—to 'keep husband happy and procreate and stay in the house', which is the key for women to enter Heaven, for Prophet Mohammad was fond of both prayer (one of the pillars of Islamic faith) and women and emphasised treating wives well, loving his wives and daughters, suggesting that 'our civilization is so wealthy, when it concerns women, that as compared to it, the Western culture seems a mere beggar' (Rashid 2006: 368). A 2003 survey conducted by the Pew Research Center for the People and the Press found that 86 per cent of Pakistanis considered that Islam should play a 'very' or 'fairly large' role in political life. According to the World Values Surveys (2000–2003) the percentage response of the people to the following question: 'Should a good government implement only the laws of the Shari'ah?' was as under (Davis and Robinson 2006: 178):

Very important	–	36.4
Important	–	25.1
Somewhat important	–	30.9
Least important	–	6.3
Not important	–	1.2

Compared to the Bangladesh situation, where 9.2 per cent of respondents did not give any importance to the *Shari'ah* (see p. 185), in Pakistan there was only a very small minority of 1.2 per cent who thought so. One explanation could be the influence in Bangladesh of Hindus who constituted over 9 per cent of the population (Davis and Robinson 2006: 178–79).

Pakistan is in a peculiar bind. It is not a theocratic state, yet it does not have the political will to extricate itself from the forces of political

The South Asian Mosaic 157

Islam because of the complex set of vested interests of the ruling military clique. As a result, the evolution of law suffers considerably. It has been argued that, unlike the Turks, the Pakistani lawmakers had neither a clear vision of the future nor a defined programme. Thus, while the Turks transplanted a set of new legal rules that had foreign origin and nurtured them so that they gradually emerged as a new 'living law', Pakistanis satisfied themselves by merely making general programmatic statements such as the Objectives Resolution of 1949. As such, their experiments with legal modernisation of family law remained halfhearted. Even the Islamisation process that started in the late 1970s could not assert itself as a coherent legal policy, resulting in some massive failures of justice. Early observers like Coulson were probably prophetic when they said that the Pakistanis were not serious enough with their Islamisation drive. The result was that, because of the particular socio-cultural and historical position of Pakistan, there could be only a combination of a juristic reassessment of the Qur'an and some piecemeal efforts at lawmaking. According to Menski:

> Pakistan is manifestly not a theocracy, but it has also resolutely declared itself to be an Islamic country. Having made that ideological as well as religious commitment, the arena for conflicts and tensions was entirely within the realm of human law-making. Apart from providing gruesome example of how men's law can go wrong, the Pakistani policies of Islamisation strongly confirm the ancient truth that nobody knows for sure what God's will actually was in all points of detail. This deepest of all legal problems in human law-making among Muslims received new illustrations through the inconsistent and incomplete processes of Islamisation in Pakistan. Given the 'margin of error' in all of Muslim jurisprudence, no other result could have been expected'.
>
> —(Menski 2000: 323–24)

To conclude this argument, the present status of Muslim personal law in Pakistan can be seen in the following chart (Table 5.1) prepared by the London-based WLUML, which gives a broad overview of the situation.

Hindu/Minority Personal Laws

The Islam-based nation-building strategy of Pakistan has completely cast aside the minorities, which primarily include Hindus and

158 *The Politics of Personal Law in South Asia*

Table 5.1 The Status of Miuslim Personal Law in Pakistan

The Constitution	Other Laws	Muslim Laws	Customary Laws	General Comments
The structure and principles of the 1973 constitution have been subverted by repeated amendments during martial law, military governments and elected governments since the 1980s. The 1985 Eighth Amendment (A. 8) made the Objectives Resolution (OR) preamble a substantive part of the constitution. The OR also talks of social justice; but in the regressive political atmosphere since the 1980s, it has been emphasised and used to attack women's fundamental rights. The constitution has inherent	Following the British colonial policy of leaving family law to be guided by personal laws, each religious community has separate laws, although all cases are heard by general family courts established under the 1964 Family Courts Act. To marry under the secular 1872 Special Marriages Act, couples are required to renounce their faith, now effectively impossible for Muslims given restrictive blasphemy laws. Family court judges do not have to be Muslim to hear cases of Muslims but, increasingly, non-Muslim judges declare	Promulgated following recommend-ations by the 1955 Rashid Commission, the Muslim Family Laws Ordinance (MFLO) 1961 gave substantial protection to women's rights within the family, but stopped short of many women's demands. The MFLO has remained the focus of attack, since its intro-duction, by regressive politico-religious forces. in 2000, although provisions relating to polygamy and to registration of marriage were upheld, certain provisions relating to registration of divorces were held 'repugnant to	Not justiciable for Muslims, courts routinely reject recourse to custom in family law cases. Family laws for Hindus are largely un-codified and are heard on the basis of long-established custom.	Numerous cases under the Zina (Enforcement of Hadd) Ordinance 1979 involve family law matters such as registration of marriage and divorce. While attem-pting to save women from the extreme punishments provided under the ordinance, the courts have under-mined the protective spirit of the MFLO. The MFLO has also been the focus of a highly charged debate over whether the statute law or the injunctions of Islam are to be supreme, and whether the superior courts have the power to declare a law repugnant.

The South Asian Mosaic 159

Table 5.1 Continued

The Constitution	Other Laws	Muslim Laws	Customary Laws	General Comments
contradictions. A.8 states that all laws and customs in violation of fundamental rights guaranteed in the constitution are void yet, for example, amendments introducing the Federal Shariat Courts are discriminatory. Meanwhile several discriminatory laws and customs remain and have not been challenged on the basis of A.8.	themselves incompetent. Women may be judges. The Guardians & Wards Act, 1890, the Child Marriage Registration Act, 1929 and the Dowry Registration Act, 1976 apply to all communities.	Islam' and to be amended by the legislature. The government has now gone in appeal.		

Christians, from the political process as if they do not exist at all. In any case, the non-Muslim minority groups in Pakistan are very small in number. According to the last Census conducted in 1981, the Hindus are 1.5 per cent of the population (and must be even less now), the Christians 1.6 per cent and the Ahmediyas 0.1 per cent. The population of Hindus had gone down significantly ever since the establishment of Pakistan. According to the 1951 Census they constituted 12.7 per cent of the population (Birnbaum 1956: 6). Most Hindus now live at, or below, the poverty line and as such they are socially and politically on the fringes of national life. A decade-old report in the Karachi-based

160   *The Politics of Personal Law in South Asia*

journal, *The Herald,* noted: 'Since Hindus are not "people of the book", most Muslims consider them to be inferior. Even today as the twentieth century comes to a close, most Muslims will not eat or drink with Hindus, nor will they touch Hindu's [*sic*] eating utensils. This intense discrimination is manifested at all levels and in all forms. Thus, Hindus form one of the poorest and most exploited communities in the country' (The *Herald Annual,* Karachi, January 1993: 87). A recent *Outlook* (New Delhi) report recounts the pathetic story of many Hindu girls in Sindh villages abducted, converted into Islam and married away to Muslims, a development about which human rights activists in Pakistan have raised an alarm. According to I. A. Rehman, the director of the Human Rights Commission of Pakistan, 'general marginalisation, discrimination, economic hardships and religious persecution have resulted in many Hindus leaving Pakistan, especially those in Sind. The Musharraf-led government needs to stop the continued social oppression of the religious minorities here'. The general liberal response in Pakistan to the *Outlook* report was the same (*Outlook,* 23 January 2006: 39, 30 January 2006: 26; see also HRCP 2006: 122). Christians too, like the Hindus, are a marginalised community, a large section of which comprises menial labourers or sweepers.

Against this background it is unthinkable that the political class in Pakistan would show any interest in reforming Hindu personal law. One may argue, in line with the argument of those in India opposed to the Indian state's interference with Muslim personal law, that even in non-democratic Pakistan the state does not interfere with minority personal law, although the state there is Islam-centric. But this logic is skewed. In Pakistan the case is not one of non-interference, but of sheer indifference and utter neglect. In Pakistan there has been little effort to introduce reforms in the personal laws of non-Muslim communities. Almost all laws governing these communities are from the pre-Independence period. The following is a list of some such laws: the Christian Marriage Act, 1872, the Parsi Marriage and Divorce Act, 1936, the Hindu Widow's Remarriage Act, 1856, the Hindu Marriage Disabilities Removal Act, 1946, the Buddhlst Law, the Arya Marriage Validation Act, 1937, the Hindu Inheritance (Removal of Disabilities) Act, 1928, the Hindu Disposition of Property Act, 1916, the Hindu Inheritance (Removal of Disabilities) Act, 1928, the Hindu Law of Inheritance (Amendment) Act, 1929, the Hindu Married Women's Right to Separate Residence and Maintenance Act, 1946, the Hindu Women's Rights to Property (Sind Extension to Agricultural Land) Act, 1943 (Abid 2000).

The South Asian Mosaic 161

So far, there have been three commissions and one committee that have been set up (the Commission on Marriage and Family Laws, 1955–56; the Pakistan Women's Rights Committee, 1976; the Pakistan Commission on the Status of Women, 1983–85; and the Commission of Inquiry for Women, 1994–97) to address the issue of women's rights; however, none of the first three have concerned themselves with minority women, barring very small and insignificant changes recommended in respect of the Divorce Act of 1869 and the Christian Marriage Act of 1872, both of which concerned the Christian community alone. It was only the 1994 Commission that recommended that 'the government should immediately set up a task force to prepare proposals for reforms in the area of family laws for non-Muslims; this task force must be representative both along gender and along minority group lines' (Government of Pakistan 1997: 21). But given the texture of Pakistan politics, which had provided no space for secular or minority politics, these recommendations remained on paper only.

The only post-Independence family law is the West Pakistan Hindu Women's Rights to Agricultural Land Ordinance 1959. Since the MFLO was meant for only Muslims, its positive aspects did not benefit Hindu women. Although there is no technical difficulty for minority communities to approach the regular family courts established by the Family Courts Act of 1964, since their jurisdiction is not restricted to Muslims alone, the religiously charged political atmosphere of Pakistan pushes these minorities to continue with their traditional laws and customs. A research study conducted in the district of Rahim Yar Khan, one of the three districts that comprise the Cholistan desert region (the other two districts are Bahawalpur and Bahawalnagar), which has a 20 per cent Hindu and a 10 per cent Christian population, has revealed that, unlike Muslim women, who have at least taken some advantage of the progressive provisions of the MFLO, the Hindu and Christian women are still languishing in their traditionally oppressed conditions (Mirani 2006). Since their economic condition is very low in general, there is no significant middle class voice to articulate their grievances, barring a handful of activists associated with the human rights movement of the country. Moreover, given the growing influence of Jamaat-i-Islami and Tabligh-i-Jamaat in the society, both of which are opposed to granting more legal rights to even Muslim women, it is unthinkable that the political class would find time to reform the family codes of the minority communities.

162 *The Politics of Personal Law in South Asia*

Bangladesh

Societal Evolution

In Bangladesh, the subject of a common civil code for all communities occupies a substantive intellectual, although not political, space. But before discussing that, it would be instructive to briefly trace the social history of the country, to put the matter in perspective. In this connection the story of the Islamisation of Bengal is relevant. The assimilation of North Indian political traditions by the Mughals, accelerated during the time of Akbar, who admitted the Rajputs into the ruling class, led to a virtual Rajputisation of the Muslim aristocracy in due course. In far-flung Bengal the dilution of the strict Muslim code was even more noticeable. While this was true of the urban-dwelling Ashraf classes, Islam was built upon indigenous roots at the mass level. Tracing the socio-economic as well as ecological processes that led to the gradual Islamisation of eastern Bengal, Richard Eaton writes:

> Although today one habitually thinks of world religions as self-contained and complete systems, with well-defined borders, such a state or fixed understanding does not apply to Bengal's pre-modern frontier, a fluid context in which Islamic superhuman agencies, typically identified with local superhuman agencies, gradually seeped into local cosmologies that were themselves dynamic. This 'seepage' occurred over such a long period of time that one can at no point identify a specific moment of 'conversion', or any single moment when people saw themselves as having made a dramatic break with the past. Islam in Bengal absorbed so much local culture and became so profoundly identified with the delta's long-term process of agrarian expansion that the cultivating classes never seem to have regarded it as 'foreign'—even though some Muslim and Hindu literati and foreign observers did and still do.
>
> —(Eaton 2003: 92)

This resulted in the growth of Muslim Sufism and Hindu *sahajiya* or folksy *Vaisnavism*, which contributed to an efflorescence of the Bengali language and a wearing down of religious distinctiveness between Bengali Muslims and Bengali Hindus. Since Chaitanya (1495–1533), the Bengali language achieved the status of a literary language and in course of time became enriched with words and phrases borrowed from Persian and Arabic. This was made possible by active encouragement

The South Asian Mosaic 163

from both Muslim and Hindu kings. The *Bhagavad Gita* was translated from Sanskrit into Bengali with the encouragement of Muslim rulers, who patronised men of letters irrespective of their faith. As a result of this secular trend, social mobility was also uniform for both religious groups. The professions came to be shared by both groups and the elites also belonged to both. According to social anthropologist Ramkrishna Mukherjee, 'the Bengali ethnic unit . . . was on the verge of attaining nationhood in the sixteenth–eighteenth century. The people of Bengal had now a territorial identification, a common history, a cultural and linguistic community, a common economic organization based on agriculture and industry (mainly the production of cotton and silk textiles for the international market through the agency of the European and East India Companies), and a distinct psychological identity assertive against superior or analogous powers' (Mukherjee 1976: 289).

Widening Schism

It was at this juncture that the British intervened; it was owing partly to imperial considerations and partly to societal circumstances that the seeds of Hindu-Muslim cleavage were sown. Gradually, conflicts of interest between the communities started getting articulated in sectarian terms. Though there was no dearth of Bengalis across the communities to talk of Bengalis as one social unit, the influence of those who talked in terms of Muslim and Hindu identities was becoming increasingly strident. The extraterritorial connection of the Bengali Muslims became an important theme of social discourse in which the role of Urdu, the anthropological heritage of the Muslims, the comparison of Islam with other religions, most notably Hinduism, and the differentiated approach to the anti-imperialist struggle became important variables. As the Muslim elites made no careful efforts to adapt their pan-Islamic ideas to the main currents of Indian life, the phenomenon, in due course, nourished separatism (De 1995: 21).

The partition of Bengal in 1905 was a significant landmark. Although it was annulled in 1912 in response to nationalist opposition, it was evident that Hindus and Muslims of Bengal did not necessarily share the same platform on the issue (Ahmed 2006: Gopal 1965: 268–69). From 1905 till the partition of India in 1947 is a long story, which need not be recapitulated here as the subject has already received considerable academic attention. Still, the following quotation from a noted authority on the subject may be useful.

164   *The Politics of Personal Law in South Asia*

[Notwithstanding democratic ideals fostered by several individuals,] various orthodox Muslim organisations, such as, Jamaat-e-Islam (1941), Jamaat-i-Ulama-i-Islam (1945) and different other centers of the Pirs in Bengal, strengthened the 'Muslim identity' among the 'Bengali Muslims' and directly and indirectly helped the Muslim League leaders to build it up as a mass organisation. With the help of the Ulama, the League leaders tried to destroy the multi-lingual character of Islam by imposing Urdu as the language of the Indian Muslims and to popularise the demand for a separate homeland for the Indian Muslims. The League-Ulama combination was so powerful that the promoters of 'Muslim identity' could easily crush the liberal democrats and rationalists and silence the voices of those nationalists who tried to build up a modern India in close association with the Congress. The process, however, started from 1936 when several powerful Muslim writers came forward to oppose the secular democrats. . . . Their ranks were swelled with the formation of the Proja-League Ministry in Bengal in 1937. . . . As the 'Muslim identity' was revealed within this separate state structure comprising the Muslim majority provinces, the 'Bengali identity' was naturally side-tracked.

—(De 1995: 21)

The Calcutta and the Noakhali riots between Hindus and Muslims in the wake of Partition considerably mauled inter-communal harmony, which was further aggravated by millions of Hindus and Muslims becoming refugees in each other's lands. Still, owing to the inherent contradictions in the inter-communal social formation of the Bengalis, the Pakistan experiment remained extremely fragile in the eastern wing of the country, where people's love for the Bengali language posed a considerable challenge to the two-nation theory which was at the core of the demand for Pakistan. Early in 1948, it became clear that the imposition of Urdu (which had a particular ideological connotation in the context of the Pakistani state [Ghosh 1989: 16–18]) on the people of East Pakistan would be potentially disruptive for Pakistan's nation-building project. It was this conflict that culminated in the liberation of East Pakistan in 1971 from the so-called ' colonialism' of West Pakistan. The most significant aspect of this liberation struggle was the fact that both Muslims and Hindus fought side by side. No wonder that when the first constitution of Bangladesh was framed in 1972, it could not have been anything but secular in its orientation and contents.

The South Asian Mosaic 165

Given the experience of the last hundred years, it would, however, be too simplistic to think that secularism was the only credo that the nation nurtured. Alongside linguistic nationalism, there was also a parallel stream of Islamic nationalism, a dichotomy that scholars have explained in terms of Bengali nationalism versus Bangladeshi nationalism (Jahan 1980). Sociologist T. N. Madan had prophetically written in 1971: 'It is not at all unlikely that in the years to come, the salience of religion will re-emerge among the Muslims of Bengal though in a changed context—for Bangladesh exists independently of the Indian state of West Bengal because it is predominantly Muslim' (Madan 1998: 976).

If the first few years of Bangladesh witnessed the ascendancy of Bengali nationalism, the succeeding phase was marked by a massive tilt towards Bangladeshi nationalism. Ever since the restoration of democracy in 1991, the two phases have alternated, with varying degrees of success depending upon which party controlled the reins of power—the Awami League (AL) or the Bangladesh Nationalist Party (BNP). Broadly speaking, the AL led by Sheikh Hasina Wajed represents Bengali nationalism while the BNP led by Begum Khaleda Zia represents Bangladeshi nationalism. Among the other parties, the Jamaat-e-Islami and the Islami Oikyo Jote (Islamic Unity Front) are resolutely Islamic. Though the mass base of the Islamic parties is limited, they bolster, because of their vocal and visible presence, the forces of Bangladeshi nationalism. In its foreign policy orientation, Bengali nationalism stands for friendly relations with India and, during the days of the Soviets, with the Soviet Union. The rhetoric of the B angladeshi nationalists is anti-Indian and pro-Islamic. Their ideology draws heavily from countries like Saudi Arabia, of course more for money than for anything else. There is also a clear tilt towards Pakistan. During the Cold War, they were pro-America. In the post-Cold War phase, both Bengali and Bangladeshi nationalists are in favour of good relations with the United States. So far as their respective approaches to India are concerned, although the AL-BNP dichotomy remains, it is much less pronounced, if the parliamentary elections of 2001 were any indication.

Given the centuries-old tradition of popular Islam and popular Hinduism in the country, and their continuation even during the twentieth century when serious disruption in the process was noticeable, it is intellectually challenging to grapple with the recent developments that indicate a manifest rise of Islamic conservatism. How much of it is homespun and how much of it is internationally influenced is anybody's guess. The fact, however, remains that there has

166   *The Politics of Personal Law in South Asia*

been an unprecedented growth of madrassas, which number about 100,000, and Saudi Wahabism and pro-Pakistanism are swelling (Ahmar 2003). The most visible expression of pro-Pakistanism is the rehabilitation of forces that opposed the liberation war. In the growing Islamic assertiveness, Jamaat-e-Islami and its students' wing, the Islami Chhatro Shibir (Islamic Students' Camp), are in the forefront (Ghosh 2005: 251).

Against this background, the minorities are getting systematically marginalised. They never actually had a fair share of representation in the public life of Bangladesh, including the first phase, that is, the Mujib era. Still, it was then better than the one that followed his assassination. At present the situation is much worse, as the statistics show. Out of 300 elected parliamentary seats only seven belong to the minorities. Incidentally, the record was much better during the Pakistan days, when there was minority quota system. In the 1954 general election, when there was the scheme of a separate electorate, minority members were as many as seventy-two out of a total of 309 parliamentary seats. Now the situation is such that even the AL is reluctant to give tickets to Hindus, leave alone other parties. Minorities now regret that, for the larger cause of democracy, they sacrificed this advantage in 1954 when the Joint Front was making its bid for power and the minorities gave away their separate representation arrangement so as to join mainstream politics. It is an irony that, in the name of democracy, they lost their leverage in the country's democracy, which systematically became majoritarian. According to the 2001 Bangladesh Census, Hindus constitute a little over 9 per cent, a drop by 6 per cent since the creation of Bangladesh. Many of them are leaving for India, a trend that commenced before the assassination of Mujib and picked up after that (Ghosh 2005: 254).

Samaddar's survey amongst the Bangladeshi Hindu migrants in India explodes the myth that democracy promotes inter-communal harmony: 'Hindu migrants . . . told us repeatedly that their position was better in the Pakistan era than in independent Bangladesh; that even in independent Bangladesh, the Hindus felt more secure under Army rule than under a democratically elected government, for "attitude towards the Hindus and (therefore) India determine [*sic*] the fate of a political party during elections"' (Samaddar 1999: 132). The fact of the matter is that no government in Bangladesh has been able to ensure the safety and security of Hindus there. Here is probably a representative statement of Hindu insecurity during the anti-Hindu riots in Bangladesh that followed the demolition of the Babri mosque in India on 6 December 1992:

The South Asian Mosaic   167

I remember that during the Pakistan's regime, the radio used to blart that—'the Hindus are our sacred *amanat*, we have to see to the security of their lives and property'. Broadcasts came not before but only after the mass killings were gone through and the looting of Hindu properties in the Dhaka Narayanganj areas took place during the 1964 communal uprising. It was widely said that it was the Biharis who caused the riot. During the communal attacks of 1990, it was also said that Ershad had instigated it through hired hoodlums. But does the responsibility of the government end by just bringing such charges in one sentence and doing nothing else to firmly deal with the situation?
—(Nahar 1994: 55–56, cited in Guhathakurta 2002: 80)

According to the Hindu leadership in Bangladesh, the situation now has become so bad that the community has been forced to assert its Hindu identity lest it be totally obliterated from the soil of Bangladesh (Ghosh 2005: 256).

Personal Laws

It is against this communal background that we will analyse the debate over the reforms of personal laws and the uniform civil code, which in Bangladeshi parlance is called the uniform family code (UFC). Table 5.2, prepared by the London-based Women Living Under Muslim Laws (WLUML), will indicate in brief the status of Muslim personal law in Bangladesh (WLUML 2003: 39).

The majority of Bangladeshi Muslims follow the Hanafi school of jurisprudence. Their personal law is primarily the one that was in practice during colonial rule, though there were some modifications introduced during the Pakistan days after liberation. Broadly, there were three codified structures in this regard, prior to liberation, namely, (a) the Muslim Personal Law (Shari'at) Application Act 1937, (b) the Dissolution of Muslim Marriages Act 1939, and (c) the Muslim Family Laws Ordinance 1961. After its independence, Bangladesh inherited Pakistan's legal system through the retrospective operation of the Bangladesh (Adaptation of Existing Bangladesh Laws) Order 1972. In 1985, Bangladesh amended the East Pakistan Muslim Family Law Rules 1961, though the changes were essentially administrative. In 1988, the Dissolution of Muslim Marriages Act 1939 was amended to modify the law on option of puberty.

There is no equivalent of the Special Marriage Act of India in Bangladesh; as such, both partners retaining their respective faiths,

Table 5.2 The Status of Muslim Personal Law in Bangladesh

Constitution	Other Laws	Muslim Laws	Customary Laws	General Comments
Secularism was one of the fundamental principles underlying Bangladesh's constitution (1972). The principle has since been repealed. Equality provisions in the constitution are interpreted as being limited by others that protect freedom of religion. In practice, even wher a discriminatory law is not based on religious laws, the courts have not used equality provisions to strike the law down.	The Indian subcontinent was under British colonial rule, for about 200 years, until 1947. During this period English Common Law was imported into the region and codified. Religious communities maintained various personal status laws, some of which were ultimately codified. Following an end to colonial rule in 1947 and independence from Pakistan in 1971, most of Bangladesh's laws continue to be based on English Common Law. Citizens may marry under the secular Special Marriages Act 1872. However, to do so they must renounce their existing faith.	The various religious communities are governed by separate personal status laws. These include pre-Independence laws such as the Dissolution of Muslim Marriages Act 1939, the Muslim Family Laws Ordinance 1961 (MFLO) as well as the post-Independence Muslim Marriages and Divorces Act 1974. All Bangladeshi Muslims are to be governed by the MFLO. Although Bangladesh is dominated by the Hanafi School, laws governing the Muslim community are derived from various schools. There are no separate Muslim courts of judges.	For Muslims, custom is not justiciable in the area of family matters.	In the area of family laws, there is an interaction between the laws based on Muslim laws and those based on other sources. This interaction includes both the substantive and procedural aspects of the laws. For example, the Guardian and Wards Act 1890, which governs all communities, is applied in conjunction with the rules of guardianship under Muslim laws in the case of disputes involving Muslims. A wife's right to *mehr* is governed by Muslim laws, facilitated by the standard marriage contract established under the Muslim Family Laws Ordinance of 1961. This is enforced through the family courts which are not specified as being available only to Muslims.

which may be different, is not possible. Marriage between a Muslim woman and a non-Muslim man is dealt with under the general principles of Muslim laws. Such a marriage is considered void and the legal paternity of the children is not recognised. However, these couples can marry under the colonial Special Marriage Act of 1872, but in that case both partners are required to make a declaration of 'non-faith'. The act's preamble states that, 'Whereas it is expedient to provide a form of marriage for persons who do not profess the Christian, Jewish, Hindu, Muslim, Parsi, Buddhist, Sikh or Jaina religion and to legalize certain marriages, the validity of which are doubtful . . .', Muslim men can contract a valid marriage with a Kitabia woman. Also, a Muslim man may marry a Hindu woman but the marriage would be considered irregular. In an irregular marriage, the legal paternity of the children is recognised but there are no rights of inheritance or maintenance established between the spouses (WLUML 2003: 102).

Regarding the personal laws related to marriage and divorce amongst Buddhists, Christians and Hindus, no law has been passed in Bangladesh to influence them. There are certain laws passed in respect of preventing cruelty to women (1983), deterring child marriage (1984), and prohibiting the practice of dowry (1984), but they are meant for all communities and so are not part of personal law. In order to promote religious activities of various faiths, the government has established the Religious Affairs Ministry, which in turn established the Hindu Religious Welfare Trust and the Buddhist Religious Welfare Trust to cater to the welfare needs of the communities. The complex politics of nation building, however, continuously impinges upon the legal discourse in the country.

The Discourse on the UFC

The discourse on the uniform family code (UFC) started in the 1980s, when a democracy movement was picking up to get rid of the dictatorship of Lieutenant General Hussain Mohammad Ershad. Given the ban on political activity, the democratic forces had no option but to employ tactics that were least prone to attract the wrath of the dictator. Agitations for human rights, legal rights and women's rights were the possible options. Against this backdrop, the Bangladesh Mahila Parishad (BMP) and some other women's organisations pushed their case for justice for oppressed women belonging to all communities.

In the aftermath of the Third International Conference on Women held in Nairobi in 1985, BMP took upon itself the task of drafting a UFC. Other like-minded women's groups joined the exercise, the

170   *The Politics of Personal Law in South Asia*

most notable being the Ain O Shalish Kendra (ASK— Legal Aid and Mediation Centre). Given the religious makeup of the country, where about 90 per cent were Sunni Muslims and the rest Hindu (Buddhists, Christians and animists form small numbers), the task was daunting. Since the proposed code was asking for gender justice it was potentially provocative for orthodox elements, both Muslim and Hindu. While Muslims believed that traditional Islamic law had enough safeguards for their women, Hindus believed the code would further corrode their identity. The result was that the idea remained largely confined to progressive women, both Muslim and Hindu, and indeed progressive men as well. In the late 1980s, when the movement for democracy became strident, these women organised a workshop in Dhaka in October 1989 under the title 'A Preliminary Proposal for a Common Family Law for All Men and Women of Bangladesh', which, in a way, became the first tangible step in the direction of a UFC.

Ironically, however, the return of democracy in 1991 served the cause little. Neither the BNP nor the AL showed any interest. Still, the women activists went ahead with their agenda and, between 1993 and 1996, fine-tuned the model code after a series of consultations with intellectuals. Lately, it has been given final shape and has been circulated for public debate. The basic features of the draft UFC are as under.

1. In matters of marriage, divorce, inheritance, and custody and guardianship of children, men and women are to be treated equally by law.
2. All marriages are to be registered irrespective of whatever rituals have been followed to solemnise them.
3. Child marriage is to be declared illegal and the minimum age for marriage should be eighteen for both boys and girls.
4. Polygamy is to be abolished.
5. During the subsistence of marriage, maintenance would depend on the following: irrespective of which spouse is the earning member, both spouses will participate equally in matters of family finance. If either, whatever be the gender, is unemployed, s/he would be entitled to maintenance from the other spouse.
6. Both mother and father will be the natural as well as legal guardians of children. In the absence of parents, either the closest relatives or persons designated by the parents will be the guardians.
7. Following the dissolution of marriage, the responsibility for maintaining the children will be the joint responsibility of the parents dependlng upon their financial situations.

The South Asian Mosaic   171

8. Equal conditions and standards will be applicable to both spouses to effect a dissolution of marriage. It would, however, be mandatory for both spouses to find ways and means for reconciliation and mediation. Therefore, there has to be a minimum lapse of time before divorce becomes effective.
9. The practice of enforcing restitution of conjugal rights will be abolished.
10. Property acquired during the subsistence of marriage will be divided as equitably as possible after the dissolution of marriage.
11. After the dissolution of marriage, if either spouse opts to take care of the chlidren the other spouse will make adequate compensation to her or him.
12. There is to be no gender discrimination in the case of inheritance.
13. Every adult male and female, whether married or unmarried, will have the right to take a child in adoption. However, in matters of adoption, the welfare of the child, and the financial capacity and custodial qualities of the adopter will be of vital consideration. The consent of the natural parents of the child being adopted, where applicable, would have to be obtained (Pereira 2002: 188–90).

Political Islam in Bangladesh is opposed to any form of UFC. In 2000, when the Bangladesh High Court ruled that mere utterance of the word 'talaq' thrice was not enough to divorce one's wife, and ordered the arrest of the *mullah* who had forced the so-divorced woman to marry her husband's paternal cousin, the orthodox Muslim political combination, Islami Oikyo Jote, was up in arms against the judgment and issued a ' death fatwa' against Justices Mohammed Gholam Rabbani and Nazmun Ara Sultana (Ahmed 2001: 618–19). Since the Bangladesh Mahila Parishad, which is in the forefront of demanding the UFC, is comprised of progressive women, many of whom have Leftist credentials, it is an eyesore to the Islamic fundamentalists.

But the opposition to the UFC is not confined to Muslim conservatives alone. It is quite broad-based. At best most Bangladeshis are indifferent to the whole issue. To understand this general indifference, an understanding of the communal scene of the country is necessary, to which we have referred above. Why are both Muslims and Hindus opposed to the UFC? Being a predominantly Muslim country the logic cannot be, as is the case with the Indian Muslims, that the identity of the Bangladeshi Muslims would be threatened because personal law is one of the important markers of identity. Already, in 1961, when Bangladesh was part of Pakistan, significant changes were brought

172   *The Politics of Personal Law in South Asia*

about in the prevailing Muslim personal law, although not outside the ambit of *Shari'ah,* by the then Ayub Khan regime. These changes are still operational in Bangladesh. It can be argued, therefore, that personal law can be modified without threatening Muslim identity. The possible explanation for East Pakistani Muslims' acceptance of the 1961 changes could, therefore, be that General Ayub Khan was not only the undisputed dictator of the land, he was a male and his Islamic credentials were not suspect. Four factors—Ayub's political authority, his gender, his Islamic credentials and Bangladesh's yet-to-crystallise anti-Pakistanism—made the situation conducive for the reforms. Over the years, Muslims of Bangladesh have become habituated to these changes. But now at play are two new factors. One, the demand for the UFC has emanated from secular women's groups with little political backing, and two, Bangladesh has been witnessing a conservative Islamic ascendancy, which is not conducive to any change in Muslim personal law that a conservative interpretation of the *Shari'ah* would provide. Generally speaking, the first reaction of most Bangladeshi Muslims is that the Qur'an is the compilation of the words of the Allah, which no human on earth has the authority to question. In a 2003 survey conducted by the Pew Research Center for the People and the Press, it was found that 74 per cent people believed that Islam should play a 'very' or 'fairly' large role in political life. The World Values Surveys (2000–2003) noted that in response to the question: 'Should a good government implement only the laws of the *Shari'ah*?, the Bangladeshis responded as under (Davis and Robinson 2006: 178):

Very Important	–	21.7%
Important	–	23.6%
Somewhat Important	–	23.8%
Least Important	–	21.8%
Not Important	–	9.2%

Still, what is to be noted is that compared to Pakistan (see p. 167) there is a much larger section of the Muslim population in Bangladesh to which Shari'ah is not the guiding principle of life.

Hindu Responses

The opposition to the UFC is not confined to Muslims alone. Hindus too are opposed to it, as I noticed through my interactions with the Hindu community leaders. But before we politically analyse the situation let us discuss the status of Hindu personal law in Bangladesh.

The South Asian Mosaic 173

Generally speaking, Hindu law in Bangladesh is frozen in its 1947 state. It is the Anglo-Hindu law insofar as its official operation is concerned. All Hindus by birth, whether Bengali or non-Bengali, are governed by it. The definition of Hindu is rather vague. It is quite broad-based, and only formal conversion to Islam or Christianity changes one's legal position as a Hindu. Unlike India where the Buddhists, Jains and Sikhs are all considered Hindu for the purposes of civil law, it is not clearly laid down in Bangladesh whether the Buddhists (in the Chittagong area they are generally called Baruas) are to be governed by Hindu law. Anglo-Indian law recognised the different position of the Chittagong Baruas and that of the Buddhists of Burmese origin in Cox's Bazar area. In Bangladesh there are three different legally definable Buddhist communities, the largest following the Dayabhaga school of Hindu law, while the remaining two follow different variants of Buddhist law (Menski and Rahman 1988: 116).

Hindu law in Bangladesh not only remains frozen, there is a widespread ignorance about it even in legal circles. There are very few Hindu litigations and mostly Hindu judges are chosen to hear them. In the lower courts they are haphazardly decided, on the basis of questionable 'authoritative' sources. Whatever clarity of law there is, is based on case law in respect of the validity of marriage, divorce, adoption and succession. There is a significant number of reputed cases on the Hindu joint family, and what has emerged from these judgments is that a new case law has been developed mainly in the context of general law, with little reference to traditional Hindu law (*ibid:* 125). Still, since there is not much judicial activism in the country, the possibility of legal reforms under such pressure is limited. Even legislative action (which could bring in reforms) is non-existent in this case, because it is considered politically unwise to interfere with minority personal laws.

In spite of the fact that Hindu law in Bangladesh remains totally unreformed, there is no demand from the community at large to reform it. More than the religious factor, their opposition is identity-centric. Leaders of the Hindu community, who also happen to be the office-bearers of the Hindu-Bouddha-Khristan Oikyo Parishad (Hindu, Buddhist, Christian Coordination Council), argue that Hindu personal law, having its base in the Hindu shastric tradition, is the most important marker of Hindu ethnicity in Bangladesh and, if it surrenders that marker then nothing can prevent it from extinction from the soil of Bangladesh. Their logic is twofold, one cultural and the other economic, though essentially both draw their sustenance from the communal divide to which reference has been made above.

174 *The Politics of Personal Law in South Asia*

One of the major components of the UFC is the issue of equal property rights for women. Hindu leaders argue that though theoretically there cannot be any debate that civil law should be gender neutral, when translated into ground realities it tells a different story. They argue: imagine that a Hindu homestead in a Bangladeshi village is divided amongst brothers and sisters. In all probability the sisters who are married into families from other villages will sell their shares of the property, which would not necessarily be purchased by the brothers. Some Muslim neighbour might buy it. If so, during the Eid festival, which attaches so much importance to the institution of *Qurbani* (the sacrifice of cows in the Bangladesh context), he would slaughter the sacrificial cow in the courtyard, the spilled blood of which would reach the *tulsitola* (the basil plant, considered sacred by Hindus; almost all rural Hindu households have it in their courtyards). Such slaughtering takes place during every Eid everywhere in the country and Bangladeshi Hindus are used to living with this reality, but would definitely not like that to happen in one's own courtyard, they argue. One may consider these fears farfetched, but given the growing Islamisation of the society, particularly in the countryside, such possibilities may not be totally imaginary. In this connection it was also mentioned that, sometimes, by throwing cow bones or cow blood in the village ponds, mischievous Muslims deliberately make the water undrinkable for Hindus.

Not all within the Hindu community, however, buy these sorts of logic to oppose the UFC. Younger Hindu men and women with whom I interacted believe that the above logic is flawed. Islamic conservatism is indeed a threat to the Hindu community but depriving Hindu women of their property rights is not a solution. Moreover, even sons can sell their properties, including their portions of homesteads. The real issue that should bother Hindus is the institution of polygamy and the absence of any legal recourse to divorce. While a Hindu man can terminate a marriage and marry again, his deserted wife is condemned to live as a widow for the rest of her life. Notably, Bangladesh has never seen any change in Hindu personal law. Bangladeshi Muslim women thus have better protection against polygamy after the passage of the Muslim Family Laws Ordinance of 1961, than their Hindu counterparts. On this specific issue, community leaders have no answer. Their suggestion is that such problems can be taken care of through affidavits submitted by both parties in courts. But technically speaking, these affidavits have no legal sanctity in the eyes of the prevailing Hindu personal law, and when husbands want to be troublesome, their deserted wives have no legal protection.

The South Asian Mosaic   175

That Hindu community leaders do not necessarily represent the Hindu viewpoint at large is evident from the fact that almost 50 per cent of the Bangladesh Mahila Parishad's 133,000-strong membership spread across the country is Hindu. It is one of the constant refrains of the Bangladesh Mahila Parishad that whenever the UFC is discussed in its conferences, Hindu community leaders, though invited, are conspicuous by their absence. Yet they always claim that they have a grassroots understanding of the situation, implying that members of the Bangladesh Mahila Parishad do not have any. In fact, these women have a much better knowledge of the ground reality—it is they who handle such cases in villages and towns as a matter of routine. The misfortune is that though female literacy is higher amongst Hindus than Muslims, Hindu women are worse off than their Muslim counterparts, both on account of the existing personal law as well as shortsighted Hindu community leadership.

The Muslim-Hindu Conservative Nexus

Religious conservatism and fanaticism thrive when there are similar trends in the rival faith. This is true anywhere in the world and Bangladesh is no exception. Two tendencies are noticeable in this connection. One, Hindus are becoming more communal, and two, communal Hindu leaders are getting co-opted by their Muslim counterparts, for it serves the political purposes of both groups. We have discussed the Hindu leadership's opposition to the demand for the UFC. We also find that Hindu leaders' efforts to go back to tradition is being actively encouraged by pro-Islamic political forces, for it not only gives them legitimacy to promote their pro-Islamic ideology, it also gives them some additional votes at the cost of their rival, the Awami League. Jagannath Hall, the only minority students' hall of Dhaka University, is a case in point.

Jagannath Hall houses about 2,500 students, mostly Hindus. There is also an *upasana ghar* (prayer hall) in the hostel. The idea is to encourage Hindu residents to retain their religious tradition. Saraswati Puja and other Hindu festivals are celebrated with fanfare. BNP leaders show interest in these events by paying advertised visits to them. In their speeches they do not fail to display their commitment to allow other religions to thrive in the country and also their desire to be in touch with the large Hindu minority. The government does not object to the celebration of Gandhi *Jayanti* (Gandhi's birthday) (Gandhi is the paradigm of religious coexistence in South Asia) in the hall, in which even government functionaries participate. During

176 The Politics of Personal Law in South Asia

the convocation ceremony of Dhaka University held in December 2004, in which Mahathir Mohammad, the former prime minister of Malaysia, was honoured with the doctorate degree, excerpts from all religious texts were read, namely, the Qur'an, the Gita, the Bible and the Tripitak. Hindu leaders of the Hindu-Bouddha-Khristan Olkyo Parishad indirectly take credit for these developments on behalf of their organisation.

Hindus have realised that it would be a tactical mistake to put all their eggs in the AL basket. They are, therefore, entering the BNP fold as well, for the way Bangladesh politics is developing, BNP appears to be poised to play a longer innings in power. This new realisation is noticeable in the fact that earlier the *puja* (idol festivals such as Durga, Kali, Saraswati, etc.) committees were controlled by pro-AL Hindu youth only but now the pro-BNP presence is evident. Of course, this has much to do with the overall lumpenisation of Bangladesh politics. Hindu leaders increasingly feel that they should get out of the syndrome of viewing India as the safety valve, which heretofore came in the way of their mustering, unlike the Indian Muslims, enough fighting spirit to live and thrive in Bangladesh in spite of all odds.

International Covenants

Reference to international covenants and declarations to which Bangladesh has been the signatory has not been of much use in convincing the political class to agree to the UFC. The CEDAW (Convention on the Elimination of All Forms of Discrimination Against Women) is a case in point (discussed in Chapter I). Many Muslim-majority countries have expressed their reservations in respect of specific provisions of the covenant, though they have signed the instrument. Bangladesh is one of them. Although it has trimmed down its reservations from the original set of objections, it has not budged on certain critical issues, primarily with regard to Articles 2 and 13. Article 2 is one of the most definitive provisions of the covenant aimed at eradicating discrimination against women. It dictates and guides the signatory states to bring in necessary domestic legislation in tune with this basic objective. Article 13 requires that the signatory state should take measures to eliminate discrimination in areas of economic and social life. For example, it is discriminatory against women that while male employees are entitled to medical benefits for their parents, the women employees are not.

The champions of UFC would have probably been more successful in their efforts had there been commensurate concern shown by

The South Asian Mosaic   177

the donors. In a country where a major portion of the development budget is dependent on foreign aid, donors can, if they so want, effectively influence the discourse on social development, an important component of which is gender justice. But in their virtually one-point programme of ensuring political stability in Muslim-majority countries by somehow co-opting the potentially destabilising Islamic conservatives, particularly after Islamic fundamentalism has emerged as a threat to the global order ever since the Iranian revolution of the late 1970s, they opt to keep off this slippery terrain. In Bangladesh this tends to create a complex nexus amongst the donors, the state and pro-Islamic forces, at the cost of women's rights (Guhathakurta 1994: 112–13; for a critique of globalised feminism, Siddiqi 2003).

To conclude, the UFC does not seem to have an immediate future in Bangladesh. Still, thanks to the relentless efforts of women's groups, the struggle is on and an increasing number of people are getting sensitised to the necessity of a common family code based on gender justice. But so long as the pro-Islamic forces call the shots, there is little likelihood that Islamic law will be further reformed or Hindu law be reformed at all. The UFC seems to be a pipe dream.

Nepal

Nepal has a uniform civil code operative since 1963, notwithstanding the fact that it is a multi-ethnic and multi-religious state. That this code is essentially a Hindu code is another matter, which we will discuss later in this section. No wonder, therefore, that the 1990 constitution of Nepal (which presently stands abrogated) is silent on the issue of personal laws of different communities for the 'Constitutional Monarchical Kingdom' of Nepal itself is 'Hindu' (Article 4). Indeed, the constitution also provides that 'every person shall have the freedom to profess and practise his own religion as *handed down to him from ancient times having due regard to traditional practices*' (Article 19; emphasis added). That the underscored words should contradict the essential elements of the (Hindu) code is once again another matter, which we will discuss here.

It may be argued that the 1990 Constitution may not have mentioned personal laws because the matter had already been settled through the enactment of the 1963 national legal code. A comparison with the Indian situation should clarify the point. The Constitution of India too guarantees freedom of conscience to all communities, yet advises the state to try to achieve the objective of a uniform civil code as contained in its Directive Principles of State Policy. Unlike

178   *The Politics of Personal Law in South Asia*

this, Part IV of the Nepalese constitution, which is almost similarly titled 'Directive Principles and Policies of the State', does not mention anything in respect of civil laws, as if the matter is settled for good. For sure, apparently, there is no controversy in Nepal over the personal laws. The politics of the country is so charged with the basic question of democracy and the Maoist challenge to both democracy and monarchy that the political class has little time to understand that the issue of civil law is also an integral element of the entire discourse. Already there are straws in the wind pointing to such debates though, at the moment, they are confined to women's rights and the demands relating to ethnic identity put forward by indigenous communities.

The story of the 1963 national code (Muluki Ain) started in 1854 when the first Muluki Ain was promulgated by Jang Bahadur Rana on 5 January 1854. The 1854 code underwent several changes till it was replaced by the 1963 code. During the course of its journey it had abolished the institution of sati in 1924, during the reign of Trichandra Samsher Bahadur Rana, who ruled Nepal from 1901 to 1929. It was the national code of 1854 that had introduced a National Caste System by allocating a certain rank to each ethnic and religious group as per the ruler's political requirements. The code was drafted by two Brahmins, who were rewarded with 500 *bighas* of land (about 300 hectares) for their job. Based on the tenets of *Manusmriti* the code did away with many of the egalitarian practices of the indigenous communities. One may argue that it was a nation-building strategy through the use of Hindu caste hierarchy. To suit this requirement, a fivefold classification was introduced, which was as follows.

At the top of the hierarchy were the *Tagadharis* (literally meaning the wearers of the sacred thread, the so-called twice-born). The communities that were included in this category were the Parbate Bahuns/ Chhetris, Newar Hindus and Brahmans (of Indian origin). This was followed by the so-called Matwalis, the non-enslavable alcohol drinkers. The groups that constituted this category were the Magars and Gurungs (associated with Gorkhali army), Hinduised Sunuwars and Newari Buddhists. In this category were also Included the progeny of freed slaves known as Ghatris. In the third category were the enslavable alcohol drinkers, namely, Bhotes (Buddhist), Chepangs/Kumals/ Hayus (ethnic minorities) and Tharus (Terai ethnics). This was followed by the 'water unacceptable' caste, the people who were not entitled to serve water to higher castes but whose touch did not defile the latter. The low caste Newars, Muslims and Christians figured in this category. At the bottom were the untouchables like Parbate artisan

The South Asian Mosaic 179

castes, Newar scavengers, etc. The justice system of the land had to respect this social stratification while dispensing justice, which was not equal for all (Dastidar 1995: 83–114; Gurung 2005: 143; Limbu 2005: 41–43). In spite of this social stratification on Hindu caste lines, certain customary practices of the communities were allowed to operate if they did not grossly violate Hindu norms like the butchering of the cow.

The 1854 code is an extremely significant document to understand the society and politics of contemporary Nepal. The code was amended from time to time. Andras Hoefer, the German scholar, who, for the first time, brought out the most detailed commentary on the code, which still remains the most authentic study on the document, wrote in the preface to the second edition of his book in 2004 (the first edition was publlshed in 1979):

> When I encountered the Legal Code (Muluki Ain) of 1854 for the first time [in 1971, following the availability of its reprint done in 1965] . . . it revealed itself as a grand, astonishingly comprehensive attempt at 'society building' in a particular country and a particular period of history, unique in its kind, above all in view of the, in part, detailed substantiation it gives for establishing and sanctioning the hierarchical stratification of social groups within a multi-ethnic society. It was rewarding to see to what extent and with what degree of consistency the opposition pure/impure had been applied in the Code, long before Western sociology came to recognise it as a basic, generative structuring principle of caste—and even more rewarding to learn from a tradition-guided Nepalese legislator that caste in South Asia was an intrinsic social category, rather than a mere construct of colonial administrators or 'orientalist' intellectuals, as some authors would have it today.
>
> —(Hoefer 2004: xxx)

The code of 1854 continued to remain the mainstay of Nepal's legal system till 1951, when 'it fell into a state of limbo' when the prime ministerial Rana dynasty fell from power following a popular revolt. Subsequently, following the return of monarchical authority in its 'panchayati' incarnation in 1960, King Mahendra, in 1963, replaced the 1854 code by a new one that did away with the caste hierarchy (Sharma 2004: 165).

The 1963 code declared all citizens equal for the purposes of the law. But since this code too was essentially a Hindu code the preeminence

180   *The Politics of Personal Law in South Asia*

of Hinduism continued. This was manifest in the clause pertaining to conversion, which said:

> Inside Nepal, nobody is allowed to preach creeds like Islam and Christianity which destroy the *dharma* practised by the Hindu people; or to convert to those creeds people practicing the *Hindu* dharma. If anybody attempts to convert people, he should be imprisoned for three years; if he has actually [converted people] he should be imprisoned for six years; and then, if he is a foreigner, he should be expelled from the country. If anybody practising the *Hindu dharma* becomes converted to any of the above mentioned creeds, he should be imprisoned for one year, and then if he is a foreigner, he should be expelled from the country. If he has only attempted to become converted, he should be punished by a fine of a hundred rupees. When somebody has become converted, the conversion is nullified, and he remains in the Hindu dharma.
> —(Quoted in Ahmad 2000: 103)

Since the subsequent constitution (1990) also declared the state as Hindu, the hierarchy continued to exist at the social level and, insofar as gender relationships were concerned, even at the legal level. Declaring the state as Hindu was indeed not a smooth affair. Opposition was expressed by religious minorities like Buddhists, Christians and Muslims. But due to pressure from dominant Hindu conservative forces, behind which was the Palace, these oppositions remained ineffective. Achyut Raj Regmi, the Minister for Housing in the interim government and a firebrand Hindu chauvinist, even threatened a hunger strike if the state was declared secular. Evidently, he had the support of the Hindutva forces in India. On 11 August 1990, BJP leader L. K. Advani visited Nepal and spoke strongly in favour of Nepal remaining a Hindu state (Ahmad 2000: 116; Sudhindra Sharma 2004: 129). The nexus between the Palace and the Hindutva forces in India was evident even in the early 1980s. One of the three main processions of the Ekatmata Yagna of 1983 (discussed in Chapter III) was flagged off by the then King Birendra in Kathmandu. This procession was to terminate at Rameshwaram. It makes political sense for the royalty in Nepal to align itself with the Hindutva forces in India to thwart the democratic opposition to it. The fact that the Nepali Congress has a political bond with the Congress Party in India contributes to this tie-up.

There are two ways of grappling with the controversies surrounding the 1963 code, one in terms of gender justice, and the other in terms

The South Asian Mosaic   181

of minority misgivings. While the first is not so much concerned with its Hindu orientation, the second is primarily in respect of that. In the forefront of the women's rights movement in Nepal is the Legal Aid and Consultancy Center (LACC), which was established in 1987 by a group of women lawyers, attorneys and law teachers with the aim of promoting and protecting the rights and interests of women and children. The other organisation with notable contribution to the movement is the Forum for Women, Law and Development (FWLD). It goes to the credit of these organisations that on 14 March 2002 the Eleventh Amendment to the 1963 code was introduced, which was a landmark step towards gender equality. Although certain lacunae still persisted, the amendment guaranteed equal rights to brothers and sisters in ancestral property. It also provided that married women would have full rights in their husbands' property and might, without any restrictions of age or duration of marriage, take their share of property and live separately from their husbands. A divorced woman was entitled to a share of property from her husband at the time of divorce. It was also provided that a wife separated from her husband could adopt a child if she did not have any of her own. One significant shortcoming of the amendment, however, was that a bigamous marriage was not declared void, only the punishment and rate of fine were increased. In spite of these achievements, women's rights groups feel that there are two major bottlenecks in their march to gender equality, one, the lack of political will across the board, and two, the continued political uncertainty in the country (Pradhan-Malla 2004: 69).

Presently the challenge to the code comes from the ethnic minorities and the Maoists, both of which have been incessantly demanding a secular Nepal. Although the exact position of the Maoists on the specific question of the civil code is not clear, the ethnic nationalities of Nepal consider the code to be an infringement upon their traditional customary practices. This issue is relevant for about 85 per cent of the disputes at the village level, including family disputes, do not reach the formal legal system (Chhetri and Kattel 2004: 4). Most indigenous communities have their traditional dispute settlement mechanisms in place and presumably the national code of 1963 has nothing much to do with this. According to Om Gurung, the general secretary of the Janajati Mahasangh (Nepal Federation of Indigenous Nationalities—NEFIN), the Manang and Mustang districts are known to have never taken their disputes to the formal courts (Interview with author, 23 February 2006). Now that large parts of Nepal are under the effective control of the Maoists, who also run their jana *adalats* (people's courts), and given the fact that the Maoists are demanding a secular

182　*The Politics of Personal Law in South Asia*

state, the 1963 code must be having little meaning to these jana *adalat* 'judges'. The reasons for people taking recourse to informal methods, more often than the formal institutions, for dispute resolution are more or less the same as in the rest of the South Asian region; the formal system is expensive, time consuming and involves long journeys, which the rural folk can hardly afford.

What is, however, more relevant, according to Gurung, who is also a professor of social anthropology at the Tribhuvan University in Kathmandu, is that the 1963 code is too Hindu oriented, which does not respect the traditional legal systems of 'indigenous' communities. For example, according to the code a man cannot marry his father's sister's daughter. The fine for such a marriage is Rs 6,000 and three months in jail, besides the annulment of the marriage. But in many communities there is no restriction on such marriages. Likewise, the code does not recognise polyandry but it is an accepted practice amongst the Humlas and Dolpos. While addressing the Nepal Bar Association on Civil Code Day, 5 August 2005, Gurung called upon appropriate amendments in the 1963 code to give due cognizance to various customary laws of indigenous nationalities (Interview with author, 23 February 2006).

It is important to fathom these opinions from the perspective of Nepal's mind-boggling ethnic politics. According to the 2001 Census, Nepal has 100 caste/ethnic groups. In May 2002, the National Committee of Nationalities of Nepal (NCNN) identified fifty-eight cultural groups divided into three ecological regions, namely, Mountain, Hill and Terai. In the same year the National Foundation for the Development of Indigenous Nationalities (NFDIN) defined indigenous nationalities as 'a tribe or community having its own mother language and traditional rites and customs, distinct cultural identity, distinct social structure and written and unwritten history'. Although the Hindus constitute 80.62 per cent of the population (2001 Census) and the state is 'Hindu', still, the politics of the country is increasingly being seen in caste and ethnic terms. As a result, it is not a politics of majority versus minorities but one amongst the minorities. Every community is a minority in Nepal *vis-à-vis* the rest put together. Thanks to the democratic resurgence in the late 1980s leading to the drafting of the 1990 constitution, a new awakening is being noticed among marginalised communities, who question the Bahun-Chhetri (combinedly making for 28 per cent of the population) political domination as well as that of the royal palace. The Maoist insurgency must also be seen in this light, particularly because of its ideological agenda, and not because of its ethnic composition, which is quite mixed (Gurung 2005: 146–48).

The future of Nepal as a Hindu state is under threat, following the 2006 democratic upsurge that has abolished the monarchy and declared Nepal a secular state pending the final decision by the constituent assembly that is in the process of being convened. As a natural corollary to this, the 1963 code would inevitably be questioned. According to Shanker Limbu, an advocate associated with the Lawyers' Association for Human Rights of Nepalese Indigenous Peoples (LAHURNIP):

> The provisions of Article 11 of the present [1990] constitution allow for discrimination on the basis of language and origin. Article 19 provides for the freedom to follow one's traditional *(sanatan)* religion. But since the word *'sanatan'* has not been defined in the appropriate laws (in this case the *Kanun Byakhya SamDandhi Ain* 2010 BS) and given that *'sanatan'* is used by some synonymously with Hindu religion, this had led to lack of clarity about whether the followers of other religions can practice their religions freely or not. This ambiguity is compounded further by the accompanying restrictive provision in the same article, which states that 'no person shall be entitled to convert other person from one religion to another'. The Constitution thus appears to indirectly support the primacy of the Hindu religion
> —(Limbu 2005: 45)

To empirically support his concern, Limbu highlights the fact that, in the judicial administration of Nepal, the 8.6 million indigenous people, comprising 37.19 per cent of the population, are represented by only 3.6 per cent personnel (excluding Newaris who account for 9.7 per cent of the national population). In contrast, the Bahun-Chhetris, who are 28 per cent of the population, account for 84 per cent of the personnel in the judicial administration (*ibid.*: 46). In the present politics of Nepal, when all the democratic and Maoist forces are pitted against the monarchy, one significant rallying point is secularism because King Gyanendra is widely seen as an epitome of the Hinduist assertion through his over-advertised ritualistic performances. He often makes it a point to sacrifice all kinds of animals at whichever shrine he visits, prompting the noted Nepali commentator, Kanak Mani Dixit, to designate it as his *'bali* (animal sacrifice) project'. In this project the king was actively supported by the Major General Bharat Keshar Simha, a retired ADC to the king, who was the president of the Vishwa Hindu Mahasangh.

184   *The Politics of Personal Law in South Asia*

It would be instructive to see where the Muslims of Nepal figure in this discourse, particularly because the general conception around the world after 9/11 is that Muslims are most orthodox about their religious values and can seldom adjust to a non-Muslim majority. Indeed, they consider the *Shari'ah* an integral part of their faith, which is true of Muslims in the rest of South Asia as well.

According to the 2001 Census, Muslims constitute 4.2 per cent of the population (in 1991 they were 3.53 per cent), of which 95 per cent live in the Terai region. (Curiously, *Muslim India*, an Indian journal dedicated to the cause of Muslims in India, unquestioningly accepts a website information that Nepali Muslims constitute 8 per cent of the country's population [January 2004: 115].) There is nothing like a Muslim vote bank, although in some districts they are in preponderance. Broadly speaking, the Muslims of Nepal can be divided into two categories in terms of social hierarchy. The first is those having Arab, Turkish or upper-caste Hindu backgrounds (such as Brahmins or Rajputs), who have close associations with the ruling class and are called Ashrafs. The second is Ajlafs, the local converts from low castes (Sudhlndra Sharma 2004: 114–15). By and large, the community profile is low and, like the Teral people (known as Madheshis), the Muslims too are not proportionately represented in jobs and professions. A survey conducted in 1989–90 of the caste and ethnic representation in the Nepalese bureaucracy and in Tribhuvan University revealed the peripheral space that the community occupied. There was no representation of Muslims at the secretary and deputy secretary levels. Only 0.29 per cent of the posts of section officers were occupied by them. Amongst the Tribhuvan University teachers only 0.87 per cent were Muslims and amongst the graduates they were only 0.37 per cent. The marginality of the community is reflected even in the casualty figures of the armed conflict between the Maoists and the security forces. Between 13 February 1996 and 31 December 2000, only one Muslim each was killed by the Maoists and the security forces (Pathak 2005: 308–9).

This political marginality of the community can explain why there has been hardly any demand for either the introduction of the *Shari'ah* or necessary amendments in the 1963 code. There are certain provisions in the latter which are at variance with Muslim personal law, like the simplicity of the divorce procedure in Islam and the unequal share in the parental property for daughters (following the 11th amendment to the 1963 code, brothers and sisters have equal rights). Since the Nepali legal system is essentially Hindu-oriented, the Muslim community at best avoids taking its personal law matters to the judiciary.[2]

The South Asian Mosaic   185

Most of these matters are settled at the community level with the assistance of community elders and the mullahs. There is, however, an evidence that in 1963–64, in the aftermath of the promulgation of the 1963 code, the All Nepal Anjuman Islah (ANAI) demanded an amendment in the code to make marriages among patrilineal cousins legal, which was granted (Ansari 2003). Beyond this, the Nepali Muslim community is not unanimous in its demand for personal law reforms. While a section believes that the Nepali code should recognise the traditional Islamic divorce system, others think that these are non-issues. The real issue is the uplift of the community. For example, the Nepal Muslim Ittehad Organisation (NMIO), founded in 1998, talks only of the general welfare of Muslims and does not refer to either protection or reform in Muslim personal law. Some even believe that the Muslim sense of security would be better taken care of in 'Hindu Nepal' rather than a 'secular Nepal'. If the state were declared secular it would soon lead to the growth of Hindu 'fundamentalism', leading eventually to the rise of Muslim 'fundamentalism', causing HinduMuslim conflicts that Nepal is not known for (author's discussion with Dr Mohammed Mohsin, an eminent Muslim leader and former cabinet minister, 27 February 2006).

Is there any tendency pointing towards the growth of Islamic identity amongst Nepal's Muslims? This question is critical because, if so, the demand for *Shari'ah* would only be a matter of time. According to Sudhindra Sharma, a scholar working on Nepali Muslims, a new kind of conversion is taking place, in spite of the fact that conversion is strictly prohibited in the country. Amongst those Muslims who go to West Asia, some return to Nepal as 'fundamentalists' and try to indoctrinate the local Muslims. *Mullahs* who come from India do the same thing. As a result, the Muslim community is in danger of alienation from the Hindus. The distinction between the two approaches is reflected in the two mosques in Kathmandu, the Kashmiri Takia and the Nepali Jama Masjid. The former represents the liberal Islam of the Barelvi school while the latter represents the orthodox Islam of the Deobandi school.

Hindutva politics of India during the 1980s and 1990s have also contributed to the growth of the Islamic identity, particularly by such acts as the bringing of anointed Ram-temple bricks to different Terai districts (Sudhindra Sharma 2004: 116–20). It is also alleged that the Pakistan intelligence agency, ISI, is operating in the region to indoctrinate its Muslims to oppose India. Given the fact that during the India-Pakistan wars the Nepali Muslims have supported Pakistan (Gaborieau 2001: 205–27), the ISI may not find it altogether difficult

186   *The Politics of Personal Law in South Asia*

to use Nepal as an important base for its anti-India activities. Because of the open border of 800 km between India and Nepal, it is not only easy to smuggle contraband into Indian territory but also to coordinate the subversive activities of secessionist groups operating in Kashmir and the Northeast. There are also Muslim groups like the Islamic Yuva Sangh (IYS) or the Muslim Ekta Sangh (MES) but one does not know for certain how much actual support Pakistan has amongst these groups or amongst Nepal's Muslims in general. There are some cases of Muslim youth being lured by money and Islamic ideology to indulge in subversive activities. Salim Ansari, a Terai Muslim leader, attributes such activity largely to the socio-economic backwardness of the community, in which situation they become tools in the hands of foreign conspirators (Dastidar 2000: 768–69). According to a report in the Indian press, in recent years *madrassas* have mushroomed in the bordering districts of Nepal, some of which have become prosperous overnight, thanks to massive grants made available to them by the Islamic Development Bank (Siddiqui 2001). However, not even a fraction of the anxiety expressed in India about ISI activities in Nepal is noticeable in the Nepali press or in discussions of Nepali intellectuals.

Sri Lanka

The population of Sri Lanka may be divided into six main groups: Sinhalas, Sri Lanka Tamils, Moors, Indian Tamils, Malays and Burghers. According to the Census of 1981 (last held), Sinhalas are in a preponderant majority (74 per cent). The percentages of other ethnic groups are as follows: Sri Lanka Tamils (12.5 per cent), Moors (7.1 per cent), Indian Tamils (5.6 per cent), Malays (0.3 per cent), and Burghers (0.3 per cent). Sinhalas are mostly Buddhists, Sri Lanka and Indian Tamils mostly Hindus, Moors and Malays are Muslims, and Burghers are Christians. Religion-wise, broadly speaking, Buddhists constitute 70 per cent of the population, Hindus 15 per cent, Christians 8 per cent, and Muslims 7 per cent.

Sri Lanka has a tradition of religious tolerance. From ldrisi's account of the Sinhalese court of the twelfth century it may be seen that Christians, Jews and Muslims enjoyed complete freedom of worship and a measure of internal jurisdiction to be governed by their own laws and customs (Jaldeen 2004: 229–30). Barring the Portuguese interlude (1597–1658) when religious tolerance was considerably marred, this tradition has more or less been maintained. The present Sri Lankan constitution (1978) is secular, though it gives primacy to

The South Asian Mosaic 187

Buddhism. Article 9 of the constitution says that 'the Republic of Sri Lanka shall give to Buddhism the foremost place and accordingly it shall be the duty of the State to protect and foster the Buddha *Sasana,* while assuring to all religions the rights granted by Articles 10 and 14 (1) (a).' In spite of the essential secular thrust of the constitution there is no reference in the constitution to a uniform civil code for the country. The Directive Principles of State Policy (Article 27), unlike the Indian constitution, is silent on the matter. Evidently, the question of the personal law of different communities is not a political issue in the country and the different communities are governed by their specific family laws. The Sri Lankan legal system is based on a complex mixture of English common law, Roman-Dutch law, Sinhalese law (more commonly referred as the Kandyan law), Buddhist law, Hindu law, Thesavelamai law, Islamic law and Mukkuvar law. An individual may, in respect of different transactions or legal relations, be governed by different systems of law (Cooray 1992: 1). While the civil law, as developed during the colonial period based on Roman-Dutch law, is the most dominant system of law, three streams of personal law/customary laws govern a significant section of the population. These streams are: Kandyan law, Muslim personal law, and Thesavelamai law.

Kandyan Law

Kandyan law has its origin in the Kandyan kingdom, which covered large parts of Sri Lankan territory barring the coastal areas and the Jaffna peninsula. In 1815 the British defeated the Kandyan king and extended their authority over the entire Island. But even after that Kandyan civil law continued to operate with people belonging to the erstwhile Kandyan kingdom. However, some amount of confusion continued for decades, regarding whether this was a personal law meant for Kandyan Sinhalese to be carried with them even if they migrated to other areas, or whether it was a territorial law meant for both Sinhalese and Tamils who continued to live in the erstwhile Kandyan kingdom. The Kandyan Marriage Ordinance of 1870 set out in its Schedule the area to which the ordinance applied. But several changes in the provincial boundaries in subsequent years continued to influence the jurisdiction of the Kandyan law. Following Sri Lanka's independence, the Kandyan Marriage and Divorce Act of 1952 referred to the following four provinces out of nine: the Central Province, the North-Central Province, Uva and Sararagamuwa. It left out the north-western Province, which had been governed by Kandyan law earlier.

188   *The Politics of Personal Law in South Asia*

The act made detailed provision for the formalities to be observed preparatory to and during the marriage ceremony. The act became effective from 1 August 1954 but did not affect the validity of earlier marriages. Certain legal enactments that have general application in the country, such as the Prevention of Frauds Ordinance of 1840, the Age of Majority Ordinance of 1865, as amended by Act No. 17 of 1989, and the Wills Ordinance of 1844 apply to Kandyans as well. In case of matters where the Kandyan law is silent, the law to be resorted to is the Roman-Dutch law (Cooray 1992: 114–29).

Muslim Law

The Dutch colonial administrators codified the rules of inheritance, marriage and divorce in order to facilitate the application of Muslim family law. This Code was preserved and adapted by the British after their victory over the Dutch in 1799. The British later enacted the Registration of Muslim Marriages Ordinance 1896, replacing parts of the earlier Anglo-Dutch Code. In 1906, a semi-official code of Shafi law was prepared (there are some Hanafi school followers also). In 1929, on the recommendation of the Akbar Committee, the government issued a Muslim Marriage and Divorce Registration Ordinance, which is still in force. Following the country's independence in 1948, the Muslim Marriage and Divorce Act was passed in 1951, which essentially reinforced the principle that, in matters of personal status, the rights and duties of the parties involved were to be determined by the school of law to which the parties belonged. Under the provisions of the act, a Muslim Marriage and Divorce Advisory Board was set up to advise the government on the matter. The act was amended thrice during 1954–56. In 1969, the act was once again amended to incorporate a Supreme Court ruling that the Judicial Commission would appoint the *qadis* (Mahmood 1995b: 91). Table 5.3, prepared by WLUML, gives a broad picture of the situation as obtaining with the Muslim community of Sri Lanka (WLUML 2003: 54).

Muslim law in Sri Lanka has some progressive elements. It is largely codlfled and all marriages have to be registered but, on the whole, it is still traditional. Although Sri Lanka does not have an equivalent of the Special Marriage Act of India, a Muslim woman can validly marry a non-Muslim under the General Law of Sri Lanka. Subsequent to the marriage, she will be governed by General Law and not Muslim laws. The two types of law differ greatly in their provisions concerning divorce and inheritance. Two Muslims, however,

Table 5.3 The Status of Muslim Personal Law in Sri Lanka

Constitution	Other Laws	Muslim Laws	General Comments
The 1978 Constitution contains clauses on basic human rights, including non-discrimination on the grounds of sex. These rights are justiciable, provided violation is by administrative/ executive action. The right of equality can be restricted on the grounds of national security and in the interest of religious and racial harmony. All laws including gender discriminatory laws in existence before the 1978 constitution cannot be challenged for non-conformity with constitutional provisions. Article 9 of the constitution gives Buddhism 'the foremost place' in the republic, and requires the state to protect and foster Buddhism, subject to guarantees of freedom of belief for all religious communities.	Roman-Dutch law, introduced by Dutch colonisers, is considered the residuary law, although it also applies as an independent system of law in certain areas of civil law. Many statutes, such as the Penal Code, are based on English law, inherited from a subsequent period of British colonial rule. Parallel personal status laws apply to different communities. The General Law, which is an amalgam of Roman-Dutch and English Common Law principles, applies to the general population, but Kandyan law and Thesavelamai law apply to certain sections of the population. A Muslim can marry a non-Muslim under the General Law, but two Muslims cannot validly marry under the General Law.	Muslims (including the Malays) are governed by Muslim laws. These were first codified in 1806 during Dutch colonial rule. The current Muslim Marriage and Divorce Act of 1951 draws heavily on the Shafi School. The act contains both substantive and procedural law but is not comprehensive; wherever the act is silent, the law of the sect to which the party belongs is to be used as the basis for decisions. The *Qazi* Courts hear matters governed by Muslim laws; appeal lies to the Board of *Qazis* and ultimately to the Supreme Court. Only Muslim males can be *Qazis*. A 1992 commission to examine the MMDA included two women but the Board of *Qazis* did not accept their recommendations.	Muslim women and children have benefited from legal values in the General Law applicable to the majority non-Muslim community. Recent reform in favour of women (on child marriage, marital rape and abortion) has not been extended to Muslims because of the growing influence of identity politics and Muslim lobbyists within Parliament. Sri Lanka has ratified CEDAW and has also formulated a Women's Charter to implement CEDAW locally. *Qazi* Courts have few powers of enforcement. To have decrees in their favour enforced, women married under the MMDA have to approach the civil courts. There have been instances of conflict of law. Muslims may adopt under the 1941 Adoption Ordinance, but under case law, inheritance matters will be governed by Muslim laws.

190   *The Politics of Personal Law in South Asia*

cannot marry under General Law. Some Muslim couples have married under General Law to avoid the *wali* requirement, but their marriages are not valid because Muslims must marry under the MMDA (WLUML 2003: 75, 102, 208). Although the law recognises polygamy, an MWRAF survey found 83 per cent of *qazis* felt that there should be law requiring the permission of a *qazi* before polygamy is performed. The courts generally uphold a wife's right to separate residence, but 'separate residence' has not been clearly defined. Earlier case law permitted conversion to Islam as a valid means to practice polygamy but, since a leading case of 1997, it is no longer possible. The 1806 Mohammedan Code recognised the legality of keeping concubines but the MMDA does not recognise sexual relationship outside marriage (*ibid.*: 215).

For more than a decade, the MWRAF has been constantly demandlng progressive changes in the present law of Muslims within the Qur'anic precepts and Sunnah. It has also been regularly dialoguing with the *qazis* in this respect. The organisation hopes that these *qazis* will be an important ally in MWRAF's advocacy for Muslim personal law reforms in Sri Lanka in the future (*ibid.*: 266).

Muslim personal law in Sri Lanka is viewed from three different angles. Progressive Sri Lankan Muslim women, having networks with international women's groups, find many flaws in the law from a gender and human rights perspective and plead for their eradication in line with the General Law of Sri Lanka and international conventions. As opposed to this, traditionalists within the community want to cling to the law to assert their identity which has particularly been under threat ever since the LTTE has subjected the community in Tamil-majority provinces to severe violence, resulting in their flight to safer areas and state-run refugee camps for survival. The Sinhala-dominated Sri Lankan state, which is pitted against the LTTE onslaught on the territorial integrity of the nation, finds it necessary to align with the traditionalists within the Muslim community, which alone can command influence on the community at large. In the given situation, it is unlikely that the state would oblige progressive Muslim women and reform Muslim personal law. For example, in September 1995, the minimum age of marriage for persons in other communities in Sri Lanka (i.e., those falling under the General Law and Kandyan law) was raised to eighteen years for both males and females. No corresponding change was made in laws governing Muslims. Muslim women's organisations demanded the inclusion of Muslims into the act, but the state did not oblige. The minister for justice justified this exclusion in the name of protecting the cultural traditions and

The South Asian Mosaic 191

aspirations of the Muslim community. In a statement made in the Parliament, he said:

> We recognize that the Muslim community is entitled to be governed by their own laws, usages and customs and it would not be productive to aim at a level of uniformity which does not recognize adequately the different cultural traditions and aspirations of the Muslim community. It is through respect for a diversity of cultures for a whole plethora of cultural traditions, which enrich our land that the government is making that exception. This is not a sign of weakness or prevarication. It embodies the essence of democratic traditions. These are very difficult questions, especially in a country like Sri Lanka where different segments of the population are governed by different laws. I think it is not something that detracts from the value of our legal system but rather something that enhances and augments the value of our legal system to recognize the different cultural values and to seek to incorporate them all in a comprehensive body of jurisprudence that we give effect to in our country.
> —(*Hansard* [101] 2, 20 September 1995: 209–210, quoted in WLUML 2003: 122)[3]

It may be noted that this was at the height of the third Eelam war that commenced in April 1995 following the collapse of the peace talks between the Chandrika Kumaratunga government and the LTTE, when the Sri Lankan state could hardly afford any rift with the Muslim community, which had been systematically distancing itself from the Tamil Tigers and coming closer to the Sri Lankan government. In November 1995 Jaffna was recaptured by the Sri Lankan armed forces by defeating the LTTE there.

The Sinhalese-Muslim political alliance is in place as Tamil-Muslim tensions continue. According to the report of a fact-finding mission undertaken in December 2003 by the Human Rights Commission of Sri Lanka, 'a Muslim registry of land recently compiled points to 490 locations in the North and East and over 100,000 acres of paddy lands that are affected by LTTE control of territory. . . . Many Muslims . . . feel the strategy of the LTTE is to forcibly evict them from the North and East as part of an exercise to change the demographic pattern (text of report in *The Island* [Colombo], 13 and 14 May 2004). With the virtual collapse of the ceasefire agreement between the Sri Lankan government and the LTTE, and the resumption of hostilities in 2006

192 *The Politics of Personal Law in South Asia*

the Muslim-LTTE relations have further deteriorated, with the former at the receiving end once again.

Thesavelamai Law

The word Thesavelamai means 'customs of the land'. The origin of these customs can be traced to those of the Dravidians from the Malabar coast of South India. During their rule on Jaffna, the Portuguese allowed the customs to continue. But their successors, the Dutch, found it necessary to codify them as there were no clear principles for the proper administration of justice. Much of the codification of Thesavelamai in the twentieth century has been through case laws. The Thesavelamai applies to all persons who come within the description of Tamil inhabitants of Jaffna. But certain sections of the law apply to lands in the Northern Province, irrespective of the race or nationality of the owner. In essence, it applies to transactions relating to land owned by Jaffna Tamils. It does not apply to Tamils from other areas. Under the law, land has to be offered to either the co-owners or the persons having hereditary rights before it is sold to others (Cooray 1992: 140–49; Goonesekere 1984: 113–23; Jennings and Tambiah 1952: 261–75). Is Thesavelamai a personal law or a territorial law? According to Cooray:

> The Thesavelamai is not a personal law in the real sense of the term. The application of a personal law depends on the existence of a personal link among a class of persons who are subject to a single system of law. But unlike Muslim law which applies to all who answer to the description of Muslims, Part I of the Thesavelamai applies to a class of persons namely Tamils, who are bound together by a personal link, but who must in addition be resident in a particular territory. It is thus a personal law in some respects, with a territorial limitation. Persons subject to the Thesavelamai could change the law by which they are governed by changing their inhabitancy. All persons subject to Kandyan law however cannot rid themselves of its incidence except by marriage.
>
> —(Cooray 1992: 147–48)

From the above discussion it is clear there is legal pluralism in Sri Lanka, which is inevitable in a country with different ethnic groups that are conscious of their respective identities. This pluralism has been a source of strain and conflict among citizens, conflict which

The South Asian Mosaic 193

the legislature has sometimes tried to resolve by applying General Law, and the courts by applying the Roman–Dutch law; however, such efforts have been limited. In 1844, the British government tried to introduce a uniform marriage law but it did not work. A century later, the Marriage and Divorce Commission made yet another effort but failed. Sri Lanka's progress towards a uniform civil code is even less compared to India, because of two reasons. First, it has no comprehensive secular marriage act like India's Special Marriage Act of 1954; and second, it has, unlike India, allowed the *qazi* courts to adjudicate Muslim law cases. In the present politics of Sri Lanka, which is overburdened by the unresolved Sinhala-Tamil ethnic conflict, it is most unlikely that there would be the slightest dilution of the ethnicity markers, which is the first requisite before any uniform civil code can be attempted. In any case, family law is not a political issue in Sri Lanka.

The Maldives

The Republic of Maldives, situated about 900 km off the southwest coasts of India and Sri Lanka, consists of a group of twenty-six atolls in the Indian Ocean. The atolls encompass a territory featuring 1,192 islets, roughly 200 of which are inhabited by people. Though small in size, the country has been populated for well over 2,000 years. Because of its strategic location, the people of the Maldives are of different ethnic origin. The language of the country is Dhivehi, which is of Indic origin. In 1153, the Maldives converted to Islam, prior to which it was Buddhist. Because of the distances from one to another islet, conversion did not take place simultaneously and it took many years before the entire country became Muslim (Mohamed 2002: 109–10). At present all Maldivians are Muslim and no non-Muslim can become its citizen. Secular marriages are not recognised and if a Maldivian girl marries a non-Muslim while abroad, she cannot return to her country. The *Shari'ah* is the only legal system in the country and is interpreted and administered by the authorities (Maloney 1980: 211).

The origin of Muslim law in the Maldives is traced to the arrival of Ibn Battuta in the island in the year 1343. Ibn Batuta was the great Moorish traveller from Tangier, who had interrupted his journey to occupy, for several years, the position of Maliki chief *qazi* at the court of the Sultan of Delhi. Since there was no qualified judge in the Maldives, he was asked to serve as chief judge. He spent only one and a half years in the country as he fell out of favour of the Maldivian prime minister. Ibn Batuta was quite impressed by the Maldivian

194   *The Politics of Personal Law in South Asia*

people and their pious nature but he found their adherence to Islamic legal precepts deficient: 'The first bad custom I changed was the practice of divorced wives staying in the houses of their former husbands, for they all do so till they marry another husband. I soon put that to rights.' As *qazi* he tried to make women wear a breast cover, but failed to implement that (*ibid.*: 228).

Over the centuries, saints and sultans who visited the country tried to force higher Islamic standards that included men growing beards, women wearing veils and covering their bodies, and banning the use of silver belts but they never fully succeeded. Following the Portuguese rule in Male from 1558 to 1573 there was a religious resurgence in the country, in the wake of which the Maliki system of jurisprudence was replaced by the stricter Shafi school. This school, which was founded in the early nineteenth century, was first introduced in the central Islamic lands and South Yemen, from which it was brought to the Maldives by Sheikh Muhammad Jamal-ud-din. Its rules are different in minor ways: one cannot touch a marriageable person after ablutions before praying, women should wear the veil in the presence of men (not observed in the Maldives) and some of the hours for praying are different. The concept of ritual pollution is derived from the Hindu-Buddhist background as well as from Islam (Maloney 1980: 233). Lately, the Saudi Wahabi influence has been gaining in strength, reflected in the female dress. On the whole, however, Maldivian society is quite modern in terms of gender equality; women are found in all professions, though the country provides only limited opportunities. The cultural impacts of Bollywood and Hindi TV serials are noticeable everywhere.

Evidently, there is no reason for any controversy over the personal law of the Maldivians, particularly because the state is authoritarian and the *Shari'ah,* as noted above, can be interpreted by the authorities alone. But this situation may not continue for long because lately there has been a democratic upsurge in the country and the present authoritarian regime led by President Maumoon Abdul Gayoom, who will complete thirty years in office in 2008 (six five-year tenures as president), has agreed under pressure to allow political parties to register themselves. In 2005, four political parties were registered, namely, the Maldivian Democratic Party (MDP), the Dhivehi Payyithunge Party (DPP, or the Maldivian People's Party, led by President Gayoom), an Islamist party called Adalat (meaning 'court of justice') and the Islamist Democratic Party (IDP). Although it is not yet clear whether these parties will be allowed to put up their candidates in the next parliamentary elections (they were not allowed to do so in the three by-elections that

The South Asian Mosaic 195

were held in December 2005), the process of democratisation, once started, cannot be stalled for long (Chakma 2006: 75–76; Velezinee 2006: 97–98). Once the Maldives is in the throes of democratic churning it is inevitable that family legal issues will be caught in the political vortex. One must note that two of the four registered parties are Islam-oriented and may insist on stricter adherence to the *Shari'ah*.

Bhutan

It is difficult to trace the evolution of the Bhutanese legal system during ancient and medieval times. Given the scattered habitation of people in geographically separated valleys, it can be presumed that local Buddhist priests must have been the propounders of the tenets of law based on customs and usage, as well as, dispensers of justice. After the consolidation of Drukpa supremacy in the fifteenth and sixteenth centuries, political authority came to be represented by the Deb Raja and religious authority by the Dharma Raja. It was only under this diarchy that the administration of justice started taking shape. Still, as the emphasis was primarily on the spiritual aspect of life, spiritual considerations governed civil and criminal laws. Following the establishment of the Drukpa hereditary monarchy in 1907 under the title Druk Gyalpo, all spiritual and temporal authorities got centralised. Druk Gyalpo thus became the highest court of appeal. From the 1950s onwards, a process of modernisation set in and in 1972 the Speaker of the National Assembly made the following significant statement:

> Giving consideration to the fact that in the face of modern development our country would not derive any benefit unless its legal codes were suitably reformed, and in view of the fact that our ancient laws did not of course take into account present day legal systems, His late Majesty took upon himself the difficult task of drafting a new legal code containing about 17 sections. This was examined by the National Assembly over a period of three years and it was finally passed in 1969. All citizens were made equal in the eyes of the law, regardless of personal status, and this has contributed greatly to the strengthening of the Kingdom's integrity.
> —(Singh 1985: 142–43)

This codification, however, was more in respect of the administration of justice and less about the law itself. As a result, the law of the land remained largely unwritten, based on religion, custom and usage, which is still the case, with only marginal attempts at codification.

196 The Politics of Personal Law in South Asia

In present day Bhutan the question of personal law is a non-issue. Since almost all controversies surrounding personal laws in South Asia start and end with women's rights and gender justice and since in Bhutan women are practically equal to men in all respects, it has reason to continue as a non-issue. The situation is rooted in two socio-logical phenomena; one, Bhutan accords the same legal rights to both men and women, and two, it has a 'fluid marriage system'. What is meant by the latter is that people can live together like married couples without entering into any formality and men and women choose their partners freely and can leave them freely as well. As such, divorce in cases of formal marriages is also rather simple. Since women retain their individual ownership of property, they are financially independent (Crins 2004: 581–82). No wonder the women's rights movement is virtually non-existent in the kingdom. The existence of something called the National Women's Association of Bhutan is more an apology for the movement rather than its effective organ.

Polygamy is prevalent in Bhutanese society, though it is increasingly becoming rare. A man can have a maximum of three wives but the consent of the first or both the first and second wives has to be obtained before a second or third marriage. (Ironically, the Bhutanese king has four wives, all sisters.) The institution of polyandry is no longer legal (Harris 1973: 369). Most marriages in Bhutan are still performed in the traditional way and most disputes, if any, are to be settled traditionally through some kind of pan-chayat system. But in case any such dispute has to be adjudicated, then the marriage needs to be registered. If a marriage is not already registered, it can be done by paying a fine (or fee) of Nu 50 (equivalent to fifty Indian rupees).

The judicial system is structured as a three-layered system. The lowest level is the sub-district court (Drungkhag), above which is the district court (Dzongkhag) and at the top is the high court (Thrimkhang Gongma). The judicial rules are still uncodified and, largely, the tradition-based Ngalong norms apply across the board irrespective of whether one is Ngalong (elite Buddhists of Tibetan origin), Sarchop (the majority population, living mostly in the eastern and central parts, who, though Buddhist, have little say in government) or Lhotshampa (ethnic Nepalese of southern Bhutan). As noted above, presumably the disputes arising within the Nepali, who are mostly Hindus too, are settled at the local levels by the community elders or the village headmen, who are officially appointed. Since hardly anything exists in written form including judgements, case law has little significance. The lawyers pleading a case can never, therefore, refer to an earlier precedent. It is possible that judges may be aware of some earlier cases and their judgements may be influenced by these precedents; however, they are not bound to quote or follow them. Each judgement is thus an individual and independent exercise. Increasingly, however, disputes are being settled in formal courts. The reason is that court procedures are being streamlined and made cost-effective. For example, in 2002, 709 cases were decided in the Phuntsholing court alone (Dubgyur 2004: 380). The legal profession is also systematically getting professionalised. A lawyer is supposed to possess an IL. B. degree or its equivalent from a foreign university, plus eighteen months of course work as an internee in a Bhutanese court.

One of the rare codified situations is in respect of the maintenance to be paid for children in case of divorce (Marriage Act 1980). All such children must be with the mother till they are nine, after which they can choose either of their parents to stay with. Earlier, the father was supposed to pay 20 per cent of his salary or income to the mother for each child, with a ceiling of 40 per cent. But there has been a change in the law. Now, if the divorce is on account of the adultery of the wife, then the rate is 10 per cent, the ceiling, however, remaining at 40 per cent.

From the above discussion it seems to be clear that personal law is not an issue in Bhutan, and nor is anything that smacks of politics or minority rights. The Druk Gyalpo favours moving slowly towards democracy and has abdicated in 2006 in favour of his son. In the draft constitution that is now being debated and discussed nationally, there is nothing on minority rights; the emphasis is entirely on Gross National Happiness based on one country, one culture. In this context there is a reference to Tsawa-Sum in Article 6.3.g dealing with citizenship. But the concept of Tsawa-Sum is not clarified, nor is it otherwise clear. A Bhutanese scholar located in a western university argues that it could well mean the king, country and culture put together; essentially, it negates pluralism (Phuntsho 2004: 356–58).

Bhutanese society is fast changing under the pressures of development in general and globalisation in particular. There is an increasing tendency towards migration from rural areas to urban centres, most notably to Thimpu, but also to Paro and Phuntsholing. With these movements of people, traditional family bonds are getting weakened and nuclear family structures are emerging. Property disputes might become more common, warranting reforms in family laws. One probable demand that can emanate from the Lhotshampa minority is with regard to modification of the code to abolish polygamy. But since even within Nepal polygamy is a legally accepted system such a demand

198 *The Politics of Personal Law in South Asia*

would not hold water, or may not even be put forward partly because in Lhotshampa politics the female voice is virtually non-existent.

The Lhotshampas are now interested in their survival in Bhutan and they want to see to it that what happened to their community in the early 1990s, when thousands of them were evicted from Bhutan and rendered into refugees in Nepal, should not also happen to them. This is particularly so because Bhutan is in no mood to take back any one of them, some cosmetic efforts notwithstanding. Between October 1993 and December 2003, fifteen rounds of talks between Bhutan and Nepal have been held to work out modalities to repatriate the refugees, who are more than 100,000 in number, but the talks have yielded little result. The only achievement of these talks has been the categorisation of the refugees into four groups, namely, 'genuine' Bhutanese forcefully evicted, 'voluntary emigrants' (a difficult call because many such signatures were extracted when they were leaving Bhutan in panic), non-Bhutanese, and Bhutani criminals. This is a clear indication that even if some repatriation takes place it would involve only a small fraction of the refugees and that Nepal is not in a position to extract a better deal from Thimpu. On the whole, therefore, the Bhutanese family code is in no danger of being questioned by any section of Bhutanese society.

Notes

1 It may, however, be noted that the name 'Pakistan' was not coined by the Muslim League; it was rather thrust upon it. Addressing the annual session of the League on 24 April 1943, Jinnah said: 'You know perfectly well that Pakistan is a word which is really foisted upon us and fathered on us by some section of the Hindu press and also of the British press. Now our resolution was known for a long time as the Lahore Resolution, popularly known as Pakistan Resolution. But how long are we to have this long phrase? Now I say to my Hindu and British friends: We thank you for giving us one word' (Conrad 1997: 122–23).

2 A contrast may be referred to here between Nepal and Kashmir. Till 1947, when Kashmir acceded to India, it too was a Hindu kingdom like Nepal, the difference being that Kashmir had a majority Muslim population while Nepal had a small Muslim minority. In Kashmir, till the enactment of the Laws Consolidation Regulation of 1872, it was customary law, not personal law, that governed both the Hindu and Muslim communities in respect of family matters and succession to landed property. In 1872 it was for the first time that personal law was given precedence over customary law. Subsequently, this practice was duly codified as the Sri Pratap Jammu and Kashmir Laws (Consolidation) Act of Samvat 1977 (AD 1920). Henceforth the law courts were required to uphold personal laws of different communities unless either of the litigants proved successfully

The South Asian Mosaic 199

that 'personal law [was] abrogated by such customs as [were] found to be prevailing' (Rai 2004: 176–77).

3 Under the MMDA there is no minimum age for marriage. Under S. 23 the marriage of a girl younger than twelve requires the permission of a *qazi* for the purposes of registration. Under S. 82, it is a punishable offence for a registrar/abettors to register the marriage of a girl younger than twelve if they know that permission from a *qazi* has not been obtained as required by S. 23. Under S. 363 of the Penal Code 1883 as amended in 1995, sexual intercourse between a man and his wife, who is younger than twelve, constitutes statutory rape. An unregistered marriage is nevertheless considered valid (WLUML 2003: 126).

6   The Wider Context

The interest in life does not lie in what people do, nor even in their relations to each other, but largely in the power to communicate with a third party, antagonistic, enigmatic, yet perhaps persuadable, which one may call life in general.

—Virginia Woolf, *The Common Reader*

Family Law and South Asia

Law is evidently a political subject and family law is more so, as we have noted in the previous chapters. In plural South Asia, therefore, no discussion on reforms in family law or on the uniform civil code, which is integrally connected to the discussion on nation building, is possible without reference to the texture of politics of the concerned nation, civilisational similarities notwithstanding. Although the region consists of seven countries (with Afghanistan eight), the overall impact of Indic culture pervades the region which the interventions of other such great traditions, most notably those of Islam and Christianity, did influence but could not supplant. On the contrary, they were themselves influenced by Hindu social formations. This is evident from the fact that the Hindu caste system did not spare these traditions, which were known to be egalitarian in most other places to which they had travelled. Moreover, South Asian Islam developed its own variety of caste system; the Muslim OBCs (other backward classes), corresponding to the so-called backward castes within the Hindu fold, have even been granted constitutional recognition. The same is true of the Dalit Christians, corresponding to the Scheduled Castes, the erstwhile 'untouchable' castes amongst the Hindus, though their demand for constitutional recognition has not yet been granted. In western countries most of the restaurants run by Bangladeshis or Pakistanis advertise their menu as 'Indian'.

The Wider Context   201

Keeping these broad realities in mind, our study suggests that the nature of the state matters the most in the way the politics of law is played out in each country. From this perspective, South Asia can broadly be divided into three segments—the first consisting of India, Sri Lanka and lately Nepal, all democratic states giving scope for discourse on minority legal rights, as well as, as in the case of India in particular, on the viability of introducing a uniform civil code; the second consisting of Bangladesh and Pakistan, where politics has an Islamic thrust with little interest shown in reforms of minority personal laws, with the notable exception of an intellectual fringe asking for a uniform family code; and the third consisting of Bhutan and Maldives, both of which are undemocratic in one way or the other, resulting in some kind of majoritarian notion of law with a total indifference to minority legal rights even in theory.

The complexity of the relationship between the state, both democratic or otherwise, on the one hand and personal law on the other hinges upon the issue of citizenship. Theoretically there cannot be two opinions, that on the assertion in a modern state, all citizens are expected to enjoy equal rights and privileges and must be covered by the same criminal and civil laws. The Indian Penal Code or the penal codes of all the South Asian countries, which are by and large the legacies of the British colonial domination of the region, are universally applicable to all citizens irrespective of their religion, caste or social status. In the sphere of civil law, however, variations occur. Also, even when a uniform civil code is available, it has not necessarily attracted the masses. For example, Indians have the option across the board to marry under the provisions of the Special Marriage Act of 1954. But not many Indian citizens have opted for marriage under this Act. All Indian communities are seemingly too traditional to substitute their conventional/religious ceremonies by the secular ones. Seldom do they bother to get their marriages registered under this act unless they want to travel abroad and the host country insists on a marriage certificate before issuing a visa. The recent Supreme Court directive too, which makes registration of marriages mandatory, may have limited efficacy given India's mass illiteracy and its rural base. Particular difficulty would arise in respect of the majority Hindu community, which, unlike other communities, has no system of registration at all, as Hindu marriages are not contractual but sacramental. In a similar vein, though Nepal and Bhutan have uniform civil codes or justice systems, the minorities, in most cases, prefer to avoid taking their family disputes to the state-run judicial system, because of the majoritarian tenor of politics.

202 *The Politics of Personal Law in South Asia*

South Asia Abroad

The South Asian social reality is not confined to South Asia; it has migrated beyond the region, together with its settlers abroad. In the United Kingdom, for example, with the growing number of Bangladeshis, Indians, Pakistanis, and Sri Lankans, together known as Asians, and their increasing ethnic assertions, the centrality of British law is under pressure and there are evidences of the latter making compromises. Sebastian M. Poulter's 1986 study entitled *English Law and Ethnic Minority Customs* for the first time highlighted this emerging plurality in the British legal system. Certain divorce procedures that have been added to British legal practice in respect of Asians seem to be equivalent of divorce by mutual consent under Section 13–B of the Hindu Marriage Act, 1955 (as amended in 1976) and Section 28 of the Special Marriage Act, 1954. Werner Menski, who wrote a review essay around the book, mentioned the interesting practice of appropriation of the British law by the Hindu marriage custom. From his fieldwork he found that the registration ceremony of English law was cleverly built into the customary 'Asian' patterns of marriage solemnisation. In the eyes of the ' Asian' spouses and their families, the registration ceremonies were no more than just engagement ceremonies. Even after the registration of marriage which declares the couple as lawful husband and wife as per the British law, the rights of the spouses as husband and wife, such as the sexual relationship, are kept in abeyance till they undergo the religious and customary wedding ritual. Till then, the 'wife' is supposed to stay with her parents, and the 'husband' is denied his conjugal access. Menski humorously concluded: 'The day of the "Asian" wedding is later remembered as the wedding day, the now-famous videos are shot then, while the registered marriage tends to be a rather dry and almost unimportant procedure that can be dealt with in a lunchbreak' (Menski 2001: 364). (Parenthetically, it may, however, be mentioned that everywhere in the western world practising Christians or Jews regard the religious ceremony as the real marriage, although for legal purposes they too will consider the date of the civil marriage as the operative date. From the perspective of the British legal system, which draws certain lines between state law and the custom, the simultaneous systems of marriage through customary practice and civil law may look weird but it is not so in South Asia and many of the countries of the world.)

The institution of arranged marriage, the most popular system of organising marriages in South Asia, has also influenced British legal ingenuity. The question is whether to respect this cultural tradition or

The Wider Context 203

to uphold the right of a bride or bridegroom to marry only according to her or his own wish. In the *Kaur v. Singh* case (1981), Singh, the husband, pleaded that his marriage be annulled because it was against his consent. But the court of appeal not only rejected his petition on the grounds that the evidence of pressure fell short of the threat to his 'life, limb or liberty' but it also made explicit reference to the institution of arranged marriages in Asiatic societies. But the same judge took a different position on a similar case only two years later. In the *Hirani v. Hirani* case, Ormrod L.J upheld the right of consent in favour of the would-be bride and thought this to be a ' classic case of a young girl, wholly dependent on her parents, being forced into marriage with a man she has never seen in order to prevent her (reasonably from her parents' point of view) continuing in association with a Muslim which they would regard with abhorrence' (Bainham 1995: 242).

Even in the United States, there is a tendency of late to give space to community customs in respect of marriage and divorce. Ordinarily, religious marriages have no legal sanctity in America. As such, a Hindu, Muslim, Buddhist or Christian of South Asian origin, whether or not a national of the United States, must have a civil marriage for it to be legally valid. But it is increasingly entering into the legal discourse whether it may be advisable to follow the Jewish institution of Beth Din in respect of Muslim system of mehr. Beth Din, which has operated for over a hundred years in the United States, is the Rabbanic court that hears and resolves cases involving Jewish law. It gives *gittin* (Jewish divorce), certificates of *geirut* (conversion), and *teudot ravakut* (certificates attesting to the status of the Jewish person), which are accepted by the Israeli Rabbinate, and are also internationally recognised. The approach of the judiciary of New York state, in contrast with that of California, is accommodative in respect of certain Muslim customs. Without fundamentally bending the rules, it is open to the idea that mehr as a prenuptial agreement could itself be seen as a contract in some sort of civil legal sense and as such can form an evidence in cases such as divorce. But before such an idea receives legal sanctity, three conditions must be fulfilled. First, Muslim couples must draft prenuptial agreements meeting all the requirements of a legally valid and binding contract. Second, the respective state legislatures must cooperate in re-examining public policy goals, specifically in the light of the *mehr* agreements. Third, courts must agree to adjudicate these agreements as contracts, irrespective of the religious context (Qaisi 2000–2001: 80–81).

But in both the above cases, that is, the Hindu marriages in England and the growing legal relevance of mehr in respect of Muslims in

204 The Politics of Personal Law in South Asia

America, what ultimately holds good is the supremacy of the national law, and not that of community custom. In the case of the religious marriage following the registration of marriage that Menski has talked about, the fact remains that, in the eyes of the law, say, when a divorce suit, is lodged in the court, the valid marriage is dated from the time of the registration and not from the date on which the community feast was organised or the religious rites were performed or the marriage was actually consummated. The community cannot dispute this factuality and that makes all the difference in the eyes of law. The same fact of the matter can be noticed in the context of mehr as a contract. In the eyes of American law, it may be treated as a useful Islamic custom but in the ultimate analysis it must fulfil all the requirements of a legally enforceable contract within the structure of the American legal system.

Legal Plurality in the Muslim World

Whatever be the reality in western democracies, customary laws have validity almost everywhere else in the world. Even in some Arab countries, which are theoretically expected to subscribe to and promote legal centralism based on Islamic *Shari'ah*, there are evidences of legal pluralism—laws that are beyond the pale of the state law. In their edited volume *Legal Pluralism in the Arab World*, Baudouin Dupret, Maurtis Berger and Laila al-Zwaini have shown, through case studies drawn from Egypt, Morocco and Palestine, that in the dispensation of law the structure is pluralistic (Goldberg 2000–2001: 447–49). If so, the Muslim leadership in India has a point, though through a convoluted logic: If it is not possible to introduce legal centralism even in *darul Islam* (the abode of Islam) how could it be possible to do it in India, which is *darul aman* (a specially coined word to suit the Indian situation, meaning 'state of peace', which is in contrast with *darul harb* meaning the 'state of war'). But to look at it from another angle, if there is legal pluralism in the Islamic world then it proves that *Shari'ah* itself is pluralistic and, as such, reforming Muslim law in India cannot be against Islam. Does the problematic as to which should get precedence: Islam or culture, have any relevance to our understanding of the situation in this regard?

On the one hand it is argued that, doctrinally speaking, whenever there is a conflict between Islam or culture, the former must get precedence because while the Qur'an, the ultimate source of everything Muslim, is the revealed word of God dictated to the illiterate Prophet Muhammad through the archangel Gabriel, culture is merely a human fabrication. As such, a Muslim is bound by every letter and phrase of the Qur'an. Cultural values, therefore, can be rejected because they are not divine. On the other hand, it has also been argued that one does not need to reject all cultural values; a person who rejects some of them does not cease to be part of that culture. The very fact that different Muslim societies have different Islamic laws shows that this is so because of cultural diversities. Stretching the logic further, it may be said that the Anglo-Muhammedan law is yet another school of Islamic jurisprudence, for it is based on case law as it evolved during the colonial period and as such is an amalgamation of religion and culture. But Muslims in general would agree that when a conflict pertaining to a legal situation between Islam and culture is to be resolved in favour of one or the other, it is Islam that gets preference. The scholarly articulation of the position goes this way: 'Cultural assumptions and customs have often been introduced legitimately into the Islamic legal system. The Qur'an celebrates ethnic, racial and other forms of diversity; and the *hadith* (reported words of the Prophet) emphasises the equality of all human beings. For this reason, jurists have encouraged various cultures to retain their cultural identity by including their customs in their legal systems. *The only condition for such inclusion was that these customs be consistent with the basic tenets of Islam itself. In case of inconsistency, the cultural customs must be rejected*' (Yahia al-Hibri: 2000–2001: 41, emphasis added). If this is so, then the pluralism of the law in the Arab world that we have discussed above has its inherent limits.

The Supremacy of National Law?

Whether in an advanced democracy, as, say, it obtains in the West, or in a Muslim majority *Shari'ah* state in the Arab world, no one would accept anything that is not within its national legal structure. It is an altogether different matter that a particular community may choose to do some value addition to make a legal situation more socially acceptable by following certain customary practices. But what about India and other South Asian states, which do not fall in either category? As a staunch critic of those who champion the cause of a uniform civil code for India, Menski would argue that no personal law, including Muslim, is completely religious in origin, nor is it all that undesirable. Historically in India, there has been a tradition of tolerance of other communities and their customary laws and, as such, the introduction of a uniform civil code would destroy that tradition. He questions: 'Why are scholars arguing that the modern state law needs to dominate people's lives right down to the household level

206   *The Politics of Personal Law in South Asia*

by providing uniform legal regulation? Looking at the matter from this angle, we may realise that calls for uniform legal regulation are in effect underwriting legal centralist aspirations which can easily slide into dictatorial abuses' (Menski 2001: 352). His main point is that the distinction between 'official law' and 'living law' must be recognised and respected. It can be empirically proved that if people at the grass-roots levels are not prepared to accept a so-called 'progressive' law, no amount of codification and standardisation will help. The Kerala Joint Hindu Family System (Abolition) Act, 1975 can be taken as a case in point. The Act was not effective as far as most Kerala villages were concerned *(ibid.*: 373–74).

Law at the Top and Law at the Grass-roots

Viewed from the above perspective, one must refer to yet another aspect of the legal discourse which is probably even more crucial, that is, how law is viewed from the top and how it is absorbed at the user level. I recall that when I visited Bhagalpur in the aftermath of the blinding episode[1] that had shaken the conscience of the nation, I found an altogether different response from all I interacted with. Instead of considering it as an obnoxious crime perpetrated by the Bihar police, everyone seemed to justify the action on the grounds that the criminals got what they deserved and that the law and order situation in the town had visibly improved after the incident. Now a quarter century later, when I am revisiting that memory while writing this book, I appreciate the fact that the law at the top and the law at the bottom are often quite different experiences and this has always been so in India. In the film *Courts and Councils: Dispute Settlement in India,* directed by Ron Hess and distributed by the South Asia Center of the University of Wisconsin, the headman of the Nandiwalla caste expresses his utter contempt for government courts which routinely transform lies into truths and truths into lies and, therefore, he has no need for them. Lariviere underlines this dysjunction between the law at the top and the local law, as an ever-continuing phenomenon in Indian history, commenting: 'What Chief J ustice Bhagwati said the law was and what the police in Bhagalpur say the law is can be very different matters' (Lariviere 2005: 469–70).

The reality being so, it may be argued that even if all personal and customary laws in India are replaced by one uniform civil code, one is not sure how effective that would be in terms of people taking recourse to the legal system, which is not only cost intensive and time consuming but also not necessarily justice producing. In India, as such, two

The Wider Context 207

parallel legal systems operate—one is the state legal system (SLS) and the other the non-state legal system (NSLS). The latter is often more functional. Upendra Baxi has convincingly argued that in rural India, this system is more commonly in operation. The same is the case in the entire South Asia, India only providing the best example. There are only 183 lawyers per one million people in India as against 1,595 in the United States, 947 in New Z ealand, 769 in Canada, 638 in Australia and 507 in the United Kingdom. Some areas in India have no lawyers at all while the distribution of lawyers in general reveals striking disparities (Baxi 1982: 344–45; see also Appends 12).

The controversy over the *Shari'ah* courts in India that surfaced in 2005 can be seen from the above perspective as well as from the perspective of Vasudha Dhagamwar, who argues that personal laws have intruded into the criminal justice system of the country, which we have discussed above (see pp. 123–24). In June 2005, a controversy surfaced over the alleged sexual assault on Imrana Bibi and the fatwa ordering her to split with her husband. Imrana was allegedly raped by her sixty-year old father-in-law, Ali Mohammad, in Muzaffarabad in UP. The Deoband-based seminary Dar-ul-Uloom decreed that she could not live with her husband any more because the latter had become a sort of son to her. Against this fatwa, a practising Supreme Court advocate, Vishwa Lochan Madan, filed a PIL in the Supreme Court seeking to restrain the *nizam-e-qaza* (the so-called parallel judiciary) from adjudicating in civil and criminal matters involving Muslims, on the grounds that the 'religious judiciary' could not perform a 'sovereign function' in a democracy. To this the Supreme Court wanted to know from the central government, the governments of Assam, Delhi, Haryana, Madhya Pradesh, Rajasthan, Uttar Pradesh and West Bengal, and the All India Muslim Personal Law Board whether the *Shari'ah* courts were interfering with the justice system of the country.

In its response, the law ministry of the government clarified that no parallel judicial system existed in the country but, indeed, the *Shari'ah* courts played the necessary role in family matters where Muslim personal was to be applicable. Evidently, what the government meant was the NSLS that Baxi talked of. Zafaryab Jilani of the AIMPLB, also a legal expert, said that the *Shari'ah* law was used in accordance with the Shariat Application Act of 1937 but the verdict of the *qazi* courts could always be challenged in the civil courts. According to him, almost 99 per cent of judgments delivered by the oldest *Shari'ah* courts in Bihar and Orissa were upheld by the civil courts when challenged. Some of the letters to the editor clarified that the *fatwa* of the

208   *The Politics of Personal Law in South Asia*

Deoband seminary was only selectively interpreted to give it a communal colour (*Telegraph*, 29 August 2005). The essential point is that these *Shari'ah* courts reduce the burden on the overloaded judiciary, and if every case had to reach the formal judiciary, the system would collapse in no time.

Society in India is still highly stratified, particularly at the village level. As such, a caste and community-based justice system is more a norm than an exception. Such systems can operate at the village level, the inter-village level or beyond. Baxi has identified four main types of non-state legal systems (NSLS) in India, namely, caste-based, community-based, tribe-based and reformative. Reformative NSLS are like the lok adalats (people's courts), which are ideologically oriented, meant to generate *lokshakti* (people's power) for socioeconomic transformation. Baxi explains that the liberal democrats who have been urging for political pluralism as their fighting faith tend to forget their own message when they deal with the law. The state, which effectively means the bureaucracy and the armed forces, is only one of the many social formations, howsoever powerful and dominating it may be. As such, the state needs a technique of social ordering and social control as much as the non-state groups do. 'I do not deny', writes Baxi, 'the importance for the liberal political thought of using the state as their " punching bag"; nor do I deny (who can?) the increasing power of state over all other groupings. But the latter exist; nay, sometimes they are even resilient. To refuse to conceptualize their regulatory systems as law (in any significant usage of that term) is to commit a kind of genocide by definition. If not that, at least, it is a goodbye to pluralism' (Baxi 1982: 330–31).

There are many takers of Baxi's logic in India, with Muslims probably in the forefront. Almost all Muslim writers discussing the subject of Muslim personal law find no fault with the law as enshrined in the Q ur'an and hence no reason to bring changes in it, leave alone having a uniform civil code, which is seen as an extension of the Hindu Code that does not necessarily have a proven record of being more egalitarian. A sample survey conducted in the early 2000s of 1,015 Muslim respondents (722 women and 293 men) from Ajmer, Aligarh, and Delhi, belonging to different socio-economic classes in both urban and rural areas, revealed that 81.9 per cent women and 90.4 per cent men felt that Muslim personal law was gender just. They felt that no change in the system was needed; what was needed was its proper implementation (Tabassum 2003: 9, 75, 106–9).

The argument that can be advanced in support of the Muslim sentiment for *Shari'ah* is that Islam is the first legal system to liberate women

The Wider Context 209

from the concept of coverture and recognise the female right to property at the time of marriage. It was introduced, as early as the seventh century, a system of marriage that was based on mutual consent. It is contractual and, therefore, dissoluble, unlike the Hindu sacramental marriages prior to the passage of the Hindu Code bills. After a thousand years of the Islamic innovation of contractual marriage, the idea spread to Europe and from there to European colonies, including India. The contractual aspect of marriage facilitated women specifying their condition in the *nikahnama* (marriage contract) or entering into pre-marriage agreements (*kabin nama*) regarding their personal property, access to their husband's income and property, location of the matrimonial home, housekeeping allowance, and several other mundane rights and duties of married life (Agnes 2002).

The Global Connection

Since our discussion on personal law has close connection with such issues as religious and ethnic identities, it is unavoidable to view the problematic in its global context as well. In the present globalised world, where even a small political development has its international linkage, the question of personal law is too important an issue to remain unaffected by global developments. The phenomenon of Islamic resurgence across nations on the one hand, and, say, the war in Iraq and Afghanistan on the other, are as much intertwined as India's or Bangladesh's or Pakistan's position on these questions and the majority-minority sectarian relations in these societies. A brief discussion, therefore, on the global scenario, particularly in the context of international terrorism at one end and anti-terror inter-state networking on the other will be in order here.

It is, however, not easy to agree on a particular date or event from where to start the story of the so-called Muslim rage. Still, one can arguably concede that the initial symptoms of Muslim disaffection started manifesting themselves in the early 1970s. It was around this time that the Libyan President Muammar al Qaddafi spread the notion of Islamic radicalism and terrorism worldwide. By the end of the decade, the 440 days of the Iranian hostage crisis of 1978–81 proved that the phenomenon was no longer merely academic. The two-week-long takeover of the Grand Mosque at Mecca by rebellious Islamists in 1979 was yet another flashpoint. Other developments of similar kinds followed in quick succession—the assassination of President Anwar Sadat of Egypt in 1981, the violent attacks against American personnel and installations in Lebanon and Kuwait in the

210 *The Politics of Personal Law in South Asia*

mid-1980s, and the bombing of the World Trade Center in 1993. The events of 9/11 were of course the climax. Samuel Huntington's clash of civilisations seemed to make sense to many.

The heat of Muslim rage was felt in South Asia in no mean measure. We have already noted that the region houses the maximum number of Muslims compared to any other region of the world (see Chapter I). Coinciding with global Islamic assertions, the region witnessed an unprecedented growth of militant separatism in India's Punjab and Kashmir in the late seventies and early eighties. In those states, Pakistan contributed to the creation of a state of insurgency through covert interventions, and thereby waged a low cost low intensity undeclared war against India through a band of terrorists trained by its intelligence agency, the Inter Services Intelligence (ISI). According to India's intelligence sources, there were about 39,000 Pakistan-sponsored terrorist incidents in J&K between 1988 and 1998, compared to only 5,000 in the rest of the world. Increasingly, terrorism, particularly in the Kashmir valley, got internationalised a fact evident from the sophistication of the operations, the undrying source of their funding and the actual arrest of terrorists belonging to other nationalities. Even a few Chechen rebels were killed in encounters. The highest watermark of the Muslim terrorist threat was the attack on Indian Parliament House on 13 December 2001, barely three months after 9/11.

It is difficult to authentically gauge the minds of South Asian Muslims, in the absence of any scientifically conducted regional survey. Still, going by what appeared in the local press and what one could see and feel, it appeared that, in general, Muslims were unhappy with the way the United States conducted its foreign policy. By and large, they were convinced that the US had found a *bête noire* in Muslims after the end of the Cold War. They seemed to believe that the improved relationship between the US and the Hindutva-oriented Vajpayee government of India was part of a global conspiracy against the Muslims. In the Muslim majority states of Bangladesh and Pakistan, the governments' pro-US stance became an anathema for the militant Islamic fringe, making it an extremely difficult tightrope exercise for the ruling elites in those countries to ensure their political survival. At the core of this general Muslim distrust was their conviction that the US policy towards the Muslims, read Arabs in particular, was dictated by its commitment to the security and welfare of Israel at the cost of the Arabs, most notably the Palestinians. Another reason for their anti-Americanism was that the US was least concerned with the welfare of the Muslim masses; its policy was

The Wider Context 211

meant to pamper dictators who had no mass base. In this connection, they referred to what happened to the election results in Algeria or Turkey. There, legitimately elected leaders were prevented from forming governments just because they belonged to some Islamic political parties.

To establish a connection between this broad global picture and the subject of this book, it is important to briefly examine the social forces that contributed to the Islamic resurgence of sorts. Discussing the Iranian revolution and the subsequent hostage crisis, some scholars have argued that Islamic revivalism in general drew its basic strength from the fact that modernisation had created cleavages in essentially traditional societies. Karl Deutsch's theory, for example, is that if the rate of social mobilisation did not exceed the rate of assimilation, the prevailing culture would survive and would actually be strengthened. But if the rate of mobilisation exceeded the rate of assimilation, the prevailing culture would be overwhelmed by the rapid intrusion and be replaced by the new culture. In the case of Iran there was an unprecedented spurt of modernisation from the 1950s onwards. The process of urbanisation and the process of modernisation of the army, which the Pahelvis introduced, created a cleavage with the religious elite, which had traditional links with the society (Yapp 1980: 189). During the eighties, when more cases of Islamic extremism were reported, another school of thought emerged, which argued that where there was no democratic outlet, democratic forces took recourse to religion. America was criticised for its shortsighted understanding in this regard. One commentator wrote that the way the US reacted to the anti-democratic coup in Algeria tended to show that it preferred a police state to an Islamic democracy. It was further argued that, more often than not, the Islamic movements had a domestic agenda and were opposed to dictatorial regimes on their own soils. Their anti-Americanism essentially sprang from the linkages these regimes had with the US (Fuller 2002; Wright 1992: 137–42).

In the aftermath of 9/11 the America-based Pakistani social anthropologist Akbar Ahmed, more or less on the lines of Karl Deutsch, argued that probably Muhammad Ibn Khaldun's concept of *asabiyya* could explain contemporary Muslim rage. Ahmed described it in the context of what was happening to traditional societies, particularly Muslim, in the age of globalisation. *Asabiyya* essentially meant 'group loyalty', 'social cohesion', or ' social solidarity'. The changing social order across the Muslim world had led to a social breakdown, resulting in a sense of loss of honor and dignity. 'Rapid global

212 *The Politics of Personal Law in South Asia*

changes are shaking the structures of traditional societies. Groups are forced to dislocate or live with or by other groups. In the process of dislocation they have little patience with the problems of others. They develop intolerance and express it through anger. No society is immune. Even those societies that economists call "developed" fall back to notions of honor and revenge in times of crisis' (Ahmed 2003: 13–15). Ahmed seems to be certain that the traditional concept of *asabiyya* will not be able to arrest the process of decay because the technological changes are too rapid. He writes: 'Tribal and rural groups can no longer provide *asabiyya;* urban areas in any case are inimical to it. The result is loss of vigor and cohesion. Muslims everywhere are voicing their alarm at the breakdown of society. They know that something is going fundamentally wrong but are not sure why' (*ibid*.: 79). In Muslim societies *asabiyya* was breaking down because of

> massive urbanization, dramatic demographic changes, a population explosion, large-scale migrations to the West, the gap between rich and poor (which is growing ominously), the widespread corruption and mismanagement of rulers, the rampant materialism coupled with the low premium on education, the crisis of identity, and, perhaps most significantly, new and often alien ideas and images, at once seductive and repellent, and instantly communicated from the West, ideas and images which challenge the traditional values and customs. This process of breakdown is taking place at a time when a large percentage of the population in the Muslim world is young, dangerously illiterate, mostly jobless, and therefore easily mobilized for radical change. The consequence is the difficulty of creating a society based on justice, knowledge, and compassion.
>
> —(Ahmed 2003: 81)

It is against this theoretical backdrop that one may analyse the popular Muslim outbursts against America. In October 1998, at a seminar in the University of Colorado, one of the most respected liberal scholars of Pakistan, the late Eqbal Ahmad, virtually justified terrorism against America on the grounds that it was promoting dictatorships in many Muslim countries. He wrote: 'In 1990 the US goes into Saudi Arabia with forces. Saudi Arabia is the holy place of Muslims, Makkah and Madinah. There had never been foreign troops there. In 1990, during the Gulf War they went in, in the name of helping Saudi Arabia defeat Saddam Hussaln. Usama bin Laden remained

The Wider Context 213

quiet. Saddam was defeated, but the American troops stayed on in the land of the Kaaba. Foreign troops' (Ahmad 2001).

During the last quarter century there has been an ascendancy of the religious right in many parts of the world; almost all religions have been victim to this process. Islam in particular has shown an additional, globally networked, tendency to militancy because of several factors. First, whenever anyone makes any suggestion in respect of Qur'anic law, it is deemed an intrusion into the religion and, since Muslim clerics have a structural communication with the masses, the news spreads. What is ignored is that Islam too, as any other religion, needs to adapt itself to changing circumstances, a point that was highlighted by no less than the president of Iran, Ali Akbar Hashemi Rafsanjani. He said:

> The important point here is that the Islam which developed 1,400 years ago on the Arabian peninsula—in a settlement where the people were fundamentally nomads—was a legal code specific to that society. And even that code was promulgated slowly over a period of seven or eight years.... Islam ... now desires to become the fulcrum of (modern) social administration and (our) nation wants to use this fulcrum (as a weapon) to wage war on the entire imperialist world, testing its mettle by those means. Unique circumstances have arisen during course of time. How can Islam (without adaptation) cover all these contingencies?
> —(Quoted by Noorani 2001: 72)

Second, according to Islamic theory there is no territorial nation state. The concept is that of an Islamic *umma*. As such, any event anywhere affecting the interests of Muslims finds reverberations in the entire Muslim world. It clashes with the concept of the modern state system based on territorial sovereignty. Third, the major portion of the global oil reserve is in the hands of the Muslim states. This tends to make them feel that they should be the masters of the world. But in reality they find themselves the underdogs of western nations. They refuse to understand that they lack the necessary finances and technological knowhow to extract the resource from the earth. Fourth, in their historical understanding of the evolution of Islam they think that in the present phase their real challenge comes from Judaism. Israel as the representative of Judaism is therefore their *bête noire*. Since America stands by Israel, America too becomes their enemy. Fifth, since many Muslim countries are located in the Arab world, traditional tribal values determine their behavioural patterns. According to

214   The Politics of Personal Law in South Asia

those values, life has little meaning without faith and honour—faith in religion, faith in friendship, and so on. According to the same value system, once a friend always a friend. It is for this reason that they do not understand why the same America that promoted *jehadi* resistance against Soviet intervention in Afghanistan could now wage a war against *jehad*. They do not understand that *jehad* for America was a means to an end and not an end in itself.

All the points made above are valid for South Asian Muslims too, for there is an inherent concept of *umma*. In the intra-Islamic sphere *umma* has no meaning but, when it comes to dealing with non--Muslims, it assumes significance. But for this, it is difficult to explain this sudden spurt of sympathy and support for Usama bin Laden and the Taliban, and lately Saddam Hussain, about whom ordinary South Asian Muslims knew little. Thanks to the electronic media, Usama bin Laden has become a household name in the region. Since he mouths pro-Islamic slogans laced with highly charged anti-American sentiments, there is reason for many Muslims to believe that America is the enemy of Islam. Because America represents certain values that may be capsuled as Americanism, their ire is against Americanism as an ideology. At the core of the ideology is the individual and not groups of individuals.[2] Islam, however, espouses the opposite where individual interests are subordinated to group interests. Individual interests translated into applied politics connote western-style democracy— freedom of opinion, gender justice, separation of religion and state, free market and plurality. No wonder the Islamic fundamentalists have targeted the dynamo behind these values, that is, free enterprise based on the theory of the 'pursuit of happiness'. In America, it is the World Trade Center. In rest of the world, including South Asia, it is Coca Cola, Pepsi, McDonalds, KFC, and so on.

In short, Muslims in general have become distrustful of the United States and all those who side with it. Although the governments in most Muslim majority countries have remained pro-US for their own survival, they continue to placate conservative sentiments in their respective countries so as not ruffle bruised sentiments. In this milieu it is not conceivable that the governments, say, in Bangladesh or Pakistan, would listen sympathetically to women's activists to usher in reforms in the *Shari'ah*. In the case of democratic states with Muslim minority populations such as India, Sri Lanka or Nepal, the governments there are extra cautious about meddling with Muslim personal law lest such moves unnecessarily provoke anti-government reactions. In the given political climate, discretion seems to be the better part of valour for regimes across the region.

The Proactive Role of the State

From the above discussion it is possible to argue in favour of legal pluralism, and also to suggest that, in spite of codification and reforms in personal laws, social pressures would sometimes negate the advances achieved in the realm of family law. Still, it should not be anybody's case that the state does not have any proactive role to play. It has often been seen that the state takes a decision on some enlightened premise and public opinion in due course approves that decision. The codification of Hindu law is a case in point. Left to society, little would move, and even less so in a stratified and feudalistic society, which is basically traditionalistic, opposed to any change and innovation. Even the invention of railways and their appearance in rural England in the nineteenth century was not welcomed, and led to protests from English farmers. They feared that the roar of the steam engines would terrify cows which would cease yielding milk. Not only were such fears utterly unfounded, today's Britain boasts of the railways as part of its heritage, with ninety-one steam railways and museums in England and thirty-six elsewhere (Bhagwati 2004: 112). Moreover, it is not the case that the state gets some vicarious pleasure in interfering in the personal affairs of communities. Quite often it is the state that is called upon to respond to demands of disgruntled elements within communities who are unhappy with the way their affairs are managed by the community elders through community norms. In such situations, the state cannot shirk its responsibility to intervene and to ensure justice to the aggrieved party. Moreover, it is also not true that the state alone can behave in a highhanded fashion; community leaders can be even more oppressive. The way the Mumbai-based social activist and scholar Asghar Ali Engineer is treated by his Bohra community patriarch (Syedna) is a case in point. Engineer has been socially ostracised to such an extent that even his own sisters are reluctant to meet him in public, fearing that they too might be excommunicated.

In India's journey towards the distant goal of a uniform civil code, can the Special Marriage Act of 1954 and the Hindu Code of 1955–56 be considered the first steps? If so, was the Muslim Women (Protection of Rights on Divorce) Act, 1986 the second step? Was the Parsi Marriage and Divorce (Amendment) Act, 1988, which was on the pattern of the Hindu Marriage Act of 1955, yet another step? And similarly, is the current exercise to codify the tribal laws of the Northeast also another step forward? That is what some scholars would argue. Their logic is that, it is only after one has a complete picture of the standardised versions of personal and customary laws

216 *The Politics of Personal Law in South Asia*

of different communities that one would be in a position to identify the commonalities and good points in them, making the task of blending these laws into a uniform code simpler. This was exactly what L. K. Advani had argued to dodge the criticism of his penchant for a uniform civil code. But there is a serious flaw in this logic. These codifications may not at all contribute to any integrative tendency; on the contrary, they may rigidify ethnic identities contributing to the celebration of India's plurality. Insofar as feasibility is concerned, if India has achieved only this much after half-a-century, it will probably take many decades to first complete the codification of all personal and customary laws and then blend them into a uniform code. Evidently, as we have discussed in the previous chapters, everything will depend upon the political climate, where the variable that would matter the most is the majority-minority equation.

The communal question in India has interesting, and often conflicting, dimensions. Although it is not true that minorities, Muslims in particular, are a pampered lot in India, a large number of Hindus think that way. In this misplaced majority notion, the personal law of Muslims figures prominently, as if the system of allowing more than one wife is a privilege that Hindus are deprived of. Muslims, too, give too much importance to their personal law, as if it alone can ensure the retention of their communal identity. Since, at the core of both premises is the sense of one's religious identity, Muslims tend to assert theirs more vocally and the Hindu-dominated state hesitates to question the premise directly and forcefully. Often it succumbs to minority pressure lest it be accused of negating social pluralism. There is evidence of religion taking precedence over the nation. Operation Blue Star, for example, was seen purely as an assault on the Sikh religion totally ignoring the fact that the pro-Khalistan anti-Indian militants had taken shelter in the Golden Temple in Amritsar and there was hardly any way other than to flush them out by using military force. It might have been an error of judgement on the part of the Indira Gandhi administration to use such massive fire power but it was certainly not her intention to denigrate Sikhism. In the aftermath of Operation Blue Star, there was revolt in some Sikh battalions and many Sikh soldiers deserted the army. Though desertion is unpardonable according to military traditions, many deserters were reinstated in the military or paramilitary forces, because the controversy had religious overtones. No such mercy was shown to the *jawans* of the Central Reserve Police Force (CRPF) revolting in 1978 in Bokaro. They were all sentenced to life (Dhagamwar 1989: 65).[3]

Revisiting the Women's Question

Considering the fact that the state has a proactive role to perform in bringing in reforms in personal laws, there is no escape from conceding that it would effectively mean improving the legal status of women across communities. In the first chapter, we discussed the 'centrality of women's rights'. In this section we will revisit the issue from the perspective of women's empowerment, for, after all, if the legal status of women has to be bettered it has to be bargained off politically *vis-à-vis* male dominance.

The discourse of women's political empowerment is at various stages of its evolution in South Asia. For obvious reasons, India is at the forefront of the movement, strangely, not followed by Sri Lanka, it is the only other South Asian country with an uninterrupted record of democracy. That second slot is occupied, once again strangely, by Pakistan, followed by Bangladesh. Nepal figures next on the list, while the discourse is virtually non-existent in Bhutan and Maldives, maybe because their women are not all that oppressed.

In India, which means Pakistan and Bangladesh put together till 1947, the articulation of political demands by women has a long history, going back to the nationalist movement. It was as early as in 1917 that a delegation of Indian women put up before the Secretary of State Edwin Montagu their demand for franchise. The result was the right to vote granted, in the 1920s, to at least propertied women. Still, women were not allowed participation in the legislatures, a right that was granted in 1930 in response to constant lobbying by the Women's Indian Association. The first woman to be nominated to the legislature was Muthulakshmi Reddi (Mumtaz 2005: 7).

In the Round Table Conference held in 1930, Begum Jahanara Shah Nawaz and Radhabai Subbarayan, the two active members of women's organisations who were nominated to the conference, pleaded in favour of 5 per cent reservation for women in the legislatures. The idea, however, was not well taken by other activists, who denounced this sort of favour-seeking. They were in favour of universal adult suffrage through which women, they argued, would automatically carve out their political niche. Though the idea of universal adult franchise gradually emerged as a consensus demand, other controversies, such as the representation of women on a communal basis and the modality of election, direct or indirect, to the federal assembly, tended to overshadow the issue of women's political participation. The Government of India Act of 1935, which broadened the franchise base, provided for formal induction of women in the political process, both in the reserved

218 *The Politics of Personal Law in South Asia*

and general seats. The provincial elections that were held under the act returned fifty-six women against 1,500 seats—forty-one from reserved constituencies, ten from general constituencies and five nominated. Besides, thirty women were elected to the central assembly, including Begum Jahanara Shah Nawaz. In the 1940s when the Pakistan movement picked up momentum, there was large scale political participation of women, though it was mostly on communal lines (*ibid.*: 8).

In the constituent assemblies of India and Pakistan, the women's issue was discussed in divergent voices. While in India the idea of reserved seats or special concessions for women found no favour with the members, in Pakistan the women members pushed for reservation of seats for women. As a result, the constitution of Pakistan (1956) provided for 3 per cent reserved seats for women in the national and provincial legislatures to be directly elected by special women's constituencies (Mumtaz 2005: 10). One must not, however, read too much into the success of the women's movement in Pakistan in the 1950s. The constitution of 1956 was supplanted by General Ayub Khan, who assumed dictatorial powers, even his family law reforms of 1961 indicated his political compulsion to placate conservative forces, a subject that we have examined in the previous chapter. It may be noted here that he was happy (one does not know whether he engineered it himself) that the ulema had issued *fatwas* against women seeking the office of head of state, given the fact that Fatima Jinnah had posed a serious challenge to his power by becoming a candidate in the presidential election of 1966 (*ibid.*: 9).

The issue of the political empowerment of women through reserved seats was prominent debate in large parts of South Asia. Although the Committee on the Status of Women in India (1975) rejected the idea of reserved seats, activist-scholars like Vina Mazumdar and Lotika Sarkar felt strongly that reservation was a necessary affirmative action for women. The year 1980 was the landmark year in the history of women's empowerment, for in that year the women's lobby was able to force the Indian Planning Commission to allocate 30 per cent funds in poverty alleviation schemes with women as specific target-group beneficiaries, a departure from the earlier family-centred approach (Agnihotri 2001). It, however, took many more years before women were granted reserved seats, though this was only at the village and district level local bodies. Through the 73 and 74 amendments to the Indian Constitution (1993) it was provided that the local bodies at those levels should have at least 33 per cent seats reserved for female members, of which one-third must belong to Scheduled Castes and Scheduled Tribes. Since India was primarily a village-based society,

The Wider Context 219

the socio-political impact of the amendments was massive. There are now more than one million women who are functioning in these bodies as members, which is certainly a great experiment in political education, notwithstanding the fact that these members quite often shy away from actively participating in the deliberations, or function just as proxies for their husbands, fathers or brothers. Besides, because of the rigid caste hierarchies in the villages, women members belonging to lower castes or SC categories are often not allowed to wield any power. A fact-finding team of the National Campaign for Dalit Human Rights (NCDHR) found that even a *sarpanch* belonging to the SC community was not allowed to unfurl the national flag on Independence Day (*The Hindu*, 15 September 2006).

Like India, Bangladesh and Pakistan too, since 1997 and 2000 respectively, have introduced the system of 33 per cent reservation for women in local bodies. In Nepal every village has nine five-member wards with one seat reserved for a woman. In Sri Lanka, Bhutan and the Maldives there is no structured female representation in political institutions though this may be due to the fact that there is no noticeable gender-based discrimination in any of these societies, at least in Bhutan and the Maldives. Wherever there is reservation for women in local bodies, the overall experience of South Asia is that male domination is still pronounced, though reservation does help expose women to public life.

Women's participation in local bodies, however, means that while it promotes women's role in politics it does not facilitate their contributing to the legislative process, which is all that matters in enhancing their legal rights. That is possible only when women's representation becomes sizable in the national legislative organs, to start with by statutory reserved seats, given the otherwise male dominated social structure of South Asia. Table 6.1 provides a comparative picture of women's representation in the parliaments of South Asian states. Strangely, Pakistan has a better record than all others, though its democratic record has been dismal. Women's representation in the National Assembly of Pakistan had a checkered history, with all kinds of ups and downs till 2000, when it was raised to sixty, that is, 17.5 per cent. Significantly, even the religious parties, which were otherwise opposed to women's representation, did not forego their share and nominated women relatives of their leaders (Mumtaz 2005: 15). However, as is the case in India, women's rights activists have not given up their demand for 33 per cent reservation.

It is important to underline that while it has been a relatively smooth affair to reserve 33 per cent seats in the local bodies in India, it has

220 *The Politics of Personal Law in South Asia*

Table 6.1 Women's Representation in the Lower House of Parliament in South Asia, 1999 and 2004

Country	% Representation in 1999	% Representation in 2004
India	8.8	8.84
Pakistan	2.8	21.64
Bangladesh	12.4	2.0*
Nepal	5.4	5.85
Sri Lanka	4.9	4.44
Bhutan	2.0	9.33
Maldives	6.3	6.0

Source: Mumtaz 2005: 1–2.
* It may be noted that Bangladesh has a provision of nominating female members to parliament after every general election, in proportion to the parties' strength in the house. Earlier 30 female members were to be nominated, that is, 300 + 30 = 330. Following the 14th Amendment to the Constitution in 2004 it has been raised to 45, that is, 300 + 45 = 345. For details, see Islam 2005.

proved to be an extremely complex exercise to repeat the performance for the Parliament and state assemblies. Ever since the mid-1990s, several efforts have been made to put up the Women's Bill for legislation but it has been repeatedly stalled on account of entrenched political opposition from leading parties, barring the leftists. The present UPA government, under the leadership of Manmohan Singh, has promised to table the bill in the budget session in 2007 but it is to be seen how it ultimately fares on the floor of the house. The main controversy hinges on the envisaged sub-quotas in addition to SC and ST women so as to include the OBCs and Muslims as well. Since there is no constitutional provision for these latter categories to get quotas in the Parliament and state assemblies, the political debate is hlghly combustible.

It is evident from the above discussion that the women of South Asia have a long distance to cover before their journey towards full empowerment is completed. The present record is worse than that of many other developing regions, such as East Asia and Sub-Saharan Africa (*ibid.*: 3). The primary reason behlnd the lack of political power of South Asian women is patriarchy coupled with religion, ethnicity and caste-based politics, all of which are increasingly expanding their turf. Whether it is the Islamists of the Kashmir valley, the Khalistanis of Punjab, the United Liberation Front of Assam (ULFA), or the Bajrangis of North India, women are the chosen category to carry the identity symbol of respective communities. In Tripura, the anti-Bengali tribal militants, while raising their secessionist demands, aggressively oppose such Bengali symbols as the *sari* or the *bindi* and

The Wider Context 221

ask their women never to wear them. Both the Hindu fundamentalist groups in India and the Muslim fundamentalist groups in Pakistan actively champion the cause of traditional values, even through their women's wings (Agnihotri 2001; Rashid 2006).

All factors considered, it is unlikely that women in South Asia will garner enough political power or motivation to ask for reforms in the personal laws of respective communities, let alone a uniform civil code. For example, the present National Commission on Status of Women of Pakistan, unlike the earlier commissions, is a standing commission, and has issued reports on several legal issues pertaining to women but, given the political climate of the country, not much is expected of these suggestions. The situation is certainly more promising in India but not beyond a point because there is a tendency with some parties, most notably the BJP, to confuse the issue by simultaneously putting forward a demand for a one-third increase in the membership of the present 543–strong Lok Sabha. The budget session of the Lok Sabha in 2007 will be interesting to watch, for the Women's Bill will be put up for debate. It will be equally interesting to see what happens in Nepal, which is in the process of introducing a republican constitution through an election, in which the leaders of the current democratic movement have promised to reserve one-third of the seats for women.

Notes

1   In 1980, Bhagalpur in Bihar came into the news when it was reported that the police blinded several undertrials by pouring acid into their eyes. The incident became infamous as the 'Bhagalpur blindings' and the acid was euphemistically called *Gangajal* (the holy water of the Ganga). The incident was widely discussed and debated and human rights activist Tapan Bose's documentary on the subject, *An Indian Story,* earned international acclaim. In 2003, a Bollywood movie loosely based on the incident and starring Ajay Devgan was released under the title *Gangajal.*

2   The American census, as also that of France for example, does not record the religious affiliation of its citizens, unlike most countries, including all in South Asia.

3   In the controversy over the Muslim reluctance to sing the national song '*Vande Mataram*', some of my Muslim friends ask why it should be necessary to judge Muslim loyalty to the nation only through such symbolism. Since the song has a Hindu religious overtone it pricks the religious sensitivity of many Muslims, for whom worshipping anybody other than Allah, including one's parents, is sacrilegious. Are not Muslims prepared to sacrifice their lives in the battlefields for the Indian nation in equal measure as their Hindu counterparts or are they not participating in international sports on behalf of India as enthusiastically as others do, they ask.

7 Conclusion

> I have learnt to use the word ' impossible' with the greatest caution.
> —Wernher von Braun, a pioneering space scientist

In his celebrated Marathi play *Uddwasta Dharmashala* (meaning 'the shattered caravanserai', which the playwright renamed *Man in Dark Times* for its English translation), G. P. Deshpande portrays his central character Sridhar Kulkarni as a highly sensitive Left liberal university professor, torn between his beliefs and activism as a playwright and his limitations as a revolutionary. His social upbringing, his deep sense of propriety, and his filial piety, all merge into a sense of uncertainty about things to come, about the ultimate frailty of human effort. Is Kulkarni confused, or is it that he is too sure that life is not mathematics—its algebra can point to 'only a possibility, [and] no more'? As he confesses to his son: 'Ultimately we are liberals. We constantly see the other side of the coin. It takes the passion out of us. Pledges melt away.'

Social science is essentially liberal arts and so should it be studied. Most of our social science questions must, therefore, have 'yes and no' answers. Twenty years ago, at the height of the Shah Bano controversy, when the debate on the uniform civil code was high on India's popular consciousness, my position on the matter was categorical—India must adopt a uniform civil code. Now that I have written this book on the theme from a comparative perspective, and taking into account the experiences of other South Asian countries, I am much less categorical. I am torn between my pro-activism as a policy analyst and my appreciation of the compulsions of realpolitik, between the primacies of individual rights and group rights, between the demands of social stability and the necessity of breaking away from retrograde social practices. Making a clear choice sometimes becomes extremely difficult, as one's ambivalence is inbuilt in the epistemology of social

Conclusion 223

science. That brings into focus the larger issue—should there be only 'relevant' research in social science (as public funding generally requires), or, as Partha Chatterjee tells us, should there be 'irrelevant' research as well (for more serious social theories do sometimes emerge out of uncharted journeys into the realms of imponderables). Afterall, Karl Marx's theory of socialist revolution must have looked 'irrelevant' in the mid-nineteenth century. It took more than six decades for that theory to be applied—the Bolshevik Revolution of Russia in 1917.

Looking at the variety of family law situations obtaining in South Asia, the questions that we posed in the beginning of our study seem largely answered, without, of course, clearly indicating what is good for society, a single civil code or the retention of all personal laws. To put it another way: Does a uniform civil code contribute to nation building or does it tend to obstruct the process? Considering the generally held view that a uniform civil code is the ideal situation, one is confused to note the fact that South Asia presents a scenario where the dictatorial or totalitarian regimes like Bhutan, Maldives and Nepal have chosen it for their peoples, showing scant regard for minority rights, while the remaining four countries, Bangladesh, India, Pakistan and Sri Lanka, two of them being uninterrupted democracies and the other two being on-and-off democracies, have decided to continue with their plural legal systems. As such, no particular pattern seems to emerge. It has also been noticed that the codification of personal and customary laws, which is considered to be the most probable route to follow to attain the goal of a uniform civil code, has actually delayed the process by rigidifying the identities. In short, the crux of the problem remains at square one: What is more important—to uphold group rights or to uphold individual rights? With all the modesty at one's command, let it be tentatively argued that what is needed first in South Asia are reforms in the personal laws of the communities, keeping gender justice as the priority. Religious differences are becoming so sharp that even women's movements sometime feel the heat. Muslim women did not speak about sati; Hindu women treated Gudiya's pleas with silence. By constantly harping on the theme of the uniform civil code, one simply obfuscates the real issues and plays into the hands of both orthodox and retrograde forces within the respective communities, as well as political entrepreneurs who are ever ready to fish in troubled waters.

But the problem is not that simple either. In a recent newspaper article, Tahir Mahmood suggests that the best way to deal with the plurality of Muslim personal law is to codify it by picking up the

224   *The Politics of Personal Law in South Asia*

best elements from all the schools of Islamic jurisprudence so that 'the heaps of age-long misinterpretations and widely prevailing misconcepts' could be weeded out and 'the present distorted view of the law' could be replaced (Mahmood 2006). Should not one go a step further? Why not pick up the best elements from the personal and customary laws of all the communities, prepare a draft UCC under a democratically constituted law commission, and then throw that draft code open for public scrutiny and debate? Then, it can be passed by the Parliament, with modifications as suggested during the debate. Naturally, politics will come into play at each of these stages; inevitably, politics is, and will remain, at the core of the discourse.

But since politics itself has to be the vehicle of change, it is possible, and indeed necessary, to be proactive in policy terms and steer politics into a progressive mode. Nehru's command over the Congress Party was phenomenal and his commitment to Hindu law reforms was also total (though Ambedkar had his misgivings about the latter); still, he had to manipulate contemporary Hindu politics in his favour by splitting the Hindu code bill into four parts before it could be passed, for there was serious conservative Hindu opposition to the original bill. Similarly, General Ayub Khan of Pakistan would not have been able to introduce reforms in Muslim family law in 1961 had he not first played the right kind of politics to establish his pro-Islamic credentials in the eyes of those Islamic forces that mattered politically. The Bangladesh Mahila Parishad is not making any headway in its demand for a uniform family code precisely because it has been unable to garner the support of both major parties and the Islamist forces.

If reforms in Muslim personal law in India are to be effected, it has to be done either by enlisting the support of the Muslim leadership, or else by establishing direct communication with Muslim masses through networking at the grassroots level. Fourteen per cent of the population is Muslim minority—a sizable political force. It becomes necessary to know who controls the buttons of the community mind. Progressive Muslim support for reforms has limited efficacy in terms of influencing the Muslim voting pattern. It works the same way as the responses of Muslim intellectuals, political leaders and ulema to international Islamic terrorism serve in combating the menace. They do refer to the tenets of Islam that speak of religious tolerance and abhor bloodshed but they stop short of making pointed criticisms of militant outfits, leave alone questioning their high profile leaders who too swear in the name of the Qur'an and Allah. As a result, the fire-eating militants command greater appeal with the Muslim masses, who see the militants not only quoting the Qur'an but also sacrificing

Conclusion 225

their lives at the altar of Islam. How many average Muslims can read the fine print in the Qur'an that talks of non-violence or the real meaning of jehad? No wonder, in the process, terrorism continues to thrive unabated in the name of Islam. The global war against terrorism has not been able to extract an unambiguous commitment from those Muslim leaders who actually control the command buttons of popular Islam. It is not the failure of military strategy; it is the failure of international politics. Similarly, it is the failure of domestic intercommunal politics that comes in the way of reform in personal law.

To extrapolate further, in spite of everything in the Qur'an to ensure gender justice, a fact highlighted by almost all in the community, the fact remains that there is gender injustice in Muslim society. Pointing out that there is gender injustice in the Hindu and Christian communities as well does not hold water; it does not alter the Muslim reality. Also, the root cause of gender injustice in Muslim society can be found not only in Muslim personal law but also in its interpretation by vested interests, that is, in essence, the politics of the community. If those vested interests are to be challenged, it has to be through a social revolution and political movement. Who would bell the cat? Potentially, there are only two groups that can do so—progressive women activists and enlightened Muslim leaders. Since their interests and social interactions converge they can both be clubbed into one force—the progressive and reformist force. The same formula is applicable to all minorities in South Asia, most notably the Hindu minority of Bangladesh. But before gaining the confidence of the majority in the communities, these forces would have to politically overpower the orthodox elements, who generally command wider appeal with the masses in their respective communities.

The question thus boils down to assessing the political power of this progressive section in influencing the political process, so as to take steps first to codify the tenets of the respective personal laws and then, at some unspecified future date, to agree to coordinate with other communities to work out a common civil code, for, after all, the essential idea is to find a humane and gender-just family code for all. To reach this enlightened level of intercommunity coordination, the texture of politics will have to change. Our study does not show much promise in that direction. Politics everywhere in the South Asian region is highly existential, leaving little room for enlightened innovations in personal laws acceptable to all communities. For example, as soon as the question of reform in Muslim personal law figures on the agenda, Muslim leadership is up in arms to withstand any threat to the community's identity. This provokes the Hindus and the whole debate

226　*The Politics of Personal Law in South Asia*

assumes a communal colour. Champions of the uniform civil code, led by the Hindu chauvinists, argue that the differentiated approaches to family laws breed communalism for they come in the way of the emotional integration of India into one nation. In contrast, the opponents of the uniform civil code argue that the threatened abolition of tradition instils fears in the minds of minority religious groups about their cultural identities, which lead to minority-majority distrust, breeding a communalist temper.

Both the major political forces in India—the Congress and BJP— have their own communal cards to play though there is one significant difference between them. For the Congress it is communalism of equi-proximity by targeting all communities, while for the BJP it is the politics of hate directed particularly at the Muslims, a distinciton this author has discussed elsewhere (Ghosh 1999). It is in this context that the so-called Muslim and Hindu 'vote-banks' assume importance. The concept of the Hindu vote has gained currency only of late, in the late 1980s and 1990s, when the BJP came to the centre of Indian politics. In the construction of this 'Hindu vote', the demand for a uniform civil code figured prominently. L. K. Advani, in his BJP presidential address of 1986, spoke of constituting a law commission to study all the personal laws of different communities so as to identify the progressive elements in them, draft a uniform code, and then throw it open for debate but this same prescription was damaged beyond repair with the subsequent political strategy of the party under his leadership as the union home minister and the deputy prime minister, when he gave so much importance to the demolition of the Babri mosque and the construction of the Ram temple in its place. BJP's political agenda and its electoral platforms at the 1989, 1991, 1996 and 1998 elections invariably focused on the introduction of a uniform civil code, with a clear slant against the continuation of Muslim personal law. However, at the 1999 and 2004 elections, the party, as a constituent of the National Democratic Alliance (NDA), had to keep the issue on the back burner.

Broadly speaking, Hindus and Muslims more or less share the same material condition in India. Socially and educationally, Hindus are only marginally better off than Muslims. Poverty and illiteracy stalk both communities. The cleavage between orthodox and progressive Hindus is as sharp as is the case in the Muslim community. But what makes all the difference is the majority status of the Hindus and their stratified social order based on a rigid caste system, which has a complex religious sanction. This gives better leverage to Hindu leaders to talk about reforms within the community, a fact that Nehru

Conclusion 227

exploited to the hilt in getting the Hindu code bills passed in the teeth of significant opposition from many powerful orthodox quarters. Moreover, since Hindu identity is extremely amorphous because of its caste system and doctrinal plurality, it does not consider its personal law to be as important in the construction of that identity as the Muslims do, for whom personal law (*Shari'ah*) and Islam are virtually interchangeable and, at a more theoretical level, state and religion are Indistinguishable. The BJP made the mistake of propagating Hindutva in terms of a monolithic Hindu identity to capture the so-called 'Hindu vote' in its name. But it has realised the hard way that it is extremely difficult to stretch that vote bank beyond 25 per cent.

Indian politics, which is increasingly becoming coalitional, is largely the replica of its federal politics, which is both horizontal and vertical—horizontal in the sense of India's political sociology and vertical in the sense of India's constitutional development. Thus the caste-based political formations in the first place and their alignments and realignments in the second represent social federalism while the formation of new states and the constant reworking of the dynamics of centre-state relations represent constitutional federalism (Ghosh 1997: 67–68). Barring Jammu and Kashmir, no other state has a Muslim majority. But in several states they form a sizable minority and in particular pockets their concentration is so high that they can considerably influence the electoral outcomes; the recent Assam assembly poll (April 2006) is a case in point. No political party worth its salt can ignore this reality, particularly in this coalition era when pre- and post-poll permutations and combinations alone decide whether parties will be sitting in the treasury benches or remain in the opposition. Whoever is able to garner the Muslim vote is welcome and if, in the process, Muslim personal law must be left untouched, parties accept this as political quid pro quo. If one analyses the political compulsions of Rajiv Gandhi in introducing the Muslim women's bill in 1986 and compares those compulsions with Charlés Hamilton's argument during the colonial period (see p. 55), one does not see much difference between the two approaches. But here lies the basic question: to what extent can an existential developing polity afford to be only reactive in preference to being proactive?

From India's experience over the centuries, it may be argued that the plurality of family laws has not proved an obstacle to either economic progress or political development. But can it be celebrated as the ideal situation? Or, can it be assumed to be a perpetual phenomenon? The present rural-urban ratio in South Asia is 75:25. As long as this continues, the texture of politics in the region will remain

228　*The Politics of Personal Law in South Asia*

more or less the way it is now. But under the tremendous pressure of globalisation, urbanisation is taking place at a pace not experienced earlier. Under changed circumstances, say, in a few decades, it is quite likely that family ties of the present type will be replaced by an altogether new variety, making individuals the prime units of politics and not social groups. (There may be a development opposite to that witnessed during the Iranian revolution, which we have discussed in Chapter VI, pp. 227–28, but let not that debate detain us here.) In such a scenario, it may be feasible to think of a common civil code applicable to all individuals across the board, which would ensure gender justice based on human values, a point we have referred to in the context of the Bhutanese situation. But that is a long-term speculative scenario. What is the present reality and what seems to be in the foreseeable future?

Since the achievement of a UCC is a political question, it is necessary to understand how to make the political climate conducive for the purpose. Generally there are three ways that can lead to a UCC. They are: an optional uniform civil code; the separate codification of every personal law; and a compulsory uniform civil code.

The first suggestion is a contradiction in terms, because if something else exists other than the UCC, as a means to deal with personal law, there obviously is no UCC. But the existence of the Special Marriage Act (1954) alongside all personal laws legitimising and governing marriages proves that it is possible. The problem is that, so long as both possibilities are equally available, it is likely that, in this vastly religious, poor and illiterate country, personal law would be more popular for it is at the same time religious, informal, and cheap. This has been the experience with the Special Marriage Act *vis-à-vis* other laws such as the Hindu Marriage Act. A 1978 ICSSR-funded project aimed at assessing attitudes of social groups to the uniform civil code, based on a Pune-based survey, revealed that while most of the respondents supported a uniform code insofar as the imposition of monogamy was concerned, they were not in favour of the abolition of personal laws. They considered that government interference in family law should be minimal and that marriages should be performed through religious rituals (Agarwala 1978: 281–83).

The second suggestion is what is being tried since Independence. Hindu law has been codified, Muslim law has been codified, to a very limited extent, and the customary laws of the tribes of Northeast are being codified, though it is a Herculean task to do so. But it has been argued that, instead of paving the way for a UCC, such codifications will contribute to the rigidification of community consciousness,

Conclusion 229

further creating hostility towards the idea of a UCC. The Muslim leadership feels that the passage of the Muslim Women's Act of 1986 is its victory over the UCC move in the direction of the latter. Syed Shahabuddin argues that Muslim personal law and Muslim identity are one and the same thing and cannot be separated. In an interview with Vasudha Dhagamwar in the late 1980s, Shahabuddin said:

> The Uniform Civil Code is neither a matter of priority nor of urgency, nor a sine-qua-non for national integration. It is nothing more than a distant social objective. The movement towards a Uniform Civil Code should logically pass through three stages:
>
> 1. The first stage is the codification of the personal laws of various communities so that over a period of time there is adequate basis in terms of comparative jurisprudence to serve as the foundation to evolve common principles for a Uniform Civil Code.
> 2. There has also to be a transitional phase of optionality.
> 3. If the Uniform Civil Code comes into conflict with the Shariat on any given point, the Muslim community should be granted exemption, when Uniform Civil Code becomes obligatory.

'Such opinions,' Dhagamwar concluded, 'give no hope that the objective of a Uniform Civil Code will be achieved by the three tier process being advocated' (Dhagamwar 1989: 70).

Besides women's rights in general, one major problem that is faced by law in the absence of a UCC is in respect of conversion to another religion by either spouse. The existing personal laws are often so contradictory that it becomes virtually impossible to adjudicate in cases involving conversion of either married partner. In this confusion the biggest casualty is 'clarity of law'. Dhagamwar writes:

> If a person's rights vis-à-vis another in familial relationships are to depend entirely upon the permutation and combination of their respective race, religion, caste and sex there can be no clarity. It is often said that the solution to iniquitous matrimonial laws is the Special Marriage Act, but so long as it remains one of the many laws of the land, it is not likely to clarify the situation. It will remain available only to those who are well informed and educated. It would be better to make a law declaring that no marriage would be void because of technical reasons such as different religions of the parties or rituals followed, no marriages would

230 *The Politics of Personal Law in South Asia*

dissolve because of conversion unless the parties so desired it, and that the intention of the parties, as demonstrated by their conduct would be sufficient to constitute a valid relationship.

—(*ibid.*: 63)

In the divorce case before the Supreme Court (1985) involving a Khasi woman and her Sikh husband married under the Christian Marriage Act, 1872 (discussed above), Justice Chinnappa Reddy, in his judgment, highlighted the conflicting positions of different personal laws on the matter and strongly pleaded with the government to introduce a UCC to get rid of these riddles (AIR, 1985, S. C. 935–41).

Community consensus as a precondition to reform personal law is not without precedent. When an enlightened section of the Parsi community suggested to prime minister Indira Gandhi that the archaic and discriminatory law of intestate succession (a Parsi female inheriting only one-half of the share of a Parsi male) needed amendment, she refused to introduce an amending legislation unless there was unanimity amongst the Parsis. Achieving such consensus was attempted over the next few years, and it was only when the Parsi panchayat of Mumbai ultimately said that the entire community unanimously wanted a reform in the law, to treat males and females equally, that the Succession Act of 1925 was amended in 1991 to bring it in line with the general law of intestate succession (Nariman 2005).

Even the passage of the Hindu Code was based on Hindu consent. It took several years and stopped when community consent stopped. Hindu women were not allowed to have any property rights in a joint family. Likewise, Muslim consensus needs to emerge in favour of codification and standardisation of Muslim personal law before a UCC is possible. According to Rajeev Dhavan, these matters require consent and consensus and not 'majoritarian' counsel. Let the 'fundamentalists' take back seats and allow the minority communities to start discussions within themselves 'without political weaponry being pointed at their head'. The issue is how to achieve justice—not politically coerced uniformity for the sake of uniformity (Dhavan 2003).

It is instructive here to note what the RSS chief M. S. Golwalkar had said in this regard. At the inauguration of the Deen Dayal Research Institute in New Delhi on 20 August 1972, he replied to questions put to him by a correspondent of the Delhi-based daily, *Motherland* (now defunct), the one-time organ of the Bharatiya Jana Sangh:

Q: Don't you consider a uniform civil code necessary for the furtherance of national integration?

A: No. I don't think so. You and many others will be surprised to hear it, but this is my opinion and I should express the truth the way I see it. . . . It is not that I object to a uniform civil code as such. But at the same time it must be borne in mind that something cannot become desirable only because it is mentioned in the Constitution. . . .

Q: Don't you think that Muslims are opposing the uniform civil code just to maintain their identity and individuality? [It may be recalled that this was the time when the Muslim leadership in the parliament was opposing the amendments to the Cr. PC, which later became the most critical points of debate in the Shah Bano case; see pp. 95–100.]

A: I have no grievance against any section, community or fraternity desiring to maintain its identity or individuality, provided that this 'identity' is not a hurdle in the way of sentiments for patriotism. So long as Muslims love this country and its culture, we welcome their way of life. [This is similar to the position the Congress had taken during the pre-Partition days, in favour of continuation of Muslim personal law after Independence. The Deobandis, in opposition to the Muslim League, had stood firmly behind the Congress to view India as one nation. For the Congress, this patriotism of the Deobandis was more important than whether or not the country went for a uniform civil code.]

Q: Will it be right to permit Muslim women to remain in purdah and put up with polygamy?

A: Muslims should be given an opportunity to give up their archaic laws. If they themselves conclude that polygamy is not good for them, I will be very happy. But I will not like to impose my views on them.

—(Zakaria 2003)

Whenever a Supreme Court judgement indicates that the state should endeavour to enact a UCC, the champions of the latter get a shot in the arm and redouble their efforts to argue for the same. But is there any effort to first draft a complete UCC and then present it for debate, as the Bangladesh Mahila Parishad (BMP) has done (discussed in Chapter V). Tahir Mahmood's question is valid: 'What, then, could be the pattern of a uniform civil code? Can somebody produce an ideal model not violating in any sense any provision of the Constitution? If this cannot be done, all talk about a uniform civil code—both in favour and against—remains an exercise in futility, all political polemics about it, an indulgence in gimmickry' (Mahmood 2003).

232 *The Politics of Personal Law in South Asia*

Ram Jethmalani refers to a serious practical difficulty in adopting a uniform code of marriage. Since the Special Marriage Act, 1954, is not taken recourse to by most people, who prefer religiously formalised marriages, it is extremely difficult to think of a common code by borrowing from all religions and customs. He thinks that neither the Supreme Court nor the supporters of a uniform civil code have considered seriously how this code would look like, or how different religious customs associated with the solemnisation of marriages would be simultaneously accommodated. For example, Hindus follow the *saptapadi* form in the presence of a priest and the sacred fire, while Muslims marry by *nikah* in the presence of a *vakil* who communicates the mutual consent of the parties. Would not the uniform code be a 'bizarre mixture of the two,' Jethmalani asks. Already a secular Special Marriage Act is available under which one can marry without bothering about ritualistic specifications (Jethmalani 2003). Jethmalani's argument against amalgamating Hindu and Muslim rituals is, however, misplaced. A uniform civil code would neither talk of rituals nor would it concern itself with whether the registration of marriage accompanies any ritual, the way many Hindus in England do, as noted in Chapter VI (see p. 217). As Swapan Dasgupta rightly argues: 'A uniform civil code will not undermine a marriage solemnized in a mosque or before a *maulvi*. It will merely ensure that any possible separation and future inheritance will be governed by the same laws as applicable to those who got married in a temple or—as a latest fad suggests— underwater. In short, a uniform civil code will ensure that laws are secularized and made pan-Indian' (Dasgupta 2003).

It is not easy to predict how long it will take for the Muslim community to ask for reforms in its personal law, leave alone acquiesce to a UCC. Ever since Independence, there is an undercurrent of apprehension within the community that its identity is under perpetual danger of extinction in Hindu-majority India. The partition of India and the creation of Muslim-majority Pakistan have done the greatest damage to the Indian Muslim psyche. Its clinging to tradition and thereby suspecting any move to even remotely reform Muslim personal law can be explained from this perspective. Though an extremely small example, the case of the Meos of Mewat in Rajasthan makes that point. Pratap Aggarwal's sociological study of the community in the sixties showed that the Meos, who for 300 years remained marginal Muslims following mostly Hindu religious practices, suddenly, after Independence, started asserting their Islamic identity. This being the general trend, social science research, barring a few earlier exceptions (Aggarwal 1971; Ahmad 1976, 1978, 1981; Dube 1969), has

Conclusion 233

increasingly concentrated on Islam as a construction and, of late, on the comparative status of Muslim and Hindu women. Hindu-Muslim communal tension, on the rise since the early 1980s, has seriously affected empirical research on such issues as the working of the legal system and the customary practices pertaining to marriage, divorce and inheritance (Fazalbhoy 1997: 1550).

The demand for a UCC is premature. What should precede a UCC is gender equality across communities. 'Unless we get these things sorted out,' writes senior advocate Indira Jaisingh, 'there is no point in talking about a uniform civil code or personal law reform. These are only routes to equality, and which route you adopt depends on the needs of the community.' The state and its institutions lack a vision of equality or of gender justice, and there is no political will to address the problems of women, she asserts. There is only one common civil code in operation, the 'common code of inequality,' she adds (quoted by Mody 2003a).

It may be underlined that, notwithstanding opposition to the Hindu Code by many Hindus, most notably Rajendra Prasad and Sardar Patel, it was possible because the Parliament was Hindudominated and led by a progressive leader like Nehru. The same is not true with the Muslims. Though they constitute about 14 per cent of India's population, their presence in Parliament is much less. One is not sure how much popular legitimacy the AIMPLB, nothing but an NGO, has in the community. The vocal Muslim leadership, including the AIMPLB, depends on the Indian state for its legitimacy and, by and large, this leadership has a conservative position on gender issues. Sociologist Zarina Bhatty argues that, as far as the general public is concerned, 'the community is only represented by people with beards and caps. There are other opinions, but they are negated by the media and politicians.' Danish Khan, the news editor of *Milligazette,* a community paper published from Delhi, is sceptical about any change in the situation in the foreseeable future. The leaders of AIMPLB are 'fanatics' without popular support, alleges Khan. 'They go on about the Muslim identity, but who is saying that they are not Muslim?' With the focus squarely on ' identity', they ignore issues of importance, such as health and education or women's rights, he adds (Mody 2003b).

Khan's views are echoed by M. J. Akbar, the editor of *The Asian Age.* The attitude of the AIMPLB 'towards social reform is best summed by the position it took on family planning. It is interesting that political parties ideologically close to the Board, like the Muslim League, supported the imposition of the Emergency by Mrs Indira Gandhi in 1975. But what might be called the "Muslim Parivar" changed track

234　*The Politics of Personal Law in South Asia*

when Mrs Gandhi used the Emergency to push some overdue social programmes like family planning. At an extraordinary meeting held on 17–18 April 1976 the Board declared that sterilisation *(nasbandi)* was *haram* or prohibited. In all matters of family law the Board has taken a male-oriented view' (Akbar 2003). Asghar Ali Engineer has argued that Muslim personal law can be reformed by following the Qur'an itself. Neither the triple talaq nor polygamy has any Qur'anic sanction if one reads the text carefully. Many illustrious Islamic scholars of the nineteenth and early twentieth centuries like Maulvi Imtiaz Ali Khan, Maulvi Chiragh Ali and the legal luminary like Justice Amir Ali had advocated these changes (Engineer 2003).

Assuming that a uniform civil code is a desirable ingredient for both democracy and national integration, is it the prerequisite? The Nepalese experience tells the story most tellingly. Nepal has one single official language, Nepali, through which all official transactions are conducted; it has one single national criminal and civil code (1963), through which all legal disputes are adjudicated, including those related to family matters of all ethnic and religious communities; yet the country is one of the most politically volatile nations of the world. Before the ouster of the monarchy in June 2006, as the nation was in turmoil reeling under its dictatorship, it was the argument of the Palace that the nation would be in danger without a centralised political command. But the reality was that the writ of the Royal government did not extend beyond the Kathmandu valley and that about 95 per cent of the country was and is under the effective control of the rebellious Maoists. Nepal is a divided house. Let alone smaller ethnic minorities, even the Madheshis, the people of Indian origin living in the Terai region of the country, who constitute a sizable portion of the population, some even arguing that they could be as many as 50 per cent of the population nationwide, are also a disgruntled lot, though most are Hindu. The joke amongst the Madheshis is that when the country is eventually divided between the Madheshis and the rest, no one will need to bother much about the boundary demarcation, because the Royal government has already done that by building the East-West highway, which would serve as a modern frontier with facilities for border patrolling by respective security forces. Evidently the uniform civil code of Nepal has not contributed to national integration.

A democracy, it can be argued therefore, can thrive even by respecting different personal laws of different communities. It all depends on the specific historical experience of a nation and the texture of the society—multiethnic or mono-ethnic. For example, Israel, generally considered a very modern society, has not enacted a common civil

Conclusion 235

code. It has left the Muslim and the Christian Arabs to be judged on personal legal matters by their own religious courts, as the rabbanical courts take care of the cases of Jewish Israelis. In contrast, however, predominantly Muslim Albania and Turkey have introduced secular civil codes without any reference to the Qur'an.

From the South Asian experience one can see that it is, rather, the undemocratic societies like Bhutan and Maldives, and also to some extent Nepal, that have experimented with uniform civil codes or uniform justice systems and have succeeded as well, though this success is largely because of a structured gagging of democratic opposition. In contrast, the Muslim-majority and Islam-oriented Bangladesh and Pakistan have allowed the Hindu personal law to thrive there, not out of any respect for minority rights but because of sheer indifference towards them. In Sri Lanka the controversy is virtually non-existent because the country's ethnic conflict consumes almost all the energy of the political class and the intelligentsia. The only country where the debate is politically relevant is India, and for the right reasons. What happens in this country has its inevitable impact in the rest of the region. At the present political juncture, given the inter-communal tensions arising out of two interconnected phenomena, namely, Hindu nationalism and Islamic terrorism, there is the least likelihood of a Hindu-Muslim consensus over a uniform civil code. Nothing beyond piecemeal reforms in the personal laws of different communities is anticipated. That itself is probably not a bad thing to happen; the process should be sustained till a more conducive political situation is arrived at in which to think in terms of a uniform civil code.

Also, the experiment of the 1954 Special Marriage Act should be replicated wherever possible. The Indian state should have the courage to adopt a uniform adoption law, providing at least those Muslim couples the opportunity to take recourse to the law who are not otherwise eligible to do so under Muslim personal law. The basic purpose of such secular legislations is that they provide some facilitative avenues to willing people who want to shake off their social bondage to lead lives as free citizens in a modern state. Such an exercise would be less politically demanding and in due course would be the model across the region. Amen.

8 Old Wine in the Old Bottle

> I am sorry for you the hapless women folk of India. I wonder for what sin of yours you are born in this country.
> —Ishwar Chandra Vidyasagar, the social crusader of nineteenth-century Bengal, who pioneered the movement for widow remarriage, and succeeded

In keeping with the organisation of the book, this chapter is divided into five parts. Part I (The Core Question) will address the most debated issue of the uniform civil code (UCC) against the background of Hindu–Muslim political contestations. It is inherent in India's circumstances that it pits the majority Hindu community against the minority Muslim community, although the crux of the matter is gender inequality, which only liberals and women activists across the board seem to be concerned about. In Part II (On the Fringes), we will discuss questions related to some other personal laws, such as the customary laws of large tribal communities scattered in central and north-eastern India whose numbers are only next to those of Muslims. In the same context we will also discuss the personal law of micro minorities, taking the case of the Parsi community as an example. The idea is to underline that the UCC discourse should not exhaust itself by addressing only the Muslim question. Since these minorities are politically not as relevant as Muslims, they do not figure in the debate, although theoretically they should. Part III (India's Neighbours) will look into the state of Hindu personal law in Muslim-majority Bangladesh and Pakistan. Situations in these countries are exactly the opposite of India; like mirror images, Hindu minorities are pitted against Muslim majorities. The latter accuse the former of backwardness and for their aversion to reforms. Part IV (Centrality of Politics) will analyse the UCC debate through the lenses of Indian politics, which is the crux of the matter. In this context we will raise the question whether any community, including the Hindu, is prepared to give up its personal law in favour of a UCC, which the community boastfully claims as their avowed pledge. For inevitable reasons, some cross-references will be noticeable in the first and the fourth parts. Part V (Conclusion: UCC: A Pipe Dream) will form our concluding argument that personal laws are going to stay into the foreseeable future by incorporating necessary reforms in them from time to time. In essence, therefore, a uniform civil code will be discussed and debated, but not enacted.

The Core Question

The Issue

Personal law is not personal at all; arguably, it is not even law.[1] Personal law bestows rights to a community, but its members can exercise that right only individually. A strictly legalistic proposition presupposes a set of codified rules and regulations. No personal law has any such comprehensive set; at best it has some partial codifications, Hindu law being the biggest success story. Essentially, personal law is a political question. Since identity issues and religious emotions are linked to it, either its continuation or its abrogation is not possible without the community's endorsement, meaning it has to be politically negotiated through. In India the question whether or not a UCC should be introduced by replacing all personal and customary laws is almost a century old, yet there does not seem to be any end to it. It has been our experience that the controversy is raked up from time to time either by the judiciary or the BJP. For the latter it happens either when it is in power or when it faces an election, particularly in north India.

The politics of personal law operates at two levels, at the inter-community level, and at the intra-community level. The first is by and large confined to the conflict between the majority community on the one hand and the largest minority community on the other. In Indian context the relevant categories are Hindus and Muslims, respectively. In Bangladesh and Pakistan it is the opposite, although in those countries the discourse is not at the popular level. In the intra-community context it is between the traditionalists and the reformists, in other words, between the conservatives and the liberals. But the politics of civil law should not exhaust itself in these narrowly focused binaries. In the deeper sense it is a contestation between the concept of patriarchy on the one hand and that of feminism on the other. The bottom line is: assertion of women's rights; in a nonoffensive term—for justice

238 *The Politics of Personal Law in South Asia*

across the genders. Over this fulcrum is constructed the superstructure of communal identity, an important marker of which is personal law. It is no surprise, therefore, that the debate is unending, for it rotates in a circular motion; in the name of ending identity politics, it consolidates it.

It is nobody's case that the idea of a UCC is intrinsically wrong. That it is morally correct and socially desirable is indisputable. But since India is socially and culturally diverse, it is not easy to convince all communities, actually their leaderships, to agree to it at one go, notwithstanding the fact that it is one of the directive principles of state policy as enshrined in the Constitution of India (I prefer to view them as 'deflective' or 'diversionary' principles).[2] According to Veerappa Moily, who was the law minister of India from 2009 to 2011, there are 200 to 300 personal laws in India (Khan 2016). Most of the minority communities fear that if a UCC is implemented it would poach into their personal laws, thereby tampering with their identity markers. Although the impression given is that it is an issue to concern the Muslims alone and that it is they who unilaterally oppose it, the truth is more complex. Not only do several other communities in India, most notably the tribes, follow their multiple customary laws, even the Muslim community does not follow one single personal law. Leave alone the several jurisprudential streams in Islam (four Sunni schools are Hanafi, Maliki, Shafi and Hanbali; and two Shia schools are Ja'fari and Zaidiyyah), even otherwise the community is highly plural, as Imtiaz Ahmad has demonstrated, leading to a curious situation that one can talk in the same breath of a Qur'anic law and a Muslim Personal Law (see pp. 109–110). Different customs and rites among Hindus are in any case mind-boggling.[3] Furthermore, not only are there community-wise differences in the application of personal laws, even within individual personal laws there are variations from place to place. For example, Jammu and Kashmir, which is although a Muslim majority state, does not recognise the Muslim Personal Law (*Shari'ah*) Application Act, 1937 and the Dissolution of Muslim Marriages Act, 1939. Similarly, the Hindu Marriage Act, 1955 and the Hindu Adoption and Maintenance Act, 1956, have no legal application in the state. J&K has its own versions of some of these laws. Similarly, in 1976 Kerala abolished joint family property altogether, but in the Hindu Succession Act, 1956, even after its amendment in 2005, it was retained (for more information, visit https://blog.ipleaders.in/important-indian-laws-that-dont-apply-in-jammu-kashmir/, accessed on 19 October 2017, and *Times of India*, 19 September 2017).

Old Wine in the Old Bottle 239

Evolution of the Debate

Before the British arrived in India, the Mughals, who carved out a huge empire that included even large parts of Afghanistan, had established a well-organised justice system. Just like there is a widespread Hindu belief (after 9/11, Western Christian as well) that Muslims as a community are monolithic, that they are backward-looking, and that they resist social reforms, there is also the notion that their legal thinking is frozen ever since the days of Islamic ascendancy, as reflected in their blind faith in the Quranic law, or *Shari'ah*. But the fact that, leave alone Islamic jurisprudential plurality, even the *Shari'ah* has undergone evolutionary changes is little known and, therefore, seldom appreciated. There are ample evidences to this effect in the experiences of the two largest Muslim empires, the Ottoman and the Mughal. These experiences are a study in contrasts. While the Ottoman Empire was a massive Muslim majority state with many non-Muslim minorities scattered all over the empire, the Mughal Empire had a minuscule Muslim minority ruling a massively non-Muslim majority consisting mostly of Hindus, who are not 'a people of the book'. But there was one significant similarity. In both the empires, *Shari'ah* was constantly discoursed and reformed, in keeping with contemporary requirements. Our concern primarily being the Mughal legal system, it may be noted that it was a hybrid system as it allowed 'widespread "permissive inclusion" into *shari'a*, whereby in non-criminal matters the *qazis* courts allowed and attracted, but did not require, all Mughal subjects [including Hindus] to avail of their civil jurisdiction' (Chatterjee 2014, p. 396). The *Shari'ah* included didactic texts together with modern rules of procedure. This was so even during Aurangzeb, who was otherwise recognised as a no-nonsense Islamist. The *qazi* followed the rules of due investigative procedure, which made even some Hindus approach them to settle their family quarrels over inheritance. During the time of Akbar we have evidence to the effect that he had decreed to respect some local Hindu customs against killing of birds, in spite of the fact that they were not repugnant to Islamic custom (for a scholarly discourse on the subject, see Chatterjee 2014).

Because of this well-oiled legal structure, the British merely had to adapt their own methods, keeping in view their imperial interests. This was a departure from their conventional colonial practice as followed in the New World (North America) and the Caribbean, where they had replaced the native laws by a new set of laws. In India they scrupulously refrained from doing so. They appreciated that although religion-based, the Hindu and the Muslim personal laws could

240 The Politics of Personal Law in South Asia

purposefully serve their interest. Still, they needed to read the Hindu and Islamic religious texts in the English language, for which their translation into English was imperative. In this project four individuals contributed immensely. They were Warren Hastings (1732–1817), Sir William Jones (1746–1794), Charles Hamilton (1753?–1792) and H. T. Colebrooke (1765–1837). Jones tried to achieve the almost impossible, to codify the Hindu and the Muslim laws. These codifications, however imperfect, became the bases of adjudication by British judges, though Hindu pundits and Muslim qazis present in the courts were expected to endorse the judgments. Gradually the compilation of these case laws came to be called the Anglo-Hindu law and the Anglo-Muhammadan law. Over the years, as more and more new interpretations of these laws took place, they increasingly became more Anglo. From 1864, even the system of pundits and qazis being present in the courts was discontinued (De 2009: 124).

Five landmark events would give some clue to the politics–law interface during the British period. They were: the Suttee (Sati) Regulation, 1829; the Hindu Widows' Remarriage Act, 1856; the Muslim Personal Law (*Shari'ah*) Application Act, 1937; the Lahore High Court's judgment of 1938 in the Shahidganj Mosque case; and the Dissolution of Muslim Marriages Act, 1939. These events underlined the influence of three forces at work, namely, the conservative/orthodox social order, the progressive/reformist fringe of that order (including women activism), and the growing Hindu–Muslim political divide. To perpetuate their imperial project the British modified their socio-legal strategy from time to time. The Bengal renaissance of the early nineteenth century had created an English-speaking pro-British Bengali elite class. Naturally when the demands for the abolition of *sati* and the introduction of widow remarriage were pushed forward by this group, the East India Company supported their moves. But the company had not realised that the social milieu of Bengal was yet to be conducive to accepting these changes. On the ground, therefore, neither the abolition of sati nor the introduction of widow remarriage had any impact.

The revolt of 1857 against the company rule, though ruthlessly crushed, made the British government in London realise that something was amiss in their colonial governance approach. The message they got from the Hindu–Muslim unity in the revolt was that they must refrain from interfering with India's social customs. The British Crown, which replaced the company in 1857, proclaimed in unmistakable terms that not only would it not interfere with India's social life, it would even safeguard the religious beliefs of the Indians.[4] This policy continued till the end of the British rule. The Government of

Old Wine in the Old Bottle 241

India Act of 1935, the most significant landmark in India's constitutional history, underlined this attitude. The act contained a clause making it mandatory to seek permission of the viceroy before any bill was tabled in the central legislature which could affect the 'religion, or religious rights and usages of British subjects of India'. To make this work effectively the British ensured that the number of official members and government-nominated members together outnumbered the private members (De 2009: 110–11, 125). During this time the British also started taking advantage of the growing tension between the Hindus and the Muslims as two separate communities. The separatist Muslim politics came handy to them. If the Muslims could be put up as a unified force against the Hindu-dominated Congress, it made common sense to the British that it would go in their favour.

The passage of the Shariat Act of 1937 and the Dissolution of Muslim Marriages Act of 1939 reveal how complex Indian politics had become prior to the Pakistan resolution of 1940 among the contending interest groups, namely, the nationalists, the champions of Muslim identity, women's groups, and, the overarching British government. Insofar as the first act was concerned, it was a political ploy on the part of Mohammad Ali Jinnah and the Muslim League to unite the Muslims under one law. But it was not simple. Many Muslims used to follow different family laws depending upon their social status and locations; sometimes they followed even the Hindu local codes. The last mentioned advantaged the Muslim landlords because it debarred daughters from inheriting paternal properties. They had reason, therefore, to oppose the bill. Jinnah, the quintessential politician that he was, saved the bill by introducing a proviso that landed property would not fall within the purview of the act. It was sufficient to enlist the support of the wealthy Muslim landlords, the potential supporters of Jinnah's future Pakistan demand. The successful use of the *Shari'ah* as a tool to promote the sectarian interests of the Muslim League, however, was tempered by the Lahore High Court judgment in January 1938 in the Shahidganj mosque dispute. The judgment upheld the supremacy of British Indian law over the *Shari'ah* by drawing its authority from the Punjab Law Act, which in 1872 had overruled Muslim personal law. The Muslims of Lahore were upset by the judgment, and tried to register the support of Jinnah. But in this case Jinnah considered discretion the better part of valour, being no doubt conscious of Sikander Hayat Khan's disinterest in the affair owing to his alliance with Hindu and Sikh landlords, who had a stake in the judgment.

The debate over the Dissolution of Muslim Marriages Act of 1939 was instructive in several respects. Adhering to the *Shari'ah* as per

242 The Politics of Personal Law in South Asia

the 1937 act, however, had its own problems. According to it, if either party in a conjugal situation abandoned his or her religion, the marriage automatically stood dissolved. To rid themselves of their oppressive husbands, some Muslim women chose to give up Islam. To prevent losing Muslim women to other communities, the 1939 act provided Muslim women with the option of divorcing their husbands without having to give up their religion. The 1939 act, however, had much more to offer relevant for the present times, namely, the complexity of personal laws, demand for a uniform civil code, the logic behind the women's rights movement, and most importantly, why it is necessary to develop a consensus among the stakeholders to make any social legislation possible. Let us look into each of these dimensions with the antecedents of the act in mind.

First, it is a largely misplaced notion that Muslim personal law is retrograde compared to other personal laws. It was definitely not so prior to the promulgation of the Hindu Code in the 1950s. The 1939 act had given Muslim women the right to dissolve their marriage 20 years before their Hindu counterparts got it. Even prior to that it was more progressive compared to Hindu and Christian laws, as testified by privy councilor Sir James Colville in the mid-1860s. Other British law reporters testified to the same. It was as recent as 1960 that an Allahabad High Court judgment had unequivocally praised the Muslim law. At that point in time, even Christian women, whether in India or in Britain, had no such right. The 1939 act also highlighted that Muslim personal law was not to be just Hanafi law, which would not allow any intrusion from other Islamic schools of jurisprudence as it included certain provisions from the Maliki law as well (De 2009: 106–07, 114–15, and 117).

Second, there was no demand for a UCC that was put forward by Hindu leaders, nor by the Congress, given the growing tensions between the Congress and the Muslim League. Both were eyeing for the same support base among the Indian Muslims. Indeed, many nationalist leaders were aware of the complexity of having several personal laws in independent India, but the then-political compulsions dictated the Congress to pledge to the Muslims that after independence their personal law would not be in jeopardy. Such commitments came from Gandhi on 28 October 1931, Nehru on 6 April 1937 and from the Congress Party in October 1937. Gandhi even assured of 'specific provisions' in the constitution as and when it would be drafted.

Third, one may say that a community-neutral women's rights voice was for the first time heard in these debates. Because of the spread of secular education women were emerging as a pressure group. In 1929,

Old Wine in the Old Bottle 243

two women's groups came into being, namely, the All India Women's Conference (AIWC) and the All India Muslim Ladies Conference (Anjuman-e-Khwateen-e-Islam). Soon after their establishment they passed identical resolutions asking for rights to inheritance and right to divorce (De 2009: 113). Here too, contrary to popular notions, Muslim women earned more brownie points than their Hindu counterparts. The antecedents leading to the passage of the 1939 act would throw some light in this regard, which is our fourth point. The act underlined why it is necessary to develop a consensus among the stakeholders if one seriously wants to bring reforms in personal law, whatever be the community. As noted by one scholar, it 'was the product of the combined efforts of an unlikely coalition of socially conservative *ulema*, reformist clergy, newly elected legislators of the Muslim League and the Congress, colonial civil servants, and activists of the national women's organisations.' For example, Dr. G. V. Deshmukh, who wanted reforms in the Hindu law, knew that he needed to broaden his base of support among Muslims and as such supported the 1939 bill (De 2009: 107, 113).

In the Constituent Assembly debates it was cerebrally discussed why as a democratic and secular state India should not enact a UCC. Equally cerebral was the discussion as to why it should not continue to allow its ethnic and religious minorities to retain their personal and customary laws. The debate was intense because these two positions were not contradictory to the logic of democracy and secularism. Ultimately, plurality of family laws was recognised as a policy choice because it was found to be historically rooted and politically consensual. As a compromise between idealism and realism it was inserted through Article 44 of the Indian Constitution in its Directive Principles of State Policy: 'The State shall endeavour to secure for the citizens a uniform civil code throughout the territory of India'. In short, it was cold-stored.

In the 70 years of India's independent existence only one marriage-related act has been passed by the parliament which is uniformly valid across communities. It is the Special Marriage Act, 1954. It is a secular act, but it is optional. As per record, Indians have seldom taken recourse to it and many a time when they have done so their respective families have disapproved of such marriages, sometimes even making the lives of the newly wed couples miserable, if not putting an end to their lives. Still, it is the only recourse that two adult male and female citizens of India can take to marry inter-religion (there are still problems in its interpretation which we have discussed below in our subsection dealing with Parsi law). Insofar as legislations in respect

244   *The Politics of Personal Law in South Asia*

of personal laws are concerned, there have been only two cases in post-independence India. The first was the four-part Hindu Code of 1955 and 1956 (Hindu Marriage Act, 1955; Hindu Adoptions and Maintenance Act, 1956; Hindu Succession Act, 1956; and Hindu Minority and Guardianship Act, 1956), and the second, the Muslim Women (Protection of Rights on Divorce) Act, 1986.[5]

Contrary to the popular Hindu imagination that Hindus are liberal minded, it may be underscored that there was a vociferous opposition to the efforts aimed at streamlining the Hindu personal laws both before and after India's independence. In 1949, Rashtriya Swayamsevak Sangh (RSS) organised as many as 79 public meetings in Delhi against the Hindu Code bill. In the same year the Hindu right formed an All-India Anti Hindu Code Bill Committee under the leadership of Swami Karpatri Maharaj, for whom even Ambedkar's dalit background was an issue. The *Kalyan* magazine, published by Gita Press, which was known for its Hindu chauvinistic orientation, published a series of articles favouring polygamy, opposing daughters' right to inheritance, and more importantly, questioning the authority of the parliament to legislate on issues pertaining to Hindu personal law (Mustafa 2016c).[6] Not only the Hindu Mahasabha leader and Industry Minister Syama Prasad Mookerjee, who subsequently formed the Bharatiya Jana Sangh, even such eminent Congress leaders like President Rajendra Prasad, Home Minister Sardar Vallabhbhai Patel, Madan Mohan Malaviya, K.N. Katju, Ananthasayanam Ayyangar and the Congress President Pattabhi Sitaramayya were opposed to the idea. So much so, that N. Natesa Iyer of the Hindu Law Committee went to the ridiculous extent of saying that the draft code was '90 per cent Muhammadan law' (De 2009: 127).

The only persons who championed the cause of a UCC were Prime Minister Jawaharlal Nehru and his law minister B. R. Ambedkar. The latter even prepared a draft UCC and presented it to the cabinet, which approved it. Nehru, however, realised that it would not be acceptable to the parliament, which profoundly annoyed Ambedkar. The latter was so disillusioned with Nehru that he resigned from his cabinet saying: 'I have never seen a case of chief whip so disloyal to the Prime Minister and the Prime Minister so loyal to a disloyal whip' (Jaffrelot, 2005, pp. 116–17). But history will judge Nehru as politically more suave. When the first effort collapsed, Nehru thought of moving slowly by taking recourse to a two-pronged strategy: first to enact an optional secular code for all Indians and then to table the Hindu code piecemeal so as not to invite a unified Hindu opposition. The first found expression in the passage of the Special Marriage

Old Wine in the Old Bottle 245

Act (1954) and the second in the four-part Hindu Code (1955–56). The importance of the Hindu Code lay in the fact that it underlined that the Indian parliament had the authority to legislate on matters of personal law, a point that was made in the Constituent Assembly in the context of the Muslim demand that parliament should be dis-empowered to deal with personal law questions (even Hindu leaders made that point, as we have mentioned above), which Ambedkar had successfully countered.

Three decades later, in 1986, parliament asserted its authority for the second time when it passed the Muslim divorced women's bill. It may be noted that the political climate then was different. Hindu nationalism, which had already been on the rise since the early eighties, was getting more and more aggressive. That its mass base was expanding was evident from the success of the *Ekatmata Yagna* of 1982–83 (Ghosh 2016: 88–89). Against this background it was inevitable that Muslim insecurity would rise and their political space would shrink. Already, in 1972, under the leadership of the All India Muslim Personal Law Board (AIMPLB), the community had resolved 'to thwart any effort to interfere, by either the government or the courts, with its interpretation of the Islamic law (or *Shariah*)'. Against this background when the Supreme Court made a reference to the *Shari'ah* in its judgment in the Shah Bano case (1985) the community reacted sharply. Although there were similar references earlier also, by mid-1980s the Hindu–Muslim politics had become more vitiated. The Congress government under the leadership of Rajiv Gandhi could not politically handle the controversy, though its policy was all right. The act did greater justice to divorced Muslim women as some empirical studies in UP showed.[7] But neither this reality nor the fact that that it was the second incident when India's parliament could legislate on a personal law question were adequately publicised as the success of the Rajiv Gandhi government. On the contrary, it allowed the popular notion to gain currency that it had given in to Muslim conservative pressures. In the process it stoked the Hindu communal fire. After a decade when BJP made it to power, L. K. Advani attributed his party's victory to the pro-Hindutva mood, which was bolstered by the passage of the Muslim Women's Bill.

Between 1986 and 2014 no major personal law issue hit the head-lines to attract political attention, though significant Muslim family matters were adjudicated by the courts. For example, in the aftermath of the Muslim Women's Act of 1986 a controversy arose as to whether the divorced Muslim women's right to maintenance was restricted only up to the *iddat* period. As such, the constitutional validity of

246   *The Politics of Personal Law in South Asia*

the act was challenged on the grounds that it violated Articles 14, 15 and 21 of the Indian constitution. The basic legal question was how the act could segregate a section of the population when a secular remedy was available under Section 125 of the CrPC. The Supreme Court resolved the matter for good in 2001 in the *Danial Latifi vs. Union of India* case (Latifi was the lawyer for Shah Bano also). On the one hand it upheld the constitutionality of the 1986 act, while on the other it held that maintenance must be provided to the divorced wife for life, and not merely during the *iddat* period. Though it was a landmark judgment, it evoked little interest for the BJP, which was then in power. In any case, there was no major election around the corner which could have made it figure in the campaigns. There were other court cases also which had nullified the instant triple talaq (discussed below) and on one pretext or another, the courts had advised the government to enact a uniform civil code. But none of them made political news, although three BJP-led coalition governments ruled the country, the first for 13 days from 16 to 28 May 1996, the second for 14 months in 1998–99 and the third for a full five-year term from 1999 to 2004. The party seemed to be satisfied by merely putting on its agenda its commitment to introduce a UCC. Of course, it should be conceded that being a member of the National Democratic Alliance (NDA) and by itself not commanding the majority in the parliament, it was obliged to keep the item on the back burner. The 2014 election changed the situation.

BJP's UCC Politics

The BJP won the 2014 election massively. As always, its election manifesto had committed the party to work for a uniform civil code: 'Article 44 of the constitution of India lists Uniform Civil Code as one of the Directive Principles of state policy. The BJP believes that there cannot be gender equality till such time India adopts a Uniform Civil Code, which protects the rights of all women, and the BJP reiterates its stand to draft a Uniform Civil Code, drawing upon the best traditions and harmonizing them with the modern times (page 41).'[8] It was a pious commitment. The BJP had made that commitment in the previous elections of 1998, 1999 and 2009 (in 2004 it was an NDA Manifesto which had certain ideas contained in the BJP's Vision Document that did not include UCC). But behind this routine commitment there was a blow cold, blow hot political strategy. Its cold strategy was reflected in its theorisation in respect of majority–minority relations, while its hot strategy was reflected at the level

Old Wine in the Old Bottle 247

of mass politics with no holds barred insofar as Muslim bashing was concerned. For example, in respect of its blow cold strategy, in the 2004, 2009 and 2014 manifestos there were promises aimed at promoting 'Urdu language,' 'increasing [the] representation of minorities in administration and public bodies' (2004 Manifesto), 'setting up of a permanent inter-faith consultative mechanism to promote harmony among and trust between communities' (2009 Manifesto), preserving 'the rich culture and heritage of India's minority communities, alongside their social and economic empowerment,' saying clearly that it was the duty of the party to 'ensure that all communities are equal partners in India's progress as . . . India cannot progress if any segment of Indians is left behind,' and ensuring for the minorities 'a *peaceful* and *secure* environment' (2014 Manifesto). Later, Narendra Modi as the prime minister popularised the slogan '*sabka saath, sabka vikas*', meaning development through togetherness.

But BJP's blow hot strategy nullified all the pious and democratic pledges, if the party's campaign speeches were any indication. They routinely indulged in vitriolic mud-slinging against Muslims. Seemingly, the job was neatly divided between the high-profile leaders on the one hand and the party's foot soldiers on the other. The first would target Muslims through tongue-in-cheek insinuations as Prime Minister Modi did during the UP assembly election of 2017—if the graveyards of the Muslims could be lighted, why not the cremation grounds of the Hindus as well? There were two political messages here. One, that the ruling Akhilesh Yadav government was pampering the Muslims, and two, how his administration was a failure. The first was politically more loaded. It was to highlight how the Hindus were being neglected, which the BJP would not tolerate. In a similar vein, after the BJP won the election, the UP chief minister Yogi Adityanath, famously asked his audience in a Lucknow rally on 19 August 2017 that if Muslims could occupy the streets for their Eid prayer, why should the UP police stations not celebrate *Janmashtami* (a Hindu religious festival)? That it was a flagrant mockery of India's secularism seemed to have little meaning for him. That all these were meant to whip Hindu sentiments against Muslims made ample common sense to the party. Against this background, insofar as their UCC rhetoric was concerned, it was couched in the party's commitment to do away with all the oppressive anti-women elements in the Muslim personal law, most notably the practice of triple talaq, once again making the tongue-in-cheek political point that the Muslim community was anti-women, which a gender-just Hindu community would not allow to continue. To an average Hindu it was honey to his ears. But that the

248   *The Politics of Personal Law in South Asia*

Muslim social reality is not as obnoxious as it is made out to be does not seem to interest most Hindus, largely because of sheer ignorance, or refusal to see through the apparent. Here are some facts.

Barring Goa, Hindus are not supposed to be polygamous, as per law. But according to 1974 official data, that means 22 years after the introduction of the Hindu Code, the incidence of polygamy was higher among Hindus than Muslims. While 5.6 per cent Muslims were polygamous, 5.8 per cent Hindus were so. There is even now an upper-caste Gujarati version of bigamy called *maitri karaar* (friendship commitment) in which the male is married. It is bigamy in all practical sense (Aakar Patel in *Mint*, 29 October 2015). The tribals accounted for the maximum (15 per cent), followed by Buddhists (7.9 per cent) and Jains (6.7 per cent). No reliable data for the subsequent decades is available. A 2006 National Family Health Survey revealed that as many as 2 per cent Indian women had said that their husbands had more than one wife. In short, polygamy still existed in spite of legal prohibitions. Insofar as the most maligned Muslim practice of triple talaq is concerned, it may be noted that as per the census of 2011, only 0.49 per cent Muslim women were divorcees and they all were not given triple talaq. Based on the data collected from Darul Ifta (institutions which issue fatwas), in 10 states it was found that out of 340,206 fatwas that were sought in 2016, only 6.50 per cent were for triple talaq, that too many of them were seeking some clarifications. Similarly, based on data collected from 74 *Shari'ah* Courts (Arbitration Councils) run by the Muslim Personal Law Boards in 15 states, it was found that these courts rarely granted triple talaq and that divorce was permitted only through one pronouncement preceded by efforts at reconciliation through arbitration (Mustafa 2016a, and also his interview in https://scroll.in/article/836751/people-will-accept-triple-talaq-out-of-fear-of-god-legal-expert-faizan-mustafa, accessed on 11 August 2017; Mustafa is a legal scholar and vice chancellor, NALSAR Law University, Hyderabad).

The BJP, however, did not have to wait for too long to push its Hindutva-loaded UCC agenda. Some court rulings of 2015 came its way quite uncannily. On 16 October 2015, in an unrelated case (*Prakash and Others v Phulvati and Others*) concerning certain aspects of the Hindu Succession Act of 1956, a two-judge bench of the Supreme Court consisting of Anil R. Dave and Adarsh K. Goel held that the provisions of the act, as amended in 2005, could not apply retrospectively. But in the second part of the judgment, the judges referred to the injustices faced by Muslim women. They sought responses from the attorney general of India and the National

Old Wine in the Old Bottle 249

Legal Services Authority on whether 'gender discrimination' suffered by Muslim women should be considered a violation of fundamental rights. This paved the way for an appeal under the system of PIL (Public Interest Litigation). A notice was sent to the attorney general for his response. Soon thereafter another bench, while hearing a case under the Christian law, requested Chief Justice H. L. Dattu to set up a Special Bench to consider gender discrimination suffered by Muslim women owing to 'arbitrary divorce and second marriage of their husbands during the currency of their first marriage'. The Supreme Court wanted an answer from the government whether 'gender discrimination' suffered by Muslim women should not be considered a violation of the Fundamental Rights under Articles 14, 15 and 21 of the constitution and international covenants to which India was a signatory. The Supreme Court specifically referred to the BJP electoral promise of 2014 to ask 'what happened to it [UCC], if you want to do it then why don't you frame and implement it'. The BJP government's rejoinder was that 'it is very sensitive issue and needs wider consultation'. Reflecting upon this 'wider consultation' phrase, Tahir Mahmood, the ex-chairman of the National Minorities Commission, said that many a time such questions had already been answered in the constitution most unequivocally. For example, the government in its affidavit to the Supreme Court said: 'The fundamental question for determination by this court is whether in a secular democracy religion can be a reason to deny equal status and dignity available to women under the Constitution.' But did not Article 25, which provided for the right to freedom of religion (within Part III that deal with fundamental rights), say at the outset that this freedom was subject, inter alia, to 'other provisions of this part' and those 'other provisions' included the *right to equal protection and gender justice* (see his article in *Times of India*, 27 October 2016, emphasis added).

Seeking an answer from the Supreme Court in respect to specific gender-unjust provisions in the Muslim personal law was largely unnecessary. Several times in the past the High Courts and the Supreme Court had given their verdicts against unjust Muslim practices, such as triple talaq. For example, in 1971 Justice V. R. Krishna Iyer had ruled in the Kerala High Court that

> the view that the Muslim husband enjoys an arbitrary, unilateral power to inflict instant divorce does not accord with Islamic injunctions ... Indeed, a deeper study of the subject discloses a surprisingly rational, realistic and modern law of divorce ... It is a popular fallacy that a Muslim male enjoys, under the

250 *The Politics of Personal Law in South Asia*

Quranic law, unbridled authority to liquidate the marriage . . . Commentators on the Quran have rightly observed—and this tallies with the law now administered in some Muslim countries like Iraq—that the husband must satisfy the court about reasons for divorce. However, Muslim law as applied in India, has taken a course contrary to the spirit of what the Prophet of the Holy Quran laid down and the same misconception vitiates the law dealing with the wife's right to divorce.

In 1978, Justice Baharul Islam held the same view in the Guwahati High Court:

In my view the correct law of talaq as ordained by the Holy Quran is that talaq must be for a reasonable cause and be preceded by attempts at reconciliation between the husband and the wife by two arbiters—one from the wife's family, the other from the husband's. If the attempts fail, talaq may be effected.

Both the above judgments were upheld in 2002 by the Supreme Court in the Shamim Ara case (Noorani 2016).

Wider Consultation: Law Commission Questionnaire

On 1 June 2016 the Modi government asked the Law Commission of India to examine the question of UCC in-depth and submit its report to the law ministry. The idea had its antecedents. In December 2015, Ashwini Upadhyay, a spokesperson of BJP's Delhi unit and a Supreme Court lawyer, had filed a PIL in the Supreme Court asking it to instruct the government to introduce a UCC as advised in the Directive Principles of the Constitution. The court dismissed the PIL on the grounds that it was none of its business to instruct the government on a legislative matter. A bench headed by Chief Justice T. S. Thakur told Upadhyay: 'How can a mandamus [a court order] be issued on such an issue? Constitutional goal is one thing, and possibility of them being fulfilled is yet another thing. These are things in [the] realm of Parliament and the Supreme Court cannot do anything. You go to the go the government.' Thakur also said: 'Let people aggrieved in a community come to this court alleging discrimination. Has anybody come forward? What cannot be done directly, you are trying to do indirectly . . . We cannot ask Parliament to bring the common civil code. It is up to the law makers to discuss and take a decision.' Encouraged by the Supreme Court, Ashwini Upadhyay shot a letter to

Old Wine in the Old Bottle   251

Sadananda Gowda, the Union Law Minister, urging him to seek the opinion of the Law Commission in this regard to which the minister responded positively (http://indiatoday.intoday.in/story/how-modi-government-set-wheels-of-uniform-civil-code-in-motion/1/705962.html, accessed on 2 August 2017).

The ruling of the Supreme Court in the case of *Prakash and Others v Phulvati and Others*, to which we have referred above, came as a godsend to the BJP government. It had been building up a political climate in the country in favour of a Hindu nationalistic state and anything that helped to corner the Muslim community fitted well into the scheme. The party suddenly became a great champion of the cause of Muslim women, knowing well that this would stir the hornet's nest among the 'patriarchs' of the Muslim community, providing further fuel to anti-Muslim and pro-Hindutva fire. Since BJP was always in an election mode and the crucial UP elections had to be fought, the Modi government not only made its attorney general appropriately reply to the Supreme Court query but also asked the Law Commission of India to circulate a questionnaire seeking people's opinion on the question of whether the nation should go for a uniform civil code. Two points to be noted here; one, whether the Law Commission was the appropriate body to undertake the job, and two, why not did the parliament itself, an elected body, take the call on such a critical legislative matter as enacting a UCC when the BJP had an absolute majority there.

Pursuant to the government order, the Law Commission circulated an appeal on 7 October 2016 under the signature of its chairman, Justice B. S. Chauhan, saying that it

[W]elcomes all concerned to engage with us on the comprehensive exercise of the revision and reform of family laws, as the Article 44 of the Indian Constitution provides that 'the state shall endeavour to provide for its citizens a uniform civil code throughout the territory of India'. The objective behind this endeavour is to address discrimination against vulnerable groups and harmonise the various cultural practices. The commission invites suggestions on all possible models and templates of a common civil code.

The Commission hopes to begin a healthy conversation about the viability of a uniform civil code and will focus on family laws of all religions and the diversity of customary practices, *to address social injustice rather than plurality of laws*. Responding to the demands of social change, the Commission will consider the

252 The Politics of Personal Law in South Asia

opinions of all stake-holders and the general public for ensuring that the norms of no one class, group or community dominate the tone or tenor of family law reforms. (See Appendix 7 for the full text of the chairman's letter and the questionnaire, emphasis here is that of this author.)

It is unthinkable that the Modi government's efforts to make the Law Commission of India consider the advisability of introducing a UCC was innocently democratic and in no sense was it meant to prick the identity sensitivity of the Muslims, behind which was its desire to placate the Hindu popular opinion, which historically had provided electoral dividends to the BJP. Here is a representative sample of the Hindutva mind in this respect. The fifth question in the questionnaire which the Law Commission circulated to all political parties and concerned groups read: 'Should the uniform civil code be optional?' In reply to the question, M. G. Vaidya, the well-known RSS ideologue and former editor of Nagpur-based RSS magazine *Tarun Bharat* (meaning: Young India), wrote: 'Those who are opposed to a UCC may be given an option to not follow it. But in that case they will have to forego their right to vote in the elections to the state assemblies and Parliament' (Vaidya, M. G. 2016, 'The Price of Personal Law', *Indian Express* [New Delhi], 1 November). His argument was that the Indian state was constitutionally duty bound to implement a UCC and it was the Modi government which for the first time had the courage to go for it. Vaidya should have known, and indeed he must have, that the directive principles of the Indian constitution had mentioned many other lofty ideals, none of which had been implemented. (Was he equally agitated by the noncompliance in respect to other directives in the Directive Principles?) He, however, was charitable to the non-Muslim minorities who could be allowed to treat the UCC as optional. In this regard he specifically referred to the tribes who followed their customary laws. About Muslims and Christians his position was that they would not lose their religious identities even if they followed the UCC: 'The government, instead of getting entangled in the intricacies of various modes of inheritance, should immediately introduce a bill to enact a common law of marriage and divorce. This law will solve the problem of "triple talaq" as well as address the discrimination against Christian women seeking divorce' (Vaidya 2016).

It may be underlined that while Vaidya particularly referred to Muslim and Christian communities, he very ingeniously ignored the fact that gender-based discriminations were there also among the

Hindus.[9] For example, as the legal scholar and women's rights activist Flavia Agnes has noted, the property question in respect of the Hindu Undivided Family (HUF),[10] cultural practices such as *kanyadan* (sacrificial offering of the bride to the groom) and the atrocities committed on women for *sapinda* and *sagotra* marriages did not project the Hindu society in any glorious light. She wrote that 'the May 2016 Supreme Court judgment holding a wife's refusal to live within a joint family, and her demand for a separate residence, amounted to cruelty to the husband would never have been delivered on a marriage governed by Christian or Parsi laws. It could only have been delivered in a case governed by Hindu law since the notion of separation violates the Hindu ethos of joint family' (Agnes 2016a). BJP's political ploy, however, did the trick. It raised a huge controversy, a glimpse of which was noticeable in India's ever-ready controversy-hungry electronic media channels to boost their Target Rating Point (TRP) ratings. It directed the Hindu community to a make-believe situation that everything was hunky-dory with them and it was the Muslim community alone which should be forced to reform. Insofar as the Muslim community was concerned, it was vertically divided between the traditionalists and modernists, as was evident in the way the Law Commission questionnaire was viewed by these groups.

The traditionalists: They were up in arms against this onslaught on their Islamic ethos at the centre of which was the issue of personal law. Soon after the release of the Law Commission questionnaire, as many as ten Muslim organisations, namely, the All India Personal Law Board, Jamiat Ulema-e-Hind, Jamaat-e-Islami Hind, Markazi Jamiat Ahle Hadees, Jamiat Ulema Hind, Ettehad-e–Millat Council, All India Milli Council, All India Muslim Majlis-e-Mushawarat, Darul Uloom Deoband and the Shia Jama Masjid Kashmeeri Gate, jointly released a press statement on 13 October 2016 against the Law Commission's move. The statement categorically said that the signatory organisations 'reject the questionnaire prepared by the Law Commission'. It further noted that it 'points to the ulterior intentions of the commission and is an attempt to nullify the Muslims personal Law. The question is framed so as to confuse the respondents. By referring to article 44 of the constitution, an attempt is made to give a constitutional position to Uniform Civil Code. This is false and deceit as the clause is Directive Principle which is not bound to be implemented . . . If the central government is serious in implementing the directive principles, then it should implement such articles of the Directive Principles that are directly connected with the well-being and welfare of the people like total prohibition, universal education for all children, provision

254   *The Politics of Personal Law in South Asia*

of health facilities to all, toilets in all households etc.' Then making a strong political point the press release said:

> People of the country following diverse faiths–Hindus, Muslims, Christians, Buddhists, Sikhs, Dalits, Adivasis, etc. jointly fought [for] the freedom and liberated the nation from the clutches of the British. In spite of variations in personal laws all these groups fought with signal mind and shoulder to shoulder . . . The Indian constitution is also framed on the foundation of unity in diversity. People following different faiths and beliefs take part in the social life following their religious beliefs independently and keeping this diversity and differences they work together for the progress and security of the country as a joint nation and society . . . So such steps for forcible uniform civil practice will be a threat to the security of the nation itself. India is nation of diverse cultures and different religions. Personal laws of all these groups are derived from their religious texts or scriptures and it has unique relevance in their cultural identity. Therefore any kind of interference in this is not only a violation of religious freedom enshrined in the constitution but will put an end to their unique cultural identity . . . This is nothing but a calculated effort to disrupt the communal harmony and social fabric by raising [a] controversial issue when the country as a whole is facing so many serious and important problems. (Full statement is available at http://aimplboard.in/images/media/Press13-10-2016%20ENGLISH.pdf.)

The AIMPLB printed thousands of forms for community members, each of which could be signed by seven, to express their disapproval of the Law Commission's move. By early November 2016 it claimed to have gathered more than 550,000 signatures opposing the commission's move (*Times of India*, 5 November 2016). It was the common refrain of Muslim leaders that uppermost in BJP's mind was nothing but the forthcoming UP assembly elections in which a polarised communal vote was expected to benefit the party. But AIMPLB's predicament was how to balance the community's fear with the aggressive Hindutva on the one hand, and the growing Muslim feminist demand for intra-community gender justice on the other. One may recall a similar situation decades ago in the history of the passage of the Dissolution of Muslim Marriages Act, 1939. At that time the Muslim members who pleaded for the bill had to project their religion as one which was not at all backward-looking as their Hindu counterparts had alleged. The Muslim members underlined that it was not the

Old Wine in the Old Bottle 255

Shari'ah which was to blame, but it was the Anglo-Muhammadan law that had tampered with it to make it look conservative. In this formulation they had to take note of the Muslim feminist diatribe as well (De 2009: 119).

The progressives: There was no dearth of Muslim liberal voices. They consisted of both intellectuals and women activists. But almost none, however, asked for a uniform civil code. This nuanced positioning of the Muslim liberal view posed a difficult challenge to the AIMPLB. Forced into a tight spot, it was obliged to balance between its rather reluctant promise to put an end to instant triple talaq and at the same time dodge the promise through its 'Islam in danger' scare mongering, at the core of which was the argument that Muslim identity must be safeguarded. More than a decade ago, in July 2004, it was hoped that at its executive committee meeting held in Kanpur, the AIMPLB would announce the abolition of triple talaq, but nothing had happened then. The much-touted 'model nikahnama', which it released in Bhopal in May 2005, proved to be a damp squib. All that the nikahnama achieved was a nonbinding promise from the bridegroom. Its Section 5(vii) read: '*Jahan tak mumkin ho ek waqt mein teen talaq dene se bachna*' (to the extent possible, avoid pronouncing three divorces at one go) (Faizur 2017). No wonder that alongside their serious misgivings about the notion of a UCC as peddled by the ruling dispensation, several noted Muslim liberals expressed their opposition to the AIMPLB's affidavit to the Law Commission. These intellectuals included such names as S. Irfan Habib, Ayesha Kidwai, Gauhar Raza, Zoya Hasan, Shabnam Hashmi and many others (*The Hindu*, 24 October 2016). It was intellectually argued that the fundamental premise of AIMPLB was wrong, which emanated from two concepts, namely, *taqleed* and *tamazzhub*. The first meant the uncritical acceptance of a particular school of Islamic jurisprudence, while the second meant the idealisation of a school. The AIMPLB followed just the selective interpretation in the Hanafi law, thereby totally ignoring the tradition of plural thinking enshrined in the Quran. The organisation suffered from 'its obsessive denominationalism', said Faizur Rahman (2017).[11]

In the forefront of the Muslim women's groups, which were opposed to the AIMPLB, yet at the same time were insisting on the correct reading of the *Shari'ah*, thereby upholding the Muslim personal law, were the Awaaz-e-Niswaan (formed in 1987), the All India Muslim Women's Personal Law Board (AIMWPLB, formed in 2005) and the Bharatiya Muslim Mahila Andolan (BMMA, formed in 2007). Other activist groups were: the Bebaak Collective (Voices of the Fearless,

256 *The Politics of Personal Law in South Asia*

which included the left-leaning All India Democratic Women's Association [AIDWA]), Forum Against Oppression of Women (Mumbai), Saheli (Delhi), Jagori (Delhi), Zubaan (Delhi), Tamil Nadu Women's Jamaat and scores of concerned individuals. To counter the signature campaign of the AIMPLB, the BMMA undertook a counter signature campaign and expected to get 50,000 forms filled by women who supported its position. Noorjehan Shafia Naz of the organisation assailed both the AIMPLB and the Hindu right, according to whom both thrived at each other's success. She called the AIMPLB 'a mafia rather than religious scholars' (*Times of India*, 3 November 2016).

There was at least one voice which took a position different from the above strand by reposing hope in the constitution and law and not in the religious texts. Razia Patel, the head of the minority cell at the Pune-based Institute of Education argued: 'The path of women's liberation is through the values enshrined in the Indian Constitution. It is unfortunate that rather than leading the community towards absolute human rights, intellectuals are making the situation for the community worse by resorting to the logic of a religious framework' (*Indian Express*, 9 September 2016). This view, however, was the minuscule minority view among Muslim women activists. One important point is necessary to underline here for our understanding of the texture of the movement. In the teeth of the Hindu nationalistic upsurge, these groups have over the years diluted their secular feminism in favour of, one, postponing their advocacy for a UCC and demanding instead reforms in Muslim personal law as ordained in the Quran, and two, coordinating their demands in cooperation with Islamic scholars and religious leaders wherever possible. Many preferred to call them 'Islamic feminists'. This has been true even with the Marxist-oriented All India Democratic Women's Association (AIDWA) (Vatuk 2008: 510–13, Z. Hasan 2010: 949–52, Vatuk 2017: 154–57).[12]

Triple Talaq Controversy

It is not easy to go into the intricate meaning and history of triple talaq in this limited space as every idea expressed has been contested, which itself proves that Muslims are as plural and opinionated as any other Indian community. In his *Times of India* (23 August 2017) article Maulana Wahiduddin Khan gives a simple description which may serve our purpose here though the debate would continue. According to him the institution of instant triple talaq is not a principle of Islam. Quran does indeed provide for divorce if a conjugal relationship becomes incompatible, but there is a proper procedure for it as laid

Old Wine in the Old Bottle 257

down in Quran and which was adhered to by Prophet Mohammad and the first caliph Abu Bakr. They dismissed any utterance of talaq thrice at one go as something which must have been done in a fit of anger and therefore treated them as only one such utterance. In any case, a divorce situation should take at least three months to mature. But this practice was diluted during the time of the second caliph Umar when it became commonplace to use instant triple talaq as a complete process to effect a divorce. It may be underlined that it was not a *Shari'ah* law, therefore. His was a *hukm-al-hakim*, meaning an executive order. Such orders could be valid only in particular cases but, could not have the status of *Shari'ah* law. However, during the British time the practice was followed more commonly and Hanafi school (to which most Indian Sunni Muslims, and the entire All India Muslim Personal Law Board, belong) made the instant triple talaq the norm, more often through *fatwas*. Against the background of the Supreme Court verdict of 22 August 2017 (discussed below) Wahiduddin Khan said: 'In such a scenario, my advice to Hanafi Muslims is to take the Supreme Court's verdict as a reminder and review their practice. They should consider triple talaq in one go as a case of a decision having been taken in anger and take it as only one talaq—as had been done during the time of the Prophet.'[13]

The recent controversy started in early 2016 when Shayara Bano, a 35-year-old Muslim woman from Uttarakhand, filed a petition in the Supreme Court to declare the *talaq-e-biddat* (the unilateral and irrevocable form of divorce called triple talaq) pronounced in 2015 by her husband, Rizwan Ahmed, an Allahabad-based property dealer, as unconstitutional since it violated her fundamental rights (https:// assets.documentcloud.org/documents/2725467/Shayara-Bano-Writ-Petition-FINAL-VERSION.txt). If one goes by just the question of declaring triple talaq as unlawful, there was nothing new. Earlier court judgments had done that time and again as in the cases of *Shamim Ara v State of U.P.* (Supreme Court, 2002), *Dadgu Pathan v Rahimbi Pathan* (Bombay High Court, 2002), *Najimunbee v Sk Sikander Sk Rehman* (Bombay High Court, 2004), *Dilshad Begum Ahmadkhan Pathan v Ahmadkhan Hanifkhan Pathan* (Bombay High Court on appeal following Sessions Court judgment, 2007), *Riaz Fatima v Mohd Sharif* (Delhi High Court on appeal following Sessions Court judgment, 2007) and *Shakil Ahmad Sheikh v Vahida Shakil Sheikh* (Bombay High Court, 2016) (details of the cases are in Agnes 2016d: 13–15). Besides, since Shayara Bano was a chronic victim of domestic violence in the hands of her husband, which had continued for 15 long years before she was banished to her parental home, she

258   *The Politics of Personal Law in South Asia*

could have taken recourse to any or all the three existing secular laws, namely, the Protection of Women from Domestic Violence Act of 2005, the Muslim Women (Protection of Rights on Divorce) Act of 1986, and under Section 125 of the Code of Criminal Procedure (CrPC). She, however, chose to appeal to the Supreme Court through a PIL claiming that her husband's action amounted to a violation of her fundamental right as enshrined in the Indian Constitution. The case drew huge media attention because of three things: one, the contemporary texture of Hindutva politics; two, a short-sighted AIMPLB, ever worried about Muslim identity running into danger; and three, an over-enthusiastic electronic media waiting for any *masala* (literal meaning: spice, connotatively: socially sensitive) topic around which it could pit two or more cantankerous groups of garrulous commentators on primetime TV to boost one's own TRP score over that of the other channels.

The Supreme Court Judgment

The judgment of the five-judge bench of the Supreme Court which ran into 395 pages came two years after Shayara Bano had filed her petition.[14] While giving the judgment the court had tagged four other similar cases, as well as the petition of the Bharatiya Muslim Mahila Andolan (BMMA). The four cases were those of Ishrat Jahan, Gulshan Parveen, Aafreen Rehman and Atiya Sabri. Thus, altogether there were six petitioners. The bench consisted of Chief Justice J. S. Khehar, Justice Kurian Joseph, Justice Uday Umesh Lalit, Justice R. F. Nariman and Justice S. Abdul Nazeer. It was a 3:2 verdict, three in favour of abolishing instant triple talaq (Justices Joseph, Nariman and Lalit), two in favour of its continuation on the grounds that it formed a part of the Muslim personal law, which had the sanction of the Indian constitution as one of the fundamental rights that included religious rights (Justices Khehar and Nazeer). There was a nuanced point of difference in the majority judgment. While two (Justices Nariman and Lalit) drew their conclusion by dissecting and questioning some of the premises of the Shariat Act of 1937, Justice Joseph based his judgment on previous Supreme Court judgments and certain Quranic principles. Curiously, and probably consciously, the composition of the bench was meant to advertise it as a secular move in itself as the five judges belonged to five different religions: Hindu (Lalit), Muslim (Nazeer), Christian (Joseph), Sikh (Khehar) and Parsi (Nariman). But, strangely, although the case under adjudication was in respect of women's rights the bench did not contain a single female judge. The

Old Wine in the Old Bottle 259

only sitting female judge, Justice R. Bhanumathi, could have been included in the bench for the purposes of propriety.

Here are some important extracts from the three sets of verdicts:

- Justices Nariman and Lalit (majority verdict):

  Islam divides, [according to Justice Hidayatuallah] all actions into five kinds which figure differently in the sight of God and in respect of which His Commands are different. This plays an important part in the lives of Muslims. (i) First degree: Fard. Whatever is commanded in the Koran, Hadis or ijmaa must be obeyed. Wajib. Perhaps a little less compulsory than Fard but only slightly so. (ii) Second degree: Masnun, Mandub and Mustahab: These are recommended actions. (iii) Third degree: Jaiz or Mubah: These are permissible actions as to which religion is indifferent. (iv) Fourth degree: Makruh: That which is reprobated as unworthy. (v) Fifth degree: Haram: That which is forbidden.

  Obviously, Triple Talaq does not fall within the first degree, since even assuming that it forms part of the Koran, Hadis or Ijmaa, it is not something 'commanded'. Equally Talaq itself is not recommended action and, therefore, Triple Talaq will not fall within the second degree. Triple Talaq at best falls within the third degree, but probably falls more squarely within the fourth degree. Triple Talaq is a permissible action as to which religion is indifferent. Within fourth degree it is reprobated as unworthy. We have already seen that though permissible in Hanafi jurisprudence, yet that very jurisprudence castigates Triple Talaq as being sinful.

  . . .

  Applying the test of manifest arbitrariness to the case at hand, it is clear that Triple Talaq is a form of Talaq which is itself considered to be something innovative, namely, that it is not in the Sunna, being an irregular or heretical form of Talaq. We have noticed how in Fyzee's book (supra), the Hanafi school of *Shari'ah* law, which itself recognizes this form of Talaq, specifically states that though lawful it is sinful in that it incurs the wrath of God.

  Given the fact that Triple Talaq is instant and irrevocable, it is obvious that any attempt at reconciliation between the

260 *The Politics of Personal Law in South Asia*

husband and wife by two arbiters from their families, which is essential to save the marital tie, cannot ever take place. Also, as understood by the Privy Council in Rashid Ahmad (supra), such Triple Talaq is valid even if it is not for any reasonable cause, which in view of the law no longer holds good after Shamim Ara (supra). This being the case, it is clear that this form of Talaq is manifestly arbitrary in the sense that the marital tie can be broken capriciously and whimsically by a Muslim man without any attempt at reconciliation so as to save it.

This form of Talaq must, therefore, be held to be violative of the fundamental right contained under Article 14 of the Constitution of India. In our opinion, therefore, the 1937 Act, insofar as it seeks to recognize and enforce Triple Talaq, is within the meaning of the expression 'laws in force' in Article 13(1) and must be struck down as being void to the extent that it recognizes and enforces Triple Talaq.

Since we have declared Section 2 of the above 1937 Act to be void to the extent indicted above on the narrower ground of it being manifestly arbitrary, we do not find the need to go into the ground of discrimination in these cases, as was argued by the learned Attorney General and those supporting him.

- Justice Joseph (majority verdict):

  There are four sources of Islamic law (i) Quran (ii) Hadith (iii) Ijma (iv) Qiyas. The learned author [Asaf A.A. Fyzee in his book *Outlines of Muhammadan Law*, 5th Edition, 2008 at page 10] has rightly said that the Holy Quran is the 'first source of law'. According to the learned author, pre-eminence is to be given to the Quran. That means, sources other than the Holy Quran are not only to supplement what is given in it and to supply what is not provided for. In other words, there cannot be any Hadith, Ijma or Qiyas against what is expressly stated in the Quran. Islam cannot be anti-Quran.'

  . . .

  These instructive verses [Justice Joseph refers to three Suras in Sura II, Sura IV and Sura LXV, the last one dealing explicitly with talaq] do not require any interpretative exercise. They are clear and unambiguous as far as talaq is concerned.

Old Wine in the Old Bottle 261

The Holy Quran has attributed sanctity and permanence to matrimony. However, in extremely unavoidable situations, talaq is permissible. But an attempt for reconciliation and if it succeeds, then revocation are the Quranic essential steps before talaq attains finality. In triple talaq, this door is closed, hence, triple talaq is against the basic tenets of the Holy Quran and consequently, it violates Shariat. The above view has been endorsed by various High Courts, finally culminating in Shamim Ara by this Court which has since been taken as the law for banning triple talaq.

. . .

I believe that a reconciliation between the same [religion and constitution] is possible, but the process of harmonizing different interests is within the powers of the legislature. Of course, this power has to be exercised within the constitutional parameters without curbing the religious freedom guaranteed under the Constitution of India. However, it is not for the courts to direct for any legislation.

Fortunately, this Court has done its part in Shamim Ara. I expressly endorse and reiterate the law declared in Shamim Ara. What is held to be bad in the Holy Quran cannot be good in Shariat and, in that sense, what is bad in theology is bad in law as well.

- Chief Justice Khehar and Justice Nazeer (minority verdict):

   The whole nation seems to be up in arms. There is seemingly an overwhelming majority of Muslim women, demanding that the practice of 'talaq-a-biddat' which is sinful in theology, be declared as impermissible in law. The Union of India has also participated in the debate. It has adopted an aggressive posture, seeking the invalidation of the practice by canvassing, that it violates the fundamental rights enshrined in Part III of the Constitution, and by further asserting, that it even violates constitutional morality. During the course of hearing, the issue was hotly canvassed in the media. Most of the views expressed in erudite articles on the subject, hugely affirmed that the practice was demeaning. Interestingly even during the course of hearing, learned counsel appearing for the rival parties, were in agreement, and described the practice

262 *The Politics of Personal Law in South Asia*

of 'talaq-e-biddat' differently as, unpleasant, distasteful and unsavoury. The position adopted by others was harsher, they considered it as disgusting, loathsome and obnoxious. Some even described it as being debased, abhorrent and wretched. We have arrived at the conclusion, that 'talaq-e-biddat,' is a matter of 'personal law' of Sunni Muslims, belonging to the Hanafi school. It constitutes a matter of their faith.

. . .

Such a call of conscience as the petitioners desire us to accept, may well has a cascading effect. We say so, because the contention of the learned Attorney General was, that 'talaq-e-ahsan' and 'talaq-e-hasan' were also liable to be declared unconstitutional for the same reasons as have been expressed with reference to 'talaq-e-biddat'. According to the learned Attorney General, the said form of talaq also suffered from the same infirmities as 'talaq-e-biddat'. The practices of 'polygamy' and 'halala' amongst Muslims are already under challenge before us. It is not difficult to comprehend, what kind of challenges would be raised by rationalists, assailing practices of different faiths on diverse grounds, based on all kinds of enlightened sensibilities. We have to be guarded, lest we find our conscience traversing into every nook and corner of religious practices, and 'personal law'. Can a court, based on righteous endeavour, declare that a matter of faith, be replaced—or be completely done away with. . . . Article 25 obliges all Constitutional Courts to protect 'personal laws' and not to find fault therewith. Interference in matters of 'personal law' is clearly beyond judicial examination.

. . .

There can be no doubt, and it is our definitive conclusion, that the position can only be salvaged by way of legislation. We understand, that it is not appropriate to tender advice to the legislature, to enact law on an issue. . . . The stance adopted by the Union of India is sufficient for us to assume that the Union of India supports the petitioners' cause. Unfortunately, the Union seeks at our hands what truly falls in its own. The main party that opposed the petitioners' challenge, namely, the AIMPLB, [has agreed] . . . to incorporate

Old Wine in the Old Bottle 263

a condition in the 'Nikahnama' to exclude resorting to pronouncement of three divorces by her husband in one sitting [there are other evidences too from the AIMPLB to the same effect]. . . . We, therefore, hereby direct the Union of India to consider appropriate legislation, particularly with reference to 'talaq-e-biddat'.

. . .

Till such time as legislation in the matter is considered, we are satisfied in injuncting Muslim husbands from pronouncing 'talaq-e-biddat' as a means of severing their matrimonial relationship. The instant injunction, shall in the first instance, be operative for six months. If the legislative process commences before the expiry of the period of six months, and a positive decision emerges towards redefining 'talaq-e-biddat' (three pronouncements of 'talaq', at one and the same time)—as one, or alternatively, if it is decided that the practice of 'talaq-e-biddat' be done away with altogether, the injunction would continue, till legislation is finally enacted. Failing which, the injunction shall cease to operate.

A Political Analysis

Since all laws are political constructions, and personal law is no exception, it would be instructive to make a political analysis of the Supreme Court judgment because it is expected to have its impact on the discourse over UCC as well as on Indian politics. The beauty of the judgment was that it made everyone happy, of course for different reasons. Everyone claimed that they got what they wanted. Shayara Bano was happy that her claim that her fundamental rights had been violated was upheld by the apex court. Four other petitioners who wanted their divorces declared illegal and unconstitutional got the verdicts in their favour. The Bharatiya Muslim Mahila Andolan (BMMA)'s plea that triple talaq had no sanction in *Shari'ah* was upheld. Even the AIMPLB was pleased that the verdict underwrote the validity of Muslim personal law. The women activists in general were happy that the judgment was a step forward and if the process continued apace, discrimination against women in terms of property rights and other social taboos, as prevalent in other personal laws, including the Hindu law, would receive wider attention and eventually judicial interventions.

264   *The Politics of Personal Law in South Asia*

But politically speaking, the biggest gainer was the BJP, particularly because it could sell it as a victory by totally glossing over the fact that its position was not upheld by the Supreme Court. The Modi government had forcefully defended its affidavit in the court for a complete ban on all forms of divorce practised by Muslims under their personal law. Attorney General Mukul Rohtagi had deposed before the court that the government would enact a law to do away with all forms of divorce available to Muslims under their personal law. Court asked for a clarification as to how such a law would not interfere with the issue of minority rights as enshrined in the constitution: 'If talaq in entirety is erased, how will a Muslim man walk out of bad marriage?' The court explained that if the government wanted uniformity then it should tell all its citizens that they could marry only under the Special Marriage Act, 1954. The bench put the following poser to Rohtagi: 'Marriage is a religious ceremony. The manner in which you are arguing, it will finish all personal law rights. Some religious rights are given to all under Article 25. The way you argue, it would mean that religion and religious practices can be thrown to the wind.' Rohtagi's reply was: 'If the court takes the first step and quashes talaq in entirety, we will take the next step of enacting a new law.' Though he was reconciliatory to the extent that let other forms of talaq (excluding instant talaq) continue for the time being, but his underlying point was that 'if all three forms of talaq are struck down, then we will not have a vacuum. Triple talaq is not part of religion. . . . Do Muslim women have equality in matter of divorce within the community? Do they enjoy equal rights compared to women of other communities within the country? Do they enjoy similar rights compared to Muslim women in other countries? If the answer to the three questions are no, then that custom, even if [it is] part of religious rights, must be struck down as unconstitutional.' The bench's counter to this was that 'right to religion cannot mean that Article 25 protects only what citizens do inside a temple, mosque, gurdwara or other religious institutions but not other customs or practices they perform outside. . . . If a man gives Rs. 10 to one son and Rs. 5 to another son, does he violate the right to equality of the sons? Marriage and divorce are part of personal laws and are religious ceremonies' (*Times of India*, 16 May 2017).

From the above, it is clear that Modi government's argument in the court was at best partially upheld. But the party spoke loudly and clearly that it was their complete victory and Modi should get all the credit for steering the nation to this outcome. The party said that it was good that Muslim women would get their right and it was a matter of

Old Wine in the Old Bottle 265

pride for them and the entire country. Muslim women too would have respect like women in other communities. Modi called the judgment 'historic', which would mean 'empowerment' of Muslim women. The BJP president Amit Shah viewed it as a 'resolute step towards New India,' which gave 'the right to crores of women to live with equality and dignity. It is a beginning of a new epoch of self-respect and equality for Muslim women'. The Union Law Minister Ravi Shankar Prasad was ecstatic: 'I am proud of Narendra Modi *ji*. He stood firmly behind those who are victims of triple *talaq*. And let me say this is Narendra Modi government, not Rajiv Gandhi government.' Senior advocate Mukul Rohatgi, who as the attorney general had argued the government's case, said that the ruling had *'completely vindicated'* the government's position. This was grossly incorrect. He also claimed that it was 'a step towards achieving the ultimate goal of a uniform civil code'. This amounted to reading too much into the judgment. The VHP characteristically went a step further and said that the government not only should enact a law against the practice of triple talaq but also bring a legislation banning more than two children. It was not clear whether this proposed ban was across the board or for Muslims only. A more balanced opinion came from the Union minister of state for minority affairs Mukhtar Abbas Naqvi. Welcoming the Supreme Court verdict, he said that the Modi government would discuss with all political parties framing a law on the subject of instant divorce. He did not talk of a larger agenda like the UCC (Smriti K. Ramachandran, 'SC Ruling On Triple Talaq: Saffron Parties Call It a 'Moral Victory', *Hindustan Times*, New Delhi, 23 August 2017, www.hindustanti-mes.com/india-news/sc-ruling-on-triple-talaq-saffron-parties-call-it-a-moral-victory/story-D2j7UlE4mmPyGdh9AZa97K.html, accessed on 10 September 2017).

Any Effective Gain for Shayara Bano? A Perspective

In Chapter VII we referred to the concept of the non-state legal system (NSLS), which was all-pervasive in South Asia. On account of mass poverty, wide-spread illiteracy, the high cost of court procedures, inordinate delays in justice delivery[15] and last, but not the least, societal interventions or community pressures, a large number of cases in the region were settled outside the formal state legal system (SLS), that is, at the community level.[16] Indeed, Shayara Bano's appeal did not fall into this category as she approached the court and got justice too. But the question is, what next? Her point was well taken by the court that her fundamental right to equality had been violated and

266   The Politics of Personal Law in South Asia

that her husband's triple talaq pronounced against her should stand nullified. By itself, however, it was expected to neither help her restore a happy married life, as she had already been a victim of domestic violence and maltreatment for a long 15-year period, nor to give her any other avenue to ask for financial help in case she ultimately seeks the divorce, than asking for the benefits under the Muslim Women's Act of 1986 or Domestic Violence Act of 2005, or, Section 125 of the CrPC. But at the societal level her worries could multiply. The more she gets media attention and the more she is used by the Hindu right, which will try to earn brownie points by showing the Muslims in a bad light, the community will be prone to distance itself from her as one who has earned a bad name for the community. Given the community's general backwardness and patriarchal orientation, she may be increasingly ostracised once she is off the media glare. One may recall how in the Shah Bano case, because of social pressure, she ultimately had to withdraw her appeal. Lawyer and women's rights activist Flavia Agnes had underlined the 'Muslim-ness' of the case even when it was underway. She wrote: 'In the prevailing media frenzy . . . [the fact that] she is a Muslim woman and the domestic violence she suffered cannot be placed under a general category. It must be given a special Islamic hue for the violence to be taken seriously by the media. The violence she endured itself is not important; it is her Muslim-ness and the projection that she is the victim of archaic and oppressive personal laws which alone can give her that special status and set her apart from all other victims of domestic violence. Without such framing, the violence she suffered would command no special status, and may easily be dismissed as the "routine" violence suffered by women in India' (Agnes 2016b: 15; Faizan Mustafa shares the same concerns in his interview in https://scroll.in/article/836751/people-will-accept-triple-talaq-out-of-fear-of-god-legal-expert-faizan-mustafa, accessed on 11 August 2017 (also in conversation with this author on 26 September 2017).

But my take on the question would be as follows. Shayara Bano may have to countenance social ostracisation from her community, making her at times feel that her legal victory has been meaningless in the real sense, but to compare her situation with Shah Bano, who under social pressure had to withdraw her appeal, will be reading too much into the element of social pressure. Unlike Shah Bano, Shayara Bano is not an uneducated woman who can be taken for granted. She is a determined woman as reflected in the fact that she did not withdraw her case, though she was pressured by some AIMPLB members to do so. Besides, many women's organisations and liberals across the

Old Wine in the Old Bottle 267

communities had lent their support to her petition. Furthermore, three decades have passed between the two Bano cases during which many things in the women's worlds have changed. Even before her marriage, Shayara Bano had a Master of Arts degree (it is indeed strange that she had tolerated an oppressive husband for fifteen long years), now she is pursuing her MBA in education. She is not politically naïve either, as she insists that the BJP government should not take undue credit for the court decision: 'It was a social fight, not a political one' (Omar Rashid, 'Who Is Shayara Bano, the Triple Talaq Crusader (opinion), *The Hindu*, 2 September 2017, www.thehindu.com/news/national/who-is-shayara-bano-the-triple-talaq-crusader/article19611402.ece, accessed on 2 November 2017).

On the Fringes

Customary Laws of Tribes

Our discourse on the uniform civil code, personal law, or 'uniformisation' of civil law will remain incomplete without reference to the tribal laws which fall within the broad category of customary law. Tribal people of India, who constitute about 9 per cent of India's population, have their own customary laws. In 1955–56 when the Hindu Code was introduced, it was stipulated that the code would apply to Hindus, Buddhists, Jains and Sikhs but would exclude from its application the members of the Scheduled Tribes within the meaning of clause (25) of Article 366 of the Constitution.[17] Article 371A, which deals with Nagaland, says specifically that 'no act of Parliament in respect of religious and social practices of the Nagas', their 'customary law and procedure' and the 'administration of civil and criminal justice involving decisions according to Naga customary law' 'shall apply to the state of Nagaland unless the Legislative Assembly of Nagaland by a resolution so decides'. Barring some special cases when the Central Government gives specific directions, the tribes are governed by their customs. But since these customs are not always in consonance with modern times, the Indian legislatures have from time to time discouraged undesirable social practices. For example, Chhattisgarh has enacted the Chhattisgarh Tonhi Atyachar (Niwaran) Act, 2005. Tribal law, therefore, comprises of customary as well as state laws.[18]

For the sociopolitical control of the tribal cultural space there is a constant contestation between the central and state governments on the one end and the tribal communities on the other end. As one young tribal doctoral student of Jawaharlal Nehru University (JNU)

268   *The Politics of Personal Law in South Asia*

notes, 'the forces of assimilation have been operating upon them on a massive scale through the influences of hinduisation, westernisation and peasantisation. . . . [S]ate has been on constant negotiation, dealing with the dialectic of either enforcement of state forces to facilitate "willing acceptance" of the indomitable "nation state" or compelling tribal regions to operate within its bounded, "autonomous" and rigid boundaries. . . . The underlying passion which spells out in forms of articulations of the indigenous resistance is the need to differentiate themselves from the "other" and to hold on to their critical geographical and social spaces both at the realm of culture and politics' (Ekka 2014: 49–50). In the context of legal pluralism this discourse assumes considerable importance. The amount of criticality that the tribes attach to their customary laws to retain their respective identities comes in conflict with the idea of a nation-state, for which the control of the legal spaces of all Indians as one single community is of huge political significance.

But the conflict is also local. Tribal laws suffer from the same patriarchy and gender discrimination as do the other Indian personal laws. Voices against these injustices have been raised by women activists in the tribal communities, which have a tradition of a pedigree in the nationalist movement. Particular concern is with regard to land rights, which the multiple court cases dealing with them indicate. These cases have resulted in a number of case laws, particularly in the Chhotanagpur region. In many of them either the Hindu Succession Act or the Christian personal law have been taken recourse to depending upon whether the litigant is a Hinduised tribal or a converted Christian. To make their voices audible, the women have formed associations like the Jharkhand Mahila Mukti Samiti (founded in 1987). Sometimes the issues are not strictly confined to land rights but include such other questions as liquor consumption, witch-hunting and demands, in general, for more political space for women (Sinha 2005: 217–18). The core idea in all these movements is to resist patriarchy. Since we have discussed the broad question of tribal law in Chapter IV, let us concentrate here only on the witch-hunting issue, which did not receive our attention in that chapter. Besides the element of superstition, at the core of the problem is the institution of patriarchy. Witch-related research, however, shows two conflicting interpretations of patriarchy. At one level it is to deprive women of their equal status in society, for example, with regard to their property rights, while at the other level it is about the women's search for direct communication channels with the supernatural (God) because tribal religions by and large are male-centric, which deprive women of any

Old Wine in the Old Bottle 269

religious role. Only males can participate in religious rituals (Sinha 2005: 60–61; Sinha 2006: 133–34).

The phenomenon of 'witch' is there in the entire tribal belt of India, and sometimes even beyond. There are evidences of it in Andhra Pradesh, Bihar, Chhattisgarh, Gujarat, Haryana, Jharkhand, Madhya Pradesh, Maharashtra, Meghalaya, Orisha, Rajasthan and West Bengal. Indeed, it would be an exaggeration to claim that the institution is a part of the tribal customary law, but it cannot be disputed that it is has considerable social sanction within the village society. For example, in spite of Rajasthan's Prevention of Witch-Hunting Act, 2015, not a single conviction has taken place though several cases of witch killing and torture have been reported. Even the power available with the state to impose punitive fines on the villages indulging in such acts, as per Section 8 of the Act, has never been taken recourse to (*The Hindu*, 1 October 2017). Just like the question of whether a uniform civil code would be able to supplant the overriding influence of the caste panchayats (say, the *khap panchayats* in Haryana, Rajasthan, western Uttar Pradesh (UP) and several other parts of north India[19]), which make a mockery of citizen's rights to marry inter-community as encrypted in the Special Marriage Act, 1954, the same doubts may be cast in respect of the anti-witch-hunting legislations as our Rajasthan example above suggests. Other states having such laws are Assam, Bihar, Chhattisgarh, Jharkhand and Orisha. It has been the experience that in most cases the prosecution witnesses do not show up, resulting in the collapse of the cases before they reach the judgment stage. Also, even if sometimes punishments are pronounced against the offenders, they are so light that they hardly serve as deterrent. Shashank Shekhar Sinha, who has been researching on the subject (2005, 2006, 2007, 2014, 2015) explained this inherent problem to this author (25 August 2017). Earlier, in 2012, he had said in an interview:

> While legislation, Christian missionaries, adivasi reform movements (inspired by Hindu ideas of purity) and the realisation that such practices were considered socially degrading played a part, what [. . . is also important] is the role of ethno-regionalism. Adivasi Mahasabha (1938) and late Jharkhand Party (1950) (with many Christianised adivasis as followers) were trying to forge a pan-adivasi collective which implied toning down internal tensions (witch killings included). The strains generated by the post-colonial developmental regime led to a new wave of witch killings in 1970s–1980s onwards. . . . The violence inflicted on

270 *The Politics of Personal Law in South Asia*

the accused has become layered and recurring and incidents of rape, physical torture or disfigurement of women's bodies are fast emerging as new dynamics in witch hunts.

—(Sinha 2012, see also Sinha 2015: 114)

Between 2001 and 2012, according to the National Crime Research Bureau (NCRB), on an average 168 witchcraft-related deaths (both 'murders' and 'culpable homicides') were reported every year, mostly from Andhra Pradesh, Chhattisgarh, Jharkhand, Madhya Pradesh, Orissa and West Bengal, but also from Bihar, Gujarat and Haryana though their numbers were small. As per the Association of for Social and Human Awareness (ASHA), a reputed NGO under the leadership of Poonam Toppo, whose grandmother was deprecated as a witch, Jharkhand alone registered 371 witch killings between 2001 and 2008 annually. According to the same NGO, the state's 32,000 villages, each reporting three or more witch accusation cases, accounted for a total of about 100,000 such accusations during the said period annually (Nathan, Kelkar and Satija 2013: 2).

The issue of witch-hunting has to be seen from four perspectives, namely, patriarchy, gender discrimination in respect of women's shares in land, patrilineal descent system and the transition from subsistence economy to accumulative economy. As noted in a study done by the Institute of Human Development, 'the violence of the witch-hunt seems to have had a constitutive role in establishing women's subordination. But it also has an instrumental role in continuing to keep women subordinated. The likelihood of any woman being denounced as a witch has an effect on all women, persuading them to follow established practices and not deviate from the norm' (Nathan, Kelkar and Satija 2013). Because of increasing democratisation of tribal societies, the problem is sometimes getting more entrenched as the nexus between the village head (*mukhiya*) and the *ojha* (also known as *sokha, deonar, mati, jan*—they roughly connote an exorcist) is becoming powerful. The naming and shaming of the so-called witch is taking ridiculous forms, such as forcing them drink fresh blood of killed animals such as chicken (for purification) or eat human excreta (for shaming and humiliating). The problem is getting increasingly worse as witch-hunting is no longer merely an intra-tribe phenomenon. It has become more of a village issue in which even Dalits and Muslims are sometimes the victims or the conduits. That the hunted witch in most cases is a widow or an unmarried woman proves the element of patriarchy, as if a woman is safe only when she has a husband, although the latter's protection does not always help. The

Old Wine in the Old Bottle 271

politicisation of the problem because of panchayat elections has further complicated the situation (author's conversation with Shashank Shekhar Sinha on 25 August 2017).

Can a uniform civil code based on international human rights norms do away with this ghastly practice? As with other personal laws, in the case of tribal laws there is a systematic uniformisation of and progressive state of judicial interventions aimed at eradicating gender injustice. Some cases that point to the trend are: 2006 AIR SCW 1529: *State of Maharashtra and Others vs. Mana Adim Jamat Mandal*; 1996 AIR SC1864: *Madhu Kishwar and others vs. State of Bihar and others*; 1972 AIR 1840 SCR (3) 361: *N. E. Horo vs. Jahan Ara Jaipal Singh*; AIR 1964 [pat 201–206: *Kartik Oraon vs. David Munzni and Anr*; AIR 1931 Pat 305: *Ganesh Mahto and Others vs. Shib Charan Mahto*; AIR 2004 Jharkhand 121: *Lakshmi Narayan Tudu vs. Smt. Basi Majhian and Others*; and WP (PIL) No. 6884 of 2002 *Kapara Hansda vs. Government of India and Others*, Jharkhand High Court, Ranchi (details in Ekka 2014: 95–114). But there is still much more to be achieved as the ostracisation of the Santhal writer Hansda Sowvendra Shekhar by the Jharkhand state assembly underlines. In 2015 Hansda wrote a book called *The Adivasi Will Not Dance*. The book was critically acclaimed and in the same year the author's other book *The Mysterious Ailment of Rupi Baskey* won him the Sahitya Akademi Yuva Purashkar. But on 11 August 2017 the Jharkhand government banned the first book mentioned as it allegedly projected Santhal women 'in a bad light'. For quite some time opinion against Hansda's writings was growing on social media, saying that they were pornographic. Notably, among his stories there was one on the torture of an alleged witch who was a widowed mother (*The Hindu*, 20 August 2017).

The Parsi Scene[20]

As per the 2011 census, the Parsis in India are just 57,264 and even that small number is constantly on the decline. While the Indian population registers a 21 per cent inter-census growth, Parsis mark a 12-per cent decline. Naturally they do not matter politically in India's massively noisy democracy. Their participation at the political leadership level was indeed important during the nationalist movement and even after independence people like Feroze Gandhi were important. But not beyond that. Probably, they could have mattered more had they displayed the violent streak that some of the tiny ethnic groups in India's northeast occasionally do. The community is professionally

272 The Politics of Personal Law in South Asia

accomplished and is generally well-to-do, often noticeably. But behind this inspirational facade there is the lurking threat of a societal collapse for which their thinning population is just one factor. In spite of the community's high literacy, gender inequality ingrained in its religious dogmatism is often as bad as in other communities. Though the society is divided between the liberals and the orthodox, the latter command a greater control over the community through various trusts, which have a long history (Sharafi 2015a: 303–5). Since some of them control the entry rights to the *Agiyari* (Fire Temple) and *Dokhma* (Tower of Silence),[21] there are a few high-profile cases filed by aggrieved women and their supporters for being prevented from entering into them. One such case is that of *Mrs. Goolrokh M. Gupta* vs *Mr. Sam Rusi Chothia & Ors*, now pending in the Supreme Court as a Special Leave Petition (18889/2012). The case has two dimensions, both of which are relevant for our understanding of the Parsi personal law, one, whether Parsi women lose their premarital religion, that is, Zoroastrianism, once they marry outside the community, even if the marriage is solemnised under the provisions of the Special Marriage Act, 1954, and two, whether Parsi community trusts, like other religious trusts, can wield authority to the extent of denying entry rights to Parsi women married outside the community on the ground that they have ceased to be Zoroastrians. The first relates to women's rights, second to the rights of the trusts, both of which are guaranteed by the Constitution of India. Though apparently unrelated to the question, the trusts' authority has much to do with it, which is at the heart of the Goolrokh Gupta case. The constitution refers to religious communities' freedom to manage their own affairs rather than guaranteeing actual 'rights to trusts' (Art. 26b).

The Goolrokh Gupta case has a history. In December 2008 Dilbar Valvi, a Zoroastrain woman, had married a Hindu man under the Special Marriage Act, 1954. In December 2009 when her mother passed away, she was denied her right to attend her funeral ceremonies at the *Agiyari* and *Dokhma* by the members of the Valsad Parsi Anjuman Trust on the grounds that she had ceased to be a Zoroastrian when she married outside the religion. Goolrokh Gupta, a Zoroastrian Parsi woman, married a Hindu in 1991 under the same Special Marriage Act, 1954, took up her case. Significantly, Goolrokh Gupta had continued to practise Zoroastrianism. The issue was whether such women married outside the community ceased to be Zoroastrian.[22] On 23 March 2012 the Gujarat High Court ruled by a majority of two to one that a woman born as a Parsi (by race) and initiated into the Zoroastrian religion by her avid Zoroastrian

Old Wine in the Old Bottle 273

parents lost her Zoroastrian religion by virtue of her marriage to a non-Zoroastrian, Hindu male. This view was taken, notwithstanding that her marriage was solemnised under the liberal and secular Special Marriage Act, 1954, without her ever having renounced her Zoroastrian faith/religion. The split judgment (2:1) further noted inter alia that upon her marriage a woman is '*deemed*' and '*presumed*' (emphasis added) to have acquired the religious status of her husband unless a declaration was made by a competent court for continuation of her pre-marriage religious status.

Curiously, the High Court's views were not restricted to Parsi women alone. In fact, in the High Court's view, 'in all religion, *be it Christian, be it Parsi, be it Jews* (emphasis added), the religious identity of a woman . . . shall merge into that of her husband' and 'such principle is generally accepted throughout the world and therefore, until the marriage, after the name of the woman, the name of the father is being mentioned and after marriage, name of the husband is being mentioned for the purpose of further describing her identity'. The High Court declared that 'when marriage takes place between a male and a female belonging to different religion, it should be presumed and considered that the woman after marriage has merged into the religion of her husband and such will be the identity of their family originating from their marriage in comparison to the society at large and such identity would stand extended to their children too'. This, in the High Court's view, even applied to marriages solemnised under the Special Marriage Act, 1954—a special statute specifically enacted by the parliament to register a special form of marriage, where neither of the parties to the marriage are required to renounce their (respective) religions. The court referred to the antiquated 'doctrine of coverture'. according to which after marriage a woman's religious identity gets merged to that of her husband (Editorial, *Economic and Political Weekly*, 14 October 2017, p. 8).[23] It is this interpretation of the law that has been challenged in the Supreme Court as mentioned above. The argument is that the 1954 act was 'a special form of marriage by registration which does not require either party to the marriage to renounce his/ her religion'.[24] It amounts to the denial of Goolrokh Gupta's fundamental rights to freely profess and practise her religion as guaranteed under Article 25 of the Constitution. On 15 July 2013, the Supreme Court admitted the petition as a special leave petition, which is yet to be heard.[25] The central argument of the petition is as under:

> The High Court's decision is shocking in view of a recent judgment of the Supreme Court of India, in which, while dealing

274   *The Politics of Personal Law in South Asia*

with an inter-caste marriage issue, the Supreme Court rejected the argument that upon marriage the woman takes the caste of her husband *(Rameshbhai Dhabal Naika vs. State of Gujarat & Ors. JT 2012 (1) SC 515)*. Not only does this amount to a gross violation of woman's right to life and dignity as guaranteed by **Article 21** of the Constitution but also negates the guarantee of protecting and preserving their human rights. The High Court has taken this restrictive view despite observing that there is neither any material nor tenet, either placed on record or otherwise, of the Parsi Zoroastrian religion requiring such retrograde treatment to women. The Constitutional ideals of secularism which are meant to safeguard the right of each person, including both men and women, to profess, practice and propagate the religion of their choice seem to have been abrogated by the High Court. . . . More importantly, although the judgment was passed *in personam*, it has its effect *in rem*, inasmuch as it applies to all women who have entered into inter-religious marriages. . . . The right to practice this faith is guaranteed by Article 25 of the Constitution to every Parsi Zoroastrian including the Petitioner and the same cannot be curbed except in accordance with law and such law should be subject to morality. Any right under Article 26 of the Constitution is subject to morality and any practice against the basic notion of morality is incapable of being accorded Constitutional protection. . . . Even though the Courts in India have always attempted at saving the rights guaranteed under the Constitution of India and have also aimed at applying a Uniform Civil Code, pragmatic approach like the one adopted by the Gujarat High Court, are a hurdle in achieving the egalitarian concept of a Universal Civil Code . . .[26] In the above backdrop, I may also highlight that the present SLP which is likely to be listed soon before the Supreme court raises far reaching questions of general public importance in the context of women's rights and the constitutional guarantees granted to women in practicing and professing their religion.[27]

The related question is whether the religious or community trusts should enjoy unbridled powers to prevent individual community members from exercising their fundamental rights, such as entry to temples and so on, as happens in certain Hindu temples or Muslim mosques and darghas.[28] There are several cases of protests by liberal and women's groups against such practices, but since there are constitutional provisions that guarantee religious communities' freedom to manage

Old Wine in the Old Bottle   275

their own affairs, the matter is not as simple as it appears. In the Parsi community even the question of the exclusivity of Zoroastrian housing colonies has resulted in lawsuits. Sometimes they also indicate power struggles between groups of trustees. In one case the Bombay High Court dismissed a ban by the Parsi Punchayet against two priests who had accepted cremation, intermarriage and the initiation of the children of mixed couples. Within the community there are three groups; one, which argues that no children from mixed marriages should be initiated to Zoroastrianism, two, which argues that if either of the spouses is Zoroastrian their children can be initiated to the religion, and three, which argues only when the father is a Zoroastrian can their children be Zoroastrian. But at the core is the question how the respective trusts take the contending logics (Sharafi 2015: 305).

There is also a controversy in Parsi law with regard to the definition of 'grievous hurt', one of the grounds women use to seek divorce from their oppressive husbands as per the provisions of the Parsi Marriage and Divorce Act, of 1936, as amended in 1988.[29] The 1936 act was supposed to have used the definition of the phrase as contained in the Indian Penal Code of 1861, but due to objections from some Parsi groups, in effect its implementation was skewed. It was argued that men were prone to some acts of violence, which should not be allowed to lead wives to seek divorce. Probably, according to a Parsi woman scholar, 'the fracture or dislocation of a bone or tooth would not constitute grievous harm in Parsi matrimonial law, although it would continue to be a crime. Any injury that caused the wife to be in "severe bodily pain" for twenty days or unable to follow her ordinary pursuits would also not constitute a ground for divorce. The message was clear: forms of violence that constituted criminal offences were not serious enough to be part of Parsi wives' divorce suits.'[30]

One point that people often refer to is about the practice of jury trial among the Parsis. A 2015 BBC report talked about it, according to which usually five-member juries (earlier there were nine members) comprising retired men and women spend six hours in the Bombay High Court for up to 10 days during a single session, granting or refusing divorces to disaffected Parsi couples. They are drawn from a pool of 20 jurors nominated for a decade by the community council. There are some criticisms about the functioning of these courts primarily because of their delays in delivering judgments, which is caused by their infrequent meetings, only a few times in a year. Whatever be it, the community seems to be happy with the system for settling matrimonial disputes, although jury trial was abolished in India in 1959.[31] But a recent study shows that it is largely a myth. It notes that

276   *The Politics of Personal Law in South Asia*

'there is little or no evidence that other state governments took similar action after the Nanavati trial. Indeed, it is not until the passage of the Code of Criminal Procedure (CrPC), 1973, that the jury was written out of the criminal trial in courts of session by simply stating, "After hearing arguments and points of law (if any), the Judge shall give a judgment in the case." It was thus by an act of omission rather than an act of commission that trial by jury finally was ended in sessions courts' (Jaffe 2017: 19).[32]

India's Neighbours

It is paradoxical that if there are majoritarian interventions in minority personal laws it is considered democratically undesirable, but at the same time if there is indifference on the part of a majority to reform the minority personal laws it is equally considered undemocratic. In Chapter V we discussed the subject as it obtains in India's South Asian neighbourhood. In this chapter we will discuss some new developments that have taken place in Bangladesh and Pakistan which mirror the Indian situation—Hindus in minority while Muslims in majority, just the opposite of India. As a result, while Hindu law as the majority law has undergone reforms in India, Muslim law as the majority law has undergone reforms in Bangladesh and Pakistan. But the difference is that while in India there is a constant debate surrounding the Muslim personal law there is hardly any such debate in Bangladesh and Pakistan in respect to reforming the Hindu law, leave alone any debate on the UCC. As a consequence, the Hindu law in these majority-Muslim countries is in its pristine form, which did not provide for women's rights at all. It is only of late that there are some reforms in Hindu personal law that have been introduced.[33]

Bangladesh: The Hindu minority of Bangladesh constitutes 9 percent of the country's 165,000,000 population. They are mostly lower-caste Hindus. The more successful upper castes had largely migrated to India in the wake of Partition. With the rise of Islamic fundamentalism in Bangladesh there have been several cases of intimidation and repression of the community, though in the Sheikh Hasina-led Awami League government the problem is in leash to some extent. Still, in 2016 the US Department of Justice had reported that 'though most minority communities have seen their fair share of societal persecution, members of the Hindu minority appear to be particularly vulnerable. . . . [R]ecent reports [however] indicate that the government is trying to be more responsive and the police are actively investigating,

Old Wine in the Old Bottle 277

arresting, and prosecuting individuals for religious, political, economic, and personally motivated threats and attacks' (p. 1).[34]

Compared to the Muslim personal law, the Hindu personal law has been hardly reformed, barring some recent steps in the direction. As such, Bangladeshi Hindu women are much worse off compared to their Muslim counterparts who had benefited from the Muslim Family Law Ordinance (MFLO) reforms of 1965 during the Ayub Khan regime (Bangladesh was in Pakistan then). During my visit to the country about a decade ago I had found that in the forefront of demanding legal rights for Bangladeshi Hindu women were mostly the women's rights activists, notably the secular Bangladesh Mahila Parishad. The Hindu community leaders, all men, were ever critical of the organisation's proposed reforms (see pp. 185–88). Lately, however, some progress has been registered in the women's lot in general as reflected in such secular legislations as the Dowry Prevention Act of 1980, Nari-o-Shishu Nirjatan Ain (law against torture of women and children) of 2000, Acid Crime Control Act of 2002 and the Domestic Violence (Prevention and Protection) Act of 2010. In the realm of Hindu personal law in particular, besides the Bangladesh Mahila Parishad, the Ain-o-Shalish Kendra (law and reconciliation centre) and the South Asian Institute of Advanced Legal and Human Rights (SAILS) are also contributing to the movement for Hindu women's rights. Since there is no concept of divorce in Hindu law one of the biggest problems that the Hindu women faced was from desertions by their husbands (perpetual widowhood) as well as polygamy. One way of dealing with the problem was through legalising divorce and registering all marriages. To this effect a reform process started in 2006 when the Bangladesh Law Commission undertook an exhaustive study to find ways and means to reform the Hindu law. The commission even prepared a draft law called the Hindu Marriage, Adoption, Maintenance and Succession Related Codified Act 2006. In 2011, after conducting a large survey, an activist group by the name, Hindu Bibaho Pronoyonee Naree Jot, meaning, the Women's Coalition for the Preparation of a Hindu Marriage Law, prepared another draft on Hindu personal law. Other two groups in the forefront were, the Human Rights Congress of Bangladesh Minorities (HRCBM) and the Coalition for the Preparation of a Draft Hindu Marriage Law (consisting of 18 NGOs). Nina Goswami, the Hindu woman director of the Ain-o-Salish Kendra, lamented that since the Hindu community was the vote bank of the ruling Awami League, the latter would not go beyond tokenism in this regard lest it might lose the support of the mainstream Hindu conservative leadership (sounds so much

278 *The Politics of Personal Law in South Asia*

Indian in the reverse order). As a result, said Goswami, 'tens of thousands of Hindu men keep multiple wives, knowing that they can't be prosecuted.' The government, however, rejected such criticisms and said that it was hamstrung by hardline Hindu activists who opposed changes in the law. According to Law Minister Shafique Ahmed, the new legislation would cut down on polygamy, which was increasing among Hindu males, and would ensure maintenance rights for women whose husbands had deserted them. 'We couldn't reform Hindu personal laws further because of opposition by Hindu groups including some of their most educated people. Hardliners did not even want registration of their marriages', Ahmed said. The latter's misgiving in respect to Hindu conservative protest was not baseless. Many conservative Hindu activists indeed rejected any reforms which, according to them, would go against their religious scriptures and traditions. They feared that the institution of divorce would threaten the basic foundation of the Hindu family system. Hiren Biswas, president of the Samaj Sangskar Parishad, said: 'We don't mind optional registration because Hindu couples sometimes need the marriage certificate when they travel [abroad], but we won't accept mandatory registration, or divorce and inheritance rights to women because our scriptures and customs don't allow them.' He alleged that these reforms were a conspiracy hatched by foreign-funded charities (www.rawstory.com/2012/06/bangladeshs-hindu-women-fight-for-divorce-rights/, accessed on 8 September 2017).[35]

It was not easy, therefore, for women's rights activists to dent the well-entrenched conservative constituencies across the communities. The only hope lay in the changed atmospherics which the restoration of the secular constitution of Bangladesh in 2011 brought about. It eased the situation. Against this background, on 18 September 2012, the government of Bangladesh enacted the Hindu Marriage Registration Act, 2012 (Farhad [undated]:1–9). The first of its kind, the act was expected to provide legal and social protection to Hindu women from marriage-related fraud as a Hindu Marriage Registrar was to be appointed at every ward and *upzilla* (subdivision) across the country. Registration of marriage, however, was not to be compulsory. The minimum marriageable age was fixed at 18 and 21 for women and men, respectively. It is still premature to think that in the foreseeable future Bangladesh, being a deeply religious society, will go for a uniform family code, though the liberal fringe expects that to happen someday. It suggests that in addition to the community laws, let there be a secular option, for not everybody wants to be bound by their religious personal laws (Noman and Khalid 2011: 109).

Old Wine in the Old Bottle 279

With regard to the issue of divorce in Hindu law, it was more complex. Most Bangladeshi Hindus follow the Dayabhaga school of Hindu law, according to which there is no system of divorce. Although several NGOs and women's rights groups were demanding for this possibility, it was in early 2015 that the Bangladesh Human Rights Foundation and others filed a writ petition in the High Court demanding reforms in the Hindu personal laws related to marriage and divorce as they were inconsistent with the fundamental rights as guaranteed to the Bangladesh citizens by Articles 26(1), 27, 28, 31 and 32 of the constitution as well underlined by Articles 3, 5, 7 and 16(1) of the 1948 Universal Declaration of Human Rights. On 20 January 2015 the court ruled that the government should enact a law of divorce for Hindu women (*The Daily Star*, Dhaka, 24 February 2015).

One last point must be mentioned in the context of the Bangladesh Hindu scene. More the Hindu nationalists in India will humiliate the Muslims, today by talking about love jihad, tomorrow about *ghar wapsi* and the day after by closing down the meat shops in UP and other places on fake charges of selling beef, the day is not far when there will be an anti-Hindu backlash in Bangladesh if the events following the felling of Babri mosque are any indication. The BJP's lollypop of granting citizenship to all Hindu migrants to Assam will only not help, but it will be counterproductive. It will destabilize the region as well by jeopardising the present bonhomie between India and Bangladesh. As its fallout, the Bangladesh Hindus will find that their state-sponsored reform packages are delayed, if not totally withdrawn.

Pakistan: In Pakistan it is only lately that some efforts have been made to reform the traditional Hindu institutions of marriage, divorce and other related matters. This delay was, just like in the case of Bangladesh, due to the opposition from upper-caste Hindu males. Rana Chandra Singh, the most prominent Rajput leader from Sind, where 96 per cent of Pakistan's 5,000,000 Hindus live, used to boast that any reform in the Hindu law would take place over his dead body. Since Singh was elected to the Pakistan National Assembly for four consecutive terms from the reserved Hindu seat in the province, his opposition mattered politically. With his death in 2009, a hurdle was removed. Still, it took five long years before the process of reform could commence. But since personal law is a state subject in the Pakistan federal structure, any question of reform in Hindu law necessarily involved both state-level (effectively meaning Sind) and central-level politics. While the Sind Assembly was dominated by the Pakistan People's Party (PPP), the National Assembly was dominated

280 *The Politics of Personal Law in South Asia*

by the Pakistan Muslim League (Nawaz). In this political competition, each party tried to outwit the other, though the bone of contention was the tiny Hindu population of Sind. As such, when, in 2016, the Pakistan National Assembly took the initiative in the matter, it was obliged to seek the approval of respective states before it could pass the Hindu law reform bill. But when this process was still on, the Sind Assembly passed its own Hindu Marriage Act, 2016 to steal the thunder of Nawaz Sharif's legislative move. The PPP, which had a massive base among the Hindus of Sind, could not afford to allow the Pakistan Muslim League (Nawaz)(PML [N]) to take all the credit in the matter. In March 2017 both the houses of Pakistan parliament also passed the Hindu Marriage Act, 2016, which was applicable for the Hindus living in the Islamabad Capital Territory and the provinces of Balochistan, Khyber Pakhtunkhwa and Punjab (Sind had already passed its own law). Prime Minister Nawaz Sharif said that his government was always committed to provide equal rights to minority communities residing in Pakistan as 'they are as patriotic as any other community and, therefore, it is the responsibility of the state to provide equal protection to them.' Ramesh Kumar Vankwani, a leading Hindu MP and PML member, said: 'Such laws will help discourage forced conversions and streamline the Hindu community after the marriage of individuals' (Mehdi 2016, *The Hindu* and *Times of India*, 19 March 2017).

With these acts in place it happened for the first time in Pakistan's history that marriage laws of 5,000,000 Hindus living in the country were codified. Minimum age for marriage was fixed at 18 and all marriages were to be registered. But critics found the law lacking in several important respects insofar as divorce was concerned. Not only was the word 'divorce' not used, its effectiveness was obfuscated by legal jargons. Instead of divorce, the phrase used was 'decree of termination of marriage'. It was a complicated phrase which could be further convoluted in the court of law. It was possible only by filing a petition in the court. The process is very cumbersome and it can take two to three years for a couple to separate, though they may have mutually decided to sever their relationship. Even the relevant law for Pakistani Christians is bad in this regard, but for Hindus, the present law is even worse. Although both the PML and PPP have earned praise for fulfilling the long-standing demand of the progressive elements among Pakistani Hindus and it may have helped them sell their parties during the elections, 'but in reality—even though Rana Chandra Singh is long dead—neither dared to transgress the patriarchal Hindu elite's position on marriage and divorce' (Mehdi 2016).

Centrality of Politics

Politics in India is largely community-centric. Either it is caste or it is religion that matters politically. If so, it would be a colossal task to make all communities agree to one family code at the core of which is gender inequality, which no community can boast of having eradicated. Although as an individual citizen each Indian has a vote and everyone is expected to be self-governing, still elections are largely won by caste or communal gerrymandering. In a first-past-the-post system that India has opted for, this phenomenon thrives because a mere 35 per cent vote is good enough in most cases to make a candidate win an election. The Indian experience suggests that even when such mass-appealing issues like corruption or national security dominate the electoral scene, caste and communal cards are used to garner votes at the local levels. On a larger canvas, to whip up the Hindu sentiment it becomes necessary for Hindu chauvinistic parties to project Muslim personal law as a favour done to the community within the overall rubric of Congress's alleged Muslim-appeasement policies. The theoretical justification, however, is that the continuation of Muslim personal law militates against India's democratic ethos. From the beginning, the BJS/BJP has harped on the tune that India must go for a uniform civil code. The subtext of this demand is that the Muslims are privileged, as if polygamy is a privilege which the hapless Hindu men are deprived of. The BJP's pro-Muslim women rhetoric is also politically motivated, as if Hindu women have nothing to complain about. But a UCC ideally being the most desirable situation in a democracy, the question is whether BJP is seriously contemplating to introduce it. Its politics does not so indicate. Every passing day the party is becoming more polarising. Ever since the Partition of India, the Hindu–Muslim divide has never been so sharp as it is now.

Though Hinduism is the majority religion of India, accounting for 80 percent of the nation's population, many Hindus seem to suffer from some kind of a minority complex. This is reflected in the attitudes of all the Hindu nationalistic parties or social formations like BJP, RSS, Shiv Sena, Vishwa Hindu Parishad, Bajrang Dal and many other new outfits which are growing like mushrooms. How much they have failed to reconcile themselves to the idea of a secular India is evident in their daily rhetoric and historically unfounded hatred for Nehru, who in their reckoning is the villain of the piece. This minority complex stems from several factors, like, one, that a vast Hindu India was ruled by a small group of Muslims for centuries, whose forefathers had come from outside as mere conquers and adventurers;

282   *The Politics of Personal Law in South Asia*

two, a large portion of the historically ordained territory of India was amputated by sheer perfidy of a group of separatists who increasingly enlarged their appeal by the logic that India consisted of two nations of Hindus and Muslims; three, the community of Muslims is now as large as 500,000,000-strong, making the region, that is, South Asia, the world's largest Muslim concentration zone; and four, which is of great contemporary importance, though in many Western and other countries they are in small numbers, their terrorist groups (or lone wolves), often inspired by fire-eating Islamic radicals, are causing havoc in otherwise peaceful places. Their unhappiness with Nepal converting itself from a Hindu nation into a secular state stems from the same persecution mania. It is like the Sri Lankan situation where though the Sinhala Buddhists are in overwhelming majority (about 70 per cent), still they suffer from a minority complex vis-à-vis the tiny Sri Lanka Tamil minority.

Given the above situation, the question is whether Hindus are ready for a UCC. It has been argued that without abolishing the caste system among Hindus, it is difficult. There are many cases of honour killing for marrying outside the caste or gotra. It may, however, be noted that caste hierarchies are not confined to Hindus alone. Otherwise egalitarian Christian and Muslim communities also have them. The Indian Catholic Church officially recognised in December 2016 that untouchability existed among them; out of 19,000,000 Catholics, 12,000,000 were Dalit, and of the 5,000 bishops, 12 were Dalit (*Indian Express*, 15 and 16 December 2016). Untouchability exists even among Muslims in some areas of UP (Trivedi *et al.* 2016: 32–36). It may be necessary to amend the Constitution (Scheduled Caste) Order of 1950 so that the relevant benefits go to all Scheduled Caste origin Christians and Muslims.

Although there is nothing like any pan-Indian Muslim politics yet, the BJP considers it as a threat. Its argument is built upon that line to construct its own pan-Indian Hindu support base. Contrary to all scholarly knowledge that the Muslims are a depressed minority, they are castigated as the most pampered minority. The Sachar Committee report of 2006 had provided ample evidence about the plight of the community in economic and social spheres. Even now, as a detailed *Indian Express* report (26 November 2016) suggests, there is hardly any change in the situation. Though Muslims constitute 14.2 per cent of India's population (2011 census), their representation in bureaucracy, government and semigovernment jobs, and in the field of education is minuscule. For example, it is 3.32 per cent in the Indian Administrative Service (IAS), 3.19 per cent in the Indian Police Service

Old Wine in the Old Bottle   283

(IPS) and 8.57 per cent (including other minorities) in the central government departments and public sector undertakings (PSUs). While the overall literacy rate in the country is 73 per cent, among the Muslims it is 68.5 per cent. Overall 4.4 per cent children are school drop-outs, but for Muslims the corresponding figure is 8.7. The only silver lining is that between 2001 and 2011 while overall there was a 64 per cent increase in the number of graduates, the Muslim community registered a 98.8 per cent growth. But this positive point is offset by the fact that given their percentage in the population, there are more jailed and under-trial Muslims in India compared to any other community. There are 15.8 per cent Muslim convicts and 20.9 per cent Muslim under-trials (*Indian Express*, 3 November 2016, for a thoughtful study on this point, see Ahmad and Siddiqui 2017: 98–106). One interpretation could be that the crime rate is higher in the community, but the under-trial figure in particular can be explained by the fact that the community is more prone to suspicion in the eyes of the security agencies, more so in terrorism-related situations.

In their political representation also Muslims are disadvantaged. Between 1962 and 2017 out of 47,729 members elected to the legislative assemblies of the states only 3,254 were Muslim. Out of 6,085 BJP MLAs, only 15 were Muslim. In the UP assembly, in 2007 the Muslim representation was 14 per cent, in 2012 it was 17, but in 2017 it was as little as 6 percent against the background of a massive BJP victory (*Hindustan Times*, 30 May 2017). It may be noted that in UP the Muslim population constitutes 19.26 per cent of the population as per the 2011 census. In the election of 2014, only 23 Muslim members were elected to the 545-seat Lok Sabha. Even if one excludes the 133 seats reserved for various categories, their number should have been 60 given that they were 14.2 per cent of the country's population (*The Caravan*, September 2016: 47).

This generally depressing record notwithstanding, the community has not thrown up any credible pan-Indian leader. Mohammad Ali Jinnah was the last such leader, though he himself was an Ismaili Shia (who later became Sunni according to Akbar Ahmed) from Gujarat. In the 1980s and 1990s some chances arose of Syed Shahabuddin (1935–2017) emerging to that level, but it did not happen. Presently Asaduddin Owaisi from Hyderabad is the frontrunner for the position. His presence is noted not only in the TV debates but in also taking vocal positions on every question concerning the Muslims of India, right from the beginning of the Babri mosque controversy till the recent triple talaq controversy. He is an active member of parliament and in 2014 he was awarded the Sansad Ratna, an award

284 *The Politics of Personal Law in South Asia*

annually given by a civil society group to all those parliamentarians who are most punctual and active. His All India Majlis-e-Ittehadul Muslimeen (AIMIMS) party has a visible presence in Maharashtra. But Owaisi's biggest handicap is his disconnect with the Muslims of north India who matter the most in the Indian Muslim politics. It is possible, however, that the more the foot soldiers of the Hindutva brigade humiliatingly push the community to the corner, it will veer round him for leadership. Already his firebrand image has earned him popularity among disgruntled Muslim youth. On the issue of Muslim personal law, Owaisi's position is that of the majority Muslims that any reform must have the sanction of the community and the case for a UCC is still premature. But he does not fail to take a dig at the BJP: 'The government should focus on bringing changes to the Goa civil code and ban second marriage there [allowed to "Gentile Hindus"]'. He underlines that Goa is ruled by BJP (*Frontline*, 26 October 2016, www.frontline.in/socail-issues/code-and-caution/article92665, for a detailed report on Owaisi's politics, see Farooquee 2016: 32–51).[36]

Like the absence of a pan-Indian Muslim leadership, there is no pan-Indian Hindu leader either. But with BJP in power, and behind it the RSS and a number of Hindu organisations in shining armour, there is an increasingly militant effort to create a pan-Indian political Hinduism. Its strategy is two-fold; one to glorify the Hindu past, and two, to denigrate the minorities, Muslims in particular. The first is reflected in unscientifically claiming every great scientific invention as a Hindu feat, while the second is reflected by proving Muslim treachery *during the last thousand years*. It becomes necessary for the Hindutva forces, therefore, to rewrite India's history and social science books to *set the record straight* as per their own theories. That they do not stand up to scholarly scrutiny matters little to these champions of the Hindutva ideology. At the political level, both these strategies coalesce in high-voltage political rhetoric on the one hand, and stray violence against Muslims on the other. For example, in September 2015, on the allegation that a Muslim family in the UP town of Dadri had stored and consumed beef, the head of the family Mohammad Akhlaq Saifi was lynched by a cow-protection Hindu mob. Akhlaq's son barely survived the attack after several days of treatment in the hospital. Many more such cases of anti-Muslim violence were registered in the subsequent months from UP, Haryana, Rajasthan and Maharashtra. Also, there were the Hindu nationalistic allegations, particularly in the Hindi-speaking states, that Muslim men were forcibly marrying Hindu women with the clear objective to convert them to Islam (called as 'love jihad'). There was little evidence to support the contention,

Old Wine in the Old Bottle 285

yet politically the message was conveyed to the Hindu voters. The danger is that in places where Muslims are in small numbers they may choose to vote for BJP out of sheer fear for life, which may be advertised by the party as their expanding base among the minorities. A study that analysed Muslim votes in Gujarat in the 2014 Lok Sabha elections found that Muslims by and large did not vote for the BJP. Only in those pockets where the community was very small and it was subjected to severe violence during the carnage of 2012 had it given more votes to BJP than in the previous elections—out of fear for their security.[37]

If this is the big picture of Indian politics, it is most unlikely that any worthwhile development in reforming the personal laws, leave alone introducing a uniform civil code, would be on the political agenda in any meaningful sense. The reality is that every political party worth its salt, more so the BJP, knows that it is not simple to introduce a UCC, however much it may commit itself to the idea at the mass level. The easiest way is to let the courts take the decisions. If not for anything else, it would at least defer the job for the time being as to what exactly was done by the Modi government when it asked the Law Commission to gauge the people's mind in this regard. Tahir Mahmood was rightly sarcastic: 'Since independence they have been shunning their responsibility to bring about social reform and throwing the ball into the court of an already over-burdened judiciary. A government not comfortable with the need or demand for a particular social reform can find easy ways to keep it hanging in the air. Where there is a will there's a way, it is said–in this case where there is no will there is a survey' (*Times of India*, 27 October 2016).

Conclusion: A Pipe Dream

It is more than a year now since the Law Commission conducted its survey to gauge people's attitudes towards the uniform civil code. With 45,000 responses available with the commission, it is at a loss how to proceed from here. To all those who have knowledge about the subject, it was predictable. The commission has virtually conceded that. According to it, it is impossible to think on the lines of a comprehensive code for all. The maximum one can expect is piecemeal, issue-based codification. This was exactly what Nehru's compromise formula was in the 1950s when he had gone for a four-part Hindu Code and not one single one. Justice B. S. Chauhan, chairman of the Law Commission, is candid: 'I am of the considered view that it will yield a better result if we study the provisions of different

286 *The Politics of Personal Law in South Asia*

personal laws relating to each component, like marriage and divorce or adoption, and try to harmonise them to suggest to the government a possible uniformity. It is important to study why different religions prescribe different norms and attempt the difficult task of recommending a Uniform Civil Code *on separate compartments* within the larger issue (emphasis added)'. He had hoped that in the triple talaq case the Supreme Court would throw some light, but that was not to be. The court simply returned the ball to the government's court (rightly so), which was expected to perform its legislative duty, which was beyond the judiciary's mandate (*Times of India*, 21 October 2017).

In a *Times of India* article published on 13 September 2017 (Ghosh 2017), this author had made a dig at India's political class for taking its people for a ride all these years by promising them a UCC when they knew too well that it was not easy, if not impossible. They never felt it to be their duty to educate the masses about those difficulties. They were just unwilling to address the fundamental question: how to ensure for all Indian women status equal to that of men in every sense—political, social, material and sexual. Also, in spite of the fact that the problem was not community-specific, they almost always projected it that way. Sometimes it was Islam in danger, sometimes it was Hinduism in danger, but, barring occasional interventions by women's rights groups, it was never that the women were in danger. It is a man's world. Unless this reality is challenged head-on, all talks about the UCC are simply hot air, good-for-nothing high-voltage TV debates. The central issue is the persistence of patriarchy. That a UCC is desirable in a democracy is common sense. But it is equally the common sense that since law is a political matter, and personal law is as much so, it must be politically worked out. To do so one will have to enlist the support of all communities. In this exercise the majority community will have to take the lead by creating a conducive situation when the smaller communities will not have doubts about the former's intentions. If the BJP, which is the most popular party in India now, is truly serious about a uniform code, it must reduce the gap between its pious promises to the minorities and venomous rhetoric and actions against them, both in form and in substance. Such pronouncements of UP Chief Minister Yogi Adityanath that if Muslims can occupy the streets for *namaz*, why should police stations not celebrate *Janmashtami*? are not only unhelpful, they are outright counterproductive. There is no dearth of such anti-Muslim insinuations.

In the given situation the best model still seems to be the Nehruvian model of going step by step. He started with the Hindu Code. The

Old Wine in the Old Bottle 287

next step could be a Muslim Code. One can draw some lessons from the past in this regard. In 1937 the Muslim Personal Law (Shariat) Application Act, in 1939 the Dissolution of Muslim Marriages Act and in 1986 the Muslim Women (Protection of Rights on Divorce) Act were passed, all by elected legislatures. In the last case it was the Indian parliament. That journey has to be carried forward. To facilitate that to happen, it would be ideal if some steps are taken to address the grossly anti-women social practices which the Indian state has constantly been doing. The idea is to first ask for a more broad-based and restrictive personal law regime which should ask for many things like abolition of polygamy, humane divorce norms (triple talaq has already been declared unconstitutional), restricting the powers of the *khap panchayats* to punish, even kill, people marrying inter-caste and inter-gotra, discouraging fasting of children for days prevalent among Jains and so on. As one writer suggests, let such a code be called an RCC, Restrictive Civil Code, because 'the binding agreement is between the citizen and the country, and not with the Hindu gurus, Muslim clerics, or any other priests of the country' (Raychaudhuri 2016: 29). Once that is achieved and the present vicious communal climate, hopefully, is contained, making the minorities feel socially and physically secure, efforts should be initiated in collaboration with community leaders, including women leaders, to see how their personal laws can be codified on humanistic lines. There is no shortcut.

In the foreseeable future there is no chance of India, leave alone any other South Asian nation where in any case it is not one of the majority demands, going for legislation doing away with all personal laws and replacing them with one uniform code to which all religious and ethnic communities will adhere. But one need not be worked up too much for that. As Werner Menski, a leading scholar of South Asian law, has argued, that all plural societies, India being one of the most prominent ones in that category, will have no escape from going for a plural legal system. Even European societies which host large Asian and Africans diasporas ('ethnic implants') have reconciled themselves to making adjustments in their civil legal frameworks. It goes to the credit of India that it has found its own strategy through 'uniformisation' of the personal laws. India has followed a two-pronged strategy. On the one hand it has tried to work out a harmonious management of its age-old cultural diversities by effectively allowing the plurality of personal laws, then, on the other, it has tried to take care of the pressures of real and potential gender and cross-community inequality 'through the intricate process of gradual

288 *The Politics of Personal Law in South Asia*

harmonisation of all Indian personal laws and supervision by criminal and constitutional laws' (Menski 2008: 245, 248). In a recent newspaper article, Menski continued to underscore the point: 'India has achieved its own sophistication in 70 years, and its experience does not follow Western models. Those dissatisfied with this model should look around them, to realize that India already operates a Uniform Civil Code in its uniquely harmonized personal law system' (*Times of India*, 14 September 2017).

Let me also end this book with an optimistic note. There is a story in Shetreet and Chodosh (2015: 244). A couple is driving down in mad speed to a wedding party because they are late. Their car gets stuck in the mud. The man yells (characteristically, probably, at the wife): 'only in India'. As it is normal in India, a crowd gathers around in no time. They pull the car out. It is now the wife's turn to yell (presumably, at the husband): 'only in India'. The moral of the story for our purpose here is that whether one is conscious of it or not, whether one wants it or not, whether a UCC will be there in near future or not, it is inevitable that the process of uniformisation of personal laws will move apace. It is happening both in India's courts and legislatures through disparate secular judgments and legislations. They are challenging the age-old injustices meted out to women. Across the communities the conservatives are feeling the heat. A uniform civil code may still take many more years to come, but reforms in the personal laws will go unabated. The writing on the wall is bold and clear.

Notes

1 For a brief discussion on the point, see Desai 2017: 13–15, also see, Faizan Mustafa's views, in https://scroll.in/article/ 836745/faizan-mustafa-supreme-court-has-already-declared-triple-talaq-invalid-it-may-just-reiterate-that, accessed on 11 August 2017.

2 Directive principles are contained in Part IV and Part IVA of the Constitution. It contains 17 articles from Article 36 to Article 51A. Although one only hears of the UCC, it has a long list of desirables most of which have not been achieved, such as educating all Indians, minimizing the inequality of income, providing nutritious food to all children, providing free legal aid, ensuring right to work, and so on. Rather, when a social thinker like Amartya Sen draws the attention of Indians to them, he is ridiculed by an important section of the political class. With regard to the UCC, it may be noted, as constitutional expert A. G. Noorani says, that even an apparently uniform-law country like the United Kingdom entertains plurality of law, criminal law included. For example, Scotland recognizes the concept of 'not proven', while England does not. The latter has barristers, the former has advocates. There is no national bar. In Canada the province of Quebec has its own legal system.

Old Wine in the Old Bottle 289

In Israel, Singapore and Sri Lanka Muslim personal law is recognized (*Indian Express*, 15 December 2016). In the State of New York a Jew may go for a civil marriage as well as a religious marriage. Even if there is a civil divorce it is not valid as per the religious law (Shetreet and Chodosh 2015: 160). Also, as political scientist Gurpreet Mahajan argues, a UCC itself is no guarantee that all citizens will be treated equally in the realm of civil law, as the European experiences show ('Why the West offers no models for a Uniform Civil Code', *Times of India*, 15 September 2017).

3 The stratification of the Hindu caste system is the most discussed, but many more diversities exist. Even in respect to such a commonly understood marker of Hindu ritualistic unity like cremating its dead, there are exceptions. Not many are aware that a large number of Hindus bury their dead. This was most dramatically confirmed when a very high-profile funeral ceremony was organized on 20 December 2016 to bid adieu to the departed soul of the Tamil Nadu chief minister, J. Jayalalithaa, and again on 6 September 2017 when the murdered Kannada journalist Gauri Lankesh was buried in Bengaluru. Historian S. Settar, former chairman of the Indian Council of Historical Research (ICHR), may have overstated the point that all those Hindus who do not do *agni puja* (fire worship) during the marriage ceremony bury their dead, but it is indisputable that a large number of Hindus within certain South Indian caste categories indeed bury their departed kin. So much so that there is even a Hindu cemetery in Bengaluru with visible tombstones displaying such Hindu deities as the Nandi bull, the Shivalinga or even the busts of the deceased (Sukumaran 2017: 56–58).

4 One may recall that the British strategy of pampering the traditionalists in the Indian society was as old as the early years of the company rule. Charles Hamilton, one who translated some Islamic legal treatises from Arabic and Persian to English, had advised that the British should keep all the Indian communities in good humour for which even if their retrograde social practices had to be supported, let it be so.

5 One may add a third, the Wakf (Amendment) Act, 2013. Although it deals only with the Muslim community, it does not strictly fall within the Muslim personal law question, which essentially is concerned with marriage-related issues. The Constitution of India has recognized the institution of 'Wakf' as a concept covering 'Trusts and Trustees' and 'Charities and charitable institutions', which is incorporated in entries no. 7 and 28, respectively, of List III (Concurrent List) of the Seventh Schedule to the Constitution. Thus, both the central and state governments may make laws relating to 'Wakf'.

6 For a detailed study of how the Gita Press played a critical role in building the notion of Hindu nationalism, see Mukul 2016.

7 Ghosh 2009: 8–9, Werner Menski, 'Don't look to the West, India has evolved its own way', *Times of India*, 14 September 2017. A recent empirical study based on the records of lower courts in Delhi and Hyderabad, however, concludes that it is difficult to say with certainty whether the law harmed or benefited divorced Muslim women, since not many such women approach the courts. Research based on High Court records may be misleading because a much smaller number of women who approach them are generally well-to-do and are prepared for long-drawn hearings.

290 *The Politics of Personal Law in South Asia*

This class dimension is an important variable in understanding the issue (Vatuk 2017: 246–73).

8 www.bjp.org/images/pdf_2014/full_manifesto_english_07.04.2014.pdf.

9 Later, in the aftermath of the Supreme Court triple judgment on triple talaq, in a newspaper article the RSS clarified, without of course mentioning the tribal customary laws, that 'there is no case for the Hindu Code Bill being imposed as UCC. It may also have many infirmities. If a UCC means Hindus losing benefits like Hindu Undivided Family or extending this benefit to other communities, let it be. If it means equal inheritance rights for women, contrary to different rules in different communities, it would be great. . . . Simply put, the need for a Uniform Civil Code flows from the very definition of secularism'. Ratan Sharda, 'True Secularism Demands a Uniform Civil Code', *Times of India*, 11 September 2017. Sharda is an RSS thinker and author of *Secrets of RSS*. Should it be treated as the total reversal of the RSS position on personal law or was Vaidya more honest? Let it be recalled that RSS had organized 79 public meetings in Delhi in 1949 to oppose the Hindu Code Bill.

10 The term 'Hindu Undivided Family' has not been defined under the Income Tax Act. It is defined under the Hindu Law as a family that consists of all persons lineally descended from a common ancestor, including wives and unmarried daughters. According the Income Tax Act of 1961, as in the general case, every individual member of a HUF gets the basic exemption of Rs. 250,000 (if senior citizen, the exemption is for Rs. 300,000), including the Karta (head) of the HUF. But the latter, gets an additional exemption of Rs. 250,000, thus a total of Rs. 500,000. This causes a substantial loss of revenue to the exchequer.

11 Since the Shah Bano controversy in 1985, the AIMPLB has been requested by several state agencies to prepare a comprehensive compendium of Muslim personal law. It has produced some documents to this effect, but it has failed to do justice to all schools of Muslim personal law (Khan 2016).

12 In traditional societies it probably works better if one takes recourse to religious texts to promote a modernist idea. It blunts the traditionalist censure based on religion. Ishwar Chandra Vidyasagar did exactly that in nineteenth-century Bengal to promote his mission for widow remarriage.

13 For a more nuanced understanding of the complexity surrounding the evolution of the concept of triple talaq, see the two-part interview of Faizan Mustafa in Scroll.in, 9 and 10 May 2017, https://scroll.in/article/836745/faizan-mustafa-supreme-court-has-already-declared-triple-talaq-invalid-it-may-just-reiterate-that, and https://scroll.in/article/836751/people-will-accept-triple-talaq-out-of-fear-of-god-legal-expert-faizan-mustafa, both accessed on 11 August 2017.

14 The full text is available at http://indianexpress.com/article/india/full-text-supreme-court-sets-aside-instant-triple-talaq-in-32-verdict-4808200/. Its relevant extracts are in *Hindustan Times*, 23 August 2017.

15 In 1987 the Law Commission had recommended that there should be at least 50 judges for every one million population. But in 2016 the Law Ministry revealed that there were just 18 judges per million (M.Rajivlochan, 'Abdication Foretold', *Indian Express*, 28 August 2017. See Appendix 6).

Old Wine in the Old Bottle 291

16 The experience of Darul Kaza (Muslim arbitration councils) suggests that about 70 per cent of matrimonial disputes are settled out of the court (Faizan Mustafa in *The Hindu*, 30 May 2017). One may add here even some state-supported off-the-court settlement mechanisms. These settlements do not necessarily follow the statutory laws. The Delhi High Court Mediation Centre has some interesting cases of this kind. See Shetreet and Chodosh 2015: 236–39.

17 The clause 366 (25) reads: '"Scheduled Tribes" means such tribes or tribal communities or parts of or groups within such tribes or tribal communities as are deemed under article 342 to be Scheduled Tribes [as per presidential notification] for the purposes of this Constitution'. For details, see Ghosh 2011.

18 Inaugural talk delivered at the workshop on 'Other Areas of Law', organized by IBA-CLE chair National Law School of India University, Bangalore and Menon Institute of Legal Advocacy Training Trivandrum in association with Guru Ghasidas Central University Law School at Bilaspur, Chhattisgarh on 12 November 2013. The title of the talk was 'An Alternative LL.B. Curriculum Relevant to Tribal States', The speaker is not identified, http://Highcourt.Cg.Gov.In/Artical/Tribalandruralcommunity. Pdf, accessed on 4 August 2017

19 Intolerance of self-styled caste leaders is not confined to north India. The case of the author Perumal Murugan of Tamil Nadu tells the same story. Under social pressure Murugan declared his 'death' as an author, taking the conscious decision to give up writing for good.

20 In writing this section I have immensely benefited from the comments of Mitra Sharafi of the Law School at the University of Wisconsin, who very kindly read the original draft. Usual disclaimer applies.

21 Tower of Silence is a circular, raised structure built by Zoroastrians where dead bodies are exposed to the sun and eaten by scavenging birds such as vultures.

22 There is an opposite case also. R. D. Tata married a French woman who tried to become Zoroastrian. He pleaded for her entry into the Fire Temple and her right to have her body consigned to the Tower of Silence. There was an uproar from the orthodox Parsis and the High Court sided with them (Hoamain Nariman Vakil, 'Why Parsis need their distinct family laws', *Times of India*, 20 September 2017). For a scholarly discourse on it, see Sharafi 2007 https://media.law.wisc.edu/m/2ywnk/sharafis_judging_conversion_to_zoroastrianism.pdf.

23 It reflected the male-chauvinistic outlook of the Gujarat High Court, which was also seen in the way the Kerala High Court gave its ruling in the Hadiya case (May 2017). Hadiya nee Sruthi Meledath had voluntarily converted herself from Hinduism to Islam before marrying Anees Hamid, a Muslim. The case assumed political colour when it was alleged that it reflected a pattern of Muslims forcibly converting Hindu women to marry, the so-called love jihad. Even the Supreme Court went to the extent of seeking the services of the National Investigation Agency (NIA) to look into the allegation. Though the matter is still pending with the Supreme Court, the division bench of the Kerala High Court has in the meantime debunked the earlier judgment, thus upholding the essence of the Special Marriage Act, 1954. The judgment starts with a quotation

292   *The Politics of Personal Law in South Asia*

from the American poet, Maya Angelou: 'Love recognizes no barriers, it jumps hurdles, leaps fences, penetrates walls to arrive at its destination full of hope' (Editorial, *Indian Express*, 23 October 2017).

24 The 1872 version of the Special Marriages Act had required the parties to renounce their religion under oath, but the revised version of the act progressively omitted that requirement (in 1923 and 1954). So, one could argue that the legislative history shows that one no longer very clearly renounces one's former religion by marrying under the act. On this point, see Sharafi 2017: 97.

25 Her sister, Shiraz Padodia, a solicitor, was fighting the case. Harish Salve and Abhishek Manu Singhvi were handling the case pro bono. Adi Godrej, Jamshyd Godrej, Smita Godrej and several others submitted intervention applications. See Goolrokh Gupta's interview in *Frontline*, 6 September 2013: 20–21.

26 In an e-mail communication with this author (15 October 2017), Mitra Sharafi found it interesting 'to see this "aspirational UCC" argument made here, because from a strictly legal perspective, India does not have a UCC. I suppose the strategy here is to appeal to the judges who think India should have a UCC. But as one dour British judge once said in a moot court I was participating in as a student: "Thank you for telling us what the law should be. Now tell us what it is."'

27 Author's communication with Goolrokh Gupta's advocate, Shiraz Padodia, 5 October 2017.

28 There are problems about Hindu and Muslim religious trusts as well. The Sabarimala temple trust in Kerala and the Shani Shingnapur temple trust in Maharashtra deny rights of entry to Hindu women. Likewise, the Muslim Haji Ali shrine trust in Maharashtra prevents women's entry across religions, including Muslim. In the Sabarimala case, the Kerala High Court in 1991 had upheld the practice of not allowing menstruating women in the age group of 10 to 50 to enter into the temple. It has been challenged in the Supreme Court, which has referred the matter to the constitution bench (*Indian Express*, 14 October 2017). For a completely different take on the matter by a confirmed feminist, yet who distances herself from the mainstream feminists to champion the cause of Hindu ritualistic diversity, see Kishwar 2017.

29 For details about the relevant clauses of the act, see Shabbir and Manchanda 1991: 46–48.

30 Mitra Sharafi, 'Many think Parsis are a model minority. Are they? *Times of India*, 20 September 2017.

31 Soutik Biswas, 'Parsi matrimonial courts: India's only surviving jury trials', *BBC News*, 24 September 2015, www.bbc.com/news/world-asia-india-34322117, accessed on 6 October 2017.

32 A *Times of India* report of 17 November 2017, however, showed that some form of jury trial still continued in the form of Parsi chief matrimonial courts in Chennai, Kolkata and Mumbai. Their short annual or bi-annual meetings inordinately delay divorce petitions as was revealed by the one submitted by Naomi Sam Irani. Arguing that the problem was rooted in the provisions of the Parsi Marriage and Divorce Act, 1938 she pleaded with the Supreme Court for its replacement by the family courts, which provided for speedy settlement through reconciliation.

Old Wine in the Old Bottle 293

33 In IR (International Relations) literature all kinds of notions for regional integration are floated. Sometimes they even include civil law integration as was done by the European Union (EU) in the late 1990s. But the idea of a European Civil Code proved to be a nine days' wonder (Dario Moura Vicente, 'International Harmonization and Unification of Private Law in a Globalized Economy', in D'Souza and D'Souza 2009: 45–46). One cannot even remotely imagine of any such proposal in the South Asian region because of SAARC's dismal failure in almost every respect.

34 The state does not, however, buy any controversy potential to provoke the radicals. In May 2017, the Supreme Court removed from its frontage a statue of the Greek goddess of justice, Themis, just because it was considered un-Islamic. Members of the liberal Ganajagaran Mancha are under threat. Rajib Haider was killed. The Hindu members are ever vulnerable (*Indian Express*, 10 and 27 May 2017).

35 It would be instructive to know about the situation in India in this regard. According to 2001 Indian census, there were 2,300,000 separated and abandoned women in India, which was 260 per cent more than the number of divorced women. Of the total figure, about two million were Hindu, 280,000 were Muslim, 90,000 Christian, and about 80,000 belonged to other religions. This was based on the survey conducted by the Delhi-based Centre for Research and Debates in Development Policy (CRDDP) (Abusaleh Shariff and Syed Khalid, 'Unimportance of Triple Talaq', *Indian Express*, 29 May 2017).

36 It may be relevant here to note that that the Goa civil code, which is often touted as a successful example of a UCC, does not exist. For example, while Christian marriages are considered legally valid if solemnised in the Church, Hindu or Muslim marriages will have to be registered. Adoption is not possible for Catholics and Muslims, but it is possible for Hindus. On 14 October 2016, some eminent Muslim professionals and community leaders even petitioned to the Goa governor against the so-called Uniform Civil Code of Goa and pleaded for the Muslim personal law available in the rest of the country (Faleiro 2017: 18).

37 Dhattiwala and Susewind 2014.

Appendices

Note: There is one item in this section which is not directly related to the subject matter of the volume, namely, Appendix 7. Since the theme of the volume has multifaceted dimensions of law and society, an understanding of which is necessary to grapple with certain socio-legal complexities, we have included this item. With tangential yet critical relevance to the subject, it is a statement on the controversy on putting up a painting of Prophet Muhammad on the wall of the Supreme Court of the United States. It is an uncompromisingly liberal statement, and yet does not deviate from the basic tenets of Islam. It will be an eye opener to all conservative Muslims in South Asia.

Appendix 1
The Muslim Women (Protection of Rights on Divorce) Act, 1986

[This Act has been formulated to protect the rights of Muslim women who have been divorced by, or have obtained divorce from their husbands, and to provide for matters connected therewith or identical thereto.]

S. 1 Short Title and Extent

1. This Act may be called the Muslim Women (Protection of Rights on Divorce) Act, 1986.
2. It extends to the whole of India except the State of Jammu and Kashmir.

S. 2 Definitions

In this Act, unless the context otherwise requires,

(a) "divorced woman" means a Muslim woman who has married according to Muslim law and has been divorced by or has been divorced by or has obtained divorce from her husband in accordance with Muslim law.
(b) "iddat period" means, in the case of a divorced woman,
    (i) three menstrual courses after the date of divorce, if she is subject to menstruation; and
    (ii) three lunar months after her divorce, if she is not subject to menstruation; and
    (iii) if she is enceinte at the time of her divorce, the period between the divorce and the delivery of her child or the termination of her pregnancy, whichever is earlier.

296 *The Politics of Personal Law in South Asia*

(c) "Magistrate" means a Magistrate of the first class exercising jurisdiction under the code of Criminal Procedure 1973 in the area where the divorced woman resides.

(d) "Prescribed" means prescribed by rules made under this Act.

S. 3 Mehr or Other Properties of Muslim Woman to be Given to Her at the Time of Divorce

1. Notwithstanding anything contained in any other law for the time being in force, a divorced woman shall be entitled to:
   (a) A reasonable and fair provision and maintenance to be made and paid to her within the iddat period by her former husband;
   (b) Where she herself maintains the children born to her before or after her divorce, a reasonable and fair provision and maintenance to be made and paid by her former husband for a period of two years from the respective dates of birth of such children;
   (c) An amount equal to [the] sum of *mehr* or dower agreed to be paid to her at the time of her marriage or at any time thereafter according to Muslim law; and
   (d) All the properties given to her before or at the time of marriage or after her marriage by her relatives or her friends or the husband or any relatives of the husband or his friends.

2. Where a reasonable and fair provision and maintenance or the amount of her mehr or dower due has not been made or paid or the properties referred to in clause (d) of sub-section (1) have not been delivered to a divorced woman on her divorce, she or anyone duly authorised by her may, on her behalf, make an application to a Magistrate for an order for payment of such provision and maintenance, *mehr*, or dower or the delivery of properties as the case may be.

3. Where an application has been made under sub-section (2) by a divorced woman, the Magistrate may, if he is satisfied that—
   (a) her husband having sufficient means, has failed or neglected to make or pay her within the *iddat* period a reasonable and fair provision and maintenance for her and the children; or,
   (b) the amount equal to the sum of *mehr* or dower has not been paid or that the properties referred to in clause (d) of sub-section (1) have not been delivered to her, make an order, within one month of the date of the filling of the application

Appendices 297

directing her former husband to pay such reasonable and fair provision and maintenance to the divorced woman as he may determine as fit and proper having regard to the needs of the divorced woman, the standard of life enjoyed by her during her marriage and the means of her former husband or as the case may be, for payment of such *mehr* or dower or the delivery of such properties referred to in clause (d) of sub-section (1) to the divorced woman.

Provided that if the Magistrate finds it impracticable to dispose of the application within the said period, he may, for reasons to be recorded by him, dispose of the application after the said period.

4. If any person against whom an order has been made under subsection (3) fails without sufficient cause to comply with the order, the Magistrate may issue a warrant for levying the amount of the maintenance or *mehr* or dower due in the manner provided for levying fines under the code of Criminal Procedure, 1973 (2 of 1974), and may sentence such person, for the whole or part of any amount remaining unpaid after the execution of the warrant, to imprisonment for a term which may extend to one year or until payment if sooner made, subject to such person being heard in defence and the said sentence being imposed according to the provisions of the said Code.

S. 4 Order for Payment of Maintenance

1. Notwithstanding anything contained in the foregoing provisions of this Act or in any other law for the time being in force, where a magistrate is satisfied that a divorced woman has not re-married and is not able to maintain herself after the iddat period, he may make an order directing such of her relatives as would be entitled to inherit her property on her death according to Muslim law, to pay such reasonable and fair maintenance as he may determine fit and proper, having regard to the needs of the divorced woman, the standard of life enjoyed by her during her marriage and the means of such relatives and such maintenance shall be payable by such relatives in the proportion in which they would inherit her property and at such periods as he may specify in his order.

Provided that where such divorced woman has children, the Magistrate shall order only such children to pay maintenance to her, and in the event of any such children being unable to pay

298 *The Politics of Personal Law in South Asia*

such maintenance, the Magistrate shall order the parents of such divorced woman to pay maintenance to her.

Provided further that if any of the parents is unable to pay his or her share of the maintenance ordered by the Magistrate on the ground of his or her not having the means to pay the same, the Magistrate may, on proof of such inability being furnished to him, order that the share of such relatives in the maintenance ordered by him be paid by such of the other relatives as may appear to the Magistrate to have the means of paying the same in such proportions as the Magistrate may think fit to order.

Where a divorced woman is unable to maintain herself and she has no relatives as mentioned in sub-section (1) or such relatives or any one of them have not enough means to pay the maintenance ordered by the Magistrate or the other relatives have not the means to pay the shares of those relatives whose shares have been ordered by the Magistrate to be paid by such other relatives under the second provision to sub-section 9 of the *Wakf* Act, 1954 or under any other law for the time being in force in a State, functioning in the area in which the woman resides, to pay such maintenance as determined by him under sub-section (1) or, as the case may be, to pay the shares of such of the relatives who are unable to pay, at such periods as he may specify in his order.

S. 5 Option to be Governed by the Provisions of Section 125 to 128 of Act 2 of 1974

If on the date of the first hearing of the application under subsection (2) of Section 3 a divorced woman and her former husband declare, by affidavit or any other declaration in writing in such form as may be prescribed either jointly or separately, that they would prefer to be governed by the provisions of Section 125 to 128 of the code of Criminal Procedure, 1973 and file such affidavit or declaration in the Court hearing the application, the magistrate shall dispose of such application accordingly.

Explanation: for the purpose of this section, "date of the first hearing of the application" means the date fixed in the summons for the attendance of the respondent to the application.

S. 6 Power to Make Rules

1. The Central Government may, by notification in the official Gazette, make rules for carrying out the purpose of this Act.

2. In particular and without prejudice to the foregoing power, such rules may provide for—the form of the affidavit or other declaration in writing to be filed under Section 5, the procedure to be followed by the magistrate is disposing of application under this Act, including the serving of notices to the parties to such application, dates of hearing of such applications and other matters, any other matter which is required to be or may be prescribed.

3. Every rule made under this Act shall be laid, as soon as may be after it is made, before each House of Parliament, while it is in session, for a total period of thirty days which may be comprised in one session or in two or more successive sessions, and if, before the expiry of the session immediately following the session of the successive sessions aforesaid, both Houses agree in making any modification in the rule or both Houses agree that the rule should not be made, the rule shall thereafter have effect only in such modified form or be of no effect, as the case may be, so, however, that any such modification of annulment shall be without prejudice to validity of anything previously done under the rule.

S. 7 Transitional Provisions

Every application by a divorced woman under Section 125 or under Section 127 of the code of Criminal procedure, 1973 pending before a Magistrate on the commencement of this Act, shall, notwithstanding anything contained in that code and subject to the provisions of Section 5 of this Act, be disposed by such Magistrate in accordance with the provisions of this Act.

Appendix 2
Code of Criminal Procedure, 1973: Maintenance of Wife

S. 125 Order for Maintenance of Wives, Children and Parents

1. If any person having sufficient means neglects or refuses to maintain
   (a) his wife, unable to maintain herself; or
   (b) his legitimate or illegitimate minor child, whether married or not, unable to maintain itself; or
   (c) his legitimate or illegitimate child (not being a married daughter) who has attained majority, where such child is, by reason of any physical or mental abnormality or injury unable maintain itself, or
   (d) his father or mother, unable to maintain himself or herself.

   Magistrate of the first class may, upon proof of such neglect or refusal, order such person to make a monthly allowance for the maintenance of his wife or such child, father or mother, at such monthly rate not exceeding five hundred rupees in the whole, as such Magistrate may from time to time direct:

   Provided that the Magistrate may order the father of a minor female child referred to in clause (b) to make such allowance. Until she attains her majority, if the Magistrate is satisfied that the husband of such minor female child, if married, is not possessed of sufficient means.

   Explanation: For the purpose of this Chapter
   (a) "minor" means a person who, under the provision of the Indian Majority Act, 1875 (9 of 1875), is deemed not to have attained his majority;
   (b) "wife" includes a woman who has been divorced by, or has obtained a divorce from, her husband and has not remarried.

2. Such allowance shall be payable from the date of the order, or, if so ordered from the date of the application for maintenance.

Appendices 301

3. If any person so ordered fails without sufficient cause, to comply with the order, any such Magistrate may, for every breach of the order, issue a warrant for levying the amount due in the manner provided of levying fines, and may sentence such person, for the whole or any part of each month's allowance remaining unpaid after the execution of the warrant, to imprisonment for a term which may extend to one month or until payment, if sooner made.

   Provided that no warrant shall be issued for the recovery of any amount due under this section unless application be made to the Court to levy such amount within a period of one year from the date on which it became due.

   Provided further, that if such person offers to maintain his wife on condition of her living with him, and she refuses to be with him, such Magistrate may consider any grounds of refusal stated by her, and may make an order under this section, notwithstanding such offer, if he is satisfied that there is just ground for so doing.
   Explanation: if a husband has contracted marriage with another woman or keeps a mistress, it shall be consldered to be just ground for his wife's refusal to live with him.

4. No wife shall be entitled to receive an allowance from husband under the section if she is living in adultery, or without any sufficient reason, she refuses to live with her husband or if they are living separately by mutual consent.

5. On proof that any wife in whose favaour an order has been made under this section is living in adultery, or that without sufficient reason she refuses to live with her husband or if they are living separately by mutual consent, the Magistrate shall cancel the order.

S. 126 Procedures

1. Proceedings under S.125 may be taken against any person in any district:
   (a) where he is, or
   (b) where he or his wife resides, or
   (c) where he last resided with his wife, or as the case may be with the mother of the illegitimate child.

2. All evidence in such proceedings shall be taken in the presence of the person against whom an order for payment of maintenance is proposed to be made, or when his personal attendance is dispensed with, in the presence of his pleader, and shall be recorded in the manner prescribed for summons cases:

302 *The Politics of Personal Law in South Asia*

Provided that if the Magistrate is satisfied that the person against whom an order for payment of maintenance is proposed to be made is willfully avoiding service, or willfully neglecting to attend the Court, the Magistrate may proceed to hear and determine the case *ex parte* and any order so made may be set aside for good cause shown on an application made within three months from the date thereof subject to such terms including terms as to payment of cost to the opposite party as the Magistrate may think just and proper.

3. The Court in dealing with applications under 125 shall have power to make such order as to costs as may be just.

S. 127 Alteration in Allowance

1. On proof of a change in the circumstances of any person, receiving under S.125 a monthly allowance, or ordered under the same section to pay a monthly allowance to his wife, child, father or mother, as the case may be, the magistrate may make such alteration in the allowance as he thinks fit. Provided that if he increases the allowance, the monthly rate of five hundred rupees in the whole shall not be exceeded.

2. Where it appears to the Magistrate that, in consequence of any decision of a competent Civil Court, any order made under S.125 should be cancelled or varied, he shall cancel the order or, as the case may be, vary the same accordingly.

3. Where any order has been made under S.125 in favour of a woman who has been divorced by, or has obtained divorce from her husband, the Magistrate shall, if he is satisfied that:

   (a) the woman has after the date of such divorce, remarried, cancel such order as from the date of her remarriage;

   (b) the woman has been divorced by her husband and that she has received, whether before or after the date of the said order, the whole of the sum which under any customary or personal law applicable to the parties, was payable on such divorce, cancel such order:

   (i) in the case where such sum was paid before such order, from the date on which such order was made;

   (ii) in any other case, from the date of expiry of the period, if any, for which maintenance has been actually paid by the husband to the woman;

   (c) the woman has obtained a divorce from her husband and that she had voluntarily surrendered her rights to maintenance after her divorce, cancel the order from the date thereof.

4. At the time of making any decree for the recovery of any maintenance or dowry by any person, to whom a monthly allowance has been ordered to be paid under S.125, the Civil Court shall take into account the sum that has been paid to, or recovered by, such person as monthly allowance in pursuance of the said order.

S. 128 Enforcement of Order of Maintenance

A copy of the order of maintenance shall be given without payment to the person in whose favour it is made, or to his guardian, if any, or to the person to whom the allowance is to be paid, and such order may be enforced by any Magistrate in any place where the person against whom it is made may be, on such Magistrate being satisfied as to the identity of the parties and the non-payment of the allowance due.

Appendix 3

Relevant Excerpts from Supreme Court Judgments with Reference to the Uniform Civil Code

[A]

SHAH BANO Case [AIR 1985 SC 945]
   [Decided on 23 April 1985 by Y. V. Chandrachud, C. J., with D. A. Desai, O. Chinappa Reddy, E. S. Venkataramiah and Raghunath Misra, JJ.]

1.   This appeal does not involve any question of Constitutional importance but, that is not to say that it does not involve any question of importance. Some questions which arise under the ordinary civil and criminal law are of a far-reaching significance to large segments of society which have been traditionally subjected to unjust treatment. Women are one such segment. *'Na stree swatantramarhati'* said Manu, the lawgiver: 'The woman does not deserve independence.' And, it is alleged that the 'fatal point in Islam is the degradation of woman': *'Selections from Kuran'*—Edward William Lane, 1843, Reprint 1982, page XC (Introduction). To the Prophet is ascribed the statement, hopefully wrongly, that 'Woman was made from a crooked rib, and if you try to bend it straight, it will break; therefore treat your wives kindly'.

....

32. It is also a matter of regret that Article 44 of our Constitution has remained a dead letter. It provides that: 'The State shall endeavour to secure for the citizens a uniform civil code throughout the territory of India.' There is no evidence of any official activity for framing a common civil code for the country. A belief seems to have gained ground that it is for the Muslim community to take a lead in the matter of reforms of their personal law. A common civil code will

Appendices 305

help the cause of national integration by removing disparate loyalties to laws which have conflicting ideologies. No community is likely to bell the cat by making gratuitous concessions on the issue. It is the State which is charged with the duty of securing a uniform civil code for the citizens of the country and, unquestionably, it has the legislative competence to do so. A counsel in the case whispered, somewhat audibly, that legislative competence is one thing, the political courage to use that competence is quite another. We understand the difficulties involved in bringing persons of different faiths and persuasions on a common platform. But, a beginning has to be made if the Constitution is to have any meaning. Inevitably, the role of the reformer has to be assumed by the courts because it is beyond the endurance of sensitive minds to allow injustice to be suffered when it is so palpable. But piecemeal attempts of courts to bridge the gap between personal laws cannot take the place of a common civil code. Justice to all is a far more satisfactory way of dispensing justice than justice from case to case.

33. Dr. Tahir Mahmood in his book *Muslim Personal Law* (1977 Edition, pages 200–202) has made a powerful plea for framing a uniform civil code for all citizens of India. He says: 'In pursuance of the goal of secularism, the State must stop administering religion-based personal laws.' He wants the lead to come from the majority community, but we should have thought that, lead or no lead, the State must act. It would be useful to quote the appeal made by the author to the Muslim community:

> Instead of wasting their energies in exerting theological and political pressure in order to secure an 'immunity' for their traditional personal law from the State's legislative jurisdiction, the Muslims will do well to begin exploring and demonstrating how the true Islamic laws, purged of their time-worn and anachronistic interpretations, can enrich the common civil code of India.

At a Seminar held on October 18, 1980 under the auspices of the Department of Islamic and Comparative Law, Indian Institute of Islamic Studies, New Delhi, he also made an appeal to the Muslim community to display by their conduct a correct understanding of Islamic concepts on marriage and divorce (see *Islamic and Comparative Law Quarterly*, April–June, 1981, page 146).

34. Before we conclude, we would like to draw attention to the Report of the Commission on Marriage and Family Laws, which was appointed by the government of Pakistan by a Resolution dated

306 *The Politics of Personal Law in South Asia*

August 4, 1955. The answer of the Commission to question no. 5 (page 1215 of the Report) is that:

> A large number of middle-aged women who are being divorced without rhyme or reason should not be thrown on the streets without a roof over their heads and without any means of sustaining themselves and their children.

The Report concludes thus:

> In the words of Allama Iqbal, the question which is likely to confront Muslim countries in the near future, is whether the law of Islam is capable of evolution—a question which will require great intellectual effort, but is sure to be answered in the affirmative.

[B]

JORDEN DIENGDEH Case [AIR 1985 SC 935]
[Decided on 10 May 1985 by O. Chinappa Reddy, J. with R. B. Misra, J.)

1. It was just the other day that a Constitution Bench of this court had to emphasise the urgency of infusing life into Art. 44 of the Constitution which provides that: 'The State shall endeavour to secure for the citizens a uniform civil code throughout the territory of India.'

The present case is yet another which focuses attention on the immediate and compulsive need for a uniform civil code. The totally unsatisfactory state of affairs consequent on the lack of a uniform civil code is exposed by the facts of the present case. Before mentioning the facts of the case, we might as well refer to the observations of Chandrachud, C. J., In the recent case decided by the Constitution Bench (Mohd. Ahmed Khan v. Shah Bano Begum, 1985 Cri L. J 875):

[The judgment reproduces here, with the omission of two sentences—the first and the third—para 32 of the Shah Bano judgment: see text supra.]

....

Appendices 307

6. We may add that under strict *Hanafi* Law there was no provision enabling a Muslim woman to obtain a decree dissolving her marriage on the failure of the husband to maintain her or on his deserting her or maltreating her and it was the absence of such a provision entailing 'unspeakable misery to innumerable Muslim women' that was responsible for the passing of the Dissolution of Muslim Marriages Act 1939 (see Statements of Objects and Reasons of that Act). If the legislature could so alter the *Hanafi* law, we fail to understand the hullabaloo about the recent judgment of this court in the case of *Mohd. Ahmad Khan v. Shah Bano Begum* (1985 Cri L.J 875) the provisions of sec. 125 of the Criminal Procedure Code and the Muslim law.

7. It is thus seen that the law relating to judicial separation, divorce and nullity of marriage is far, far from uniform. Surely the time has now come for a complete reform of the law of marriage and [to] make a uniform law applicable to all people irrespective of religion or caste. It appears to be necessary to introduce irretrievable breakdown of marriage and mutual consent as grounds of divorce in all cases. The case before us is an illustration of a case where the parties are bound together by a marital tie which is better untied. There is no point or purpose to be served by the continuance of a marriage which has so completely and signally broken down.

We suggest that the time has come for the intervention of the legislature in these matters to provide for a uniform code of marriage and divorce and to provide by law for a way out of the unhappy situations in which couples like the present have found themselves. We direct that a copy of this order may be forwarded to the Ministry of Law and Justice for such action as they may deem fit to take.

[C]

SARLA MUDGAL Case [AIR 1995 SC 1531]
[Decided on 10 May 1995 by Kuldip Singh, J. and R. M. Sahai, J. (separate judgments).]

[a] Justice Kuldip Singh

1. 'The State shall endeavour to secure for the citizens a uniform civil code throughout the territory of India' is an unequivocal mandate under Article 44 of the Constitution of India which seeks to introduce a uniform personal law—a decisive step towards national consolidation. Pandit Jawahar Lal Nehru,

308 *The Politics of Personal Law in South Asia*

while defending the introduction of the Hindu Code Bill instead of a uniform civil code, in the Parliament in 1954, said,

I do not think that at the present moment the time is ripe in India for me to try to push it through.

It appears that even 41 years thereafter, the rulers of the day are not in a mood to retrieve Article 44 from the cold storage where it is lying since 1949. The governments—which have come and gone—have so far failed to make any effort towards 'unified personal law for all Indians.' The reasons are too obvious to be stated. The utmost that has been done is to codify the Hindu law in the form of the Hindu Marriage Act 1955, the Hindu Succession Act 1956, the Hindu Minority and Guardianship Act 1956, which have replaced the traditional Hindu law based on different schools of thought and scriptural laws into one unified code. When more than 80% of the citizens have already been brought under the codified personal law there is no justification whatsoever to keep in abeyance, any more, the introduction of 'uniform civil code' for all citizens in the territory of India.

....

25. The interpretation we have given to section 494, IPC would advance the interest of justice. It is necessary that there should be harmony between the two systems of law just as there should be harmony between the two communities. Result [*sic*] of the interpretation we have given to section 494 IPC would be that the Hindu law on the one hand and the Muslim law on the other hand would operate within their respective ambits without trespassing on the personal laws of each other. Since it is not the object of Islam nor is [it] the intention of the enlightened Muslim community that the Hindu husbands should be encouraged to become Muslims merely for the purpose of evading their own personal laws by marrying again, the courts can be persuaded to adopt a construction of the laws resulting in denying the Hindu husband converted to Islam the right to marry again without having his existing marriage dissolved in accordance with law.

....

30. Coming back to the question of 'uniform civil code', we may refer to the earlier judgments of this court on the subject. A Constitution

Bench of this court speaking through Chief Justice Y. V. Chandrachud in *Mohd. Ahmed Khan v. Shah Bano Begum* [AIR 1985 SC 945, para 32] held as under:

[The judgment reproduces here in full para 32 of the Shah Bano judgment: see text supra.]

31. In Ms. Jorden Diengdeh v. S.S. Chopra (AIR 1985 SC 935) O. Chinnappa Reddy, J. speaking for the court referred to the observations of Chandrachud, C. J. in *Shah Bano Begum's* case (AIR 1985 SC 945) and observed as under:

[The judgment reproduces here the opening lines in para 1 of the Jorden Diengdeh judgment; see text supra.]

32. One wonders how long will it take for the government of the day to implement the mandate of the framers of the Constitution under Article 44 of the Constitution of India. The traditional Hindu law—personal law of the Hindus—governing inheritance, succession and marriage was given a go-bye as back as 1955–56 [sic] by codifying the same. There is no justification whatsoever in delaying indefinitely the introduction of a uniform personal law in the country.

33. Article 44 is based on the concept that there is no necessary connection between religion and personal law in a civilized society. Article 25 guarantees religious freedom whereas Article 44 seeks to divest religion from social relations and personal law. Marriage, succession and like matters of a secular character cannot be brought within the guarantee enshrined under Articles 25, 26 and 27. The personal law of the Hindus, such as relating to marriage, succession and the like have all a sacramental origin, in the same manner as in the case of the Muslims or the Christians. The Hindus along with Sikhs, Buddhists and Jains have forsaken their sentiments in the cause of the national unity and integration, some other communities would not, though the Constitution enjoins the establishment of a 'common civil code' for the whole of India.

35. Political history [sic] of India shows that during the Muslim regime, justice was administered by the qazis who would obviously apply the Muslim scriptural law to Muslims, but there was no similar assurance so far [as] litigations concerning Hindus was concerned; the system, more or less, continued during the time of the East India Company, until 1772 when Warren Hastings made Regulations for the administration of civil justice for the native population, without discrimination between Hindus and Moha-medans. The 1772 Regulations were followed by the Regulations of 1781 where under it was prescribed that either community was to be governed by its 'personal' law in matters relating to inheritance, marriage, religious

310 *The Politics of Personal Law in South Asia*

usage and institutions. So far as the criminal justice was concerned the British gradually superseded the Muslim law in 1832 and criminal justice was governed by the English common law. Finally the Indian Penal Code was enacted in 1860. This broad policy continued throughout the British regime until independence and the territory of India was partitioned by the British rulers into two states on the basis of religion. Those who preferred to remain in India after the partition fully knew that the Indian leaders did not believe in two-nation or three-nation theory and that in the Indian Republic there was to be only one Nation—Indian Nation—and no community could claim to remain a separate entity on the basis of religion. It would be necessary to emphasise that the respective personal laws were permitted by the British to govern the matters relating to inheritance, marriages, etc., only under the Regulations of 1781 framed by Warren Hastings. The legislation—not religion—being the authority under which personal law was permitted to operate and is continuing to operate, the same can be superseded/supplemented by introducing a uniform civil code. In this view of the matter no community can oppose the introduction of uniform civil code for all the citizens in the territory of India.

36. The successive governments till-date have been wholly remiss in their duty of implementing the Constitutional mandate under Article 44 of the Constitution of India.

37. We, therefore, request the government of India through the Prime Minister of the country to have a fresh look at Article 44 of the Constitution of India and 'endeavour to secure for the citizens a uniform civil code throughout the territory of India.'

38. We further direct the government of India through Secretary, Ministry of Law and Justice to file an affidavit of a responsible officer in this court in August 1996 Indicating therein the steps taken and efforts made by the Government of India towards securing a 'uniform civil code' for the citizens of India. Sahal, J. in his short and crisp supporting opinion has suggested some of the measures which can be undertaken by the government in this respect.

[b] Justice R. M. Sahai

1. Considering sensitivity of the issue and magnitude of the problem [*sic*], both on the desirability of a uniform or common civil code and its feasibility, it appears necessary to add a few words to the social necessity projected in the order proposed by my esteemed brother Kuldip Singh, J., more to focus on the urgency of such a legislation

Appendices 311

and to emphasise that I entirely agree with the thought-provoking reasons which have been brought forth by him in his order clearly and lucidly.

2. The pattern of debate, even today, is the same as was voiced forcefully by the members of the minority community in the Constituent Assembly. If 'the non-implementation of the provision contained in Article 44 amounts to grave failure of Indian democracy' represents one side of the picture, then the other side claims that 'logical probality appears to be that the code would cause dissatisfaction and disintegration than serve as a common umbrella to promote homogeneity and national solidarity'.

3. When Constitution was framed [*sic*] with secularism as its ideal and goal, the consensus and conviction to be one, socially, found its expression in Article 44 of the Constitution. But religious freedom, the basic foundation of secularism, was guaranteed by Articles 25 to 28 of the Constitution. Article 25 is very wisely worded. It guarantees all persons not only freedom of conscience but the right to profess, practise and propagate religion. What is religion? Any faith or belief. The court has expanded religious liberty in its various phrases guaranteed by the Constitution and extended it to practices and even external overt acts of the individual. Religion is more than a mere matter of faith. The Constitution by guaranteeing freedom of conscience ensured inner aspects of religious belief. And external expressions of it were protected by guaranteeing right to freely practise and propagate religion [*sic*]. Reading and reciting holy scriptures, for instance, Ramayana or Quran or Bible or Guru Granth Sahib is as much a part of religion as offering food to a deity by a Hindu or bathing the idol or dressing him and going to a temple, mosque, church or gurudwara.

4. Marriage, inheritance, divorce, conversion are as much religious in nature and content as any other belief or faith. Going round the fire seven rounds or giving consent before a *qazi* are as much matters of faith and conscience as the worship itself. When a Hindu becomes [a] convert by reciting *Kalma* or a Muslim becomes Hindu by reciting certain *mantras* it is a matter of belief and conscience. Some of these practices observed by members of one religion may appear to be excessive and even violative of human rights to members of another. But these are matters of faith. Reason and logic have little role to play. The sentiments and emotions have to be cooled and tempered by sincere effort. But today there is no Raja Ram Mohan Roy who single-handed brought about that atmosphere which paved the way for sati abolition. Nor is a statesman of the stature of Pt. Nehru who could pilot

312 *The Politics of Personal Law in South Asia*

through, successfully, the Hindu Succession Act and Hindu Marriage Act revolutionizing the customary Hindu law. The desirability of uniform code can hardly be doubted. But it can concretize only when social climate is properly built up by elite of the society, statesmen amongst leaders who instead of gaining personal mileage rise above and awaken the masses to accept the change [*sic*].

5. The problem with which these appeals are concerned is that many Hindus have changed their religion and have become converts to Islam only for the purpose of escaping the consequences of bigamy. For instance, Jitendra Mathur was married to Meena Mathur. He and another Hindu girl embraced Islam. Obviously because Muslim law permits more than one wife and to the extent of four. But no religion permits delibeate distortions. Much misapprehension prevails about bigamy in Islam. To check the misuse many Islamic countries have codified the personal law, wherein the practice of polygamy has been either totally prohibited or severely restricted. Syria, Tunisia, Morocco, Pakistan, Iran, the Islamic Republics of the Soviet Union are some of the Muslim countries to be remembered in this context.

But ours is a secular democratic republic. Freedom of religion is the core of our culture. Even the slightest deviation shakes the social fibre. But religious practices violative of human rights and dignity and sacerdotal suffocation of essentially civil and material freedoms, are not autonomy but oppression. Therefore, a unified code is imperative both for protection of the oppressed and promotion of national unity and solidarity. But the first step should be to rationalize the personal law of the minorities to develop religious and cultural amity.

The government would be well advised to entrust the responsibility to the Law Commission which may in consultation with Minorities Commission examine the matter and bring about the comprehensive legislation in keeping with modern day concept of human rights for women [*sic*].

6. The government may also consider feasibility [*sic*] of appointing a committee to enact a Conversion of Religion Act, immediately, to check the abuse of religion by any person. The law may provide that every citizen who changes his religion cannot marry another wife unless he divorces his first wife. The provision should be made applicable to every person whether he is a Hindu or a Muslim or a Christian or a Sikh or a Jain or a Budh [*sic*]. Provision may be made for maintenance and succession, etc., also to avoid clash of interests after death.

7. This would go a long way to solve the problem and pave the way for a unified civil code.

Source: Mahmood, Tahir, *Uniform Civil Code: Fictions and Facts.* New Delhi: India and Islam Research Council, 1995, pp. 194–202.

Appendix 4
Muslim Personal Law in Other Countries

In most countries Muslims are still governed by their personal laws, Turkey and Soviet Central Asia being two notable exceptions. In Turkey, Muslim religious law was replaced in 1926 by a civil code drawn from the Swiss Civil Code of 1912, and in Soviet Central Asia, in the wake of the Bolshevik Revolution, Muslim law was gradually given up in favour of the newly introduced socialist laws. Elsewhere in the Muslim world, many countries have deemed it necessary to change the Shariat law while asserting that they have not acted against the spirit of Islam. The following are the major family law statues now in force:

Algeria	Code of Personal Status and Succession, 1984 (Al-Mudawwana)
Burma	Muslim Dissolution of Marriage Act, 1953 (Act 14 of 1953)
Cyprus	Turkish Family (Marriage and Divorce) Law, 1951 (Law No. 4 of 1951)
Egypt	Family Law Enactments, 1920–25 (Law No. 25 of 1920 and No. 25 of 1929) Law of Inheritance, 1943 (Law No. 77 of 1943)
Indonesia	Marriage Law, 1974 (Law No. 1 of 1974)
Iraq	Law of Personal Status, 1959 (Law No. 188 of 1959)
Jordan	Law of Personal Status, 1976 (Law No. 41 of 1976)
Lebanon	Ottoman Law of Family Right, 1917
Libya	Law of Women's Rights, 1972 (Law No. 176 of 1972)
Morocco	Code of Personal Status, 1958
Pakistan	The West Pakistan Muslim Personal Law (Shariaht) Application Act, 1962 (Act V of 1962)
Philippines	Code of Muslim Personal Law, 1977 (enforced by Presidential decree No. 1083 of February 4, 1977)

Appendices 315

Singapore	Muslims Ordinance, 1957 (Ordinance No. 25 of 1957) Administration of Muslim Law Act, 1966 (Act No. 27 of 1960)
Somalia	Family Law Act, 1975 (Law No. 23 of 1975)
Sri Lanka	Muslim Marriage and Divorce Act, 1951 (Act No. 13 of 1951)
Sudan	Judicial Circular (*man shur*) relating to Law of Marriage, 1960 (Circular No. 64 of 1960)
Syria	Law of Family Rights, 1953 (Law No. 59 of 1953)
Tunisia	Code of Personal Status, 1959 (*Al-Majaua*) Law of Guardianship and Adoption, 1959 (Law No. 58–67 of 1959)
Yemen	Family Law Act, 1975

Iran: Marriage with more than one wife is not permitted except with the permission of the *Qadi*. The grant of such permission is usually based on the condition that the husband's financial position is sound enough to care for more than one wife. The husband does not have the right to repudiate his wife without any judicial intervention.

The Marriage Law of 1931 deals with the wife's right to maintenance. It provides that if an order of the court directing the husband to provide maintenance to the wife, issued on her application, cannot be executed, she may demand dissolution of marriage by the court. It further permits the wife to live separately from her husband without losing her right to maintenance, if she has left her husband's house due to the fear of unbearable physical injury or monetary loss.

Iraq: Marriage with more than one wife is not permitted except with the permission of the *Qadi*, who grants such permission if the husband's financial position is sound and where injustice between the wives is not feared. All those who enter into a contract of marriage with more than one woman in contravention of the above conditions are liable to imprisonment for a period not exceeding one year, or fine not exceeding 100 dinars or both.

Jordan: There is a provision that a woman, at the time of marriage, can stipulate that she will have the right to divorce in specified circumstances or to live in a specified place. Indeed she can even stipulate that the husband should not saddle her with a co-wife. But such stipulation can be enforced only if the *Qadi* incorporates it in the registered marriage deed and also in the certificate.

316   The Politics of Personal Law in South Asia

Lebanon: Articles 20 to 101 of the Ottoman Law make provision for the enforcement of the wife's right to maintenance. The court can fix the amount of maintenance to be paid by the husband and in the event of his inability to do so, authorises the wife to borrow on his credit. The amount of maintenance so fixed shall be regarded a debt against the husband.

Morocco: The wife may demand from the *Qadi* dissolution of marriage when her husband is present but neglects to maintain her. In such cases, if the husband has any known property, the *Qadi* shall order for payment of maintenance from such property. Where there is no known property, who is not destitute, persists in not maintaining his wife, dissolution of marriage shall be granted to the wife. if the husband establishes that he is incompetent to provide maintenance to the wife, the *Qadi* shall give him a period of respite not exceeding three months, and after the expiry of that period if the husband still cannot provide maintenance, shall grant dissolution of marriage.

Dissolution of marriage granted under this Article constitutes a divorce revocable by the husband during the period of *iddat* if he expresses willingness for and is capable of providing maintenance to the wife. Morocco law requires the husband to pay the wife a parting amount in proportion to his means and her circumstances.

Pakistan: Under the Pakistan Family Laws Ordinance 1961, the prior permission of an arbitration council is obligatory for marriage a second time. Chief Justice of Pakistan Hameedur Rehman said that Shariat permitted the Muslims to have more than one wife, but no man in Pakistan could now marry a second time if his first wife was alive and unless she documented her consent.

The Pakistan ordinance provides that if a husband fails to maintain his wife adequately or to treat his co-wives (if he has more than one) equitably, an arbitration council will enquire into the matter. According to Kaplla Khandwala: 'Pakistan has now changed the family laws and the made plurality of wives and the pronouncement of *Talaq* (divorce) illegal; other modern Muslim states have gone still further' (*Report of the Commission on Marriage and Family Laws*, Gazette of Pakistan, Extraordinary, 20 June 1956, p. 51). The Commission is not authorised or prepared to tamper with the Sharat but its members and hundreds of Muslims who have answered the Questlonnalre issued by the Commission, have exercised their judgment freely in matters that pertain to *fiqh*. Law is ultimately related to life experiences which are not a monopoly of the theologians only.

There are recorded cases in which un-learned women corrected the Khalifa who gratefully acknowledged his error of judgment. If Muslim society has to become genuinely free and dynamic again, offering itself as a model for all other types of democracy, that original spirit of Islam has to be revived.

There is no question of amending the basis of the laws about marriage and family relations as promulgated in the Holy Book or any clear and authentic injunctions which could be derived from the *Sunnah*. The members of the Commission as well as those from all spheres of society and different intellectual levels who have pondered over the Questionnaire and sent replies have acted with the conviction that it is not explicit Islamic injunctions that are to be amended or altered; they are only to be liberally and rationally interpreted and properly implemented.

Divorce by Husband [in Pakistan]

Should it be open to a matrimonial and family laws court, when approached, to lay down that a husband shall pay maintenance to the divorced wife for life or till her remarriage?

The commission was of the opinion that such a discretion should be vested in the matrimonial court, and that a large number of middle-aged women who are being divorced without rhyme or reason should not be thrown on the street without a roof over their heads and without any means of sustaining themselves and their children. Of course it would be open to a matrimonial court to refuse to sanction any maintenance if the woman is at fault.

Having dealt with specific questions in detail we would like to make some concluding remarks to indicate that we have always kept the injunctions of the Holy Qur'an and the *Sunnah* in view in proposing certain reforms. We have given no new rights to women. An effort has been made to provide machinery for the implementation of rights that have already been granted to women and children by the Holy Qur'an and the *Sunnah* only. . . .

Islam very justly claims to be a simple and liberal creed, and apart from a very few categorical injunctions, adumbrated in broad outline its basic principles, aspirations and trends, are based on natural and substantial justice. The Qur'an says that previous societies perished because they were burdened with too much inflexible law and too much unnecessary ritual, which the Holy Book has stigmatised as chains and halters. Law is a creative and adaptive process and it requires more of vision and less of inflexible rules.

318   *The Politics of Personal Law in South Asia*

The original simple and liberal spirit of Islam must be revived and for guidance we have to go back to the beginning of Islam when it was yet free from accretions. Later multiplication's of laws and codes may be studied as facts of historical importance, but can never be identified with the totality of Islam. As the great sage-philosopher of Islam Allama Iqbal said, 'Islam is more of an aspiration than a fulfillment,' meaning thereby that its implementation at any epoch of history in any particular socio-economic pattern is only a moment in the dialectic of its history. No progressive legislation is possible if Muslim assemblies remain only interpreters and blind adherents of ancient schools of law. . . .

Bangladesh: There have been two important rulings, one from the Dhaka High Court and the other from the Supreme Court on this issue. In 1995, the Dhaka High Court ruled that a divorced woman is entitled to maintenance till her remarriage. In 1998, the constitutional bench of the Supreme court over ruled the High Court ruling that a divorced woman is entitled to maintenance for her lifetime or until her remarriage. The court ruled that mata'a couldn't be equated with maintenance. The court explained the meaning of the term mata'a as something (a provision), which a divorced woman is entitled and which the former husband is under an obligation to pay.

1995: Dhaka High Court: Justices Mohammad Gholam Rabbani and Syed Amirul Islam—9 January 1995.
Mohd Hefzur Rahman v. Shamsun Nahar Begum
47 (1995) Dhaka Law Reports 54

The parties were married on 25 March 1985. Taka 50,001 was fixed as *mehr* (dower). In 1987 a son was born to the couple. On 19 August 1988 the husband divorced the wife. On 2 November 1988 the wife filed a suit in the Family Court for recovery of *mehr* and for Taka 1,000 per month as maintenance for herself and a further Taka 1,000 per month as maintenance for her minor son. The Family Court directed the husband to pay the wife the balance of *mehr* amount being Taka 48,000. Taka 1,000 per month to the wife as maintenance for three months of *iddat* period and Taka 1,000 per month as maintenance to the minor son. In an appeal filed by the husband the amount of maintenance was reduced to Taka 600 per month for both the wife and the minor son.

In appeal, the High Court held: A woman who is divorced is entitled to household stuff, utensils, goods, chattels, provision, convenience which is known, recognised, honourable, good, befitting, a kindness.

Abdullah Yusf AN is, therefore, correct in translating the expression 'mataaoon bill maaroot' as 'maintenance should be provided on a reasonable scale'. One of the meanings of the word 'maaroof is 'recognized'. This meaning is to be considered with regard to the amount of maintenance and not with regard to the period of maintenance. This is apparent in view of the fact that Qur'an directs a woman who is divorced to undergo a period of iddat elsewhere (Second Sura Baqara, verse 228) and herein Qur'an directs a man to give maintenance in case he divorces his wife. These two legal provisions are, therefore, independent of each other and are addressed to two persons of different status.

Considering all the aspects we finally hold that a person after divorcing his wife is bound to maintain her on a reasonable scale beyond the period of *iddat* for an indefinite period, that is to say, till she loses the status of a divorcee by remarrying another person.

1998: Supreme Court of Bangladesh: Justices: A. T. M. Afzal, Mustafa Kamal, Latifur Rahman, Md Abdur Rouf and B. B. Roy Choudhury 3 December 1998.
Hefzur Rahman v. Shamsun Nahar Begum
Civil Appeal No. 130 of 1997

Over ruling the division bench decision of the Dhaka High Court, the constitutional Bench of the Supreme Court of Bangladesh held as follows:

The respondents and the interveners supporting them have not been able to show one instance from the early days of Islam till the date of the impugned judgment, where the view taken by the High Court as to maintenance has been upheld even by any authority or Court in any Muslim society/country at any time during the last fourteen hundred years.

The impugned decision appears to be *prima facie* ill-considered and ill-conceived as it apparently failed to take into consideration the whole conspectus of Muslim Law. The High Court has read the words of Verse 241 and put a meaning to it according to their own wisdom which is unique and first of its kind [*sic*] and its interpretation is rejected and set aside with the resultant decision which automatically fails through.

The mandatory Mata'a or gift due to the woman divorced both before consummation and before an amount of *mehr* has been settled is defined by the classical Hasafi jurists in terms of three items of clothing the fabric of which depends on the economic position of the husband.

320   *The Politics of Personal Law in South Asia*

The Board of Islamic Publication, Delhi translated the word mata'a as 'something'. 'Mata'a is something to which a divorced woman is entitled and which the former husband is under an obligation to pay seems to follow naturally from the Verse itself. But the whole question is whether Mata'a can be equated with maintenance as has been done by the High court. Mata'a is certainly not maintenance as can be claimed within the meaning of maintenance under the Family Court Ordinance.

The import of the word Mata'a should be understood in the sense the Holy Prophet (S) and his companions had understood it and not according to later day translations of the said word which are conflicting. In no country there is found to be any provision of granting Mata'a for a lifetime or till remarriage of the divorcee generally. In Tunisia and Turkey a married person, husband or wife, who insists on divorce against the wishes of the other spouse and without his or her fault, can be directed to suitably indemnify the other spouse.

Malaysia: In Malaysia, where Shafi law is followed, the divorced wife is entitled to Mata'a in addition to *iddat* maintenance and her *mehr*. The amounts awarded under this head are not large, but the Malaysian wife is also entitled to a division of matrimonial property on divorce. The latter is derived from Malaysian customary law and is incorporated into Malaysian Muslim Law.

Egypt: In Egypt, generally Hanafi law is followed. The codified law dealing with marriage and divorce was amended to provide that a wife divorced without fault and without her consent would be entitled to obtain (in addition to her *mehr* and *iddat* maintenance) mata, defined as an amount equivalent to not less than two years' expenses and subject to no maximum limit. The amount of mata shall be determined with reference to the means of the husband, the circumstances of the divorce, and the duration of the marriage. If necessary or convenient, the mata may be paid by installments. The Explanatory Note to the amendment observes that in the classical law payment of mata was not obligatory (except in the case of a woman divorced before both settlement of the amount of *mehr* and consummation).

Syria: A *Qadi* can refuse a married man permission to marry another women, if it is proved that he is not capable to maintaining two wives. In case of divorce, the matter is brought before a *Qadi* and where the *Qadi* considers that a husband has repudiated his wife

Appendices 321

without reasonable cause, he may ask the husband to pay his wife compensation limited to one year's maintenance and support.

Tunisia: Plurality of wives is positively prohibited in Tunisia. Any person who being already married, and before lawfully dissolving that marriage marries again, is liable to imprisonment for one year, or a fine of 240,000 francs or both. Tunisian law provides that where the husband (or the wife) is the one who insists on a divorce, the court shall decree the compensation that he (or she) shall pay.

Turkey: Muslim Law has been totally abrogated and the Swiss Civil Code has been adopted. Turkey and Albania are the only two countries with a Muslim majority, which have abandoned the Islamic law. Turkey, Cyprus, Tunisia, Algeria, Iraq and Iran do not give a Muslim husband the right to divorce his wife unilaterally. A Muslim husband seeking to divorce his wife must apply to the court of law.

It should be clear from the forgoing that modifications have been made in Muslim personal law in many Muslim countries to protect the rights of women. These modifications are designed to elevate the status of women equal to men in matters of family relations. Muslim personal law is not a static code based on rigidity of religious sources. It has grown in their countries to meet the changing conditions.

Source: Muniza Rafiq Khan, *Socio-Legal Status of Muslim Women*, New Delhi: Radiant Publishers, 1993: pp. 18–21; as cited in Tabassum 2003: 144–150.

Appendix 5

Declaration Adopted at the Conference on 'Genuine Problems of Women and their Solution in the Light of *Shariah*' Organized by the All India Muslim Personal Law Board on 7 and 8 April 2001

We, the participants of the Conference, solemnly affirm our faith in the Islamic *Shari'ah* and express our conviction that the *Shari'ah* provides judicious solution of all the problems of human life, including those related to women. We are of the opinion that the distressing problems that Muslim women are facing today are themselves due to the lack of faithful observance of the provisions of the principles of *Shari'ah*. We, therefore, feel that the solution of these problems lies in the society's endeavour to bring its practices into conformity with the norms and principles of *Shari'ah*. It requires to more vigorously pursue the campaign for educating the people of their rights and duties so as to reach a maximum number of people in a short period of time, inculcating in them the right consciousness and attitudes.

In this direction the Conference resolves to take the following measures:

1. To hold small workshops in various parts of the country with the help of *ulema, imams* of the mosques and other opinion makers for increasing awareness of rights and duties among the people at the local level.
2. To speed up the process of the establishment of Islamic courts (Darul Qaza) as much as possible, and to make them increasingly acceptable among the people so that they take recourse to these courts for the resolution of the disputes.
3. As the mosques could serve as the forum for educating people on the mutual rights and duties of the husband and wife, we appeal to the *imams* of the mosques to undertake this mission.
4. As frequent and irresponsible exercise of the rights to divorce seriously undermines the objectives of the *Shari'ah* and as it brings in

Appendices 323

its wake distress to wives, children and other relatives, a concerted endeavour is required for the eradication of this evil.

5. Apart from educating people on the issue and inculcating in them right attitudes, there is a need for some social restraint on divorce. For example, it may be impressed upon the people to seek the advice and intervention of *ulema,* imams and the community *panchayats* in case there is any genuine need for divorce.

6. Taking note of the increasing practice of the social evils of dowry and *tilak,* this Conference would like to remind the Muslims in India that such practices have been unanimously decreed as un-Islamic by *ulema.* It is, therefore, incumbent on them to try to eradicate these evils.

7. This Conference appeals to all *ulema, imam*s, and social organisations, especially women organisations to endeavour their utmost to wipe out this evil.

8. Similarly, issues like the non-payment of *mehr* and taking another wife, while doing injustice to the first wife, including desertion, needs to be addressed by the society through a process of mobilisation of opinion and consciousness raising.

9. This Conference appeals to the president of Personal Law Board to take all such measures that are required for the eradication of the social evils through intensification of ongoing efforts with the cooperation of *ulema,* organisations and intellectuals. The Conference assures our full cooperation to him in this regard.

This Conference also appeals to the Government of India to accord legal sanction to Darul Qaza (Islamic judicial *panchayats),* which will be helpful to women in securing their rights. We also appeal to the Government of India to constitute a *Shari'ah* bench within the Family Court system.

Appendix 6
Judges and Lawyers in Selected Countries

Country	Judges (number per million)	Lawyers (number per million)
Australia	41.6 (1977)*	911.6 (1975)
Belgium	105.7 (1975)	389.7 (1972)
Canada	59.3 (1970)	890.1 (1972)
Costa Rica	64.8 (1970)	293.1 (1970)
England, Wales	50.9 (1973)	606.4 (1973)
France	84.0 (1973)	206.4 (1973)
India	10.9 (1971)	323.6 (1981)
Italy	100.8 (1973)	792.6 (1973)
Japan	22.7 (1974)	91.2 (1975)
Netherlands	39.8 (1975)	170.8 (1972)
New Zealand	26.8 (1976)	1081.3 (1975)
Norway	60.8 (1977)	450.0 (1977)
Peru	23.6 (1970)	318.4 (1970)
Poland	93.6 (1975)	92.1 (1975)
Spain	31.0 (1970)	893.4 (1972)
South Korea	14.5 (1975)	23.5 (1975)
Sweden	99.6 (1973)	192.4 (1973)
United States	94.9 (1980)	2348.7 (1980)
Germany	213.4 (1973)	417.2 (1973)
Yugoslavia	481.1 (1979)	177.2 (1979)

*Years in brackets indicate years to which the figures relate.
Source: Galanter (1986: 166).

Appendix 7

A Statement on Prophet Muhammad's Picture on the Wall of the American Supreme Courtroom*

Islamic jurisprudence is vast and rich and encompasses many schools of thought. If this jurisprudence is vast enough to encompass the view that prohibits paintings and sculpture representing living souls, then it should also be vast enough to encompass the view that permits them. In every age and in most unclear religious matters, people are caught between those ultra-conservatives who interpret the law strictly so as to forbid, prohibit, or restrict the scope of what is permitted, and moderates who constantly seek to enlarge the scope of what is permitted, and restrict the scope of what is prohibited. The tendency of the contemporary reformist school of Islamic jurisprudence is to take the expansive approach as to what is permitted. At the forefront of this school are esteemed jurists such as Sheikh Rashid Ridha, Sheikh Muhammad Bakheet al-Mutaiyi'I, the former Mufti of Egypt, as well as many Islamic schools of thought too numerous to describe herein.

Indeed, the famous interpreter Ibn Kathir referred to images of Prophets in his explanation of the Qur'anic verse 7:157 (al-A'raf). He repeated a narration mentioned in Mustadrak al-Hakim about the Umayyad Hisham bin al-'Aas: In the days of Khalifah (Caliph) Abu Bakr (may God be pleased with him), Hisham al-'Aas was sent with another person to Heraclius, the Emperor of Byzantium, to invite him to Islam. According to the narration, the ruler of Byzantium showed Hisham al-'Aas and his companion pictures of a number of prophets. Among these they recognized the picture of the Prophet Muhammad, Messenger of God (SAAS).[1] When the incident was related to Abu Bakr (may God be pleased with him), he was moved to tears. He did not fault Hisham al-'Aas or his companion.

---

* This is the summary of al-Alwani 2000–2001.

326 *The Politics of Personal Law in South Asia*

The most pertinent inquiry in resolving the matter of the propriety of the frieze may not be a search of the legal rulings regarding sculpture, photography, oil painting, or other representations of living souls. Rather, it may be to ask whether the Court has the right to place among these symbols a representation of the Prophet Muhammad (SAAS), which does not reflect his true image, as descrlbed in the sirah, but which nevertheless accords him full respect.

My answer to this question is as follows: What I have seen in the Supreme Courtroom deserves nothing but appreciation and gratitude from American Muslims. This is a positive gesture towards Islam made by the architect and other architectural decisionmakers of the highest Court in America. God willing, it will help ameliorate some of the unfortunate misinformation that has surrounded Islam and Muslims in this country.

For this reason, I would like to express my gratitude and appreciation to the early twentieth century architect and his associates who brought, in their own way, the essence of what the prophet (SAAS) symbolised, namely, law with justice, to the attention of the American people. I hope that the Muslim leadership in the United States and around the world will join me in expressing this appreciation even though the frieze is over 60 years old.

God knows best what is right.

May God let you be successful in what He loves and in what pleases Him.

Peace be upon you with the mercy of God and His blessings.

Note

1 SAAS means *Salla Allahu ʿalayhi wa ala Allihi wa Sallam* (May the peace and blessings of God be upon him and upon his household members). This prayer is said by Muslims whenever the name of the Prophet Muhammad is mentioned or whenever he is referred to as the Prophet of God.

Appendix 8
Law Commission of India: Questionnaire on Uniform Civil Code

Dr. Justice B. S. Chauhan
Former Judge Supreme Court of India
Chairman, Law Commission of India
Government of India

7 October 2016

Appeal

The Law Commission of India welcomes all concerned to engage with us on the comprehensive exercise of the revision and reform of family laws, as the Article 44 of the Indian Constitution provides that 'the state shall endeavour to provide for its citizens a uniform civil code throughout the territory of India'. The objective behind this endeavour is to address discrimination against vulnerable groups and harmonise the various cultural practices. The commission invites suggestions on all possible models and templates of a common civil code.

The Commission hopes to begin a healthy conversation about the viability of a uniform civil code and will focus on family laws of all religions and the diversity of customary practices, to address social injustice rather than plurality of laws. Responding to the demands of social change, the Commission will consider the opinions of all stakeholders and the general public for ensuring that the norms of no one class, group or community dominate the tone or tenor of family law reforms.

Family law reform, *inter-alia* has to view women's rights as an end in itself rather than a matter of constitutional provisions, religious rights and political debate alone. With this in the background the Commission opens the debate on uniform civil code and seeks your valuable contribution towards social and legal reforms, religious groups, social groups, minority groups, non-government organizations,

328 *The Politics of Personal Law in South Asia*

political parties, civil society initiatives and government agencies, who are willing may present their views within the period of 45 days, to the Law Commission of India, 14th Floor, H.T. House, Kasturba Gandhi Marg, New Delhi – 110 001, by post, or by e-mail at lci-dla@nic.in. The Commission, at a subsequent stage may interact with them.

The Commission has prepared a questionnaire to solicit opinions and ideas of the public at large about the ways in which family law reforms could be introduced in the most integrative manner that does not compromise the diversity and the plurality that constitutes the core of India's social fabric.

[Justice Dr. B.S. Chauhan]

Law Commission of India Questionnaire on Uniform Civil Code

1. Are you aware that Article 44 of the Constitution of India provides that "the State shall endeavour to secure for the citizens a Uniform Civil Code throughout the territory of India"?

   a. Yes
   b. No
   In your view, does this matter require any further initiatives?

   _____
   _____
   _____

2. The various religious denominations are governed by personal laws and customary practices in India on matters of family law, should the UCC include all or some of these subjects?
   i. Marriage
   ii. Divorce
   iii. Adoption
   iv. Guardianship and Child custody
   v. Maintenance
   vi. Successions and
   vii. Inheritance

   a. Yes, it should include all these
   b. No, it should exclude _____
   c. It should further include_____

Appendices 329

3. Do you agree that the existing personal laws and customary practices need codification and would benefit the people?

   a. Yes
   b. No
   c. Personal laws and customary practices should be replaced by a uniform code
   d. Personal laws and customary practices should be codified to bring them in line with fundamental rights.

4. Will uniform civil code or codification of personal law and customary practices ensure gender equality?

   a. Yes
   b. No

5. Should the uniform civil code be optional?

   a. Yes
   b. No

6. Should the following practices be banned and regulated?

   a. Polygamy (Banned/Regulated)
   b. Polyandry (Banned/Regulated)
   c. Similar customary practices such as *Maitri-karaar* (friendship deed) et.al. (Banned/Regulated)

7. Should the practice of triple *talaq* be

   a. Abolished *in toto*
   b. Retained the custom
   c. Retained with suitable amendments

8. Do you think that steps should be taken to ensure that Hindu women are better able to exercise their right to property, which is often bequeathed to sons under customary practices?

   a. Yes, Hindu women must be made aware of this right and measures should be taken to ensure that women, under pressure from family do not forego their property.
   b. No there are adequate protections in the existing law.
   c. Legal provisions will not help in what is primarily a cultural practice, steps have to be taken so sensitise the society instead.

330 *The Politics of Personal Law in South Asia*

9. Do you agree that the two-year period of wait for finalizing divorce violates Christian women's right to equality?

   a. Yes, it should be made uniform across all marriages
   b. No. This period is sufficient and in-keeping with religious sentiments.

10. Do you agree that there should be a uniform age of consent for marriage across all personal laws and customary practices?

    a. Yes
    b. No, customary laws locate this age at the attainment of puberty.
    c. The prevailing system of recognizing 'voidable' marriages is sufficient.

11. Do you agree that all the religious denominations should have the common grounds for divorce?

    a. Yes
    b. No, cultural difference must be preserved.
    c. No, but there should be the same grounds for divorce available for men and women within personal law.

12. Would uniform civil code aid in addressing the problem of denial of maintenance or insufficient maintenance to women upon divorce?

    a. Yes
    b. No
    Give reasons:

    _____

    _____

13. How can compulsory registration of marriages be implemented better?

    _____

    _____

14. What measures should we take to protect couples who enter into inter-religion and inter-caste marriages?

    _____

    _____

Appendices 331

15. Would uniform civil code infringe in individual's right to freedom of religion?

    a. Yes
    b. No

    Give reasons:

    _____
    _____

16. What measures should be taken to sensitize the society towards a common code or codification of personal law?

    _____
    _____

    Remarks:

    _____
    _____
    _____
    _____

Please provide us with your name, contact number and address.

Glossary

Adivasi Original inhabitants, first settlers, tribes people (India).

Ahmediyas/Ahmadis Also known as Qadiyanis, they are the followers of Mirza Ghulam Ahmad, a Sunni *alim* of Qadiyan, a place near Amritsar in Indian Punjab. In the 1870s, Ahmad initiated a 'rationalist' movement claiming himself to be the Messiah, Jesus, the Prophet in his Second Coming, as well as the *mahdi*, thus challenging, or even appearing to 'fulfill', Christian eschatology. The movement soon became one of the fastest-growing religious movements in northern India and a local competitor to Christian evangelicalism and Islam (Jalal 2001: 290–98; Powell 2003:250). At present they claim to be Muslims, which orthodox Muslims object to because for Muslims Prophet Muhammad was the last prophet.

Ashraf Respectable class. In the South Asian context, a Muslim caste. (Singular: *sharif*)

Dar-ul-Aman Abode of peace.

Dar-ul-Harb Abode of war.

Dar-ul-Islam Abode of Islam.

Fatwa Religious ruling, decree or opinion, usually issued by a body of religious scholars or an individual, or even a mosque *imam*, with or without sanction by the state.

Fiqh Jurisprudence; generally used to refer to Muslim laws as developed by jurists.

Gotra Clan (Hindu).

Hadd Literally, 'the limits'. Used mainly with reference to Muslim penal laws, and the evidentiary requirements and maximum punishments as prescribed in the Qur'an. Some Hudood laws are operative in Malaysia, Nigeria and Pakistan.

Hadith/Ahadith Reported sayings of the Prophet Muhammad.

Haj Pilgrimage to Mecca.

Glossary 333

Hanafi A particular school of Muslim thought of the Sunni School attributed to Abu Hanifah Nu'man ibn Thabit. He was born in Kufah, Iraq, in A.D. 699 and is of Persian descent (d. A.D. 767).

Hanbali A particular school of Muslim thought of the Sunni School attributed to Abu Abdullah Ahmad ibn Hanbal. He was born in Baghdad in A.D. 780 (d. A.D. 855). He journeyed to Syria, Hijaz, Kufah and Basrah.

Hindutva Everything related to the Hindu—his social, political, cultural and economic life. In the political context it means the unification of Hindus in order to assert their authority. In short, the word implies political Hinduism.

Hudood/Hudud See Hadd.

Hukm-al-hakim An executive order.

Iddat/Idda/Iddah Waiting period, which begins from the time a Muslim woman is divorced or widowed. The period varies depending on the type of divorce, whether she is pregnant, whether she is still menstruating and whether she is widowed. During this time, she is not free to contract another marriage.

Ijma Consensus of scholars on an issue.

Ijtihad Independent reasoning to arrive at a legal principle.

Imam One who leads the prayers, usually male.

Jehad Striving for perfection; Muslim holy war.

Jirga A traditional adjudication forum common in parts of Pakistan.

Kabinama Muslim marriage contract prevalent amongst Bangladeshi Muslims.

Khula A form of divorce in Islamic law where the woman can initiate divorce proceedings. If solemnized by the *quazi*, it is irrevocable.

Maliki A particular school of Muslim thought of the Sunni School attributed to Malik ibn Anas al-Asbahi. He was born in Medina in A.D. 713 and lived in Medina all his life except for a pilgrimage to Mecca. He died in A.D. 795.

Mehr/Mahr/Mahari Dower. The goods and/or cash to be given by the groom to the bride as a requisite of a valid Muslim marriage. It may be given at the time of the marriage ceremony (prompt), or promised at a later date, or to be paid upon divorce or the death of the husband (deferred), or divided into prompt and deferred portions.

Mlechha Hindu derogatory term for foreigners/'non-Aryans'.

Mubarat A form of divorce in Islamic law in which both the parties desire divorce in which the proposal may emanate from either side.

Mudakhlat-fid-deen Interference in religion.

334   *The Politics of Personal Law in South Asia*

Mufti   One considered competent to give a legal decision on a question asked or a *fatwa*.

Mutatis mutandis   A Latin phrase meaning 'with necessary changes'.

Nikah Halala   Prohibition on remarriage with the divorced husband without consummating marriage with another man.

Nikahnama   Muslim marriage contract prevalent in India and Pakistan.

Nizam-i-Mustafa   Demand for an Islamic system.

OBCs   Other Backward Classes of India—a set of intermediate castes from all religious groups identified in the Mandal Commission Report (1980) as backward and, therefore, deserving positive discrimination by the state.

Panchayat   Traditional adjudication forum; formal or informal gathering of community elders, community influentials or family elders.

Polygynous   A marriage in which the husband has more than one wife at the same time.

Pir   Muslim spiritual guide.

Qadiyanis   See Ahmadiyas.

Qazi/Qadi/ /Quazi   Muslim court judge, or registrar.

SCs   Castes identified in the Schedules of the Indian Constitution as depressed and, therefore, deserving affirmative action of the state for their uplift.

Sangh Parivar   All organisations that swear in the name of a Hindu nation, namely, RSS, BJP, VHP, Bajrang Dal and Shiv Sena. *Parivar* literally means family.

STs   Tribes identified in the Schedules of the Indian Constitution as depressed and, therefore, deserving affirmative action of the state for their uplift.

Salish   Traditional and informal village mediation body. Usually comprises village elders, local influentials and occasionally the village mullah.

Shafi   A particular school of Muslim thought of the Sunni School attributed to Muhammad ibn Idris al-Shafi of the Quraysh tribe who was born in Gaza in A.D. 767 (d. A.D. 819). He travelled widely to the Hijaz, Yemen, Egypt and Iraq.

Shari'ah/Shari'a   The highway to the watering-place; the revealed law. Canonical law of Judaism, Christianity or Islam, usually used for Islamic law.

Shia   One of the seventy-two non-Sunni groups in Islam; followers of Ali and his sons: the twelve Imams. A Muslim sect, the followers of which believe that Ali b. Abi Talib was nominated by the Prophet as his sole successor, and after him the progeny

Glossary 335

of Fatimah-al-Zahra, his wife and daughter of the Prophet. The Shias have their two schools of fiqh.

Sunna/Sunnah The practice (acts, deeds/omissions and words) of the Prophet Muhammad. The word means 'a way or manner of acting', which in the early Islamic period came to stand for 'a generally approved standard or practice introduced by the Prophet as well as by the Pious Elders, the *salaf salih*' (Hartung 2006: 19).

Sunni A Muslim sect, traditionally with four main schools of jurisprudence: Hanafi, Hanbali, Maliki and Shafi.

Tabligh/Tabliq Religious preaching.

Talaq Unilateral divorce by the husband, a practice prevalent amongst Muslims.

Talaq-e-ahsan The Qur'anic form of divorce most preferred by the Prophet. It meant pronouncing *talaq* once in the presence of four respected members of society, two from each side, preferably those who witnessed the marriage. This form of divorce allowed for a three-month period when reconciliation could be attempted, failing which divorce became effective.

Talaq-e-bid'a See *Talaq-e-biddat*.

Talaq-e-biddat See Triple *Talaq*.

Talaq-e-hasan When one divorce is pronounced each month for three months.

Talaq-e-Mughallazah Triple talaq that is irrevocable.

Talaq-e-tafwid Delegated divorce which gives a wife equal rights to her husband by pronouncing divorce on herself if the husband breaches the marriage contract.*

Tamazzhub The idealization of a particular school of Islamic jurisprudence.

Taqleed Uncritical acceptance of a particular school of Islamic jurisprudence.

Triple Talaq Divorce given by the husband to the wife under Muslim personal law by saying '*Talaq*' thrice at a single sitting either by word of mouth, letter or SMS. Also known as *talaq-e-biddat*.

Thesavalamai Law A set of specific customary laws that govern the transfer of agricultural land in Jaffna. These ancient customary practices have evolved over centuries, particularly during colonial rules when efforts were also made to codify them. Much of their codification in the twentieth century has been through case laws. In brief, the law applies to transactions relating to land owned by

---

* The Orissa Mohammedan Marriage & Divorce Registration Act, 1949 provides for the registration of such divorces.

336 The Politics of Personal Law in South Asia

Jaffna Tamils. It does not apply to Tamils from other areas. Under the law, land has to be offered to either the co-owners or persons having hereditary rights over the land before it is sold to others.

Ulema/Ulama   Muslim religious scholars or jurists; singular: alim.

Umma   The (Muslim) community.

Wahabi   A puritanical sect founded in Arabia in the eighth century. It is now the dominant form of Islam in Saudi Arabia.

Zakat   Muslim alms tax.

Zina   Enforcement of Hudood.

Bibliography

Abbott, Freeland. 1968. *Islam and Pakistan*. Ithaca: Cornell University Press.

Abid, S. A. (ed.). 2000. *Manual of Family Laws in Pakistan (Amendments and Case Law up to date)*. Lahore: Civil and Criminal Law Publications.

Abrol, Anam. 1990. 'Attitude of "Hindus" and "other religious" Communities towards Uniform Civil Code', *K. L. T. Journal* (Ernakulam) 2: 65–72.

ACHR. 2005. 'Lesson Not Learnt by Assam: Ethnic Cleansing and Internal Displacement in Karbi Anglong and NC Hills', *ACHR Review* (New Delhi) 98, 9 November.

Agarwal, Bina. 1994. *A Field of One's Own: Gender and Land Rights in South Asia*. Cambridge: Cambridge University Press.

Agarwala, Rajkumari. 1978. 'Attitudes of Social Groups to Uniform Civil Code with Special Reference to Marriage' (an ICSSR unpublished pilot study, 1978, available at University of Poona Library, Pune).

Agarwala, Rajkumari and A. Ramanamma. 2004. 'Women and the Family Law', in Lotika Sarkar and B. Sivaramayya (eds), *Women and Law: Contemporary Problems*, pp. 248–69. New Delhi: Vikas Publications.

Aggarwal, Kailash. (ed.). 1999. *Dynamics of Identity and Intergroup Relations in North-East India*. Shimla: IIAS.

Aggarwal, Pratap. 1971. *Caste, Religion and Power*. New Delhi: Shri Ram Centre for Industrial Relations.

Agnes, Flavia. 1995. 'Hindu Men, Monogamy and Uniform Civil Code'. *Economic and Political Weekly* (Mumbai), 16 December: 3238–242.

———. 1996a. 'Economic Rights of Women in Islamic Law', *Economic and Political Weekly* (Mumbai), 12 December: 2832–838.

———. 1996b. 'The Politics of Women's Rights', *Seminar* (New Delhi) 441, May: 62–66.

———. 2002. 'Women, Marriage and the Subordination of Rights', in Partha Chatterjee and Pradeep Jeganathan (eds), *Subaltern Studies XI: Community, Gender and Violence*. New Delhi: Permanent Black and Ravi Dayal Publishers.

———. 2004a. 'Law and Gender Inequality: The Politics of Women's Rights in India', in *Women and Law in India: An Omnibus*. New Delhi: OUP.

338 *The Politics of Personal Law in South Asia*

———. 2004b. 'Revisiting Shah Bano and the Muslim Women's Act', *Muslim India* (New Delhi) 22 (3), March: 389–90.

———. 2016a. 'Muslim Women's Rights and the Media Coverage', *Economic and Political Weekly* (Mumbai), 51 (22), 28 May: 13–16.

———. 2016b. 'Gender Justice: In Fact', Indian Express (New Delhi), 17 November.

Agnihotri, Indu. 2001. 'Rereading Histories', *Seminar* (New Delhi) 505, September: 16–25.

——— and Veena Mazumdar. 1995. 'Changing Terms of Political Disourse: Women's Movement in India', *Economic and Political Weekly* (Mumbai), 22 July: 1869–878.

Ahmad, Aziz and G. E. von Grunebaum (eds). 1970. *Muslim Self Statement in India and Pakistan, 1857–1968*. Wiesbaden: Otto Harrassowitz.

Ahmad, Eqbal. 2001. 'The Political Terror of Those Who Want to be Heard', *Asian Age* (New Delhi), 9 October. (Reproduced from *The Dawn*, Karachi.)

Ahmad, Furqan. 1994. *Analytical Studies with Emphasis on Socio-Legal Aspects*. New Delhi: Regency.

Ahmad, Imtiaz. (ed.). 1976. *Family, Kinship and Marriage among Muslims in India*. New Delhi: Manohar Publications.

———. (ed.). 1978. *Caste and Social Stratification among Muslims in India*. New Delhi: Manohar Publications.

———. (ed.). 1981. *Ritual and Religion among Muslims in India*. New Delhi: Manohar Publications.

———. 2002. 'Urdu and Madrassa Education', *Economic and Political Weekly* (Mumbai) 37 (24), 15 June: 2285–287.

———. (ed.). 2003. *Divorce and Remarriage among Muslims in India*. New Delhi: Manohar Publications.

———. Partha S. Ghosh and Helmut Reifeld (eds). 2000. *Pluralism and Equality: Values in Indian Society and Politics*. New Delhi: Sage Publications.

Ahmad, Irfan and Md. Zakaria Siddiqui. 2017. 'Democracy in Jail: Over-Representation of Minorities in Indian Prisons', *Economic and Political Weekly* (Mumbai), 52(44), 4 November: 98–106.

Ahmad, Zafar. 2000. *Islam and Muslims in South Asia*. Delhi: Authors Press.

Ahmar, Moonis. 2003. 'Pakistan and Bangladesh: From Conflict to Co-operation', *BIISS Papers* (Dhaka) 19, March.

Ahmed, Abu Nasar Saied (ed.). 2006. *Nationality Question in Assam: The EPW 1980-81 Debate*. Guwahati: OKD Institute of Social Change and Development; New Delhi: Akansha.

Ahmed, Akbar S. 2003. *Islam Under Siege: Living Dangerously in a Post-Honor World*. New Delhi: Vistaar Publications.

Ahmed, Anees. 2001. 'Reforming Muslim Personal Law', *Economic and Political Weekly* (Mumbai), 24 February: 618–19.

Ahmed, Leila. 1992. *Women and Gender in Islam: Historical Roots of a Modern Debate*. New Haven and London: Yale University Press.

Bibliography 339

Ahmed, Sufia. 2006. 'Partition of Bengal', *Banglapedia http:// Banglapedia. search.com. Bd/HT/P_0100.HTM, accessed on 18 May 2006.*

Aiyar, Pallavi. 2006. Islam in China: No Longer Insulated', *The Hindu* (New Delhi), 2 September.

Akbar, M. J. 2003. 'How Personal is the Law?', *Asian Age* (New Delhi), 27 July.

al-Alwani, Taha Jaber. 2000–2001. 'Fatwa Concerning the United States Supreme Courtroom Frieze', *The Journal of Law and Religion* (Buffalo, NY), 15 (1&2): 1–28.

Alam, Anwar. 1995. 'Muslims in Indian Political Process', *Journal of Objective Studies* (New Delhi) 7 (2), July: 106–33.

Alavi, Hamza. 1988. 'Pakistan and Islam: Ethnicity and Ideology', in Fred Halliday and Hamza Alavi (eds), *State and Ideology in the Middle East and Pakistan,* pp. 64–111. London: Macmillan Education.

al-Hibri, Azizah Yahia. 2000–2001. 'Muslim Women's Rights in the Global Village: Challenges and Opportunities', *The Journal of Law and Religion* (Buffalo, NY) 15 (1 and 2): 37–66.

Ali, Kecia. 2006. *Sexual Ethics and Islam: Feminist Reflections in Qur'an, Hadith, and Jurisprudence.* Oxford: One World.

Ali, Mohd Moazzam. 1991. 'Death of Gandhi-Nehru Model of Secularism and Minority Rights—Need for Resurrection through New Constitutional Provisions', in Tahir Mahmood (ed.), *Minorities and the State at the Indian Law: An Anthology.* New Delhi: Institute of Objective Studies.

Amin, S. H. 1998. 'Classification of Legal Systems in the Muslim Countries', in H. S. Bhatia (ed.), *Studies in Islamic Law, Religion and Society,* pp. 133–44. New Delhi: Deep and Deep Publications.

Anderson, J. N. D. 1959. *Islamic Law in Modern World.* London: OUP.

———. (ed.). 1963. *Changing Laws in Developing Countries.* London: George Allen and Unwin.

Anderson, Michael R. 1993. 'Islamic Law and Colonial Encounter in British India', in David Arnold and Peter Robb (eds), *Institutions and Ideologies: A SOAS South Asia Reader,* pp. 165–85. London: Curzon Press.

An-Na'im, Abdullah A. 2002. *Islamic Family Law in Changing World: A Global Resource Book.* London: Zed Books.

Ansari, Hamid. 2003. 'Muslims in Nepal', *Prachi* (Kathmandu) 53. (In Nepali.)

Ansari, M. A. 1988. *Tribals and Corrective Justice.* Jaipur: Sublime Publications.

Anthias, F. and N. Yuval-Davis. 1992. *Racialised Boundaries: Race, Nation, Gender, Colour and Class and the Anti-Racist Struggle.* London and New York: Routledge.

Anveshi Law Committee. 1997. 'Is Gender Justice Only a Legal Issue? Political Stakes in UCC Debate', *Economic and Political Weekly* (Mumbai) 32: 453–58.

Austin, Granville. 1966. *The Indian Constitution: Cornerstone of a Nation.* Oxford: OUP.

340 The Politics of Personal Law in South Asia

Bainham, Andrew. 1995. 'Family Law in a Pluralistic Society', *Journal of Law and Society* (Oxford) 22 (2), June: 234–47.

Baird, Robert D. 1978. 'Religion and the Legitimation of Nehru's Concept of the Secular State', in Bardwell L. Smith (ed.), *Religion and the Legitimation of Power in South Asia*. Leiden: E. J. Brill.

———. (ed.). 2005a. *Religion and Law in Independent India*. Second enlarged edition. New Delhi: Manohar Publications.

———. 2005b. 'Religion and Law in India', in Robert D. Baird (ed.), *Religion and Law in Independent India*. Second enlarged edition. pp. 7–34. New Delhi: Manohar Publications.

Balchin, Cassandra (ed.). 1994. *A Handbook of Family Law in Pakistan*. Lahore: Women Living Under Muslim Laws.

Bandopadhyay, D. 2005. 'Nyaya Panchayat: The Unfinished Task'. Paper presented at the Rajiv Gandhi Foundation Workshop on 'Role of Women in Strengthening Panchayat Raj Institutions', 19 November.

Banerjee, Paula. 2005. 'Women's Autonomy: Beyond Rights and Representations', in Ranabir Samaddar (ed.), *The Politics of Autonomy: Indian Experiences*, pp. 49–70, New Delhi: Sage Publications.

Bano, Shah. 1985. 'Open Letter to Muslims', translated from Urdu, *Inquilab* (Mumbai), 13 November.

Barkat, Abul (ed.). 2000. *An Enquiry into Causes and Consequences of Deprivation of Hindu Minorities in Bangladesh through the Vested Property Act*. Dhaka: Prip Trust.

Barnett, Randy E. 1998. *The Structure of Liberty: Justice and the Rule of Law*. Oxford: Clarendon Press.

Barpujari, I. 2005. 'A Gendered Perspective of Indigenous Knowledge'. Briefing paper written for Gene Campaign, New Delhi.

Barpuzari, H. K. 1996. *Assam in the Days of the Company (1826–1858)*. Shillong: North Eastern Hill University.

Barooah, Jeuti (compiled). 2001. *Administration of Justice in Meghalaya*. Guwahati: Law Research Institute, Eastern Region.

Basham, A. L. 1954. *The Wonder that was India*. New York: Grove Press Inc.

———. (ed.). 1975. *A Cultural History of India*. New Delhi: OUP.

Basu, Monmayee. 2004. 'Hindu Women and Marriage Law: From Sacrament to Contract', in *Women and Law in India: An Omnibus*. New Delhi: OUP.

Basu, Srimati. 1999. *She Comes to Take Her Rights: Indian Women, Property and Propriety*. New York: State University of New York.

Baxi, Upendra, 1980. *The Indian Supreme Court and Politics*. Lucknow: Eastern Book Company.

———. 1982. *The Crisis of the Indian Legal System*. New Delhi: Vikas Publishing House.

———. 1986. *Towards the Sociology of Indian Law*. Delhi: Satvahan Publications.

Beaglehole, J. H. 1967. 'The Indian Christians—A Study of a Minority', *Modern Asian Studies* (Cambridge) 1 (1): 59–80.

Bibliography 341

Begin, M. 1998. *Towards a Critical Mass: Women in Politics*. New Delhi: CWDS.

Benei, Veronique. 1998. 'Hinduism Today: Inventing a Universal Religion?' *South Asia Research* (New Delhi) 18 (2), Autumn: 117–48.

Benton, Lauren. 1994. 'Beyond Legal Pluralism: Towards a New Approach to Law in the Informal Sector', *Social and Legal Studies* (London) 3: 223–42.

———. 2002. *Law and Colonial Cultures: Legal Regimes in World History*. Cambridge: Cambridge University Press.

Best, Steven and Douglas Kellner. 1997. *The Postmodernist Turn*. New York: Guildford Press.

Beteille, Andre. 1991. *Society and Politics in India: Essays in a Comparative Perspective*. London: The Athlone Press.

Beyond Beijing Committee. 2004. *Nepal: CEDAW Alternative Advocacy to Second and Third Combined Report Submitted by His Majesty's Government*. Kathmandu: Beyond Beijing Committee.

Bhagabati, A. C. 1997. 'Formalization of Tribal Customary Law in North-East India', in P. C. Dutta and D. K. Duarah (eds), *Aspects of Customary Laws of Arunachal Pradesh*, pp. 20–27. Itanagar: Directorate of Research, Government of Arunachal Pradesh.

Bhagwati, Jagdish. 2004. *In Defense of Globalization*. New Delhi: OUP.

Bhandare, Muralidhar C. (ed.). 1999. *The World of Gender Justice*. New Delhi: Har-Anand.

———. 2004. 'Women's Rights and Wrongs', ExpressIndia.com, 27 July, accessed on 17 September 2006.

Bhargava, Rajeev. 1994. 'Giving Secularism its Due', *Economic and Political Weekly* (Mumbai), 9 July: 1784–786.

Bhasin, Kamala, Ritu Menon and Nighat Saead Khan (eds). 1994. *Against All Odds*. New Delhi: South Asian Women's Forum, Kali for Women and ISIS.

Bhatia, H. S. (ed.). 1998. *Studies in Islamic Law, Religion and Society*. New Delhi: Deep and Deep.

Bhattacharjee, A. M. 1983. *Hindu Law and the Constitution*. Calcutta: Eastern Law House.

———. 1994. *Muslim Law and the Constitution*. Calcutta: Eastern Law House.

Bhatty, Zarina. 1976. 'Status of Muslim Women and Social Change', in B. R. Nanda (ed.), *Indian Women: From Purdah to Modernity*. New Delhi: Vikas Publications.

———. 1980. 'Muslim Women in Uttar Pradesh', in Alfred de Souza (ed.), *Women in Contemporary India and South Asia*. New Delhi: Manohar Publications.

Bhaumik, Saba Naqvi. 2001. 'Pent-up and Silent', *Outlook* (New Delhi), 5 November.

———. 2004. 'Half Crescent', *Outlook* (New Delhi), 4 October: 32–40.

342 The Politics of Personal Law in South Asia

Bilgrami, Akeel. 1992. 'What is a Muslim?: Fundamental Commitment and Cultural Identity', *Economic and Political Weekly* (Mumbai) 27 (20 and 21), 16–23 May: 1071–078.

———. 1997. 'Secular Liberalism and Moral Psychology of identity', *Economic and Political Weekly* (Mumbai), 4 October: 2527–540.

Birnbaum, Ervin. 1956. 'Some Theoretical and Practical Aspects of the Islamic State of Pakistan', Memoir No.1, Pakistan Historical Society, Karachi.

Black's Law Dictionary. 2004. (ed.) Bryan A. Garner. 8th edn. Saint Paul, MN: West Group.

Breckenridge, Carol A. and Peter van der Veer (eds), 1994. *Orientalism and the Postcolonial Predicament.* New Delhi: OUP.

Carole, Hillenbrand. 2004. *Islam—An Historical Introduction.* New Delhi: New Age.

Carrol, Lucy. 1983. 'The Muslim Family in India: Law, Custom and Empirical Research', *Contributions to Indian Sociology* (New Delhi) 17 (2): 205–22.

———. 1986. 'Muslim Women in India and England: Divorce and Alimony', *The Islamic Quarterly* (London) 33 (1), first quarter: 21–30.

Center for Reproductive Rights. 2005. *Women of the World: South Asia: Laws and Policies Affecting the Reproductive Rights.* New York: The Center for Reproductive Rights.

Cesari, Jocelyne and José Casanova (eds.). 2017. *Islam, Gender, and Democracy in Comparative Perspective.* Oxford: OUP.

Chakma, Suhas. 2006. 'Democracy Deficit in the Maldives', *Himal Southasian* (Kathmandu) 18 (4), January–February: 75–76.

Chakravartty, Gargi. 2005. 'Common Gender—Just Civil Laws: Need of the Hour', *Women's Watch* (New Delhi) 2 (4), July–September.

Chander, Harish. 1983. *Law of Adoption in India: A Study in Sociology of Law.* Project report. New Delhi: ICSSR.

Chandhoke, Neera. 1999. *Beyond Secularism: The Rights of Religious Minorities.* New Delhi: OUP.

Chandra, Satish (ed.). 2005. *Religion, State, and Society in Medieval India: Collected Works of S. Nurul Hasan.* New Delhi: OUP.

Chandra, Sudhir. 2004. 'Enslaved Daughters: Colonialism, Law and Women's Rights', in *Women and Law in India: An Omnibus.* New Delhi: OUP.

Chatterji, Jyotsna. 1996. 'Towards an Indian Family Law', *Seminar* (New Delhi) 441, May: 34–36.

Chatterjee, Manini. 1992. 'Seeds of Fascism', *Seminar* (New Delhi) 399, November: 17–21.

Chatterjee, Nandini. 2014. 'Reflections on Religious Difference and Permissive Inclusion in Mughal Law', *Journal of Law and Religion* (Atlanta, GA), 29(3): 396–415.

Chatterjee, Partha. 1993. *The Nation and its Fragments: Colonial and Postcolonial Histories.* Princeton, NJ: Princeton University Press.

———. 1995. 'Religious Minorities and the Secular State: Reflections on an Indian Impasse', *Public Culture* (Chicago) 8.

Bibliography 343

Chatterjee, P. C. 1996. 'Civil Code: Uniform or Common', *Seminar* (New Delhi) 441, May: 53–54.

Chaube, Shibani Kinkar. 2000. *Constituent Assembly of India: Springboard of a Revolution:* New Delhi: Manohar Publications.

Chhetri, Ram B. and Shambhu P. Kattel. 2004. *Dispute Resolution in Nepal: A Socio-Cultural Perspective.* Kathmandu: Centre for Victims of Torture.

Chiba, Masaji (ed.). 1986. *Asian Indigenous Law: In Interaction with Received Law.* London and New York: KPI.

Chipp-Kraushaar, S. 1981. 'The All Pakistan Women's Association and the 1961 Muslim Family Laws Ordinance', in G. Minault (ed.), *The Extended Family: Women and Political Participation in India and Pakistan.* Delhi: Chanakya.

———. 1999. *Hill Politics in Northeast India.* Patna: Orient Longman.

Choudhury, Cyra Akila. 2008. '"(Mis)Appropriated Liberty: Identity, Gender Justice and Muslim Personal Law Reform in India', *Columbia Journal of Gender & Law* 17 (1): 45–110.

Choudhury, G. W. (ed.). 1967. *Documents and Speeches on the Constitution of Pakistan.* Dacca: Green Book House.

Chowdhury, J. N. 1997. 'The Nature of Customary Law and its Relation to Statutory Law of the State', in P. C. Dutta and D.K. Duarah, *Aspects of Customary Laws of Arunachal Pradesh.* Itanagar: Directorate of Research, Government of Arunachal Pradesh: 3–19.

Cohn, Bernard S. 1996. *Colonialism and its Forms of Knowledge: The British in India:.* New Delhi: OUP.

Conrad, Dieter. 1995. 'The Personal Law Question and Hindu Nationalism', in Vasudha Dalmia and Heinrich von Stietencron (eds), *Representing Hinduism: The Construction of a Religious Tradition and National Identity,* pp. 306–37. New Delhi: Sage Publications.

———. 1997. 'Conflicting Legitimacies in Pakistan: The Changing Role of the Objectives Resolution (1949) in the Constitution', in Subrata K. Mitra and Dietmar Rothermund (eds), *Legitimacy and Conflict in South Asia.* New Delhi: Manohar Publications.

Constituent Assembly Debates, 1946–1950 (12 vols) Delhi, 1946–50.

Coomaraswamy, Radhika. 2002. 'Identity Within: Cultural Relativism, Minority Rights and the Empowerment of Women', *The George Washington International Law Review* (Washington, DC) 34 (3): 483–513.

Cooray, L. J. M. 1992. *An Introduction to the Legal System of Sri Lanka.* Colombo: Lake House Investments Ltd.

Coulson, Noel J. 1963. 'Islamic Family Law: Progress in Pakistan', in J. N. D. Anderson (ed.), *Changing Laws in Developing Countries,* pp. 240–57. London: George Allen and Unwin.

———. 1969. *Conflicts and Tensions in Islamic Jurisprudence.* Chicago: Chicago University Press.

Crins, Reiki. 2004. 'Religion and Gender Values in a Changing World', in Karma Ura and Sonam Kinga (eds), *The Spider and the Piglet,* pp. 581–95. Thimpu: Centre for Bhutan Studies.

344 The Politics of Personal Law in South Asia

Das, S. K. 1989. *Spotlight on Assam*. Chanderpur, Maharashtra: Premier Book Service.

Dasgupta, Swapan. 2003. 'Ghetto Blaster', *Hindustan Times* (New Delhi), 4 August.

———. 2006. 'Dogmatic Certitude', *The Telegraph* (Guwahati), 10 February.

Dastidar, Mollica. 1995. *Religious Minorities in Nepal: An Analysis of the State of Buddhists and Muslims in the Himalayan Kingdom*. New Delhi: Nirala.

———. 2000. 'Muslims of Nepal's Terai', *Economic and Political Weekly* (Mumbai) 35 (10), 4 March: 766–68.

Davis, Nancy J. and Robert V. Robinson. 2006. 'The Egalitarian Face of Islamic Orthodoxy: Support for Islamic Law and Economic Justice in Seven Muslim-Majority Nations', *American Sociological Review* (Washington, DC) 71 (2), April: 167–90.

De, Amalendu. 1995. 'The Social Thoughts and Consciousness of the Bengali Muslims in the Colonial Period', *Social Scientist* (New Delhi) 23 (4–6), April–June.

De, Rohit. 2009. 'Mumtaz Bibi's Broken Heart: The Many Lives of the Dissolution of Muslim Marriage Act', *The Indian Economic and Social History Review* (New Delhi), 46 (1): 105–30.

———. 2013. 'Personal Laws: A Reality Check', *Frontline* (Chennai), 6 September: 4–10.

———. 2017. 'A nuanced Judgment', *Frontline* (Chennai), 15 September.

Dena, Lal. 1988. *Christian Missions and Colonialism: A Study of Missionary Movement in Northeast India with Particular Reference to Manipur and Lushai Hills 1894–1947*. Shillong: Vendrame Institute.

Deolekar, Madhu. 1995. *India Needs a Common Civil Code*. Mumbai: Vivek Vyaspeeth.

Derret, J. D. M. 1963. *Introduction of Modern Hindu Law*. Oxford: OUP.

———. 1968. *Religion, Law and the State in India*. London: Faber and Faber.

———. 1977. 'Hindu Law in Goa: A Contact between Natural, Roman and Hindu Laws', in J. D. M. Derret, *Essays in Classical and Modern Hindu Law, 2*. Leiden: E. J. Brill.

Desai, Mihir. 2017. 'A "Safe" Judgment: Religious Rather Than Constitutional Test', *Economic and Political Weekly* (Mumbai), 52 (36), 9 September: 12–16.

Desai, Nishtha. 1996. 'Uniform Civil Code in Goa Protects Women's Rights', *Times of India* (New Delhi), 27 June.

———. 1997. 'Goa Code has Meshed Well with Muslim Culture', *Times of India* (New Delhi), 29 April.

Deshta, Kiran. 2002. *Uniform Civil Code in Retrospect and Prospect*. New Delhi: Deep and Deep Publications.

Desouza, Peter Ronald. 2015. 'Politics of the Uniform Civil Code in India', *Economic and Political Weekly* (Mumbai), 50 (48), 28 November: 50–57.

Bibliography 345

Devadasan, E.O. (ed.). 1974. *Christian Law in India: Law Applicable to Christians in India*. Chennai: DSI Publications.

Dhagamwar, Vasudha. 1989a. *Towards the Uniform Civil Code*. Bombay: N. M. Tripathi.

———. 1989b. *Women and Divorce: An Attempt to Test Awareness of law amongst Women and to Determine the Role Played by Our Education*. Project report. New Delhi: ICSSR.

———. 1992. *Law, Power and Justice*. New Delhi: Sage Publications.

———. 1994. *Essays on Christianity in North-East India*. New Delhi: Indus.

———. 1996a. *Criminal Justice or Chaos*. New Delhi: Har Anand Publications.

———. 1996b. 'A Question of Rights: The Problem', *Seminar* (New Delhi) 441, May: 12–14.

———. 2003. 'Invasion of Criminal Law by Religion, Custom and Family Law', *Economic and Political Weekly* (Mumbai) 38 (15), 12 April: 1483–92.

———. 2005. 'Women, Children and the Constitution: Hostages to Religion, Outcaste by Law', in Robert D. Baird (ed.), *Religion and Law in Independent India*. Second enlarged edition, pp. 283–324. New Delhi: Manohar Publications.

———. 2006. *Role and Image of Law in India: The Tribal Experience*. New Delhi: Sage Publications.

Dhattiwala, Raheel and Raphael Susewind. 2014. 'Spatial Variation in the "Muslim Vote" in Gujarat and Uttar Pradesh, 2014,' *Economic and Political Weekly* (Mumbai), 49 (39), 27 September 2014, pp. 99–110.

Dhavan, Rajeev. 1978. *Government by Default: Essays on Law and Democracy*. Project report. New Delhi: ICSSR.

———. 2003. 'Codifying Personal Laws', *The Hindu* (New Delhi), 1 August.

Diwan, Paras. 1972. 'Uniform Civil Code: A Projection of Equality', in Mohammed Imam (ed.), *Minorities and the Law*. Bombay: N. M. Tripathi.

———. 1985. 'Uniform Civil Code and the Supreme Court', *Annual Survey of Indian Law* (New Delhi: Indian Law Institute) 21: 132–35.

D'Mello, Pamela. 1997. 'Common Personal Law in Goa—A Critique', *Muslim India* (New Delhi) 179, November: 513, 522.

D'Souza, Anthony and Carmo D'Souza (eds.). 2009. *Civil Law Studies: An Indian Perspective*. New Castle: Cambridge Scholars Publishing.

Doley, D. 1998. 'Tribal Movements in the North-Eastern Region', in K. S. Singh (ed.), *Antiquity to Modernity in Tribal India, Vol. IV*. New Delhi: Inter-India.

Donnan, Hastings (ed.). 2002. *Interpreting Islam*. New Delhi: Vistaar.

Downs, Frederick S. 1981. 'Administrators, Missionaries and a World Turned Upside Down: Christianity as a Tribal Response to Change in Northeast India', *Indian Church History Review* (Bangalore) 15 (2): 99–113.

Dube, Leela. 1969. *Matriliny and Islam: Religion and Society in the Laccadives*. Delhi: National Publishing House.

Dubgyur, Lungten. 2004. 'Review of Judicial Reforms in Bhutan', in Karma Ura and Sonam Kinga (eds), *The Spider and the Piglet*, pp. 379–87. Thimpu: Centre for Bhutan Studies.

346　*The Politics of Personal Law in South Asia*

Dubois, Abbe J. A. 1990. *Characters, Manners and Customs of the People of India and of their Institutions—Religious and Civil.* Delhi: Daya Publishing House.

Dutta, P. C. and D. K. Duarah. 1997. *Aspects of Customary Laws of Arunachal Pradesh.* Itanagar: Directorate of Research, Government of Arunachal Pradesh.

Dutta, Sujit Kumar. 2002. *Functioning of Autonomous District Councils in Meghalaya.* New Delhi: Akansha.

Dwivedi, Pankaj. 2016. *Uniform Civil Code.* New Delhi: Vayu Education of India.

Eaton, Richard M. 1984. 'Conversion to Christianity among the Nagas, 1876–1971', *Indian Economic and Social History Review* (New Delhi) 21 (1): 1–44.

———. 2000. *Essays on Islam and Indian History.* New Delhi: OUP.

———. 2002. 'Indo-Muslim Tradition, 1200–1750: Towards a Framework of Study', *South Asia Research* (New Delhi) 22 (1), Spring.

———. 2003. 'Who are the Bengal Muslims? Conversion and Islamization in Bengal', in Rowena Robinson and Sathianathan Clarke (eds), *Religious Conversion in India: Modes, Motivations, and Meanings.* New Delhi: OUP.

Eikelman, Dale F. and James Piscatori. 1997. *Muslim Politics.* New Delhi: OUP.

Ekka, Anurag Augustine. 2014. 'Marriage, Property and Inheritance: Legal Pluralism and the Oraons in Jharkhand', M.Phil. Dissertation, Centre for the Study of Law and Governance, Jawaharlal Nehru University, New Delhi.

Ellickson, Robert. 1990. *Order without Law: How Neighbors Settle Disputes.* Cambridge: Cambridge University Press.

Elwin, Verrier. 1943. *The Aboriginals.* Bombay: OUP.

———. 1999. *A Philosophy for NEFA (Arunachal Pradesh).* Itanagar: Directorate of Research, Government of Arunachal Pradesh. (First published in 1957.)

Engineer, Asghar Ali. 1987. *The Shah Bano Controversy.* Bombay Orient Longman.

———. 1993. 'Common Civil Code: A Poser', *The Hindu* (New Delhi), 11 March.

———. 1994. 'Muslim Family Law', in Lotika Sarkar and B. Sivaramayya (eds), *Women and Law: Contemporary Problems,* pp. 50–62. New Delhi: Vikas Publications.

Engineer, Asghar Ali. 1997. 'Indian Islam and Reform Movements in Post-Independence India', *Dossier 20,* December 1997: 217–21.

———. 1999a. 'Muslim Women and Maintenance', *Economic and Political Weekly* (Mumbai) 34, 1999: 1488–489.

———. 1999b. 'Muslim Views of Hindus since 1950', in Jacques Waardenburg (ed.), *Muslim Perceptions of Other Religions: A Historical Survey,* pp. 263–69. New York: OUP.

Bibliography   347

———. 2002. 'Bombay High Court Judgement—A Landmark Judgement on Talaq', *Secular Perspective* (Mumbai), 16–31 July.

———. 2003. 'Who is for a Common Civil Code?', *Hindustan Times* (New Delhi), 3 August.

———. 2004. 'Triple Divorce—Need for Change', *Secular Perspective* (Mumbai), 16–30 June.

———. 2005. *Religion, State and Civil Society*. Mumbai: Vikas Adhyayan Kendra.

Epstein, Richard A. 1998. *Principles for a Free Society: Reconciling Individual Liberty with the Common Good*. Reading, Massachusetts: Perseus Books.

Esposito, J. L. 1982. *Women in Muslim Family Law*. Syracuse: Syracuse University Press.

Esposito, John L. and Natana J. DeLong-Bas. 2001. *Women in Muslim Family Law* (2nd ed.). New York: Syracuse University Press.

Ete, Jarjum. 1996. 'Empowering Women', *Seminar* (New Delhi) 441, May: 42–45.

Ewing, K. I. (ed.). 1988. *Shariat and Ambiguity in South Asian Islam*. Berkeley: University of California Press.

Faleiro, Eduardo. 2017. 'On Uniform Civil Code', *Mainstream* (New Delhi), 31 March–6 April: 17–18.

Farhad, Shah Ali. (Undated). 'Reform of Laws on Hindu Marriage and Related Areas in Banglsdesh: A "Legal" Take on a Very "Social" Issue', http://think legalbangladesh.com/home/uploads/article/1833115827_1484651549.pdf, accessed on 2 August 2017.

Farooqee, Neyaz. 2016. 'The Seeker: Asauddin Owaisi's Ambition to Unite India's Fractured Muslim Electorate', *Caravan* (New Delhi), September: 32–51.

Fayzee, A. A. A. 1987. *Outlines of Mohammedan Law*. New Delhi: OUP.

Fazalbhoy, Nasreen. 1997. 'Sociology of Muslims in India', *Economic and Political Weekly* (Mumbai), 28 June: 1547–551.

Fierro, Maribel. 2000–2001. An untitled review article based on four books on Islam, in *The Journal of Law and Religion* (Buffalo, NY) 15 (1 and 2): 579–87.

Fuller, Graham E. 2002. 'The Future of Political Islam', *Foreign Affairs* (New York) 81 (2), March–April.

Gaborieau, Marc. 2001. 'Muslims in the Hindu Kingdom of Nepal', in T. N. Madan (ed.), *Muslim Communities of South Asia: Culture, Society and Power*. Third enlarged edition. New Delhi: Manohar Publications. (This is a reprint of an earlier article written in 1972.)

Galanter, Marc. 1986. 'Adjudication, Litigation, and Related Phenomena', in Leon Lipson and Stanton Wheeler (eds), *Law and Social Sciences*, pp. 151–257. New York: Russel Sage Foundation.

Galanter, Marc. 1989a. 'The Aborted Restoration of "Indigenous" Law in India', in Rajiv Dhawan (ed.), *Law and Society in Modern India*. New Delhi: OUP.

348 *The Politics of Personal Law in South Asia*

————. 1989b. 'The Displacement of Traditional Law in Modern India', in Rajiv Dhawan (ed.), *Law and Society in Modern India*. New Delhi: OUP.

————. 1997. *Law and Society in Modern India*. New Delhi: OUP.

Gandhi, Nandita and Nandita Shah. 1991. *The Issues at Stake: Theory and Practice in the Contemporary Women's Movement in India*. New Delhi: Kali for Women.

Gangoli, G. and G. Solanki. 1997. 'Towards Gender Just Laws', *Economic and Political Weekly* (Mumbai) 32: 854–55.

Gangoli, Geetanjali. 2003. 'Muslim Divorce and the Discourse around Muslim Personal Law', in Imtiaz Ahmad (ed.), *Divorce and Remarriage among Muslims in India,* pp. 367–95. New Delhi: Manohar Publications.

Ganjoo, Lila Kanth. 1959. *Customary Law of Kashmir*. Srinagar: Fine Art Press.

Ghadially, Rehana. 1996. 'Women and Personal Law in an Ismaili (Daudi Bohra) Sect of Indian Muslims', *Islamic Culture* (Hyderabad) 70 (1), January: 27–52.

Ghosh, Partha S. 1989. *Cooperation and Conflict in South Asia*. New Delhi: Manohar Publications.

————. 1997. 'Hindu Nationalism, the Politics of Nation-Building and Implications for the Legitimacy of the State', in Subrata K. Mitra and Dietmar Rothermund (eds), *Legitimacy and Conflict in South Asia,* pp. 50–68. New Delhi: Manohar Publications.

————. 1999. *BJP and the Evolution of Hindu Nationalism: From Periphery to Centre*. Reprint 2000. New Delhi: Manohar Publications.

————. 2003. *Ethnicity versus Nationalism: The Devolution Discourse in Sri Lanka*. New Delhi: Sage Publications.

————. 2004. *Unwanted and Uprooted: A Political Study of Refugees, Migrants, Stateless and Displaced in South Asia*. New Delhi: Samskriti.

————. 2005. 'Conservative Ascendancy in Bangladesh', *South Asian Survey* (New Delhi) 12 (2), July–December: 247–65.

————. 2009. 'Politics of Personal Law in India: The Hindu-Muslim Dichotomy', *South Asia Research* (New Delhi), 29 (1): 1–17.

————. 2017. *BJP and the Evolution of Hindu Nationalism: Savarkar to Vajpayee to Modi*. New Delhi: Manohar.

————. 'Why nobody is sincere about UCC', *Times of India* (New Delhi), 13 September 2017.

Ghosh, Srabanee. 2011. 'Tribal Laws and Customs in India', www.legal servicesindia.com/article/print.php?art_id=847, accessed on 4 August 2017.

Glenn, H. Patrick. 2000. *Legal Traditions of the World*. Oxford: OUP.

Goldberg, Jan. 2000–2001. 'Review of Baudouin Dupret, Maurtis Berger and Laila al-Zwaini (eds), *Legal Pluralism in the Arab World*' in *The Journal of Law and Religion,* (Buffalo, NY) 15 (1 and 2): 447–49.

Goonesekere, Savitri W. E. 1984. 'Introduction to the Laws of Sri Lanka, Book I'. [Written for the Course Team of the Bachelor of Laws Degree. Nugegoda: The Open University of Sri Lanka (mimeo).]

Bibliography 349

———. 1987. *The Sri Lanka Law on Parent and Child.* Colombo: Gunasena.

——— and N. Anoma Abeyratne. 1985. 'Introduction to the Laws of Sri Lanka, Book II'. [Written for the Course Team of the Bachelor of Laws Degree. Nugegoda: The Open University of Sri Lanka (mimeo).]

Gopal, S. 1965. *British Policy in India 1858–1905.* Cambridge: Cambridge University Press.

Goswami, Atul (ed.). 2002. *Traditional Self-Governing Institutions among the Hill Tribes of North-East India.* New Delhi: Akansha.

Goswami, M. C. (ed.). 1981. *The Customary Laws and Practices of the Ao of Nagaland.* Guwahati: The Law Research Institute, Eastern Region (mimeo).

Government of India, 1973a. *Position of Divorce in India.* New Delhi: Office of the Registrar General, Ministry of Home Affairs.

———. 1973b. *The Constitution of India (As modified up to the 1ˢᵗ January 1973: Commemorative Edition).* New Delhi: Ministry of Law and Justice.

———. 1974. *Towards Equality: Report of the National Committee on the Status of Women in India,* Delhi: National Committee on the Status of Women.

———. 1980. *Recommendations of the Minority Commission on the Demand from a Section of the Parsees for Exclusion of the Parsee Community from the Purview of the Adoption Bill, 1980.* New Delhi: Minorities Commission.

———. Lok Sabha. 1999. *Constituent Assembly Debates: Official Record.* Ninth edition, third reprint. New Delhi: Lok Sabha Secretariat.

Government of Pakistan. 1948. *Quaid-e-Azam Speaks.* Karachi: Pakistan Publicity.

———. 1997. *Report of the Commission of Enquiry for Women.* Islamabad.

———. 2003. *On the Path of Women's Empowerment: A Synthesis of Reports of Commissions/Committee on the Status of Women.* Islamabad: Ministry of Women Development, Social Welfare and Special Education.

Griffiths, J. 1986. 'What is Legal Pluralism', *Journal of Legal Pluralism* (Birmingham) 24 (1): 1–55.

Guha, Ramchandra. 1996. 'Savaging the Civlilised: Verrier Elwin and the Tribal Question in Late Colonial India', *Economic and Political Weekly* (Mumbai) 31 (35, 36, 37), Special Number September: 2375–89.

Guha, Ranajit. 1997. *Dominance without Hegemony: History and Power in Colonial India.* Cambridge, MA: Harvard University Press.

Guhathakurta, Meghna, 1994. 'The Aid Discourse and the Politics of Gender: A Perspective from Bangladesh', *The Journal of Social Studies* (Dhaka) 65, July.

———. 1997. 'Bangladesh: A Land of Shifting Populations', in Tapan K. Bose and Rita Manchanda (eds), *States, Citizens and Outsiders: The Uprooted Peoples of South Asia.* Kathmandu: South Asian Forum for Human Rights.

———. 2002. 'Communal Politics in South Asia and the Hindus of Bangladesh', in Monirul Hussain and Lipi Ghosh (eds), *Religious Minorities in South*

350   *The Politics of Personal Law in South Asia*

Asia: Selected Essays on Post-Colonial Situations, Vol. I, Bangladesh, Pakistan, Nepal, Sri Lanka. New Delhi: Manak Publications.

Gulati, Saroj. 1994. 'Sati Custom—A Historical Perspective', in Lotika Sarkar and B. Sivaramayya (eds), *Women and Law: Contemporary Problems.* New Dehi: Vikas Publications.

Gupta, Kanchan. 1996. 'Towards an Equal Social Order', *Seminar* (New Delhi) 441, May: 19–22.

Gurung, Harka. 1998. *Nepal: Social Demography and Expressions.* Kathmandu: New Era.

———. 2005. 'Social Exclusion and Maoist Insurgency', in Sarah Webster and Om Gurung (eds), *ILO Convention 169 and Peace Building in Nepal.* Kathmandu: Nepal Federation of Indigenous Nationalities, 141–68.

Haksar, Nandita. 1996. 'The Political Issues', *Seminar* (New Delhi) 441, May: 52–61.

Hameed, Syeda S. 2016. 'This Reform Must Begin Within', *The Hindu* (New Delhi), 27 April.

Harris, George L. (ed.). 1973. *Area Handbook for Nepal, Bhutan and Sikkim.* Washington D. C.: The American University.

Hartung, Jan-Peter. 2003. 'The Land, the Mosque, the Temple: More than 145 Years of Dispute over Ayodhya', in Richard Bonney (ed.), *Ayodhya 1992–2003: The Assertion of Cultural and Religious Hegemony,* pp. 1–34. Leicestor: Centre for the History of Religious and Political Pluralism/ Institute for the Study of Indo-Pakistan Relations; New Delhi: Media Publishing House.

Hartung, Jan–Peter. 2006. 'Towards a Reform of the Indian Madrasa? An Introduction', in Jan-Peter Hartung and Helmut Reifeld (eds), *Islamic Education, Diversity, and National Identity: Dini Madaris in India Post 9/11,* pp. 11–36. New Delhi: Sage Publications.

——— and Helmut Reifeld (eds). 2006. *Islamic Education, Diversity, and National Identity: Dini Madaris in India Post 9/11.* New Delhi: Sage Publications.

Hasan, Farhat. 2004. *State and Locality in Mughal India: Power Relations in Western India, 1572–1730.* Cambridge: Cambridge University Press.

Hasan, Ibn. 1936. *The Central Structure of the Mughal Empire and its Practical Working up to the Year 1657.* London: OUP.

Hasan, Mushirul. 1997. *Legacy of a Divided Nation.* New Delhi: OUP.

———. 2002. *Islam in the Subcontinent: Muslims in a Plural Society.* New Delhi: Manohar Publications.

Hasan, Zoya. 1994. 'Minority Identity, State Policy and the Political Process', in Zoya Hasan (ed.), *Forging Identities: Gender, Communities and the State.* New Delhi: Kali for Women.

———. (undated). 'Religion, Feminist Politics and Muslim Women's Rights in India', http://feministlawarchives.pldindia.org/wp-content/uploads/Zoya-Hasan.pdf.

Bibliography 351

———. 2010. 'Gender, Religion and Democratic Politics in India', *Third World Quarterly* 31 (6): 939–54.

Hayley, Frederic Austin. 1993. *A Treatise on the Laws and Customs of the Sinhalese including the Portions Still Surviving Under the Name of Kandyan Law*. New Delhi: Navrang.

Hoefer, Andras. 2004. *The Caste Hierarchy and the State in Nepal: A Study of the Muluki Ain of 1854*. Kathmandu: Himal Books.

Hooker, M. B. 1975. *Legal Pluralism: An Introduction to Colonial and Neo-Colonial Laws*. Oxford: Clarendon Press.

HRCP (Human Rights Commission of Pakistan). 2006. *State of Human Rights in 2005*. Lahore: Human Rights Commission of Pakistan.

Huntington, Samuel P. 1996. *The Clash of Civilizations and the Remaking of World Order*. New Delhi: Viking.

———. 2004. *Who Are We: The Challenges to America's National Identity*. New York: Simon and Schuster.

Husain, Sheikh Abrar. 1971. *Marriage Customs among Muslims in India*. New Delhi: Sterling Publishers.

Hussain, Monirul and Lipi Ghosh (eds). 2002. *Religious Minorities in South Asia: Selected Essays on Post-Colonial Situations*. Two volumes. New Delhi: Manak Publications.

Hust, Evelin. 2004. *Women's Political Representation and Empowerment in India: A Million Indiras Now?* New Delhi: Manohar Publications.

Hutt, Michael. 2003. *Unbecoming Citizens: Culture, Nationhood and the Flight of Refugees from Bhutan*. New Delhi: OUP.

Imam, Mohammed (ed.). 1972. *Minorities and the Law*. Bombay: N.M. Tripathi.

Imam, Zafar (ed.), 1975. *Muslims in India*. New Delhi: Orient Longman.

Imchen, C. L. 2003. 'The Nagas and the Legacy of Civlilizing Mission of the Western World', in Joseph Anikuzhikattil, George Palackapillil and Joseph Puthenpurakal (eds), *Understanding Tribal Cultures for Effective Education,* pp. 48–69. New Delhi: Commission for Education and Culture, and Shillong: DBCIC Publications.

Inden, R. 1990. *Imagining India*. Oxford: Basil Blackwell.

Inglehart, Ronald and Marita Carballo. 1997. 'Does Latin America Exist? (And Is There a Confucian Culture?): A G lobal Analysis of Cross-Cultural Differences', *PS: Political Science and Politics* (Washington DC), March.

Irani, Phiroze. 1968. 'The Personal Law of the Parsis of India', in J. N. D. Anderson (ed.), *Family Law in Asia and Africa*. London: George Allen and Unwin.

Islam, Safiqul. 2005. 'Fourteenth Amendment of Bangladesh Constitution: A Review', *Chittagong University Journal of Social Sciences* (Chittagong) 23 (1), December.

Iyer, V. R. Krishna. 1987. *The Muslim Women (Protection of Rights on Divorce) Act*. Lucknow: Eastern Book.

352 *The Politics of Personal Law in South Asia*

Jaffe, James. 2017. 'After Nanavati: The Last Jury Trial in India?' *Economic and Political Weekly* (Mumbai), 52 (32), 12 August: 18–20.

Jaffrelot, Christophe. 1993. 'Hindu Nationalism: Strategic Syncretism in Ideology Building', *Economic and Political Weekly* (Bombay), 20–27 March: 517–24.

———. 1996. *The Hindu Nationalist Movement in Indian Politics*. London: Hurst.

———. 2004. 'Composite Culture is Not Multi-Culturalism: A Study of the Indian Constituent Assembly Debates', in Ashutosh Varshney (ed.), *India and the Politics of Developing Countries: Essays in Memory of Myron Weiner*. New Delhi: Sage Publications.

———. 2005. *Dr. Ambedkar and Untouchability: Fighting the Indian Caste System*. New York: Columbia University Press.

Jahan, Rounaq. 1980. *Bangladesh Politics: Problems and Issues*. Dacca: University Press.

Jain, M. P. 1990. *Outlines of Indian Legal History*. Bombay: N. M. Tripathi.

Jalal, Ayesha. 2001. *Self and Sovereignty: Individual and Community in South Asian Islam Since 1850*. New Delhi: OUP.

Jaldeen, M. S. 2004. *The Muslim Law of Marriage, Divorce and Maintenance in Sri Lanka*. Colombo: Haji Omar Foundation for Peace, Education and Research.

Jayal, Niraja Gopal. 2001. *Democracy and the State: Welfare, Secularism and Development in Contemporary India*. New Delhi: OUP.

Jeffrey, Patricia. 2001. 'A Uniform Customary Code? Marital Breakdown and Women's Economic Entitlements in Rural Bijnor', *Contributions of Indian Sociology* (New Delhi) 35 (1), January–April: 1–32.

Jeffery, P. and A. Basu (eds). 1999. *Resisting the Sacred and the Secular: Women's Activism and Politicized Religion in South Asia*. New Delhi: Kali for Women.

Jeffery, R. and P. Jeffery. 1997. *Population, Gender and Politics: Demographic Change in Rural North India*. Cambridge: Cambridge University Press.

Jennings, Ivor and H. W. Tambiah. 1952. *The Dominion of Ceylon: The Development of its Laws and Constitution*. Westport, CT: Greenwood Press.

Jethmalani, Ram. 2003. 'Haste will be Disastrous: Uniform Civil Code and the Supreme Court', *Asian Age* (New Delhi), 31 July.

Jha, M. 1998. *An Introduction to Anthropological Thought*. New Delhi: Vikas Publications.

Jha, Shefali. 2002. 'Secularism in the Constituent Assembly Debates', *Economic and Political Weekly* (Mumbai) 37 (30), 27 July: 3175–180.

Jindal, Manjula. 1996. 'The Relevance of Secularism', *Seminar* (New Delhi) 441, May: 46–52.

Jodhka, Surinder S. (ed.), 2001. *Communities and Identities: Contemporary Discourses on Culture and Politics in India*. New Delhi: Sage Publications.

Bibliography   353

Joshi, A. P., M. D. Srinivas and J. K. Bajaj. 2003. *Religious Demography of India*. Chennai: Centre for Policy Studies.

Jyrwa, E. 1996. 'Formation of the District Council in the Hill Areas of Assam', *Journal of North East Council of Social Science Research* (Shillong) 20 (1), April: 22–27.

Kairys, David. 1992. 'Legal Reasoning', in David Kairys (ed.), *The Poltics of Law: A Progressive Critique*. New York: Pantheon Books, 11–17.

Kamali, Muhammad Hashim. 1989. 'Source, Nature and Objectives of Shariah', *The Islamic Quarterly* (London) 33 (3), third quarter: 215–35.

Kannabiran, K. G. 1996. 'Whose Code is it Anyway?', *Seminar* (New Delhi) 441, May: 15–18.

Kannan, K. 2016. 'Frames of Reference', *The Hindu*, 21 October, www.the hindu.com/opinion/lead/Frames-of-reference/article16077807.ece.

Kapur, R. and B. Crossman. 1996. *Subversive Sites: Feminist Engagements with Law in India*. New Delhi: Sage Publications.

Kapur, Ratna. 1996. *Feminist Domains in Legal Terrains: Interdisciplinary Essays on Women and Law in India*. New Delhi:

Kali for Women. Karandikar, M. A. 1987. *Islam in India's Transition to Modernity*. New Delhi: Orient Longman.

Karki, Arjun and Mukunda Kattel (eds). 2005. *Nepal: The Maoist Insurgency and Beyond*. Hong Kong: ARENA [Special Issue of *Asian Exchange,* 19 (1) and 20 (1), 2005].

Karnanaikil, Jose. 1983. *Christians of Scheduled Caste Origin*. New Delhi: Indian Social Institute.

———. 1990. *Scheduled Caste Converts and Social Disabilities*. New Delhi: Indian Social Institute.

Kaur, Ravinder (ed.). 2005. *Religion, Violence and Political Mobilisation in South Asia*. New Delhi: Sage Publications.

Khan, Arif Mohammad. 2017. 'No country for Triple talaq', *Indian Express*, 6 June. http://indianexpress.com/article/opinion/columns/no-country-for-triple-talaq-4690585/, accessed on 27 July 2017.

Khan, Muniza Rafiq. 1993. *Socio-Legal Status of Muslim Women*. New Delhi: Radiant Publishers.

Khan, Wahiduddin. 1996. *Uniform Civil Code: A Critical Study*. New Delhi: Islamic Centre.

Khan, Zafarul-Islam. 2016. 'Muslim Personal Law and Uniform Civil Code, *The Milli Gazette Online*, http://www.milligazette.com/news/15084-india-muslim-personal-law-and-uniform-civil-code, accessed on 2 August 2017.

Khory, Kavita R. 2005. 'The Shah Bano Case: Some Political Implications', in Robert D. Baird (ed.), *Religion and Law in Independent India*. Second enlarged edition, pp. 149–66. New Delhi, Manohar Publications.

Kishwar, Madhu. 1986. 'Pro Women or Anti Muslim?', *Manushi* (New Delhi): 6, 4–13.

———. 1994. 'Codified Hindu Law: Myth and Reality', *Economic and Political Weekly* (Mumbai), 13 August: 2145–161.

354   *The Politics of Personal Law in South Asia*

———. 1996. 'Women and Politics: Beyond Quotas', *Economic and Political Weekly* (Mumbai), 26 October: 2867–874.

———. 1999. 'Stimulating Reform, Not Forcing It: Uniform versus Optional Civil Code', *Manushi* (New Delhi) 89, July–August: 5–14.

———. 2017. 'Fetishizing Gender Equality to Destroy Diversity & Freedom of Faith', *The Hindu*, 20 October. http://www.thehindu.com/opinion/op-ed/restrictions-on-women-at-sabarimala-it-is-complicated/article19887180.ece.

Kitch, Edmund W. 1986. 'Law and the Economic Order', in Leon Lipson and Stanton Wheeler (eds), *Law and the Social Sciences,* pp. 109–49. New York: Russle Sage Foundation.

Kohli, Atul. 1997. 'Can Democracies Accommodate Ethnic Nationalism? Rise and Decline of Self-Determination Movements in India', *The Journal of Asian Studies* (Chicago) 56 (2), May: 325–44.

Kozlowski, Gregory C. 2005. 'Muslim Personal Law and Political Identity in Independent India', in Robert D. Baird (ed.), *Religion and Law in Independent India*. Second enlarged edition, pp. 103–20. New Delhi: Manohar Publications.

Krishna, S. 2005. 'Gendered Price of Rice in North-Eastern India', *Economic and Political Weekly* (Mumbai), 18 June.

Kumar, B. B. 1996. *Reorganization of North-East India*. New Delhi: Osmos.

Kumar, Alok Prasanna. 2016. Uniform Civil Code: A Heedless Quest?' *Economic and Political Weekly*, 51 (25), 18 June.

Lariviere, Richard W. 2005. A Persistent Disjunction: Parallel Realms of Law in India', in Robert D. Baird (ed.), *Religion and Law in Independent India*. Second enlarged edition, pp. 469–78. New Delhi: Manohar Publications.

Larson, Gerald Jamers (ed.), 2001. *Religion and Personal Law in Secular India*. New Delhi: Social Science Press.

Lateef, Shahida. 1994. *Muslim Women in India: Political and Private Realities*. New Delhi: Kali for Women.

———. 1996. 'The Communal Agenda', *Seminar* (New Delhi) 441, May: 23–29.

Limbu, Shanker. 2005. 'Comparative Study of Existing National Laws Concerning Indigenous Nationalities in Nepal and ILO Convention No. 169 on Indigenous and Tribal Peoples', in Sarah Webster and Om Gurung (eds), *ILO Convention 169 and Peace Building in Nepal*. Kathmandu: Nepal Federation of Indigenous Nationalitites, 39–77.

Lindsay, Jonathan M. and Richard Gordon. 2005. 'Reflections on Law and Meaningfulness in a North Indian Hindu Village', in Robert D. Baird (ed.), *Religion and Law in Independent India,* pp. 479–504. New Delhi: Manohar Publications.

Lipson, Leon and Stanton Wheeler (eds.). 1986. *Law and the Social Sciences*. New York: Russle Sage Foundation.

LRI—Law Research Institute Eastern Region. 1987. *A Study of Administration of Justice Among the Tribes and Races of North Eastern Region (Excluding Nagaland and Meghalaya)*. Shillong: North Eastern Council.

Bibliography 355

McPherson, Kenneth. 1974. *The Muslim Microcosm: Calcutta, 1918–1935.* Wiesbaden: Franz Steiner Verlag.

Madan, T. N. 1975. 'Structural Implications of Marriage in North India', *Contributions to Indian Sociology* (New Delhi) 9 (2), 1975: 217–43.

Madan, T.N. 1998. 'Coping with Ethnicity in South Asia: Bangladesh, Punjab and Kashmir Compared', *Ethnic and Racial Studies* (London) 21 (5), September: 969–89.

———. 2001. 'The Social Construction of Cultural Identities in Rural Kashmir', in T. N. Madan (ed.), *Muslim Communities of South Asia: Culture, Society and Power.* Third enlarged edition. New Delhi: Manohar Publications.

Mahajan, Gurpreet. 2002. *The Multicultural Path: Issues of Diversity and Discrimination in Democracy.* New Delhi: Sage Publications.

Mahmood, Tahir. 1972. 'Common Civil Code, Personal Laws and Religious Minorities', in Mohammed Imam (ed.), *Minorities and the Law.* Bombay: N. M. Tripathi.

———. (ed.), 1972b. *Islamic Law in Modern India.* Bombay: N. M. Tripathi.

———. 1977. *Muslim Personal Law: Role of the State in the Subcontinent.* New Delhi: Vikas Publications.

———. 1993. 'Constitutional Ideal of Uniform Civil Code—Is Muslim Personal Law a Stumbling Block?', *Religion and Law Review* (New Delhi), 2 (2), winter: 166–74.

———. 1995a. *Uniform Civil Code: Fictions and Facts.* New Delhi: India and Islam Research Council.

———. 1995b. *Statutes of Personal Law in Islamic Countries—History, Texts and Analysis.* Second edition. New Delhi: India and Islam Research Council.

———. 2003. 'Encoded Menace', *Hindustan Times* (New Delhi), 2 August.

———. 2005. 'Interaction of Islam and Public Law in Independent India', in Robert D. Baird (ed.), *Religion and Law in Independent India.* Second enlarged edition, pp. 121–48. New Delhi: Manohar Publications.

———. 2006. 'Muslim Personal Law: Clearing the Cobwebs', *The Hindu* (New Delhi), 30 July.

Malik, Yogendra K. and V. B. Singh. 1994. *Hindu Nationalists in India: The Rise of the Bharatiya Janata Party.* New Delhi: Vistaar.

Mallampalli, Chandra S. 1995. 'Separating "Religion" from Politics: Denying or Rechanneling India's Past?', *Ethnic Studies Report* (Kandy) 8 (1), January: 73–111.

Maloney, Clarence. 1980. *People of the Maldive Islands.* Madras: Orient Longman.

Mansfield, John H. 2005. 'The Personal Laws or a Uniform Civil Code?' in Robert D. Baird (ed.), *Religion and Law in Independent India.* Second enlarged edition, pp. 207–46. New Delhi: Manohar Publications.

Massey, James. 2003. *Minorities and Religious Freedom in a Democracy.* New Delhi: Manohar Publications.

356 The Politics of Personal Law in South Asia

Mayaram, Shail. 1997. *Resisting Regimes: Myth, Memory and the Shaping of a Muslim Identity*. New Delhi: OUP.

Mehdi, Adil. 2002. 'Radicalism Among Indian Muslims in the Aftermath of September 11 Attacks and the War in Afghanistan', in Frederic Grare (ed.), *The Muslims of the Indian Subcontinent after the 11th September Attacks*. New Delhi: India Research Press.

Mehdi, Rubya. 1994. *The Islamization of the Law in Pakistan*. Surrey: Curzon.

Mehdi, Tahir. 2016. 'HYPERLINK https://www.dawn.com/news/1291835/two-laws-but-no-solution" Two Laws but no Solution', *Dawn, 24 October*. http://www.dawn.com/news/1291835/two-laws-but-no-solution, accessed on 6 September 2017.

Menon, K. D. 1991. 'Report on Codification of Tribal Customary Laws, Rites and Land Usages Pattern of Tripura' (mimeo).

Menon, Nivedita. 1998. 'Women and Citizenship', in Partha Chatterjee (ed.), *Wages of Freedom*. New Delhi: OUP.

———. 2000. 'State, Community and the Debate on the Uniform Civil Code in India', in Mahmood Mamdani (ed.), *Beyond Rights Talk and Culture Talk*. New York: St Martin's Press.

———. 2002. 'Embodying the Self: Feminism, Sexual Violence and the Law', in Partha Chatterjee and Pradeep Jeganathan (eds), *Subaltern Studies XI: Community, Gender and Violence*. New Delhi: Permanent Black and Ravi Dayal Publishers.

———. 2004. 'Refusing Globalisation and the Authentic Nation: Feminist Politics in Current Conjuncture', *Economic and Political Weekly* (Mumbai) 39 (1), 3 January: 100–04.

Menski, Werner F. 1988. 'Uniformity of Laws in India and England', *Journal of Law and Society* (Oxford) 7 (11), June: 11–26.

———. 1990a. 'Uniform Civil Code in India: A False Model for Development', *K. L. T. Journal* (Ernakulam) 2: 3–10.

———. 1990b. 'The Reform of Islamic Family Law and a Uniform Civil Code for India', in Chibli Mallat and Jane Connors (eds), *Islamic Family Law,* pp. 253–93. London: Graham and Trotman.

———. 1993. 'Legal Pluralism in the Hindu Marriage', in David Arnold and Peter Robb (eds), *Institutions and Ideologies: A SOAS South Asia Reader,* pp. 148–64. London: Curzon Press.

———. 2000. *Comparative Law in a Global Context: The Legal Systems of Asia and Africa*. London: Platinium.

———. 2001. *Modern Indian Family Law*. Surrey: Curzon.

———. 2003. *Hindu Law: Beyond Tradition and Modernity*. New Delhi: OUP.

———. 2004. 'From Dharma to Law and Back? Postmodern Hindu Law in a Global Order', *Heidelberg Papers in South Asian and Comparative Politics* 20, January.

———. (2006a) 'Asking for the Moon: Legal Uniformity in India from a Kerala Perspective'. *Kerala Law Times*, 2006(2), Journal Section, 53–78.

———. (2006b) *Comparative Law in a Global Context. The Legal Systems of Asia and Africa*. Second ed. Cambridge: Cambridge University Press.

———. 2008. 'The Uniform Civil Code Debate in Indian Law: New Developments and Changing Agenda', *German Law Journal*, 9 (3): 211–50. https://static1.squarespace.com/static/56330ad3e4b0733dcc0c8495/t/56b 84f1d859fd0b8c4b1dd30/1454919453650/GLJ_Vol_09_No_03_Menski. pdf, accessed on 2 August 2017.

———. and T. Tahmina Rahman. 1988. 'Hindus and the Law in Bangladesh', *South Asia Research* (London) 8 (2), November: 111–31.

Merry, Sally Engle. 1988. 'Legal Pluralism', *Law and Society Review* (New York) 22 (5): 869–96.

———. 2001. 'Law: Anthropological Aspects', in Neil J. Smelser and Paul B. Baltes (eds), *International Encyclopedia of the Social and Behavioral Sciences (Volume 12)*. Amsterdam: Elsevier: 8489–492.

Metcalf, Barbara D. 2004. *Islamic Contestations: Essays on Muslims in India and Pakistan*. New Delhi: OUP.

Mill, John Stuart. 1958. *Considerations on Representative Government*. New York: Liberal Arts.

Mirani, Akram. 2006. 'Implications of Family Laws on Minority Women: Research Report on District Rahim Yar Khan', Karachi: Minority Rights Commission (mimeo).

Mir-Hosseini, Ziba. 1999. *Islam and Gender: The Religious Debate in Contemporary Islam*. Princeton, NJ: Princeton University Press.

Miri, Mrinal. 2003. *Identity and the Moral Life*. New Delhi: OUP. (Particularly, Chapter 11, 'On "Mainstream" and "Marginality"'.)

Miri, Sujata (ed.), 1980. *Religion and Society of North-East India*. New Delhi: Vikas Publishing.

Mishra, S. N. 1998. 'India's Tribal Population and Its Regional Concentration', in S. N. Mishra (ed.), *Antiquity to Modernity in Tribal India, Vol. III*. New Delhi: Inter-India Publications, 1–14.

Misra, Amalendu. 2004. *Identity and Religion: Foundations of Anti-Islamism in India*. New Delhi: Sage Publications.

Misra, Udayon. 2000. *The Periphery Strikes Back: Challenges to the Nation-State in Assam and Nagaland*. Shimla: Indian Institute of Advanced Study.

Mitra, B. M. 2000. 'The Anthropological Interpretation of Customs and Customary Law', *Journal of the Anthropological Survey of India* (New Delhi) 49 (1), March 2000: 1–8.

Mitra, Subrata and Alexander Fischer. 2002. 'Sacred Laws and the Secular State: An Analytical Narrative of the Controversy over Personal Laws in India', *India Review* (Philadelphia) 1 (3), July: 99–130.

Mody, Anjali. 2003. 'It is about Equality, not Uniformity' and 'Muted Voices of Change', *The Hindu* (New Delhi), 10 August.

Mohamed, Naseema. 2002. 'Pre-Islamic Maldives', *Man and Environment* (Pune) 27 (1): 109–15.

358 *The Politics of Personal Law in South Asia*

Momin, A. R. 2004. 'Islam and Pluralism', *Studies on Islam* (New Delhi) 1(1): 9–25.

Moore, Sally Falk. 1986. 'Legal Systems of the World: An Introductory Guide to Classifications, Typological Interpretations and Bibliographical Resources', in Leon Lipson and Stanton Wheeler (eds), *Law and the Social Sciences*, pp. 11–62. New York: Russle Sage Foundation.

More, Sheshrao. 2004. *Islam: Maker of the Muslim Mind*. Pune: Rajhans Prakashan.

Mukherjee, Ramkrishna. 1976. 'Nation-building in Bangladesh', in Rajni Kothari (ed.), *State and Nation Building*. Bombay: Allied Publishers.

Mukhia, Harbans. 1991. 'Communalism and the Indian Polity', *South Asia Bulletin* (London) 11 (1 and 2).

Mukhopadhyay, Maitrayee. 1998. *Legally Dispossessed: Gender, Identity and the Process of Law*. Calcutta: Stree Publications.

Mukul, Akshay. 2016. *Gita Press and the Making of Hindu India*. New Delhi: HarperCollins.

Mumtaz, Khawar. 2005. 'Women's Representation, Effectiveness and Leadership in South Asia' (prepared for the Fifth South Asia Regional Ministerial Conference, Celebrating Beijing Plus Plan, 3–5 May 2005), February. (Downloaded from the internet.)

Murmu, Emami. 1996. 'Where Have all the Flowers Gone?', *Seminar* (New Delhi) 441, May: 39–41.

Mustafa, Faizan. 2016a. 'Multiple Ways to Equality', *Indian Express* (New Delhi), 28 October.

———. 2016b. 'The Debate on Triple Talaq Must be Based on Proper Research and Data', *The Wire*, 6 November, https://thewire.in/77923/muslim-personal-law-reforms-bmma-studies/, accessed on 2 August 2017.

———. 2016c. 'Look Who's Talking', *Indian Express* (New Delhi), 11 November.

MWRAF (Muslim Women's Research and Action Forum). 2000. 'The Need for Ijtihad or Intellectual Reasoning', *Seminar Series* No. 2, Colombo.

Nagasila, D. 1992. 'Family Courts: A Critique', *Economic and Political Weekly* (Mumbai) 27: 1735–737.

Nahar, Sultana. 1994. *Shonkhaloghu Shomprodaya* (Bengali). Dhaka: Dhaka Prokashan.

Nandy, Ashis. 1980. 'Woman versus Womanliness in India: An Essay in Cultural and Political Psychology', in Ashis Nandy, *At the Edge of Psychology: Essays in Politics and Culture*, pp. 32–46. New Delhi: OUP.

———. 2004. 'A Billion Gandhis', *Outlook* (New Delhi), 21 June: 14.

Naqvi, Rabab. 1986. 'A Setback for Indian Muslim?', *Dawn* (Karachi), 16 May.

Nariman, Fali S. 2003. 'Uniform Civil Code: Good Intentions are Not Good Enough', *Asian Age* (New Delhi), 27 July.

Nathan, Dev, Govind Kelkar and Shivani Satija. 2013. Witches: Through Changing Contexts Women Remain the Target. New Delhi: Institute for Human Development (Working Paper No. WP 004/2013).

Bibliography 359

Navlakha, Gautam. 1994. 'Triple Talaq: Posturing at Women's Expense', *Economic and Political Weekly* (Mumbai), 21 May: 1264.

Nayak, P. and S. Nayak. 2001. 'Status of Muslim Personal Law in Pakistan', in Ramakant, S. N. Kaushik and Shashi Upadhyaya (eds), *Contemporary Pakistan: Trends and Issues,* Vol. I. Delhi: Kalinga.

Nazir, Pervaiz. 1993. 'Social Structure, Ideology and Language: Caste Among Muslims', *Economic and Political Weekly* (Bombay) 28 (52), 25 December: 2897–900.

Neelakanthan, S. and Nasir Tyabji, 1991. 'The Case for a Secular Civil Code', *The Hindu* (New Delhi), 25 July.

Newberg, Paula R. 1995. *Judging the State: Courts and Constitutional Politics in Pakistan.* New Delhi: Foundation Books.

Nizam, Vahidha. 2017. 'Supreme Court Verdict on Instant Triple Talaaq— What Does It Mean for the BJP?' *Mainstream* (New Delhi), 8–14 September 2017: 9–12.

Noman, Abul Bashar, Mohammad Abu, and Saeed Ahsan Khalid. 2011. 'Uniform Family Code: An Appraisal of Viability in Pluralistic Bangladeshi Society', *The Chittagong University Journal of Law*, 16: 81–109.

Noorani, A. G. 2001. 'Islam and Violence: Slurs and Myths', *Frontline* (Chennai), 26 October.

———. 2002. *Islam and Jehad.* New Delhi: LeftWord Books.

———. 2003. 'Keep the Faith', *Hindustan Times* (New Delhi), 30 July.

———. 2016. 'The Code versus the Talaq', *The Hindu*, 15 December.

Oddie, G. A. (ed.), 1977. *Religion in South Asia: Religious Conversion and Revival Movements in South Asia in Medieval and Modern Times.* New Delhi: Manohar Publications.

Oommen, T. K. 1990. *State and Society in India: Studies in Nation Building.* New Delhi: Sage Publications.

Pakistan: The Rot Deepens (A Compilation). New Delhi: Wordsmiths.

Palriwala, R. 1996. 'Negotiating Patriliny: Intra-Household Consumption and Authority in Northwest India', in R. Palriwala and Carla Risseeuw (eds), *Shifting Circles of Support: Contextualizing Gender and Kinship in South Asia and Sub-Saharan Africa,* pp. 190–217. New Delhi: Sage Publications.

Pant, R. 2001. 'Exploring the Role of Community and Customary Law in Natural Resources Management in the Legal Pluralist Societies of North East India'. Paper prepared for NBSAP (National Biodiversity Strategy and Action Plan) of UNDP.

Pant, Ruchi. 2002. *Customs and Conservation: Cases of Traditional and Modern Law in India and Nepal.* Pune: Kalpavriksh.

Parashar, A. 1992. *Women and Family Law Reform in India: Uniform Civil Code and Gender Equality.* New Delhi: Sage Publications.

———. 1997. 'Family Law as a Means of Ensuring Gender Justice for Indian Women', *Indian Journal of Gender Studies* (New Delhi) 4: 199–229.

Parekh, Bhikhu. 2000. *Rethinking Multiculturalism: Cultural Diversity and Political Theory.* London: Palgrave.

360 *The Politics of Personal Law in South Asia*

Parthasarathi, G. (ed.). 1985. *Jawaharlal Nehru: Letters to Chief Ministers* (in 5 volumes covering the period 1947–1964). New Delhi: Nehru Memorial Museum and Library.

Pathak, Bishnu. 2005. *Politics of People's War and Human Rights in Nepal.* Kathmandu: BIMIPA Publications.

Pathak, Z. and R. S. Rajan. 1989. 'Shahbano', *Signs* (Chicago), 14: 558–82.

Peacock, Olive. 1998. 'Christian Minority in Pakistan', in Ramakant, S. N. Kaushik and Shashi Upadhyaya (eds), *Contemporary Pakistan: Trends and Issues* Vol. I. Delhi: Kalinga.

Pearl, David. 1979. *A Textbook on Muslim Personal Law.* London: Croom Helm.

Pereira, Faustina. 2002. *The Fractured Scales: The Search for a Uniform Personal Code.* Dhaka: The University Press Ltd.

Pereira, Melvil, Bitopi Dutta, and Binita Kakati. 2017. *Legal Pluralism and Indian Democracy: Tribal Conflict Resolution Systems in Northeast India.* New Delhi: Routledge.

Phillips, Roderick. 1991. *Untying the Knot: A Short History of Divorce.* Cambridge: Cambridge University Press.

Phukon, Banasree. 2003. 'Role of Civil Society in Conflict Resolution: A Case Study of Naga Hoho'. Guwahati: OKD Institute of Social Change and Development (mimeo).

Phuntsho, Karma. 2004. 'Echoes of Ancient Ethos: Reflections on Some Popular Bhutanese Social Themes', in Karma Ura and Sonam Kinga (eds), *The Spider and the Piglet,* pp. 364–80. Thimpu: Centre for Bhutan Studies.

Pleshov, Oleg V. 2004. *Islamism and Travails of Democracy in Pakistan.* Delhi: Greenwich Millennium Press.

Ponnambalam, Shirani. 1987. *Law and the Marriage Relationship in Sri Lanka.* Colombo: Lake House.

Poulter, Sebastian M. 1986. *English Law and Ethnic Minority Customs.* London: Butterworths.

Powel, Avril A. 2003. '"Pillar of a New Faith": Christianity in Late- Nineteenth-Century Punjab from the Perspective of a Convert from Islam', in Robert Eric Frykenberg (ed.), *Christians and Missionaries in India: Cross-Cultural Communication since 1500,* pp. 223–55. London: Routledge.

Pradhan-Malla, Sapna. 2004. *Inheritance Rights of Nepali Women: Journey Towards Equality.* Kathmandu: Forum for Women, Law and Development.

Prasad, R. N. 1994. *Autonomy Movement in Mizoram.* New Delhi: Vikas.

Puri, Balraj. 2003. 'Muslim Personal Law: Uniformity vs. Reform', *Muslim India* (New Delhi), January–July: 7–11.

Qaisi, Ghada G. 2000–2001. 'Religious Marriage Contracts: Judicial Enforcement of Mahr Agreements in American Courts', *The Journal of Law and Religion* (Buffalo, NY) 15 (1 and 2): 67–81.

Qureshi, Saleem M. M. 1972. 'Pakistan Nationalism Reconsidered', *Pacific Affairs* (Vancouver) 45 (4), winter.

Bibliography 361

Qureshi, Siraj. 2016. 'Oxford University Press book on Common Civil Code alarms Muslims', http://indiatoday.intoday.in/story/oxford-university-press-book-common-civil-code-muslims-bjp/1/747948.html, accessed on 2 August 2017.

Rahman, A. Faizur. 2017. 'Letting Go of Instant Triple Talaq', *The Hindu* (New Delhi), 8 August.

Rahman, Md. Ashabur. 2017. 'Protection of Right to Divorce for Hindu Woman', *Law Journal Bangladesh*, Vol. 6, January–June, http://www.law journalbd.com/2017/03/protection-of-right-to-divorce-for-hindu-woman/, accessed on 2 August 2017.

Rahman, S. Ubaidur (ed.). 2004. *Understanding the Muslim Leadership in India*. New Delhi: Global Media.

Rahman, Syedur. 1989. 'Bangladesh in 1988: Precarious Institution Building Amid Crisis Management', *Asian Survey* (Berkeley) 29 (2).

Rai, Mridu. 2004. *Hindu Rulers, Muslim Subjects: Islam, Rights, and the History of Kashmir*. New Delhi: Permanent Black.

Rajagopal, Arvind. 2003. 'The Emergency and the Sangh', *The Hindu,* 13 June.

Rajagopal, Krishnadas. 2017. 'What Is Triple Talaq', *The Hindu*, 27 May, http://www.thehindu.com/news/national/the-hindu-explains-triple-talaq/article18590970.ece, accessed on 27 July 2017.

Raju, M. P. 2003. *Uniform Civil Code: A Mirage?* Delhi: Media House.

Rashid, Tahmina. 2006. 'Radical Islamic Movements: Gender Construction in Jamaat-i-Islami and Tabligh-i-Jamaat in Pakistan', *Strategic Analysis* (New Delhi) 30 (2), April–June: 354–76.

Ratnaparkhi, M. S. 1997. *Uniform Civil Code: An Ignored Constitutional Imperative*. New Delhi: Atlantic Publishers.

Raychaudhuri, Diptendra. 2016. 'A Wider, Restrictive Civil Code', *Mainstream* (New Delhi), 54 (49), 26 November: 27–31.

Rehman, I. A. 2003. 'Another Fling at Shariaht', *The Dawn* (Karachi), 8 June.

Reyes, A. F. T. 1986. 'English and French Approaches to Personal Laws in South India, 1700–1850', Ph.D. dissertation, Cambridge University Library, St. John's College, Cambridge.

Risso, Patricia 1992. 'Indian Muslim Legal Status (1964–86)', *Journal of South Asian and Middle Eastern Studies* (Villanova, PA) 16 (2), winter.

Rizvi, Anusha, 2016, 'The Indian Media's Focus on Shayara Bano Betrays an Ignorance of Important Precedents', *The Wire*, 11 June, https://thewire.in/42276/the-indian-medias-focus-on-shayara-bano-betrays-an-ignorance-of-important-precedents/, accessed on 2 August 2017.

Robinson, Rowena. 2003. *Christians of India*. New Delhi: Sage Publications.

Rosen, Lawrence. 2000. *The Justice of Islam: Comparative Perspectives on Islamic Law and Society*. London: OUP.

Roy, Shibani and S. H. M. Rizvi. 1990. *Tribal Customary Laws of North-East India*. New Delhi: B. R. Publishing.

362 The Politics of Personal Law in South Asia

Royal Government of Bhutan. 2001. *Proceedings and Resolutions of the 79th Session of the National Assembly,* Vol. 15. Thimpu: National Assembly Secretariat.

Sagade, Jaya. 1996. 'A Common Adoption Law', *Seminar* (New Delhi) 441, May: 29–33.

Saikia, Rajen. 2000. *Social and Economic History of Assam.* New Delhi: Manohar Publications.

Samaddar, Ranabir. 1999. *The Marginal Nation: Transborder Migration from Bangladesh to West Bengal.* New Delhi: Sage Publications.

Sangari, Kumkum. 1995. 'Politics of Diversity: Religious Communities and Multiple Patriarchies', *Economic and Political Weekly* (Mumbai), 23 December: 3787–810.

————. 1999. 'Gender Lines: Personal Laws, Uniform Laws, Conversion', *Social Scientist* (New Delhi), 27 (5–6). May–June: 17–61.

Sanneh, Lamin. 1989. *Translating the Message: The Missionary Impact on Culture.* New York: Orbis Books.

Saradamoni, K. 1997. 'Matriliny Transformed: Family, Law and Ideology in 20th Century Travancore'. Project report. New Delhi: ICSSR.

Sarkar, Sumit. 2002. *Beyond Nationalist Frames: Relocating Postmodernism, Hindutva, History.* New Delhi: Permanent Black.

Sarkar, Tanika. 1993. 'Rhetoric against Age of Consent: Resisting Colonial Reason and Death of a Child-Wife', *Economic and Political Weekly* (Mumbai), 4 September: 1869–878.

————. 1999. 'Pragmatics of the Hindu Right: Politics of Women's Organisations', *Economic and Political Weekly* (Mumbai) 34 (31), 31 July: 2159–167.

———— and Urvashi Butalia (eds). 1995. *Women and the Hindu Right.* London: Zed Press and New Delhi: Kali for Women.

Sarkar, Urvashi. 2016. 'Resisting Codification of Muslim Personal Law is Denial of Muslim Women's Constitutional Rights', *The Wire,* 29 March. https://thewire.in/26521/resisting-codification-of-muslim-personal-law-denies-muslim-women-their-constitutional-rights/, accessed on 2 August 2017.

Satyamurthy, T. V. (ed.), 1994. *State and Nation in the Context of Social Change.* New Delhi: OUP.

Schacht, Joseph. 1964. *An Introduction to Islamic Law.* London: Clarendon Press.

Setalvad, M. C. 1967. *Secularism: Patel Memorial Lectures 1965.* New Delhi: Publications Division of the Government of India.

Seth, Leila. 2005. 'A Uniform Civil Code: Towards Gender Justice', *India International Quarterly* (New Delhi), 31 (4), Spring: 40–54.

Shabbir, Mohammad and S. C. Manchanda. 1991. *Parsi Law in India* (As amended by Act of 1988). Allahabad: The Law Book Company.

Shah, A. B. 1981. *Religion and Society in India.* Bombay: Somaiya.

Shah, K. T. (ed.). 1948. *National Planning Committee Report.* Bombay: Vora and Co.

Bibliography 363

Shahabuddin, Syed. 2004. 'Open Letter to Dr. Partha S. Ghosh: Understanding Islam in the Modern World', *The Milli Gazette* (New Delhi), 1–15 January: 1–7.

Shaheed, Farida. 2002. *Imagined Citizenship: Women, State and Politics in Pakistan*. Lahore: Shirkat Gah Women's Resource Centre.

Shaheed, Farida, Sohail Akbar Warriach, Cassandra Balchin and Aisha Gazdar (eds). 1998. *Shaping Women's Lives: Laws, Practices and Strategies in Pakistan*. Lahore: Shirkat Gah Women's Resource Centre.

Shakir, Moin. 1972. *Muslims in Free India*. New Delhi: Kalamkar Prakashan.

Sharafi, Mitra. 2007. 'Judging Conversion to Zoroastrianism: Behind the Scenes of the Parsi Panchayat Case (1908)', in John R. Hinnells and Annal Williams (eds.), *Parsis in India and the Disapora*, London: Routledge.

———. 2015a. 'Law and Modern Zoroastrians', in Stausberg, Michael and Yuhan Sohrab-Dinshaw Vevaina (eds.), *The Wiley-Blackwell Companion to Zoroastriansim*. Hoboken, NJ: Wiley Blackwell: 299–312.

———. 2015b. 'South Asian Legal History', *Annual Review of Law and Social Science*, 11: 309–36.

———. 2017. *Law and Identity in Colonial South Asia: Parsi Legal Culture, 1772–1947*. Ranikhet: Permanent Black.

Sharma, Prayag Raj. 2004. *The State and Society in Nepal: Historical Foundations and Contemporary Trends*. Kathmandu: Himal Books.

Sharma, Sudhindra. 1994. 'How the Crescent Fares in Nepal', *Himal* (Kathmandu) 7 (6), November–December: 35–40.

———. 2004. 'Lived Islam in Nepal', in Imtiaz Ahmad and Helmut Reifeld (eds), *Lived Islam in South Asia: Adaptation, Accommodation and Conflict*. New Delhi: Social Science Press.

Sheth, D. L. and Gurpreet Mahajan. 1999. *Minority Identities and the Nation State*. New Delhi: OUP.

Shetreet, Shimon and Hiram E. Chodosh. 2015. *Uniform Civil Code for India: Proposed Blueprint for Scholarly Discourse*. New Delhi: OUP.

Shirkat Gah. 2000. *Women's Rights in Muslim Family Law in Pakistan: 45 Years of Recommendations vs. the FSC Judgement*. Lahore: Shirkat Gah Women's Resource Centre.

Shodhan, Amrita. 2000. 'Women, Personal Laws and the Changing Juridical Practice', *Economic and Political Weekly* (Mumbai), 8–14 April.

Siddiqi, Dina M. 2003. 'Religion, Rights and the Politics of Transnational Feminism in Bangladesh', CENISEAS Papers No. 2, Guwahati: Omeo Kumar Das Institute of Social Change and Development.

Siddiqui, M. M. 1996. *A Preliminary Report of Incidence of Divorce among Muslims*. New Delhi: Institute of Objective Studies.

Siddiqui, Pervez Iqbal. 2001. 'Madrasas Multiply as Foreign Funds Flow in', *Sunday Times of India* (New Delhi), 4 November.

Sigler, Jay A. 1983. 'Minority Rights: A Comparative Analysis', *Contributions in Political Science* (Greenwood Press) 104.

364 The Politics of Personal Law in South Asia

Sikand, Yoginder. 2004a. 'The Indian Ulema and Freedom Struggle', *Muslim India* (New Delhi) 22 (1), January: 8–10.

———. 2004b. 'Militancy and the Madrasahs: The Pakistan Case', *Muslim India* (New Delhi) 22 (1), January: 10–12.

———. 2004c. 'Brahmanisation of a Sufi Saint: The Sai Baba of Shirdi', *Muslim India* (New Delhi) 22 (6), June: 616–21.

———. 2004d. 'Mardrasah "Reform" in India: State Initiatives and "Ulema Responses"', *Muslim India* (New Delhi) 20 (1), January: 13–15.

Sikand, Yoginder. 2005. '"The Glories of India": Indian Patriotism in Islamic Discourse', *Indian Journal of Secularism* (Mumbai) 8 (4), January–March: 25–31.

———. 2006. 'The Indian Madaris and the Agenda of Reform', in Jan-Peter Hartung and Helmut Reifeld (eds), *Islamic Education, Diversity, and National Identity: Dini Madaris in India Post 9/11*, pp. 269–84. New Delhi: Sage Publications.

Singh, A. 1992. *Women in Muslim Personal Law*. Jaipur: Rawat.

Singh, K. S. (ed.). 1993. *Tribal Ethnography, Customary Law and Change*. New Delhi: Concept Publishing.

Singh, Kirti. 1993. 'Women's Rights and the Reform of Personal Laws', in Gyanendra Pandey (ed.), *Hindus and Others: The Question of Identity in India Today*. New Delhi: Viking.

———. 1996. 'Combating Communalism', *Seminar* (New Delhi) 441, May: 55–58.

Singh, Nagendra. 1985. *Bhutan: A Kingdom of the Himalayas: A Study of the Land, its People and their Government*. New Delhi: S. Chand and Co.

Singh, S. N. (ed.). 2003. *Muslims in India*. New Delhi: Anmol Publications.

Singh, Yogendra. 1989. 'Law and Social Change in India: A Sociological Perspective', in J. S. Gandhi (ed.), *Law and Social Change*. Jaipur: Rawat Publications.

Sinha, A. C. 2001. *Himalayan Kingdom Bhutan: Tradition, Transition and Transformation*. New Delhi: Indus.

Sinha, S. 1965. 'Tribe-Caste Continuum', *Man in India* (New Delhi) 45 (1).

Sinha, Shashank Shekhar. 2005. *Restless Mothers and the Turbulent Daughters: Situating Tribes in Gender Studies*. Kolkata: Stree.

———. 2006. 'Adivasis, Gender and the "Evil Eye": The Construction(s) of Witches in Colonial Chotanagpur', *The Indian Historical Review* (New Delhi), 33 (1), January: 127–49.

———. 2007. 'Witch-hunts, Adivasis, and the Uprising in Chhotanagpur', *Economic and Political Weekly* (Mumbai), 42 (19), 12 May: 1672–76.

———. 2012. 'On Witch-hunting', *The Sunday Guardian*, 3 November. http://sacw.net/article3299.html, accessed on 21 August 2017.

———. 2014. 'Adivasi Movements and the Uprising in Chhotanagpur', *NMML Occasional Paper New Series 53*. New Delhi: Nehru Memorial Museum and Library.

———. 2015. 'Culture of Violence or Violence of Cultures? Adivasis and Witch-hunting in Chotanagpur', *Anglistica AION*, 19 (1): 105–20.

Bibliography 365

Siwakoti, Gopal Krishna (ed.). 2004. *Beijing + 10: South Asia NGO Regional Consultation: Report 19–20 June 2004*. Kathmandu: Beyond Beijing Committee and United Nations Development Fund for Women.

———— and Susan Ostermann (eds). 2004. *Nepal: Beijing and Beyond: Beijing + 10 NGO Country Report 2004*. Kathmandu: Beyond Beijing Committee.

Smelser, Neil J. and Paul B. Bates (eds). 2001. *International Encyclopedia of the Social and Behavioural Sciences*. Amsterdam: Elsevier.

Snyder, Francis. 1993. *Law and Anthropology: A Review*. Florence: European University Institute.

Srinivasan, Bina. 1994. *A Cry for Change: A Report on Muslim Personal Law and their Implications for Women in Baroda*. Mumbai: Women's Research and Action Group.

Stuligross, David. 1999. 'Autonomous Councils in Northeast India: Theory and Practice', *Alternatives* (New Delhi) 24 (4), October–December: 497–525.

Subramanian, Narendra. 2004. 'Family Law and Cultural Pluralism', forthcoming in Stanley Wolpert and Raju G. C. Thomas (eds), *Encyclopedia of India.*: Charles Scribner's Sons. *http://www.profs-polisci.mcgill-ca/subramanian/papers/familylawandculturalpluralism-pdf (accessed on 18 May 2006).*

Sukumaran, Ajay. 2017. 'A Flame beneath the Ground', *Frontline* (Chennai), 23 January: 56–58.

Syed, M. H. 2003a. *Human Rights in Islam: The Modern Perspective, Vol. I, Concept of Human Rights*. New Delhi: Anmol Publications.

————. 2003b. *Human Rights in Islam: The Modern Perspective, Vol. II, Social Justice*. New Delhi: Anmol Publications.

Tabassum, Suraiya. 2003. *Waiting for the New Dawn: Muslim Women's Perception of Muslim Personal Law and its Practices*. New Delhi: Indian Social Institute.

Talukdar, A. C. 1988. 'Traditional Village Councils of Arunachal Pradesh and their Role as a Village Government', *Journal of North-East India Council of Social Science Research* (Shillong) 12 (1), April.

Tamanaha, Brian Z. 1993. 'The Folly of the "Social Scientific" Concept of Legal Pluralism', *Journal of Law and Society* (Oxford) 20 (2), summer: 192–217.

The Herald Annual (Karachi) 1993. January.

The Telegraph (Guwahati). 2005. 10 May.

Tie, Warwick J. 2002. 'Legal Pluralism', in Herbert M. Kritzer (ed.), *Legal Systems of the World: A Political, Social and Cultural Encyclopedia*. California: ABC CLIO.

Times of India (New Delhi). 1994. 19 and 22 April.

————. 1995. 10 December.

Timm, Fr. R. W. 2002. 'Christian Community in Bangladesh', in Monirul Hussain and Lipi Ghosh (eds), *Religious Minorities in South Asia: Selected Essays on Post-Colonial Situations, Vol. I, Bangladesh, Pakistan, Nepal, Sri Lanka*. New Delhi: Manak Publications.

366   The Politics of Personal Law in South Asia

Tiwari, Devendra Kumar and Mahmood Zaidi. 1997. *Commentaries on the Family Courts Act, 1984.* Allahabad: Alia Law Agency.

Trivedi, Prashant K., Srinivas Goli, Fahimuddin and Surinder Kumar. 2016. 'Does Untouchability Exist among Muslims? Evidence from Uttar Pradesh', *Economic and Political Weekly* (Mumbai), 51 (5), 9 April: 32–36.

Tulzapurkar, V. D. 1987. 'Uniform Civil Code', *AIR 1987 Journal* (New Delhi): 17–24.

Tyabji, Kamala. 1982. 'Muslim Women and the Uniform Civil Code', *PUCL Bulletin,* (New Delhi), September.

Upadhyay, V. 2003. 'Customary Rights over Tanks', *Economic and Political Weekly* (Mumbai), 1 November: 4643.

Ura, Karma and Sonam Kinga (eds). 2004. *The Spider and the Piglet.* Thimpu: Centre for Bhutan Studies.

U.S. Department of Justice. 2016. *Report: Bangladesh: Treatment of Religious Minorities.* Washington, DC: The Law Library of Congress, August, https://www.justice.gov/eoir/file/882896/download

Vaidya, M. G. 2016. 'The Price of Personal Law', *Indian Express* (New Delhi), 1 November.

Van der Veer, Peter. 1994. *Religious Nationalism: Hindus and Muslims in India.* Berkeley: University of California Press.

Vani, M. S. 2002. 'Customary Law and Modern Governance of Natural Resources in India—Conflicts, Prospects for Accord and Strategies'. Paper submitted for the Commission on Folk Law and Legal Pluralism, XIII International Congress, Thailand.

Vattathara, Thomas and Elizabeth George (eds). 2004. *Peace Initiative: A North-East Asia Perspective.* Guwahati: Don Bosco Institute.

Vatuk, Sylvia. 1990. 'The Cultural Construction of Shared Identity: A South Indian Muslim Family History', *Social Analysis* (Adelaide) 28: 114–31.

———. 1999. 'Shurreef, Herklots, Crooke, and Qanoon-e-Islam: Constructing an Ethnography of "The Moosulmans of India"', *South Asia Research* (New Delhi) 19 (1): 5–28.

———. 2008. 'Islamic Feminism in India: Indian Muslim Women Activists and the Reform of Muslim Personal Law', *Modern Asian Studies*, 43 (2–3), March–May: 489–518.

———. 2017. *Marriage and its Discontents: Women, Islam and the Law in India.* New Delhi: Kali for Women.

Velezinee, Aisath. 2006. 'Waiting for a Political Tsunami', *Himal Southasian* (Kathmandu) 18 (4), January–February: 97–98.

Verghese, B. G. 1996. *India's North East Resurgent.* New Delhi: Konark Publishers.

———. 2003. 'Who is Afraid of a Uniform Civil Code?', *The Hindu* (New Delhi), 13 August.

Verma, B. R. 1998. *Muslim Marriage, Dissolution and Maintenance.* Second edition. Allahabad: The Law Book Company.

Verma, J. S. 2000. *New Dimensions of Justice.* Delhi: Universal Law Publishing Company.

Bibliography 367

Vidyaarthi, L. P. 1978. *Dynamics of Tribal Leadership in Bihar*. Allahabad: Kitab Mahal.

Vora, Rajendra and Anne Feldhaus (eds). 2006. *Religion, Culture, and Politics in India*. New Delhi: Manohar.

Waardenburg, Jacques (ed.). 1999. *Muslim Perceptions of Other Religions: A Historical Survey*. New York: OUP.

Wadud, Amina. 1990. *Qur'an and Woman: Reading the Sacred Text from a Woman's Perspective*. Oxford: OUP.

Waheed-uz-Zaman and M. Saleem Akhtar (eds). 1993. *Islam in South Asia*. Islamabad: National Institute of Historical and Cultural Research.

Warriach, Sohail Akbar and Cassandra Balchin. *Know Your Rights*. Karachi: ZA Publications.

Webster, Sarah and Om Gurung (eds). 2005. *ILO Convention 169 and Peace Building in Nepal*. Kathmandu: Nepal Federation of Indigenous Nationalities.

Williams, Raymond Brady. 1998. 'Asian Indian and Pakistani Religions in the United States', *Annals* (Philadelphia) 558, July: 178–95.

Williams, Rina Verma. 2006. *Postcolonial Politics and Personal Laws: Colonial Legal Legacies and the Indian State*. New Delhi: OUP.

Winkelman, Mareike Jule. 2006. 'Muslim Reactions to the Post-9/11 Media Discourse on the Indian Madaris', in Jan-Peter Hartung and Helmut Reifeld (eds), *Islamic Education, Diversity, and National Identity: Dini Madaris in India Post 9/11*, pp. 252–68. New Delhi: Sage Publications.

WLUML (Women Living Under Muslim Laws). 2003. *Knowing Our Rights: Women, Family Laws and Customs in the Muslim World*. New Delhi: Zubaan and Kali for Women.

Women's Feature Service. 1999. 'Muslim Family Law under Attack in Pakistan', in *Women Living Under Muslim Laws Newssheet*, Lahore.

Working Group for Women's Rights. 1996a. 'Statement on Uniform Civil Code: A Debate', *Alternatives/Vikalp* (New Delhi) 5 (3).

———. 1996b. 'Reversing the Option: Civil Codes and Personal Laws', *Economic and Political Weekly* (Mumbai) 31: 1180–183.

Working Group on Women's Rights. 1996. 'Equal Laws for Women', *Seminar* (New Delhi) 441, May: 37–38.

WRAG (Women's Research and Action Group). 1997a. *Aspects of Culture and Society: Muslim Women in India: WRAG Report*. Mumbai: Women's Research and Action Group.

———. 1997b. *Women, Law and Customary Practices*. Mumbai: Women's Research and Action Group.

Wright, Robin. 1992. 'Islam, Democracy and the West', *Foreign Affairs* (New York) 71 (3), Summer: 137–42.

Xaxa, Virginius. 1999. 'Transformation of Tribes in India: Terms of Discourse', *Economic and Political Weekly* (Mumbai) 34 (24), 12 June: 1519–524.

368 The Politics of Personal Law in South Asia

———. 2003. 'Tribal Scene in India Today', in Joseph Anikuzhikattil, George Palackapillil and Joseph Puthenpurakal (eds), *Understanding Tribal Cultures for Effective Education*, pp. 70–78. New Delhi: Commission for Education and Culture; Shillong: DBCIC Publications.

Yapp, M. E. 1980. 'Contemporary Islam: Revivalism', *Asian Affairs* (London) 6 (old series 67), Part II, June 1980.

Yusuf, K. M. 1965. 'The Judiciary in India Under the Sultans of Delhi and the Mughal Emperors', *Indo-Iranica* (Calcutta) 18 (4): 1–12.

Yuval-Davis, N. 1997. *Gender and Nation.* New Delhi: Sage Publications.

Zakaria, Rafiq. 2003a. 'The Plight of Indian Muslims', *Asian Age* (New Delhi), 28 May.

———. 2003b. 'Can a Code Ever Become Law?', *Asian Age* (New Delhi), 31 July.

Zaman, Waheed-uz-and M. Saleem Akhtar (eds), 1993. *Islam in South Asia,* Islamabad: National Institute of Historical and Cultural Research.

Ziring, Lawrence. 1999. *Pakistan in the Twentieth Century: A Political History.* Karachi: OUP.

Index

Abbott, Freeland 143
Abd al-Aziz, Umar bin 23
Adityanath, Yogi 247, 286
Advani, L. K. 104, 180, 216, 245
Afghanistan 3, 26, 36, 37, 141, 200, 209, 214, 239
Agarwala, Rajkumari 228
Age of Majority Ordinance of 1865 188
Aggarwal, Kailash 232
Aggarwal, Pratap 232
Agnes, Flavia 53, 56, 59, 84, 98, 114, 253, 266
Agiyari (Fire Temple) 272; and the Parsi community trusts 274–75; *see also* Parsi Law
Agnihotri, Indu 221
Ahl-e-Hadis 109
Ahmad, Aziz 146
Ahmad, Eqbal 213
Ahmad, Imtiaz 23, 31, 42, 109, 110, 232
Ahmad, Irfan 283
Ahmad, Mirza Ghulam 30
Ahmad, Naziruddin 68
Ahmad, Zafar 180
Ahmed, Akbar S. 211, 212, 234
Ahmed, Maulvi Nazir 61
Ahmed, Rizwan 257
Ahmed, Shafique 278
Ahmed, Sufia 163
Ahmediya 30, 147, 155
Ain O Shalish Kendra (ASK) (Legal Aid and Mediation Centre) 170, 277

Aiyar, Pallavi 42
Akbar, M. J. 63, 89
Akhtar, M. Saleem 44
Albuquerque, Alfonso de 17
al-Hibri, Azizah Yahia 205
al-Hidaya 50, 51, 54
All India Babri Masjid Action Committee 32, 105, 108
All India Muslim Majlis-e-Mushawarat 85, 87, 90, 253
All India Muslim Personal Law Board (AIMPLB) 3, 32, 88, 90–92, 100, 107–8, 110, 207, 233, 245, 254–56, 262–63, 266, 290
All India Muslim Women's Law Board 111
All Nepal Anjuman Islah (ANAI) 185
Ambedkar, B. R. 64–66, 69, 71–73, 79–81, 95, 224, 244–45
Anderson, J. N. D. 21, 50, 54, 86
An-Na'im, Abdullah A. 152
Ansari, Hamid 185
Ansari, M. A. 125
Anti-Hindu Code Committee 81
AP Bill for Protection of Customary Laws and Special Practices 1994 139
Apte, S. S. 102
Arunachal Pradesh Women's Welfare Society (APWWS) 139
Arya Marriage Validation Act 1937, 160
Assam Accord 99

370   *The Politics of Personal Law in South Asia*

Ayyangar, M. Ananthasayanam 73, 244
Ayyappa temple, 'men only', in Kochi 35
Ayyar, Alladi Krishnaswamy 69, 71
Azad, Maulana Abul Kalam 42

Bahadur, Mahboob Ali Baig Sahib 68, 69
Bahadur, Pocker Sahib 68, 69
Bainham, Andrew 203
Baird, Robert D. 82
Balban 44
Bandopadhyay, D. 116
Bangladesh: Bangladesh (Adaptation of Existing Bangladesh) Laws Order 1972 167; Bangladesh Mahila Parishad (BMP) 169, 175, 224; Bangladeshi nationalism versus Bengali nationalism 165–67; Hindu community in 172–75, 276–77; Hindu Marriage, Adoption, Maintenance and Succession Related Codified Act, 2006 277–79; Hindu Marriage Registration Act, 2012 278; multiple personal laws 167–69; Muslim–Hindu conservative nexus 175–77; reforms in Hindu law 277–79; societal evolution 162–65; uniform family code, discourse on 169–72
Bano, Shah 90, 91, 97, 99, 101, 105, 107, 245, 290; *see also* Shah Bano case
Bano, Shayara 257, 258, 265, 266, 267; and the Supreme Court verdict 265–67
Barnett, Randy 7, 22
Barpuzari, H. K. 25
Basham, A. L. 46
Basu, Monmayee 52
Bates, Paul B. 20
Baxi, Upendra 126, 207, 208
Benei, Veronique 103
Benton, Lauren 17
Berman, Harold 21
Best, Steven 20
Beteille, Andre 120, 121
Bhagwati, Jagdish 39, 215

Bhandare, Muralidhar C. 111
Bharatiya Janata Party (BJP) 27–28, 42, 93, 102, 104–5, 113–15, 180, 221, 226–27, 237, 245; position on UCC 246–54, 264–65, 279, 281–86
Bhardwaj, H. R. 114
Bhargava, Mukul Beharilal 80
Bhattacharjee, A. M. 84
Bhutan: evolution of law 195–96; judicial system 196–97; Marriage Act 1980 197; personal law as non-issue in 196; polygamy in 196
Bhutto, Zulfiqar Ali 147
Birnbaum, Ervin 143, 147
Biswas, Soutik 292
BJP *see* Bharatiya Janata Party
BJP Mahila Morcha 113
Bordoloi, Gopinath 129, 140
Bose, Nirmal Kumar 126, 127
Braun, Wernher von 222
British Legislations Intervening into Personal Laws (Table 2.1) 62
Buddhist Law 160
Buddhist Religious Welfare Trust 169

Cairo Declaration of the OIC, on Islamic concept of human rights 41
Carballo, Marita 27
Caste Disabilities Removal Act of 1850 84
Catholic Church marriages 18–19
Cattle Trespass Act 136
Chagla, Mohammadali Currim 86
Chakma, Suhas 195
Chakravartty, Gargi 80
Chandra, Satish 44
Charter Act of 1833 58
Charter of Liberty of Brahmanabad 44
Chatterji, Jyotsna 113
Chatterjee, Manini 104
Chatterjee, Nandini 239
Chatterjee, Partha 223
Chauhan, B. S. 251, 285
Chhetri, Ram B. 181
Chittagong Hill Tracts (CHT) region 126
Chodosh, Hiram E. 288, 289, 291

Index   371

Choudhury, G. W. 142, 143, 146
Chowdhury, J. N. 133
Christian and Parsi personal laws 15
Christian law 62, 80, 89, 102, 112, 126, 134, 161, 169, 173, 178, 230, 242, 249, 252–54, 268 280; Christian Marriage Act, 1872 126, 161; Christian Marriage Bill 1994, 113; Hindu conversions to Christianity in Goa 16–18; and untouchability 200, 282–83
Clinton, Bill 76
Code of Civil Procedure of 1908 134–36
Codes of Usages and Customs of Gentile Hindus of Goa 18–19
Cohn, Bernard S. 21, 48, 49, 50
Colebrooke, H. T. 48, 49, 240
Congress Party 55; alleged appeasement of Muslim by 98; loss of Muslim votes 92–93; and Muslim conservatives 100–1
Conrad, Dieter 142, 198
Constituent Assembly (India) Debates 65–74
Convention on the Elimination of All Forms of Discrimination Against Women (CEDAW) 36, 41–42, 176
Convention on the Elimination of All Forms of Racial Discrimination (1969) 11
Coomaraswamy, Radhika 12
Cooray, L. J. M. 188, 192
Coulson, Noel J. 151, 152, 157
Crins, Reiki 196
Customary law: definition of 119–21, 267; democratic churning, and 270–71; in India's North East 126–35; plural justice system in 135–37; tensions between customary and codified laws 137–38, 268–71; as tribal law 121–26; witch hunting, and 269–71; women's issues 138–40; *see also* Pakistan

Dandavate, Madhu 96
Dandavate, Pramila 96
Dar-ul-Uloom 207

Dayabhaga 49
Declaration on the Elimination of All Forms of Discrimination Against Women 36
Declaration on the Rights of Persons Belonging to National or Ethnic, Religious and Linguistic Minorities 11
Danish, Ishtiaque 42
Dasgupta, Swapan 34, 232
Dastidar, Mollica 179, 186
Dattu, H. L. 249
Davis, Nancy J. 156
Dawood, N. J. 42
De, Amalendu 163, 164
De, Rohit 241, 242, 243, 244, 255
Dena, Lal. 134
Deobandi, Mufti Muhammad Shaafi' 151
Deoras, Balasaheb 102
Derret, J. D. M. 21, 83
Desai, Nishtha 18
Desai, Sundarlal T. 12
Deshmukh, G. V. 59, 243
Deshta, Kiran 92
Deutsch, Karl 211
Dhagamwar, Vasudha 43, 67, 74, 75, 76, 77, 81, 115, 118, 207, 216, 229
Dharma Shastra 12, 45, 57
Dhattiwala, Raheel 293
Dhavan, Rajeev 83
Dhivehi Payyithunge Party (DPP) 194
Dissolution, of Muslim Marriages Act of 1939 2, 55–57, 110, 167
Divorce Act of 1869 161
Dixit, Kanak Mani 183
Dokhma (Tower of Silence) 272; and the Parsi community trusts 274–75; *see also* Parsi Law
D'Mello, Pamela 19
Doley, D. 130
D'Souza, Anthony 293
D'Souza, Carmo 293
Dube, Leela 232
Dubgyur, Lungten 197

East Pakistan Muslim Family Law Rules 1961 167
Eaton, Richard M. 162

372 The Politics of Personal Law in South Asia

Ekka, Anurag Augustine 268
Ellickson, Robert 25
Elwin, Verrier 117, 126, 127, 128, 129
Engineer, Asghar Ali 61, 86, 92, 110, 111, 234
English Common Law 15
Epstein, Richard A. 26
Ershad, Hussain Mohammad 169
Ete, Jarjum 138
Evidence Act of 1872 148

Faleiro, Eduardo 293
Family Courts Act of 1964 161
Family Law and South Asia 200–1
Farhad, Shah Ali 278
Faridi, Abdul Jaleel 85
Federal *Shari'ah* Courts 153–54
Fierro, Maribel 34
Forum Against Oppression of Women (FAOW) 107, 111
Forum for Women, Law and Development (FWLD) 181
Freud, Sigmund 141
Fuller, Graham E. 150, 211
Fuller, Lon 7, 21
Furnivall, J. S. 10

Gaborieau, Marc 185
Galanter, Marc 21, 45, 58, 59, 63, 82, 83
Gandhi, Indira 78, 88, 99, 103, 107
Gandhi, Mohandas K. (Mahatma) 13, 67, 78, 102, 242
Gandhi, Rajiv 92, 97, 98, 99, 101, 245, 265
Gandhi, Sanjay 102
Gangoli, Geetanjali 108
Gharpure, J. R. 59
Ghosh, Partha S. 78, 103, 105, 148, 164, 166, 227, 245, 286, 289
Ghosh, Srabanee 291
Ghuriye, G. S. 126, 127
gittin (Jewish divorce) 203
Goa Civil Code 17–19
Goa Muslim Shariat Organisation 18
Goldberg, Jan 204
Golwalkr, M. S. 102
Goonesekere, Savitri W. E. 192
Gopal, S. 163

Goswami, M. C. 123, 124, 125
Government of India Act of 1935 65, 121, 217
Gowda, Sadananda 251
Grunebaum, G. E. von 146
Guardians and Wards Act of 1890 84, 89
Guha, Ramchandra 126, 128
Guhathakurta, Meghna 167, 177
Gulati, Saroj 52
Gupta, Goolrokh, 272; *see also* Parsi Law
Gupte, S. V. 79
Gurung, Harka 179, 182
Gurung, Om 181
Gyanendra, King 183

Habib, S. Irfan 255
Haider, Moinuddin 149
Haj Committee Act (1959) 28
Hamilton, Charles 50, 51, 227, 240, 289
Hanbal, Imam 14
Hansda, Sowvendra Shekhar 271
Haq, Iltisham-ul- 151
Haq, Zia-ul 8, 148, 149, 154
Harris, George L. 196
Hasan, Ibn 44
Hasan, Mushirul 64, 97, 98, 111
Hasan, Zoya 255, 256
Hashmi, Shabnam 255
Hasina, Sheikh 165, 276
Hastings, Warren 47, 48, 240
Hazrat Mohammad 30
Hindu Adoption and Maintenance Act of 1956 84, 89
Hindu-Bouddha-Khristan Oikyo Parishad (Hindu, Buddhist, Christian Coordination Council) 173
Hindu Code of 1955–56 13, 49, 59–60, 79, 81–85, 209, 215, 230, 267, 285–6, 290, 308; conservative Hindu opposition to 243–45
Hindu Disposition of Property Act 1916 62, 160, 172
Hindu Inheritance Removal of Disabilities Act 1928 160
Hindu Law of Inheritance Amendment Act 1929 160

Hindu Marriage Act of 1955 81, 215
Hindu Marriage Disabilities
    Removal Act 1946 160
Hindu Married Women's Property
    right Act of 1937 59
Hindu Married Women's Right
    to Separate Residence and
    Maintenance Act 1946 160
Hindu Succession Act, 1956 81, 85
Hindu Widow's Remarriage Act
    1856 53, 81, 160
Hindu Women's right to Property
    Sind Extension to Agricultural
    Land 160
Hoefer, Andras 179
Hooker, M. B. 21
Human Rights Commission of Sri
    Lanka 191
Huntington, Samuel P. 27, 210
Husain, Tajamul 67

Iltutmish 44
Imchen, C. L. 134
India: India Centre for Human
    Rights and Law 111; Muslim
    politics 14–15, 32–34, 282–85;
    political Hinduism 1, 12–13,
    78–79, 101–7, 243–50
Indian Council of Social Science
    Research (ICSSR) 107
Indian Divorce Act (IDA) of 1869,
    anti-women provisions 112
Indian National Congress see
    Congress Party
Indian Penal Code (IPC) 60–61, 201
Indian Succession Act of 1925 16
Inglehart, Ronald 27
International Covenant on Civil and
    Political Rights 11
International Covenant on Economic,
    Social and Cultural Rights 11
International Solidarity Network
    of Women Living Under Muslim
    Personal Laws 41 (WLUML),
    37–38
Irani, Phiroze 16
Iranian revolution of 1979 8, 211
Islam, Safiqul 220
Islami Oikyo Jote (Islamic Unity
    Front) 165

Iyer, N. Natesa 244
Iyer, V. R. Krishna 97, 249

Jafar, Imam Abu 14
Jaffe, James 276
Jaffrelot, Christophe 64, 65, 80, 81,
    102, 244
Jainism 43, 84
Jalal, Ayesha 54, 56, 57
Jamaat-e-Islami/Jamaat-i-Islami 37,
    142, 147, 149, 161, 165
Jamaat-e-Ulema-e-Hind 65
Jamal-ud-din, Sheikh Muhammad 194
Janajati Mahasangh (Nepal
    Federation of Indigenous
    Nationalities) 181
Jatoi, Ghulam Mustafa 149
Jeffrey, Paticia 98
Jennings, Ivor 192
Jethmalani, Ram 232
Jha, M. 120
Jilani, Zafaryab 207
Jinnah, Fatima 218
Jinnah, Mohammad Ali 142, 143,
    241, 283
Johsi, Vinayak 59
Jones, Sir William 47, 50, 240
Joseph, Justice Kurian 258, 260
J. P. movement 102
Jyrwa, E. 129

Kairys, David 5
Kandyan Marriage Ordinance of
    1870 187
Kannabiran, K. G. 60
Katju, K. N. 64, 244
Kattel, Shambhu P. 181
Kaur, Rajkumari Amrit 66
Kidwai, Ayesha 255
Kelkar, Govind 270
Kellner, Douglas 20
Kerala Joint Hindu Family System
    (Abolition) Act, 1975 206
Khaldun, Muhammad ibn 211
Khalid, Saeed Ahsan 278
Khalid, Syed 293
Khan, Arif Mohammad 96
Khan, Ayub 147, 153, 218, 224
Khan, Danish 233
Khan, Liaquat Ali 143

374　*The Politics of Personal Law in South Asia*

Khan, Maulana Mohammad Habib Yar 91
Khan, Maulana Wahiduddin 256
Khan, Maulvi Imtiaz Ali 234
Khan, Sikander Hayat 57, 241
Khan, Sir Syed Ahmed 55
Khan, Zafarul-Islam 238
Khehar, Justice J. S. 258, 261
Khilafat movement 101
Kipling, Rudyard 1
Kirby, Michael 39
Kishwar, Madhu 12, 13, 47, 48
Koya, C. H. Mohammed 89

Lalit, Justice Uday Umesh 258, 259
Lariviere, Richard W. 206
Latifi, Danial 246
law, centrist and pluralist concepts of 19–26; evolution of 6–8; British experiments 239–40; Mughal experience 239–42
Law Commission of India: of 1958 79, 327–31; gauging public mood on UCC (2016) 250–53; liberal suspicions thereof 254–56; Mughal experience 239–42; Muslim misgivings thereof 253–55; questionnaire 250–52
Legal Aid and Consultancy Center (LACC) 181
Legal Code Muluki Ain of 1854 179
Lester, Anthony 39
Limbu, Shanker 179, 183

McPherson, Kenneth 32
Madan, T. N. 31, 42, 165
Madan, Vishwa Lochan 207
Mahajan, Gurpreet 289
Maharaj, Swami Karpatri 244
Mahmood, Sayed 85
Mahmood, Tahir 2, 90, 151, 223, 231, 249, 285, 305, 313
Malaviya, Madan Mohan 64, 80, 244
Maldives: evolution of Muslim law in 193–95; all Sunni reality 193
Malik, Imam 14, 23
Malik, Yogendra K. 104
Mallampalli, Chandra S. 78
Maloney, Clarence 193
Manu Smriti 12

Married Women's Protection of Right Bill 1994 113
Masani, M. R. 66, 67
Maududi, Maulana Abu'l A'la 37, 146, 151
Mazumdar, Vina 218
Meena, K. L. 115
Mehdi, Adil 32
Mehdi, Tahir 280
Mehta, Hansa 66, 67
Menon, Nivedita 83
Menski, Werner F. 13, 49, 107, 112, 113, 151, 157, 173, 202, 205, 206, 287, 288
Metcalf, Barbara D. 154
MFLO *see* Muslim Family Law Ordinance
Mitakshara 49
Mitra, B.M, 122
Mitter, Dwarkanath 59
Modi, Narendra 247, 265
Mody, Anjali 233
Mohammedan Code, 1806 190
Mohani, Maulana Hasrat 73
Mohsin, Dr. Mohammed 185
Moily, Veerappa 238
Moinuddin-Chisti 30
Momin, A. R. 23
Mookerjee, Syama Prasad 80
Moore, Sally Falk 21
Mukherjee, Ramkrishna 163
Mukhia, Harbans 45
Mukul, Akshay 289
Mumtaz, Khawar 37, 218, 220
Munshi, K. M. 65, 66, 69, 70, 71, 72
Musawat-i-Mohammadi 147
Musharraf, General Pervez 149
Muslim Family Law Ordinance (MFLO) of 1961 151–55, 158, 161, 168, 277; *see also* Bangladesh; Pakistan
Muslim Marriage and Divorce Act 188
Muslim Marriage and Divorce Registration Board 188
Muslim Satyashodhak Mandal 97
Muslim Satyashodhak Samaj 87
Muslim Women (Protection of Rights on Divorce) Act in 1986 2, 101, 105, 215, 295–99

Index 375

Mustafa, Faizan 244, 248, 255, 256, 266, 288, 290, 291

Nadri, Syed Abdul 92
Nadwi, Syed Abdul Hasan Ali 99
Nandy, Ashis 13, 35, 78
Naqvi, Maulana Sayed Rabey Al-Hasani 111
Naqvi, Rabab 97
Nariman, Fali S. 230
Nariman, Justice R. F. 258, 259
Nasr, Syed Hossein 86
Nathan, Dev 270
National Campaign for Dalit Human Rights (NCDHR) 219
National Committee of Nationalities of Nepal (NCNN) 182
National Commission on Status of Women of Pakistan 221
National Foundation for the Development of Indigenous Nationalities (NFDIN) 182
Native Marriage Act of 1872 53, 85
Navlakha, Gautam 108
Nayak, P. 154
Nayak, S. 154
Naz, Noorjehan Shafia 256
Nazeer, Justice S. Abdul 258, 261
Neelakanthan, S. 40
Nehru, Pandit Jawaharlal 13, 66, 79, 80, 82, 85, 101, 224, 242, 244
Nepal: caste hierarchy in 178–79; evolution of law in 177–79; family law and the nationalities 181–83; Muluki Ain of 1954 178–79; Muslim personal law 184–86; predominance of Hindu law 180; women's rights movement 180–81
Nepal Muslim Ittehad Organisation (NMIO) 185
Newberg, Paula R. 149
Noman, Abul Bashar Mohammad Abu 278
Noorani, A.G. 146, 250, 213
Northern Area and the Federally Administered Tribal Areas (FATA) 118
North-West Frontier Province (NWFP) 118

Objective Resolution of 1949 157
Owaisi, Asauddin 283, 284

Pakistan: customary and minority (non-Hindu) laws 157–61; evolution of Islamic ideology 142–50; Hindu Marriage Act 2016, 280; Hindu personal law 157–60, 279; Muslim personal law 150–57; PML–PPP competition over Hindu Law reforms 280; tribal laws in, reforms in Muslim personal law 150–57; women's rights 161
Pant, K. C. 95
Pant, Ruchi 124, 125
Parekh, Bhikhu 8, 9
Parsi Law: community profile 271–72; and the issue of 'grievous hurt' 275; and the jury trial 275–76; Parsi Intestate Succession Act 16; Parsi Law Association 16; Parsi Law Commission 16; Parsi Marriage and Divorce Act 1936 17, 160; Parsi Marriage and Divorce Amendment Act 1988 215; Parsi personal law 15–17; and the Special Marriage Act of 1954 272–75
Parthasarathi, G. 81, 82
Pataskar, H. V. 81
Patel, Aakar 248
Patel, Razia 256
Patel, Sardar Vallabhbhai 80, 233, 244
Pathak, Bishnu 184
Patodia, Shiraz 292
Pereira, Faustina 171
Phuntsho, Karma 197
Pleshov, Oleg V. 143, 146
Portuguese Civil Code (PCC) 18
Poulter, Sebastian M. 202
Pradhan-Malla, Sapna 181
Prasad, Rajendra 80, 83, 233, 244
Prasad, Ravi Shankar 265
Prevention of Frauds Ordinance of 1840 188

Qaddafi, Muammar al 209
Qadiyanis *see* Ahmediyas
Qureshi, Saleem M.M. 153

376   The Politics of Personal Law in South Asia

Rabbani, Mohammed Gholam 171
Rafsanjani, Ali Akbar Hashemi 213
Rahid, Mian Abdul 150
Rahman, Tahmina 173
Rahman, Ziaur 8
Rai, Mridu 199
Rajagopal, Arvind 102
Rajagopal, G. R. 79
Rajivlochan, M. 290
Ramachandran, Smriti K. 265
Rana, Jang Bahadur 178
Rana, Trichandra Samsher
    Bahadur 178
Rashid, Omar 267
Rashid, Tahmina 150, 156, 221
Rashid Commission of Marriage and
    Family Laws 150–52
Rashtriya Swayamsevak Sangh (RSS)
    81, 101–5, 109–110, 230, 244,
    252, 281, 284, 290, 334
Ratnaparkhi, M. S. 51
Rau, B. N. 59, 77
Ray, Renuka 64
Raychaudhuri, Diptendra 287
Raza, Gauhar 255
Registration of Muslim Marriages
    Ordinance, 1896 188
Regmi, Achyut Raj,180
Rehman, I.A. 154
Rehmani, Minnatwala 99
Report of the Basic Principles
    Committee, 1952 146
Risso, Patricia 56, 87
Rizvi, S. H. M. 134
Robinson, Robert V. 156
Rohtagi, Mukul 264, 265
Roy, Ram Mohun 52
Roy, Shibani 134
RSS see Rashtriya Swayamsevak
    Sangh
Rushdi, Salman 34

Sabur, A. K. M. Abdus 31
Sahib, Haji Abdul Gaffar 91
Sahib, Mohamad Ismail 68, 72, 73
Saifi, Mohammad Akhlaq 284
Sait, Ebrahim Suleiman 89, 92, 99
Sangari, Kumkum 39
Sanneh, Lamin 42
Santhanam, K. 59

Sarkar, Lotika 218
Sarkar, Sumit 47
Sarkar, Tanika 53, 54, 75, 113
Satija, Shivani 270
Sen, A. K. 94, 95, 116
Sen, Amartya 288
Setalvad, M. C. 43, 63, 64, 84, 85
Shah, A. B. 87
Shah, Amit 265
Shah, K. T. 78
Shah Bano case 90–93; see also
    Bano, Shah
Shahabuddin, Syed 90, 92, 96, 99,
    101, 229, 283
Sharafi, Mitra 272, 275, 291, 292
Shaheed, Farida 35
Shakir, Moin 85, 87
Shamim, Shamim Ahmed 89
Shankaracharya, Jagatguru 104
Sharda, Ratan 290
Shariat Act of 1937 72
Sharif, Nawaz 149, 217, 218, 280
Shariff, Abusaleh 293
Sharma, Prayag Raj 179
Sharma, Sudhindra 180, 185
Shetreet, Shimon 288, 289, 291
Shukla, B. N. 42
Siddiqi, Dina M. 177
Siddiqui, Md. Zakaria 283
Sigler, Jay A. 10
Sikand, Yoginder 30, 66, 99, 150
Singh, K. S. 137
Singh, Kirti 115, 138
Singh, Manmohan 220
Singh, Nagendra 195
Singh, Rana Chandra 279, 280; see
    also Pakistan
Sinha, Shashank Shekhar 268, 269,
    270, 271
Singh, V. B. 104
Sinhalese-Muslim political alliance 191
Sitarammya, Pattavi 244
Sleeman, Sir W. H. 61
Smelser, Neil J. 20
Snyder, Francis 21, 24
South Asian Association for
    Regional Cooperation (SAARC) 3,
    141, 293
Special Marriage Act of 1872 51,
    53, 85, 169

Index 377

Special Marriage Act of 1954 84–85, 201, 215, 232, 235
Sri Lanka: evolution of law in 186–87; Kandyan Law 187–88; Muslim personal law 188–92; religious groups in 186; Thesavelamai Law (for Jaffna Tamils) 16, 130, 192–93
Strange, Thomas 49
Stuligross, David 127, 129
Sukumaran 289
Sultana, Nazmun Ara 171
Sultana, Rehana 111
Supreme Court of Judicature, establishment of, at Fort William in Calcutta 47
Susewind, Raphael 293
Suttee Regulation Act of 1829 51, 53
Syed, M. H. 41

Tabassum, Suraiya 92, 97, 208
Tabligh-i-Jamaat 148, 161
Talaq controversy 107–11, 256–58; Supreme Court judgment on 258–63
Tambiah, H. W. 192
Tayyab, Qazi Mohammed 88
Thakkar, Amrit V. 126, 127
Thakur, T. S. 250
Thesavelamai law of the Jaffna Tamils 16, 130, 192–93
Thomas Christians, converted Goa Indians 17–18
Tie, Warwick J. 20, 24
Tikait, Mahendra Singh 115
Toppo, Poonam 270
Tribal law *see* Customary law
Triple Talaq *see* Talaq controversy
Tripura Tribal Areas Autonomous District Council Act 1979 136
Tyabji, Nasir 40, 90

UN Declaration of Human Rights of 1948 36, 40–41
Uniform Civil Code (UCC) 1–6, 11, 19, 20, 27, 34–36, 39, 50, 64–74,

78–79, 98, 101, 106, 113, 116, 141, 205, 224, 228–38, 242–44, 246–48, 256, 263, 265, 276, 281–84, 292; BJP's politics over 246–58; in nationalist discourse on 64–74
Universal Declaration of Human Rights 36, 40–41
Upadhyay, Ashwini 250
Upadhyay, V. 124, 137

Vaidya, M. G. 252, 290
Valvi, Dilbar 272
Vani, M. S. 45, 57
Vasudeo, Rajaratna 50
Vatuk, Sylvia 256, 290
Velezinee, Aisath 195
Venkwani, Ramesh Kumar 280
Verma, J. S. 23
Vidyasagar, Ishwar Chandra 52, 236
Vishwa Hindu Parishad (VHP) 101–5, 113, 265, 281, 334

West Pakistan Hindu Women's Rights to Agricultural Land Ordinance, 1959 161
West Pakistan Muslim Personal Law (Shariat) Application Act, 1962 152
Williams, Raymond Brady 27
Williams, Rina Verma 89, 105
Woolf, Virgina 200
Wright, Robin 211

Xaxa, Virginius 120, 130

Yadav, Akhilesh 247

Zachariah, Mary Sonia 112
Zahra, Abu 14
Zakaria, Rafiq 81, 98, 203, 231
Zaman, Waheed-uz 44
Zia, Begum Khaleda 165
Zina Ordinance 154, 155, 158
Ziring, Lawrence 147
Zoroastrians 15